Studies in Interactional Soc

General Editor: John J. Gumperz

MW00340187

Discourse markers

Companions to this volume

Discourse strategies John J. Gumperz

Language and social identity edited by John J. Gumperz

The social construction of literacy edited by Jenny Cook-Gumperz

Politeness: some universals in language usage by Penelope Brown
   and Stephen C. Levinson

*Talking voices: repetition, dialogue, and imagery in conversational
   discourse* by Deborah Tannen

Discourse markers

Deborah Schiffrin

Department of Linguistics,
School of Languages and Linguistics,
Georgetown University

CAMBRIDGE
UNIVERSITY PRESS

Published by the Press Syndicate of the University of Cambridge
The Pitt Building, Trumpington Street, Cambridge CB2 1RP
40 West 20th Street, New York NY 10011–4211, USA
10 Stamford Road, Oakleigh, Melbourne 3166, Australia

First published 1987
Reprinted 1987
First paperback edition 1988
Reprinted 1988, 1990, 1992, 1994, 1996

British Library cataloguing in publication data
Schiffrin, Deborah.
Discourse markers
(Studies in interactional sociolinguistics; 5)
1. English languages – Discourse analysis
I. Title   II. Series
425   PE1422

Library of Congress cataloguing in publication data
Schiffrin, Deborah.
Discourse markers.
(Studies in interactional sociolinguistics; 5)
Includes index.
1. Discourse analysis. 2. Sociolinguistics. I. Title II. Series
P302.S335 1986   401'.41   86-18846

ISBN 0 521 35718 7 paperback

Transferred to digital printing 2001

To LOUIS

Contents

Acknowledgements

Many people have helped me during various stages of this work. At its earliest stages, my professors at the University of Pennsylvania, Erving Goffman, William Labov, Ellen Prince, and Gillian Sankoff, were sources of unending patience, guidance, and inspiration. I thank all of them, although I deeply regret that I can no longer convey my appreciation to Erving Goffman in person. A special thank-you is due to William Labov, who allowed me to help collect and analyze the data forming the basis of my analysis as part of his project on linguistic change and variation in Philadelphia (National Science Foundation Grant 75–00245), and to two sociolinguistics students (Sally Boyd and Val) whose two previous interviews supplemented the N.S.F. data.

At its later stages, my students and colleagues at Georgetown University have been invaluable in facilitating my continuing interest in discourse markers. I thank, in particular, my colleague Deborah Tannen, and my students Susan French and Susan M. Hoyle. A Georgetown University Faculty Research Grant allowed me a summer of uninterrupted time during which I was able to complete a great deal of the work needed to turn a dissertation into a book. Penny Carter and Jean Field at Cambridge University Press have been models of editorial care and assistance, and I am grateful for their help. Acknowledgement is also given to the Linguistic Soiciety of America for permission to reprint my article 'Conversational coherence: The role of *well*' which appeared in *Language*, 61:640–67.

I also want to thank the people who invited me into their homes for the evenings of tape-recorded talk which provided the basis of my analysis. It was not only linguistic interest that allowed me to analyze their talk in such detail, but human interest: they offered me much of their lives and their selves through what they said. Had they not been such interesting people, this book would not have been possible.

Finally, my husband Louis Scavo has provided so much patience, tolerance, and understanding that it is sometimes a wonder to me that he has managed to pursue his own work. Our son David has provided new and important meanings to lives too often consumed almost totally by work. These contributions cannot be measured or described in words.

Intonation and transcription conventions

The role of intonation in my analysis

Although my analysis of discourse markers is primarily an analysis of how particular expressions are used to organize/conversational interaction, the impact that a single expression has in conversation may differ depending upon the way in which it is said. For example, *oh* with a rising intonation might be interpreted as a request for confirmation, as in:

> A: I think the party's called for six o'clock.
> B: Oh?

But the same expression with a falling intonation might be interpreted not as a request for confirmation, but as an acknowledgement:

> A: I think the party's called for six o'clock.
> B: Oh.

Because the role of intonation is important, I have paid attention to it in my transcription conventions (see below). I have also discussed intonation when it makes a systematic contribution to the interpretation of an expression. But intonation has not received nearly as much attention as two other factors in my analysis: the expression being used as a marker (its linguistic properties) and the conversational (textual, interactional, etc.) context of the expression. It is my hope that an understanding of these two factors will act as a foundation for a more thorough analysis of the prosody of discourse markers.

Key to transcription conventions

> falling intonation followed by noticeable pause (as at end of declarative sentence)
>
> ?   rising intonation followed by noticeable pause (as at end of interrogative sentence)

,   continuing intonation: may be slight rise or fall in contour (less
than '.' or '?'); may be followed by a pause (shorter than '.' or '?')

!   animated tone

. . .   noticeable pause or break in rhythm without falling intonation
(each half-second pause is marked as measured by stop watch)

–   self interruption with glottal stop

:   lengthened syllable

italics   emphatic stress

CAPS   very emphatic stress

Bold   is used in the examples to highlight those discourse markers being

type   discussed in the text

When speech from A and B overlap, the starting point of the overlap is
marked by a left-hand bracket, and the ending point of the overlap is
marked by a right-hand bracket.

> A: Do you know what time the party's supposed ⎡ to start? ⎤
> B: ⎣ Six o'clock. ⎦

When lack of space prevents continuous speech from A from being presented on a single line of text, then '=' at end of A1 and '=' at beginning of
A2 shows the continuity.

> A1:   Do you know what time the party's supposed ⎡ to start?= ⎤
> B: ⎣ Six o'clock. ⎦
> A2:   =Because I have to work late tonight.

When speech from B follows speech from A without perceptible pause,
then ◨ links the end of A with the beginning of B.

> A: Do you know the time? ⤸
> B: Six o'clock.   ⌐Six o'clock.

When speech from B occurs during what can be heard as a brief silence
from A, then B's speech is under A's silence.

> A: I can't wait to go to the party!   It'll be fun.
> B: Oh yeh!

1 Background: What is discourse?

1.1 Discourse analysis

Discourse analysis is a vast and ambiguous field. Consider two recent definitions. First, Brown and Yule (1983: 1) state that:

the analysis of discourse, is necessarily, the analysis of language in use. As such, it cannot be restricted to the description of linguistic forms independent of the purposes or functions which these forms are designed to serve in human affairs.

Second, Stubbs (1983a: 1) states that discourse analysis consists of:

attempts to study the organization of language above the sentence or above the clause, and therefore to study larger linguistic units, such as conversational exchanges or written texts. It follows that discourse analysis is also concerned with language in use in social contexts, and in particular with interaction or dialogue between speakers.

Brown and Yule emphasize a particular **perspective** toward language (functional versus structural) which is tied to a focus on *parole* (versus *langue*); Stubbs' emphasis on a particular **unit of analysis** ('above the sentence') leads him toward a similar pragmatic emphasis on 'language in use'. The authors then observe a definitional problem similar to the one noted above. Brown and Yule (1983: viii) observe that the term discourse analysis

has come to be used with a wide range of meanings which cover a wide range of activities. It is used to describe activities at the intersection of disciplines as diverse as sociolinguistics, psycho-linguistics, philosophical linguistics and computational linguistics.

Stubbs (1983a: 12) continues:

no one is in a position to write a comprehensive account of discourse analysis. The subject is at once too vast, and too lacking in focus and consensus. . . Anything at all that is written on discourse analysis is partial and controversial.

The vastness and ambiguity of discourse analysis is also suggested by textbooks on different approaches to language, such as pragmatics, which define this field as 'the study of the general conditions of the communicative use of language' (Leech 1983: 10) and which include chapters on conversation analysis (Levinson 1983: Chapter 6), and by edited collections in sociolinguistics (e.g. Baugh and Sherzer 1984, Giglioli 1972) which include articles that could fit as comfortably into readers on discourse analysis.

It should not really be surprising that discourse analysis is so vast and diffuse: like pragmatics and sociolinguistics, it has its intellectual roots not only in linguistics, but in the social sciences and in philosophy. Discourse analysis began within linguistics through the work of Harris (1951, 1952), a structural linguist who used distributional methods of analysis to discover recurrent patterns of morphemes which would differentiate a text from a random collection of sentences. Within the social sciences, anthropology has promoted interest in naturally occurring discourse as a culturally relative realization of ways of acting and being (Hymes 1974). In addition, the distinction between referential and social functions of language which is so important to discourse studies had its roots in anthropologist Malinowski's (1930) concept of phatic communion. Sociology also shares responsibility for promoting interest in discourse. From Durkheim's (1895) notion of social fact (a constraint external to the individual) which was adapted by de Saussure in his characterization of *langue*, to Simmel's (1911) focus on forms of social life including conversation and small group interactions, discourse has long been one of the natural interfaces between sociology and linguistics. More recent work by Goffman (e.g. 1959, 1971, 1974, 1981a, 1981b) focused attention on microanalytic frames of social interaction, including the use of language as a sign-vehicle in discourse. The phenomenological movement within philosophy (Schutz 1970) was an impetus for a school of sociology (ethnomethodology) in which the focus of attention is on the common sense procedures used by individuals to construct social worlds: discourse not only provides one of the procedures, but it is part of the social world under construction. And also within philosophy, work by Austin (1962) and Searle (1969) on speech acts, and by Grice on conversational maxims (1975) forced attention to language use.

Because discourse analysis is so vast a field, readers of discourse analyses may find themselves unexpectedly confronted by terms, concepts, and perspectives borrowed from a home turf which is different from their own. (Of course, an equally disorienting problem faces discourse analysts: they may need to wander into analytic terrain which is far from their own initial starting point!) I therefore want to begin this book on discourse markers – words like *oh, well, and, but, or, so, because, now, then, I mean,* and *y'know* – by discussing some assumptions that I will be making about discourse (1.2) and some properties of discourse (1.3). Although I am sure that some readers will find even these assumptions and this discussion of basic properties to be disputable, I then go on to still more controversial ground: I discuss how discourse properties are to be integrated (1.4) within a model of coherence in discourse (1.5).

Note, then, that although this first chapter will say nothing about discourse markers *per se*, it is important background not only for the orientation reason mentioned above, but because it provides a theoretical background for the study of discourse markers, and a model upon which I will base both my analysis of specific markers (Chapters 4–9) and my general conclusions (Chapter 10).

1.2 Assumptions of discourse analysis

The key assumptions about language which I take to be central to current discourse analysis concern context and communication.[1]

1. Language always occurs in a context.
2. Language is context sensitive.
3. Language is always communicative.
4. Language is designed for communication.

1.2.1 Language always occurs in a context

A great deal of sociolinguistic and psycholinguistic research has detailed the specific contexts in which language is produced and interpreted – contexts which range from cultural contexts of shared meanings and world views, to social contexts through which definitions of self and situation are constructed, to cognitive contexts of past experience and knowledge. Understanding how language is used and how it is structured depends on consideration of how it is embedded in all of these contexts. In fact, the role of context is so pervasive that it figures even in grammatical analyses whose data consist of individual intuitions about idealized isolated sentences. Not only is the introspection which accompanies intuition actually a special kind of cognitive context in and of itself, but (as teachers of introductory syntax can no doubt attest) individuals are very adept at imagining discourse contexts in which ungrammatical sentences find a natural home.

And as Goffman (1981a: 30) states, the grammarian's effort to analyze single, isolated sentences requires a general understanding 'that this effort is an acceptable, even worthy, thing to do'. Goffman (1981a: 30–1) goes on to say that:

> The mental set required to make sense out of these little orphans is that of someone with linguistic interests, someone who is posing a linguistic issue and is using a sample sentence to further his argument. In this special context of linguistic elaboration, an explication and discussion of the sample sentence will have meaning, and this special context is to be found anywhere in the world where there are grammarians. . . So all along, the sentences used by linguists take at least some of their meaning from the institutionalization of this kind of illustrative process.

As Goffman's point suggests, it is not only intuitions about the grammaticality of sentences which are inherently contextualized: so too, are intuitions about semantic meaning. Gazdar (1979: 3–4) suggests that Katz's (Katz 1977, Katz and Fodor 1963) effort to invent a sentence which is totally decontextualized (and would thus be free for semantic interpretation based solely on referential meaning) is futile precisely because inferences about contextually provided non-referential meanings can never be totally excluded. In fact, one of the problems for current research in pragmatics is to successfully limit which of the many features of context actually **do** enter into utterance interpretation.[2]

Thus, I assume that language always occurs in some kind of context, including cognitive contexts in which past experience and knowledge is stored and drawn upon, cultural contexts consisting of shared meanings and world views, and social contexts through which both self and others draw upon institutional and interactional orders to construct definitions of situation and action.[3]

1.2.2 Language is context sensitive

Not only does language always occur in a context, but its patterns – of form and function, and at surface and underlying levels – are sensitive to features of that context. Analyses from a variety of perspectives have documented systematic relationships between language and context which penetrate to all levels of language; see, for example, the quantitative sociolinguistic analyses which focus on how constraints drawn from cultural, social, psychological, and textual domains affect phonological, morphological, and syntactic variation (Fasold 1983, Fasold and Shuy 1975, Labov and Sankoff 1980, Sankoff and Cedergren 1981). Examples of the context sensitivity of language could be almost endlessly multiplied from studies of the internal and external pressures on language change, to studies of how cultural presuppositions influence narrative structure, to studies of how different degrees of mutual knowledge influence language use and expression.

In sum, I assume that language is potentially sensitive to all of the contexts in which it occurs, and, even more strongly, that language **reflects** those contexts because it helps to constitute them.

1.2.3 Language is always communicative

Because language is always addressed to a recipient (either actual or intended) it is always communicative. Note that I am considering communication in a very broad sense here. Some analysts have argued that communication occurs only under certain conditions of speaker intentionality. Ekman and Freisen (1969), for example, differentiate messages which are informative from those which are communicative: the former elicit similar interpretations in observers but may be inaccurate information about the sender; the latter need not be informative (i.e. may not receive consistent interpretations) but are those which a sender consciously intends to send. Still other messages are interactive: they modify another's behavior, even though they need be neither consistently interpreted nor consciously intended toward a particular modification. MacKay (1972) offers another differentiation: communication is necessarily goal-directed and interpreted as goal-directed; whatever is either not goal-directed, or not interpreted as such, falls into the category of conduct. Similar to MacKay is Grice's (1957) well known concept of meaning-nn (an abbreviation for non-natural meaning): speaker's intended meaning which receives an interpretation and a response because a recipient recognizes the intention (rather than the meaning *per se*). A much broader view of communication is that of Ruesch and Bateson (1951) and Watzlawick, Beavin and Jackson (1967) who suggest that whatever occurs within the presence of a sender and a receiver is communicative: so long as it becomes available to another within a shared domain, it need not have been intended as message to count as communication. Goffman (1959) makes the distinction between information given and information given-off: the first is communication in the narrow (intended and received) sense; the second is information which is interpreted for meaning, and assigned significance, simply because it occurs in the presence of another and because it resides within a shared sign system – regardless of its intentional transmission.

I assume that communication occurs when a sender either gives, or gives

off, information. Thus, I assume that language is always communicative
either because it is directed toward a recipient (immediate or eventual),
because it is intended to be so directed, and/or because it is attended by a recipient.

1.2.4 Language is designed for communication

My final assumption is that language is designed to reflect its communicative basis. Consider, for example, the design features of language discussed
by Hockett (1958): some certainly contribute to the ease with which
language can be used as a system of communication (e.g. the fact that
language is a code with unrestricted displacement in time and space). (See
also discussion in Lyons 1972, 1977a: 70–85.) Or consider those features of
language which respond to the need for ease of comprehension: Slobin
(1975) suggests, for example, that the tremendous amount of redundancy
in language is designed to ease the comprehension process. Such features
may be interpreted as designed to aid the recipient's end of the communication process (also Leech 1983: 64–70). Many features of language use are
also recipient designed (Sacks 1971): for example, choice among reference
terms (e.g. DuBois 1980) and the organization of information in sentences
(e.g. Prince 1981) takes recipients' current information state into account,
i.e. what information can be assumed to be shared. Furthermore, communicative processes guide the emergence and development of syntactic
structures in language, both diachronically (Givón 1979, Sankoff and
Brown 1976, Sankoff 1984) and ontogenetically (Bates and MacWhinney
1979, 1982, Ochs and Schieffelin 1979). And at another level of communication – the communication of social information and group membership –
studies of sociolinguistic variation show how the communication of group
identity leads to the maintenance or change of the sound system of language
(e.g. Labov 1972d, Downes 1983).

In sum, I assume that language is designed for communication, or as
Lyons (1977a: 638) states, that 'there is much in the structure of languages
that can only be explained on the assumption that they have developed for
communication in face-to-face interaction'.

1.3 Properties of discourse

I now discuss several properties of discourse: discourse forms structures
(1.3.1), conveys meanings (1.3.2), and accomplishes actions (1.3.3). It
will become obvious that these properties concern slightly different aspects

of discourse. The first two properties are largely concerned with discourse as extended sequences of smaller units, e.g. sentences, propositions, utterances. The third property is more concerned with language as it is used within a social interaction; included is speakers' use not only of extended sequences, but their use of a single unit (e.g. an utterance) within a social interaction. By examining relationships among these properties of discourse (1.4), I lead into a discussion of coherence (1.5) – which I view as an integrative property of discourse.

1.3.1 Structure

Studies of discourse structure have dealt with two related issues: is discourse structure a linguistic structure? Can discourse structure be studied with methods inherited from linguistics? One of the earliest analysts of discourse, Harris (1952), attempted to extend the methods of structural linguistics into discourse analysis: the structure of a text was produced by recurrent patterns of morphemes independent of either their meaning, or their relationship with non-textual factors. More recent approaches have based discourse grammars on transformational generative sentence grammars: van Dijk (1972), for example, claims that texts can be treated as extensions of sentences and that a text grammar can be written in the same form as a generative sentence grammar. Within such a text grammar, the acceptability of a discourse would be determined by a set of rules acting as formal criteria for the interpretability of sentences within the text. Several studies take a more liberal approach to non-textual factors in their suggestion that discourse structure reflects the informational content and structure of what is being talked about. Linde and Labov (1975) and Linde and Goguen (1978) show that the structure of specific discourse units (apartment descriptions, plans) is modelled after their informational structure and content. Grosz (1981) shows that the process of focusing on specific entities throughout a discourse is modelled after the structure of a specific task in which the referred-to entities are used.

Although the studies mentioned thus far differ in terms of their inclusion of non-textual factors, they all view discourse as a structured composition of linguistic constituents (morphemes, clauses, sentences) within a monologue. Other studies of discourse structure differ either because they focus on linguistic units within dialogue, or because they focus on non-linguistic units. Some analysts take the position that linguistic units are the basic constituents of dialogue structure. Polanyi and Scha (1983), for example, argue that discourse has a syntactic structure in which clauses belong to discourse units ranging in size from local turn-taking exchanges, to more extended semantic units, such as narratives, and even to speech events and exchanges.

Many other studies of dialogue structure focus on units which are not strictly linguistic. Key to an ethnomethodological approach to discourse, for example, is the concept of adjacency pair: a sequentially constrained pair of turns at talk in which the occurrence of a first-pair-part creates a slot for the occurrence of a second-pair-part (a conditional relevance), such that the non-occurrence of that second-pair-part is heard as an official absence (Schegloff and Sacks 1973). Examples are question/answer pairs, compliment and response pairs. Evidence for the constraining influence of first-pair-parts comes from various observations about the consequences of absent second-pair-parts: first-pair-parts are repeated when their attendant expectations are violated, delayed second-pair-parts are accompanied with explanations for the delay (Schegloff 1972). Adjacency pairs exhibit structure not only because they strongly constrain linear sequence, but because they provide a basis for formal modifications of dialogue: insertion sequences (Schegloff 1972), for example, can be characterized as one adjacency pair embedded within another.

Other research takes us still further from a dependence on purely linguistic constituents of discourse structure to show how sequences of actions are formally constrained and modified. Goffman (1971) and Merritt (1976) demonstrate that sequences of particular conversational moves, e.g. requests, remedies, acknowledgements, can undergo formal modifications ranging from embedding to ellipsis to coupling, as can many ritual interactions, such as greetings (Irvine 1974, Schiffrin 1977). In these analyses, the formal modifications of action sequences are explicitly linked to variation in non-textual, situational factors.

In sum, whether monologue and dialogue structures are composed of linguistic constituents, and whether such structures can be studied with methods inherited from linguistics, are questions which are central to ultimate decisions as to whether discourse structure is purely linguistic, and whether that structure parallels other types of language structure (see Levinson 1981, Stubbs 1983a: Chapter 5).

1.3.2 Meaning

Our discussion of structure showed that some analysts apply methods used in sentence analysis to discourse, while either maintaining or rejecting the notion that it is linguistic units *per se* (morphemes, clauses, sentences) which form the basic constituents of discourse. Other discourse analysts argue that texts are so different in kind from smaller linguistic units that methods used for analyzing such units should not be expected to provide a model for discourse analysis. Halliday and Hasan (1976) argue, for example, that although structure may be one definitional source of a text – a source that specific genres of texts share with sentences – a more compelling source is at the level of semantic relationships underlying the text. Thus, particular items such as pronouns, adverbs, and conjunctions help create discourse not because of their rule-governed distribution, but because they indicate an interpretive link between two parts within the text. And although we can recognize a cohesive element by its surface appearance in a clause, what such an element actually displays is a connection between the underlying propositional content of two clauses – the clause in which the element appears and a prior clause. In short, the cohesive link is established because interpretation of an element in one clause presupposes information from a prior clause.

Cohesion can be found not only in monologue, but in dialogue. A convenient way to locate conversational cohesion is to examine dialogic pairs whose propositional completion depends on contributions from both speaker and hearer. Question/answer pairs are an example. In asking a question, a speaker presents a proposition which is incomplete either as to polarity (a yes–no question) or as to who, what, where, why, when or how (a WH-question). Completion of the proposition is up to the recipient of the question, who either fixes the polarity or fills in the WH-information. Analyses of communicative development in children also suggest that shared responsibility for conversational cohesion extends to propositional completion in general (Ochs and Schieffelin 1979), discourse topic (Keenan and Schieffelin 1976) and reference (Atkinson 1979, Scollon 1979).

In sum, studies of cohesion indicate that the meaning conveyed by a text is meaning which is interpreted by speakers and hearers based on their inferences about the propositional connections underlying what is said. Cohesive devices do not themselves create meaning; they are clues used by speakers and hearers to find the meanings which underlie surface utterances.

Before closing this section, it is important to note that the underlying propositional connections cued by cohesive ties are not posited as the only source of textual meaning. Not only do Halliday and Hasan (1976: 23–6) make this point clear, but Halliday's (1973) model of language explicitly views cohesion as only one component of a broader textual function of language (a function which includes both thematic and informational components). Thus, propositional meaning does not exhaust the meaning of a text. Nor is cohesion supposed to supply all the inferences and understandings made available through a text. (Pragmatic perspectives, including analyses of speaker intention (Grice 1957), communicative strategies (Gumperz 1982, Leech 1983), and cooperative maxims (Grice 1975) help to provide a principled account of these additional inferences.) Thus, a complete analysis of the meaning of a text would specify both the propositional meanings displayed by cohesive ties, and the inferences and understandings derived through application of contextual and pragmatic principles.

1.3.3 Actions

Structure and meaning are properties of discourse when discourse is considered as a linear sequence of smaller units, e.g. sentences, turns, propositions. Although action – or more accurately the accomplishment of action – is also a property of discourse, it is a property which emerges not so much from arrangements of underlying units, as from the organization of speaker goals and intentions which are taken up and acted upon by hearers, and from the ways in which language is used in service of such goals.

Four branches of study contribute to our understanding of discourse as a means of action. The most general contribution is from theoretical discussions of the functions of language. Many linguists distinguish a referential (also referred to as descriptive, representational, or cognitive) function of language from a social function (e.g. Gumperz 1964). Others suggest a three-part division in which a referential function is differentiated from social and expressive functions (e.g. Bühler's 1934 terms 'conative' and 'emotive'). Jakobson (1960) differentiates six functions of language, arguing that each is based upon a different component of the overall speech situation, i.e. emotive (the addressor), conative (the addressee), phatic (the addressor/addressee relationship), meta-linguistic (the code), poetic (the message form), referential (the context). These functional classifications share two insights. First, language is a vehicle through which a range of different functions can be realized – functions which differ markedly from the referential function, i.e. the transmittal of information about the world to one who does not share that information. Second, the various functions of language influence its structure, i.e. the different parts and patterns of language can be understood only by reference to the role which they play in the overall system. (See Lyons 1977a: 50–6 for discussion of these and other functional classifications, and Halliday 1973 for a model of language which explicitly bases structure on function.)

The second source of insight about discourse as action is speech act theory. Since Austin's (1962) discussion of how to do things with words, and Searle's (1969) elaboration of speech acts, felicity conditions, and constitutive rules, there has been a great deal of effort to incorporate into formal linguistic theory the insight that language is used to perform actions (e.g. Cole and Morgan 1975, Sadock 1974), to account for how one can say and mean one thing but do quite another (e.g. Searle 1975), and to discover the procedures by which hearers interpret the actions that are performed by speakers' words (e.g. Bach and Harnish 1982). Although work in speech act theory and analysis has often focused on the actions performed (more accurately performable) by single sentences (often isolated and idealized from their contexts of use, see Stubbs 1983b), sociolinguists have begun applying the insights of speech act theory to the range of naturally occurring utterances which perform actions (e.g. Ervin-Tripp 1976).

The third source of insight on language as action comes from conversation analysis which is sociological in orientation. (See van Dijk (1985: 1–7) on the differences between sociological and linguistic interests in, and perspectives on, conversation.) Conversation analysts provide the critical insight that although actions are situated in a fairly broad sense of being performed by a particular speaker to a particular hearer in a certain social situation, they are also situated in two very local senses. First, they emerge in locally negotiated settings in which interactional identities may play as crucial a role as the institutional identities often focused upon by more macro-level sociolinguistic analyses. Second, what occurred in the immediately prior exchange of talk may play as critical a role in allowing the recognition of an action – and in influencing the form of its performance – as the set of static mutually known preconditions typically focused on by speech act theorists. Such insights also lead toward the identification of action structures (1.3.1), including those in which sequences of acts which differ markedly on the surface can be seen as similar in their underlying interactional structures and ritual functions (Goffman 1974).

The final source of insight about discourse as action is from the ethnography of communication (Bauman and Sherzer 1974, 1982, Saville-Troike 1982). Many ethnographies of communication have shown that cultures differ dramatically in terms of what speaker goals are culturally encoded in patterns of speaking, as units of speech (acts, events), and in situations for speech. Not only do different speech communities have widely divergent meta-languages for describing speaker goals, speech units, and speech situations (e.g. Abrahams 1974, Stross 1974), but the rules for accomplishing what might at first seem to be the same act often differ tremendously, greatly complicating efforts for cross-cultural comparisons of speech acts.

These four branches of scholarship differ quite markedly in focus. Taken together, however, they show that language is used by its speakers for a tremendous amount of social work. Not only is language used for a referential function (to transmit information about the world), but it is used for a social function (to establish, maintain, and adjust relationships with others), and an expressive function (to display various selves and their attendant feelings, orientations and statuses). And not only is language used to accomplish the well-documented actions of promising and requesting, but also to perform the less well-understood actions of threatening, confiding, boasting, complaining, complimenting, insulting, and so on. And just as this tremendous amount of social work is both locally oriented and organized within an interaction, it is also more globally oriented and organized within cultural world views and sets of moral assumptions about being and acting.

In addition, these branches of scholarship all have applications (potential in some cases, and actual in others) not just to sentences, but to discourse. Speech acts, for example, are realized in and through social interaction: for example, there may be certain acts which emerge in particular interactions (Zimmerman 1984). Similarly, the patterns and norms of speaking isolated by ethnographers are situated in ongoing interactions (a point made quite emphatically by Gumperz 1981, 1984). Or, responsibility for the accomplishment of an action may be shared by both actor and acted-upon: Labov and Fanshel (1977: 93–7) suggest, for example, that a repeated request is a challenge because of the prior failure of the acted-upon to comply with a request whose appropriateness had been assumed to be guaranteed by assumptions about his social competence. And finally, because actions are directed by one person toward another, they become the basis for further action from their recipient; the actions accomplished by language are treated by recipients as a basis upon which to build interaction.

In sum, we have seen in this section that language is used to accomplish social actions. Such actions are an integral part of discourse: actions are accomplished in culturally defined interactional contexts in which what one person does is treated as a basis for what another does.

1.4 Relationships among properties

The fact that language has structure, creates meaning, and is used to perform actions is of course not limited to units of discourse. Indeed, we are more familiar with the syntactic structures of sentences than we are with structures of discourse. And although cohesion is defined by Halliday and Hasan (1976) as a textual property, linguists deal with similar phenomena whenever they address questions about semantics: questions about word-meaning and sentence-meaning both reside in the more encompassing problem of how language-texts provide information which allows language-users to make sense. Thus, cohesion actually depends on a general process of semantic inferencing by language-users who make sense not only out of texts, but out of sentences and words as well. Similarly, discourse is hardly the only domain of language through which speakers perform actions: in fact, speech act theory developed the notion that rules of use constitute the actions performed by sentences, and later developments of speech act theory continued to focus on sentences through attempts to explain syntactic restrictions by appeal to constituted actions.

Although speakers and hearers create and search for structures, meanings, and actions in domains other than discourse, examining these properties in discourse suggests that such properties are not autonomous: no one of these properties can be understood without attention to the others. Many discourse analysts readily acknowledge, for example, that the particular property of discourse on which they focus cannot be thoroughly described without attention to other properties. Van Dijk (1972) acknowledges that textual structure is partially determined by pragmatic, referential, and non-linguistic aspects of communication. Halliday and Hasan (1976) admit that although texture is produced primarily by cohesion, particular discourse genres or registers also gain their textuality through structure. Labov and Fanshel (1977: 350) argue that it is underlying actions which provide participant understandings of utterance connections; but they also acknowledge the role of surface structures in establishing actual sequencing patterns.

Studies of the function of particular discourse features also point out the necessity of not limiting attention to any single aspect of discourse. Meta-linguistic phrases (Schiffrin 1980), and paraphrases (Schiffrin 1982a), for example, both contribute to discourse at levels of structure, interpretation, and action – binding discourse units, marking structural transitions, conveying speakers' attitudes, and displaying conversational adjacency-pair relations. Similarly, studies of discourse ordering options – referentially

equivalent ways of ordering discourse units – show the difficulty of separating the effect of semantic from pragmatic constraints, suggesting instead
that what does influence clause order in discourse is prior surface information which contributes both semantically and pragmatically to the
emerging text (Schiffrin 1985b).

Very similar questions about the integrated nature of discourse are confronted in two specific areas of discourse analysis: the study of narrative
and the study of argument. Narrative study is one of the most developed
areas of discourse analysis. The story grammar approach, formulated initially by Propp (1928), formalized by Rumelhart (1975) and expanded by
cognitive scientists (e.g. Thorndyke 1977) and literary theorists (e.g.
Prince 1973), raises questions about the feasibility and the consequences of
treating stories purely as structural objects. Do stories really share the
structural properties of sentences (Fillmore 1982, Wilensky 1982)? Or
should the notion of story grammar serve more as a metaphor for story
comprehension, to which are added factors as varied as goals of storytellers
(Meehan 1982), the cultural base of stories (Colby 1982), and the affective
forces of stories as vehicles of entertainment (Brewer and Lichtenstein
1982) or instruction (Calfee 1982)? Even the definition of story is complicated by uncertainty over the feasibility of assuming that structure, meaning, and action can be separately considered. Stein (1982) concludes, for
example, that what is critical in differentiating stories from other discourse
is not just structure, but context, semantic content, and sequencing. And
Polanyi (1982) goes so far as to distinguish different genres of oral narrative, relying not only on linguistic factors, but on social constraints, such as
speaker/hearer deference, and turn-taking.

Although the discourse analysis of argument is less well developed, some
of the same questions about structure, meaning, and action are confronted
as in narrative analysis. For example, a central problem for the analysis of
arguments concerns their underlying organization: are they sequences of
logically related steps? Why do some propositions allow the deduction of
others? Which inference steps result in fallacious reasoning? Such
questions concern both the structure and the meaning of arguments – the
steps in an argument form a logical sequence because their semantic content allows particular inferences. Another problem for the analysis of arguments concerns how speakers use arguments to persuade others of a point
of view, although here analysts often speak of the field of rhetoric (e.g.
Perelman and Olbrechts-Tyteca 1969) rather than logic. It is when the persuasive aspects of arguments are analyzed that their study touches on the
study of actions, i.e. persuasive actions. The initial source of work on both

logical and rhetorical aspects of argument is Aristotle, who labels 'the faculty of observing in any given case the available means of persuasion' (1355–25) as the field of rhetoric, and who suggests that one element of persuasion is 'the proof, or apparent proof, provided by the words of the speech itself' (1356–5), i.e. the form of the argument in which all the logical steps are explicit. Thus, even from its inception in Aristotelian logic and rhetoric, the study of argument can be seen to focus upon the interplay among structure, meaning, and action.

It will be helpful to review the way in which analyses of narrative and argument approach structure, meaning, and action for two reasons. First, this work illustrates my point that different dimensions of talk work together by showing that specific discourse tasks are accomplished through an integration of structures, meanings, and actions. Second, I will be using examples drawn from both narratives and arguments throughout my analysis of markers – since telling stories and arguing are two speech activities frequently engaged in by my informants (Schiffrin 1984a, Chapter 2 in this book). Thus, it is useful to know something about these two discourse modes prior to that analysis.

My discussion of narrative presupposes some familiarity with the framework proposed by Labov and Waletsky (1967) and Labov (1972a) in which narratives are composed of five different parts: (1) an abstract which prefaces the point and/or topic of the story, (2) an orientation which provides descriptive background about who, where and when story events occurred, (3) a complicating action in which the story events are recounted in temporal order, (4) a coda which closes the story by moving from the past story world to the present conversational world, and (5) an evaluation whose diffuse location throughout the complicating action, and within the syntax of complicating action clauses, shows the way in which the storyteller is using the particular experience to make a point. (See also Hymes 1981, Polanyi 1979.)

I will consider four discourse tasks which figure prominently in conversational storytelling: initiating the story, reporting events within the story, conveying the point of the story, accomplishing an action through the story. At first glance, each task might seem to require the speaker's attention to just one aspect of talk. But upon closer examination, each task actually requires simultaneous attention to several dimensions of talk from both the speaker and hearer.

Consider, first, story initiation. Because stories take more time to tell than turns at talk typically allow, they require that the storyteller enlist from the hearer tacit agreement to bypass many potential turn-transition

points (Sacks 1971). In short, if a storyteller is to situate and complete the
story, turn exchange has to be temporarily suspended. But more than the
mechanics of turn exchange is involved: to gain a turn long enough for a
story, speakers can project an anticipated turn length through strategies
which manipulate several levels of discourse (e.g. Jefferson 1978, Sacks
1971): The prototypical story beginning *y'know what happened?*, for
example, requires a listener not only to answer the question (*no*), but leads
him/her to ask another question (*what?*). This question then opens both a
conversational space for the storyteller's answer, and a proposition for the
storyteller to complete, both of which can be accomplished by telling a
story which does no less than describe *what happened*. In short, such a
story-beginning builds on the adjacency pair organization of question/
answer pairs, and on the propositional completion accomplished by an
answer to a question, to create a turn-taking space for the story. Or consider story prefaces which abstract an evaluative component of the story,
e.g. *a funny thing happened the other day*. Such an abstract helps to create
a conversational space for a story by alerting listeners as to what to listen
for: something funny. Thus, by foreshadowing the evaluative meanings to
be conveyed through the story events, it proposes that listeners refrain
from exchanging speaking roles until something funny has been reported.

Second, consider reporting story events. This task seems to be, at least
in part, a semantic and structural task: speakers present a set of event
clauses in a basically linear structure, a set whose order is assumed to match
the temporal order of events. But this linear structure has interactional consequences which may very well figure in its motivation: the linear structure
seats the listener in the narrator's perspective, thus creating out of the listener an audience, and even more, a vicarious participant in the narrator's
experience (Goffman 1974: 504).

Third, indicating the general point conveyed by the specific experience
reported in the story (Labov 1972a) might be seen as a semantic task
because it involves the hierarchical organization of a set of propositions into
a larger schema. But, in fact, what is intended and understood as the point
is strongly dependent on social, cultural, conversational, and personal contexts (Polanyi 1979, Tannen 1984), such that we cannot really speak of the
point until we have grasped the larger schemas in which the story takes
shape. In addition, speakers use prosodic, lexical, grammatical, and
discourse modifications of the textual norm (Labov 1972a, Polanyi 1979)
to convey the point, suggesting that multiple facets of language are used in
service of what at first seemed to be a semantic task.

Finally, to propose the performance of the story as a specific interactional move, speakers not only situate their story as a response to prior conversational actions, and in conformity with participant understandings as to what constitutes the performance of particular actions, but they modify the syntactic structure of constituent clauses, of repair structures, and of discourse referents in service of that action. And by repeating key phrases from prior conversation within the complicating action and evaluation of the story, they use a cohesive device to show that understanding the interactional meaning of the story requires reference to prior conversation (Schiffrin 1984b discusses these ideas in more detail).·

Consider, now, that these discourse tasks – opening a story, reporting events, making a point, performing an action – are accomplished not only through speakers' manipulation of different aspects of talk, but through a finely tuned process of hearer participation: by withholding their own turn-incomings, displaying their appreciation and evaluation of the story at critical junctures, responding appropriately to the action, and in general making evident a receptive stance toward the story (Goffman 1974: 504), it is hearers of the story who ultimately provide the turn, realize the point, and endorse the action. In short, speakers have only partial responsibility for the construction of narratives: speakers can propose the form, meaning and action of what they are saying, but to be established as part of the discourse, such proposals need hearer endorsement.

Let us turn now to arguments. Since the discourse analysis of argument is less well developed than that of narrative, many of the issues considered here are of a definitional nature. Let us consider, first, whether there are two distinct modes of argumentative discourse – the first a monologue, and the second a dialogue. The first mode of argument would share features with other expository discourse, e.g. explanations, but the second mode of argument would share features with disagreements, e.g. disputes, confrontations, and quarrels. Although the monologue/dialogue distinction is useful in many discourse analyses, it does not seem to be readily applicable to analyses of argument. Many discussions that seem to focus on monologic argument, for example, assume that the point being established either has not been openly accepted or has already been disputed; once the question of hearer reception is raised, however, we are in the realm of dialogue. And many discussions that seem to focus on dialogic argument nevertheless describe how speakers support and defend positions through logical reasoning and personal evidence; attention to how speakers support a position, however, takes us back into the realm of monologue. Thus, argument seems to be a mode of discourse which is neither purely monologic nor dialogic.

How can we define argument in such a way as to capture both its textual properties as a monologue, and its interactive properties as a dialogue? In previous work (Schiffrin 1982b: Chapter 9, 1984a, 1985a), I have defined argument as discourse through which speakers support disputable positions. This definition incorporates both monologic and dialogic properties: the textual relations between, and arrangement of, position and support is monologic, and the interactional organization of dispute (challenge, defense, rebuttal, and so on) is dialogic.

Discussion of the three parts of argument central to my definition – position, dispute, support – suggests that the understanding of arguments requires attention to as many aspects of discourse organization as those to which we were forced to attend in discussion of narrative. Let us start with **position**. Although a key part of a position is an idea, i.e. descriptive information about situations, states, events, and actions in the world, another important part is speaker commitment to that idea. The simplest display of commitment is through an assertion, i.e. a claim to the truth of a proposition. In more complex displays, speakers indicate their confidence in that truth, e.g. by hedging or intensifying what they say. Still another part of a position is its presentation. Positions are often verbally presented in what Labov (1972c) has called soapbox style: the speaker uses increased volume, maintains the floor for an extended period, and seems to be addressing an audience larger than those in his immediate co-presence. Although positions are often personally held beliefs about the way the world is, they may also be beliefs about the way the world should be. Thus, it is not surprising that speakers often adopt a verbal style in which they seem to be addressing as wide an audience as possible. Nor is it surprising that the presentation of such claims can reveal not only ideas, but moral values and claims to competence and character. (Goffman 1959 argues that all performances have this capacity.)

In **dispute** of a position, individuals can address their opposition to any one (or more) of its parts: a dispute can be centered around propositional content (the accuracy with which a position represents a given state of affairs), speaker orientation (challenging the speaker's stance *vis-à-vis* the facts), or personal and moral implications of the verbal performance (the kind of person the speaker is revealed to be). Sometimes oppositions are obscured because they are presented indirectly (Labov and Fanshel 1977) or mitigated through accommodative devices (Pomerantz 1984). Oppositions are also obscured because they may be definable only by reference to a framework of background knowledge which speakers bring to their understanding of a discourse – reference to information going well beyond the surface meanings of the text itself. Some topics of talk, for example, seem to be culturally defined as disputable (e.g. politics, religion); other topics are sources of dispute only within particular relationships. In either of these cases, understanding the source of an opposition requires reference to background knowledge which is not explicitly presented within a text.

The final component of argument is **support**. A speaker can support a position on any of the levels at which it can be disputed: one can explain an idea, justify a commitment, defend a presentation. Support at any one of these levels can of course be labelled as different speech acts, e.g. one might speak of an explanation, a justification (or an account), or a defense. (None of these speech acts are restricted to arguments: explanations, for example, can be used to clarify; justifications to apologize, and so on.) Each such act, however, consists of the provision of information through which a speaker induces a hearer to draw a conclusion about the credibility of the position.

The examination of support in an argument touches not only on speech acts, but on inferential relations between ideas. Although a main source of insight about the semantic relation between support (premises) and position (conclusion) has been logical analyses of argument, other approaches challenge the applicability of such analyses to everyday arguments. Allwood *et al.* (1977: 104–5) mention some general problems in applying logic to everyday argument, e.g. the role of hidden premises, the need for background information. Toulmin (1958) rejects a formal syllogistic model, arguing that a jurisprudential model of argument provides a less ambiguous framework – since the traditional units of premises and conclusion obscure the more differentiated units of data, warrant, backing, qualification, claim, and rebuttal. Furthermore, in many of the arguments which I have examined, both the content of support, and the inferential relationship between support and position, are widely variable: modes of support as different as personal example, analogy, and appeal to authority require different modes of reasoning if they are to be interpreted as validating a position. Scribner (1979) finds cultural differences responsible for the use of the two different modes of support, i.e. empirical evidence rather than syllogistic proofs. She also locates the problem of learning to 'speak in syllogisms' firmly within communicative competence, arguing that we know little about the social or cultural conditions which give rise to the logical genre, nor how cultures define occasions for its use. The growing literature on children's arguments (Adger 1984, Brenneis and Lein 1977, Eisenberg and Garvey 1981, Lein and Brenneis 1978, Genishi and DiPaolo 1982, Maynard 1985) also provides insights into the wide range of circumstances which can be responsible for the emergence of particular means of support.

Although the issues raised by narrative and argument analysis differ in detail, the general point illustrated by analysis of either discourse genre is the same: speaker and hearer divide responsibility for the construction of discourse at several levels of talk simultaneously. This point conforms to the overall thrust of this section, that is, that discourse cannot be considered the result of any single dimension or aspect of talk from either speaker or hearer alone. If we attempt to analyze the structure (or syntax) of discourse without also analyzing the meaning that is conveyed (both semantic and pragmatic) or the action that is performed (the interactional force), and without also viewing such properties as joint accomplishments of both speaker and hearer, we may not get very far in understanding what quality (or qualities) distinguish discourse from a random collection of sentences, propositions, or actions.

Halliday (1978: 134) states the importance of integration not just for discourse, but for linguistics in general:

a linguistic description is not just a progressive specification of a set of structures one after the other, ideational, then interpersonal, then textual. The system does not first generate a representation of reality, then encode it as a speech act, and finally recode it as a text.

Just speaking of the need for integration, however, specifies neither the precise way in which it should be accomplished, nor the precise shape which it should take. In fact, there are numerous ways that structures, meanings, and actions could be integrated, with each assigning a different degree of autonomy to the individual components. For example, one might argue that meaning and action are inherently separate aspects of discourse, but that one influences the other (or that they influence each other). Alternatively, one might argue that actions are a type of meaning, and thus that the relationship is not one of influence, but of identity. In short, the same diversity of solutions that have been proposed for integrating different components of language in general – phonology, morphology, semantics, pragmatics, syntax – are faced by discourse analysts. (See, for example, the current debates concerning the semantics/pragmatics boundary, e.g. Gazdar 1979, Kempson 1975: Chapters 7–9, 1984, Leech 1983: 5–7, Levinson 1983: Chapter 1.) But because of the vastness and ambiguity of discourse analysis (recall my comments in 1.1), scholars are able to specify neither the route toward, nor the eventual shape of, discourse integration in a way that allows the empirical testing of different predictions.

In the next section, I suggest that we approach the task of understanding how different dimensions of discourse are integrated through a model of

discourse coherence. The model will not only specify different planes of talk, but it will allow us to suggest several different ways in which those planes are integrated with one another.

1.5 A model of discourse coherence

Although the concept of coherence is of central importance to discourse analysis, it is notoriously difficult to define. We often have an intuitive feeling about why one discourse is coherent, and another is incoherent, but it is difficult to provide a principled account for these different judgements, and even more difficult to predict which sequences will be interpreted as coherent. Greetings, for example, form an adjacency pair: an initial greeting constrains the next available interactional slot such that whatever occurs there will be heard as (or examined for its adequacy as) a second greeting. One would not expect, however, that a second part from a **different** adjacency pair would turn up in the second-greeting slot. Yet, I recently returned a telephone call to someone who responded to my 'hello' and self identification with 'thank you'. When I later asked her why she had said this, she said she was thanking me for returning her telephone call so quickly. The point is not that this kind of sequence is typical; the point is only that although it might not be predicted to be so, it can be produced and interpreted as a coherent sequence.

Difficulties of this sort have led discourse analysts away from direct definitions of, and accounts for, coherence. Yet many acknowledge a need for a theory of (or theories of) coherence. Stubbs (1983a: 147) suggests a need for multiple theories of discourse coherence:

> we need accounts not only of surface lexical and syntactic cohesion, and of logical propositional development. We also need an account of speech acts, indirect speech acts (in which the illocutionary force of an utterance is overlaid by markers of mitigation or politeness), the context-dependence of illocutionary force, and the sequential consequences (predictive power) of certain speech acts. In other words, we have to have multiple theories of discourse coherence.

Gumperz's recent work (1982, 1984) suggests an integrated view of coherence. Gumperz suggests that communicative meaning is achieved through a process of situated interpretation in which hearers infer speakers' underlying strategies and intentions by interpreting the linguistic cues which contextualize their messages. Such cues are called contextualization cues: they are the verbal (prosodic, phonological, morphological, syntactic, rhetorical) and nonverbal (kinesic, proxemic) aspects of a communicative code which provide an interpretive framework for the referential content of a message. Crucial to Gumperz's model is the idea that such devices are reflexive: not only are they constrained by the larger interactional frames in which they are situated, but they actually create interpretive contexts through which a speaker's underlying communicative intention can be inferred. Thus, production and reception of a message depend upon shared access to culturally defined repertoires of verbal and nonverbal devices which are both situated in, and reflexive of, the interactional frames within which they occur. Coherence, then, would depend on a speaker's successful integration of different verbal and nonverbal devices to situate a message in an interpretive frame, and a hearer's corresponding synthetic ability to respond to such cues as a totality in order to interpret that message.

I suggest that the properties of discourse discussed in the previous section also contribute to the overall sense – to the coherence – of discourse. Not only do speakers and hearers use many different kinds of contextualization cues to situate their communicative intentions, but they do so within an integrated framework of interactionally emergent structures, meanings, and actions. This peripatetic tendency of language-users would help account for the peripatetic tendencies of discourse analysts, who acknowledge the need for analyses of meaning and action in their analyses of structure, or who wander from cognitive expectations (e.g. Brown and Yule 1983) to social actions (e.g. Labov and Fanshel 1977) in their analyses of coherence.

I also propose that both language-users and language-analysts construct models of the relations between units (sentences, propositions, actions) based not only on how such units pattern relative to other units of the **same** type, but on how they pattern relative to units of **other** types. In other words, both users and analysts of language build models which are based on a patterned integration of units from different levels of analysis. Such models are what allow them to identify discourse segments with parallel patterns, and more importantly for my current point, to make overall sense out of a particular segment of talk – to define it as coherent.

Any such model faces two immediate difficulties. First, it is almost impossible to identify a pattern which is categorically prohibited, that is, formally disallowed to the same degree as an ungrammatical sentence is not generated by a sentence grammar. Second, it is almost impossible to identify a pattern which is categorically required: there always exist multiple candidates which can fill any particular slot within a pattern, and even worse, there usually exist multiple slots.

Another way of saying this is that multiple options for coherence are always available for both speakers and hearers. Indeed, even when coherence options are relatively limited, there still exist multiple candidates for what can be heard as a coherent response. Take the limitation of coherence options through the form and content of a question. Asking someone's age with the tag question *you're twenty one, aren't you?* constrains coherence options for an answer fairly strongly, but many responses are still possible, and more important, coherent (e.g. *Thanks!* or *Here's my identification card*). And, of course, even silence can still be interpreted as a response to such a question and imbued with meaning, simply because of its sequential location in an adjacency pair (Schegloff and Sacks 1973; see also Tannen and Saville-Troike 1985). Or consider the limitation of coherence options set by the first part of a ritual interchange: saying *Hi how are you* delimits what will conventionally follow, but answers as varied as *Fine*, *Hi*, and *Bye* can all be understood as coherent (Goffman 1971, Schiffrin 1977).

Of course responses which do not draw from the conventional range of coherence options (however that is to be defined) may require hearers to undertake substantial inferencing if they are to construct for them a coherent interpretation (Grice 1975). But it is partially the availability of just such context dependent, defeasible inferential procedures that so expands the range of coherence options. In addition, as Goffman (1974, 1981a) has pointed out, gaps between utterance and action, or between contiguous utterances, may be resolved by participants only because they understand other moves to have been deleted or re-arranged, or because they share a focus of attention which is several utterances (or several interactions) prior to their current focus of attention. That individuals can draw upon such understandings also creates an expanded range of coherence options.

Bateson (1953) makes a point which suggests a solution for some of these worries about coherence options: one cannot see the outline of a conversation when one is in the middle of it, only when it is finished. The solution is this: one may not have anticipated the range of coherence options created by one speaker's utterance until after that utterance has received a response which has drawn from that range. In other words, it is because discourse has emergent structure that one cannot always know from what system an option will be selected until the choice has been made.

My overall point in this section has been that speakers' and hearers' efforts to build coherence face the same problems, and rest on the same principles, as analysts' efforts to describe discourse. Conversationalists devote a great deal of joint effort toward the accomplishment of coherence; discourse analysts devote great effort toward description of how discourse differs from random collections of smaller units. Both efforts depend on the integration of different dimensions of talk, and both efforts are greatly complicated by the near lack of either categorical prohibitions or requirements. Of course the conversationalist's immediate goals differ from those of the analyst: he or she is expected to be an active participant in a conversation through construction of a next unit, which will in turn be assessed as a candidate upon which to base still another unit. But regardless of the immediate communicative or contextual importance of their models, both language users and language analysts use essentially the same procedures in its construction.

I now want to propose a model of coherence in talk, which I also take to be a model of discourse. The model focuses on local coherence, i.e. coherence that is constructed through relations between adjacent units in discourse, but it can be expanded to take into account more global dimensions of coherence. It not only summarizes (at the risk of great reduction) and adds to much of what we have been discussing in this chapter, but it will also be a source of definitions, as well as a framework, for the analysis of markers in the rest of this book. Furthermore, I will be viewing markers as indicators of the location of utterances within the emerging structures, meanings, and actions of discourse. The model will thus also show the contexts to which utterances are indexed. (I expand this aspect of the model in Chapter 10.)

Figure 1.1 presents the model. I first distinguish two kinds of non-linguistic structures: an **exchange structure** and an **action structure**. The top part in each structure is from an initial speaker, the bottom part is from a next speaker. Later on in the model, I'll bring in these two participants more explicitly.

The units of talk in an **exchange structure** are the sequentially defined units attended to by ethnomethodologists: I've labelled them turns (because this is the primary unit) but they include conditionally relevant adjacency-pair parts – in other words, questions and answers, greetings. In general, then, exchange structures are the outcome of the decision procedures by which speakers alternate sequential roles and define those alternations in relation to each other (hence, an answer is defined in relation to a question). In addition, an exchange structure is critical in fulfilling what Goffman (1981a: 14–15) called the system constraints of talk. System constraints are concerned with the mechanical requirements of talk: a two-way capability for transmitting acoustically adequate and readily interpretable

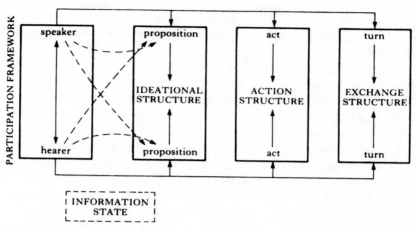

Figure 1.1 *A discourse model.*

messages, feedback capabilities, contact signals, turnover signals, preemption signals, framing capabilities, such as rekeying signals.

Next is an **action structure**. I am using this term to indicate that speech acts are situated – not only in terms of speakers' identities and social setting, but in terms of what action precedes, what action is intended, what action is intended to follow, and what action actually does follow. Thus, I use the term structure here for the same reasons that I used it in discussion of exchange structure – to direct attention to orders of occurrence and to the decision procedures through which such orders emerge. In short, actions occur in constrained linear sequences – they are not randomly ordered, there is a pattern and a predictability to their occurrences – and they are interpreted as situated. Finally, although the distinction is not absolute, action structures revolve more around fulfilling what Goffman (1981a: 21) has called ritual constraints (than the system constraints fulfilled by exchange structures). Ritual constraints are concerned with the interpersonal requirements of talk: the management of oneself and others so as not to violate appropriate standards regarding either one's own demeanor or deference for another; they are designed to 'sustain and protect through expressive means what can be supportively conveyed about persons and their relationships'.

Another structure of discourse is **ideational**. In contrast to exchange and action structures (which I view as pragmatic because of the central role which speakers and hearers play in negotiating their organization), the units within this structure are semantic: they are propositions, or what I'll just call ideas. Three different relations between ideas contribute to the overall configuration of idea structures: cohesive relations, topic relations, and functional relations.

Cohesive ties are established when interpretation of an element in one clause presupposes information from a prior clause (Halliday and Hasan 1976) because of the semantic relationships underlying a text. Another part of an idea structure is its organization of topics and subtopics – what is being talked about. Unfortunately, I have no solution to propose as to how to find topics and subtopics, although it often seems intuitively very clear, especially when topics shift. In addition, although the topics of sentences clearly contribute to the topic of discourse, it does not seem to be a cumulative process such that adding all the sentence topics produces the discourse topic. More promising is the view that topic is a summary of the important parts of discourse content – like a title. (See Brown and Yule 1983: Chapter 3 for an excellent review of topic.) Functional relations between ideas are also part of an idea structure. These are somewhat easier to identify, for they concern the roles which ideas play *vis-à-vis* one another, and within the overall text: for example, in a narrative, some ideas may serve as a descriptive background for others; in explanatory discourse, some may provide specific instances to illustrate a generalization, or reasons which support a position.

As I noted above, idea structures differ from action and exchange structures because they consist of linguistic units (propositions with semantic content), whereas exchange and action structures emerge through units (turns and acts) which are realized by the use of language, but are not linguistic *per se*.

Another difference concerns whether these three structures are definable in relation to both monologues and dialogues, or just to one. Exchange structures, for example, emerge only in dialogue (even though a particular turn may be oriented toward its eventual completion, and thus, oriented toward its role in an exchange). But action structures can emerge in either dialogue or monologue: for example, a pre-request and a request ('are your hands free?', 'can you hand me that ladder?') touch on both. In contrast, idea structures are clearly found in both monologues and dialogues. Examples of monologues with clear idea structures are narratives, descriptions, and explanations. Question/answer pairs illustrate a dialogue with a specific idea structure: in asking a question, a speaker presents a proposition which is incomplete either as to polarity (a yes–no question) or as to WH-information (a WH-question).

The next plane of discourse is the **participation framework**, a term introduced by Goffman (1981b). The terms 'speaker' and 'hearer' here are a gross oversimplification of the various levels of identity which are reflected, and allowed to emerge, through talk. Goffman differentiates, for example, among different 'production formats', including an animator (who presents talk), a figure (who is presented through talk), and a principal (who is responsible for the content and implications of talk). (See also Clark and Carlson 1982.) The term 'hearer' is also underdifferentiated for it fails to discriminate among different 'reception formats', for example, hearers who are intended recipients of talk (addressees) from those who are unintended recipients (overhearers), and passive listeners from those who are expected to contribute to talk. The terms 'speaker' and 'hearer' also ignore the ways in which institutional aspects of identity – teacher/student, doctor/patient – and interpersonal differences of power and solidarity influence the allocation of participant roles. Keeping in mind all the intra and inter-individual differences the terms 'speaker' and 'hearer' capture, I will merely define this aspect of participation framework as the different ways in which speaker and hearer can relate to one another.

There is another aspect to participation frameworks. Although speakers and hearers are related to each other, because of their mutual presence and shared responsibility for talk, they are also related to talk – to what they are producing. The ways in which speakers and hearers can be related to their utterances – to their propositions, acts, and turns – is another part of the participation framework, and these relationships also influence the ways in which speakers and hearers relate to each other. For example, speakers are oriented toward ideas: they evaluate them, or present them neutrally; they express commitment to them, or distance from them. Speakers take stances in performing actions: they may perform an action indirectly and thus deny responsibility for its consequences. And finally, speakers are related to their turns: they may claim them, fight for them, relinquish them.

All of these relations between speaker and utterance influence the relations between speakers themselves. A good example of this is what happens when speakers are telling a story and shift from reporting the events (narrative actions) to selecting a subjective interpretation and assessment of the events (narrative evaluation). Although this is a shift in the relation between 'speaker and utterance', it also opens the story for audience evaluation – which is a shift in speaker/hearer relations. So, participation framework captures both speaker/hearer relations, and speaker/utterance relations.

Recall, now, that I mentioned that I will consider exchange and action structures to be basically pragmatic in nature because of the central role played by speakers and hearers in their negotiation. Participation frameworks are also pragmatic because they involve speakers' relations to each other and to what is being said, meant, and done. Thus, I am taking a very broad view of the scope of pragmatics in which pragmatics concerns the relation of language to its users. (This follows Morris' (1938: 6) initial definition of pragmatics as the study of 'the relation of signs to interpreters'.) Furthermore, I will also be considering these three pragmatic components as more interactional in nature than the others – again, because of the central role played by speakers and hearers in their negotiation.

The final component in my model is **information state**. Here we also find speaker and hearer playing a central part, but unlike the participation framework, they do so not in their social interactional capacities, but in their cognitive capacities. This cognitive focus is because information state involves the organization and management of knowledge and meta-knowledge.

Speaker/hearer knowledge concerns what a speaker knows and what a hearer knows: a speaker may have complete access to information, a hearer may have complete access, both speaker and hearer may have complete access (Labov and Fanshel 1977). Speaker/hearer meta-knowledge concerns what speakers and hearers know about their respective knowledge, and what parts of each knowledge base one knows (or assumes to know) the other to share.

Both knowledge and meta-knowledge vary in terms of their certainty and their salience. Although individuals make assumptions about each other's knowledge and about each other's meta-knowledge, the certainty of those assumptions varies, depending on such factors as the source of information, recency of mention, and so on. Knowledge and meta-knowledge also vary as to their salience for a current discourse. Obviously, not all information to which speaker and hearer share access – and know one another to share access to with different degrees of certainty – is relevant (either directly or indirectly) for the production and interpretation of a particular message. Thus, only parts of speaker/hearer knowledge need to be activated for a hearer's successful decoding of a speaker's message.

Note, now, that although information state involves speakers and hearers in their cognitive capacities, there is still an interactional relevance to knowledge and meta-knowledge. Because discourse involves the **exchange** of information, knowledge and meta-knowledge are constantly in flux, as are degrees of certainty and salience. Another way of saying this is that information states are constantly evolving over the course of a conversation: what speakers and hearers can reasonably expect one another to know, what they can expect about the other's knowledge of what they know, how certain they can expect one another to be about that knowledge, and how salient they can expect the other to find that knowledge are all constantly changing. In short, information states are dynamic interactive processes which change as each one of their contributing factors change.

Since information states are interactively emergent, they **can** become pragmatically relevant so long as speakers display their knowledge and meta-knowledge to one another. But in contrast to turns and actions, which are constituted only through talk, and to participation frameworks, which emerge only because speaker and hearer are orienting their communicative conduct toward each other, knowledge and meta-knowledge can also be essentially internal states (and this includes not only the static organization of knowledge but the dynamic internal processes by which inferences are drawn). It is because an information state is only **potentially** externalized that I speak of it as pragmatically relevant, rather than as pragmatic *per se*.

In sum, my discourse model has both non-linguistic structures (exchange and action) and linguistic structures (ideational). Speaker and hearer are related to each other, and to their utterances, in a participation framework. Their knowledge and meta-knowledge about ideas is organized and managed in an information state. Local coherence in discourse is thus defined as the outcome of joint efforts from interactants to **integrate** knowing, meaning, saying and doing.

How and where does such integration occur? There are three different possibilities. First, different parts of one component are related to each other: ideas to ideas, actions to actions, and so on. Second, different components are related to each other: action structures to exchange structures, information states to participation frameworks, and so on. Third, a part of one component can be related to a part of another component. But since each component has been conceptualized as forming a structure **individually**, these latter sorts of mutual dependencies might challenge an assumption left untouched by the other means of integration, i.e. the assumption that each component is autonomous. Although I will not attempt to describe exactly how and where these different means of integration occur, I will return to the general issue again in Chapter 10, where I suggest that discourse markers have a role in accomplishing the integration needed for discourse coherence.

1.6 Summary

In this chapter, I have tried to define discourse by briefly summarizing the scope of academic interest in discourse, outlining some assumptions which

play a critical role in my view of discourse, and describing several properties of discourse. I then argued that discourse structure, meaning, and
action are jointly integrated by speaker and hearer in their efforts to find
coherence, and suggested a model of local coherence.

   This first chapter has said nothing about discourse markers *per se*. Yet it
provides a theoretical background for the study of discourse markers, as
well as a model upon which I will base both my analysis of specific markers
(Chapters 4–9) and my general conclusions (Chapter 10). Furthermore, it
provides a background for my operational definition of discourse markers
and description of data (Chapter 2) and for my discussion of the questions
which are raised by discourse markers (Chapter 3).

2 Prelude to analysis: Definitions and data

This chapter has two aims. The first is to present an operational definition of the items I analyze as discourse markers: *oh, well, and, but, or, so, because, now, then, I mean, y'know* (2.1). This definition will allow us to identify markers by some principled set of criteria: we need to know not only how to find the markers that we are analyzing, but why we are proposing their similarity. The second aim is to describe the data that I am using in my analysis (2.2).

2.1 Operational definition of markers

I operationally define markers as **sequentially dependent** elements which bracket units of talk.[1] In (2.1.1), I motivate the decision to define markers in relation to units of talk, rather than a more finely defined unit such as sentence, proposition, speech act, or tone unit. In (2.1.2), I define brackets as devices which are both cataphoric and anaphoric whether they are in initial or terminal position. In (2.1.3), I discuss sequential dependence.

2.1.1 Units of talk

Defining markers in relation to 'units of talk' is a deliberately vague way of beginning our definition. To be sure, there have been many efforts to more precisely define units of language, as well as units of speech. In fact, we discussed many such units in Chapter 1: units defined because of their structural relations with other units, their cohesive relations, or their interactional relations. Yet, because there are many units of talk which influence the use of markers, basing our definition on a more precise unit would place a tremendous limit on our analysis by restricting our attention to just that unit.

Consider first, a syntactic unit. Although markers often precede sentences, i.e. syntactic configurations of an independent clause plus all clauses dependent on it, they are independent of sentential structure. Removal of a marker from its sentence initial position, in other words, leaves the sentence structure intact. Furthermore, several markers – *y'know, I mean, oh, like* – can occur quite freely within a sentence at locations which are very difficult to define syntactically (see, however, James 1972, 1974). Basing the definition of such elements on the sentence *per se* would imply a dependence on, and relationship with, syntactic structure which is just not evident. (See also, discussion on sequential dependence in 2.1.3.)

Another reason for bypassing the sentence as the unit of talk by which to define markers is that sentences are not the unit most germane to understanding language use and social interaction. It is well known, for example, that speech acts can be realized through a variety of sentence structures: a request can be enacted through a declarative sentence (*The door should be closed*) or an interrogative (*Would you please close the door?*) as well as an imperative (*Close the door*). This lack of fit between act and syntactic form suggests that interactionally situated language use is sensitive to constraints quite independent of syntax (as, indeed, many speech act theorists have shown). Goodwin (1981) goes so far as to propose that sentences themselves are interactionally constructed: his argument is based on the ways in which conversationalists use verbal and nonverbal signals (especially gaze) to negotiate syntactic boundaries.

Still another reason for not basing our definition of markers on the sentence is that sentences are often difficult to identify in everyday conversation. Notwithstanding Labov's (1975) observation that the great majority of sentences in everyday talk are grammatical, Crystal (1980) presents striking examples of how indeterminate connectivity, ellipsis and intercalation of structures may so obscure syntactic boundaries as to make the identification and classification of sentences in everyday conversation almost impossible.

Defining markers relative to propositions raises other problems. Many occurrences of markers would be excluded were we to consider them just as propositional modifiers, or only in relation to propositional meaning. The causal conjunction *because*, for example, is regularly used as a link between a speech act and a reason for performance of the act. Addressing the question *Is that your newspaper?* to a commuter next to whose seat is a newspaper which he is not reading is hardly just a question about ownership: it is a request for permission to read the newspaper. Such a request can be followed by a reason – *because I haven't seen the headlines yet today* – in which *because* links the semantic content of the reason (which itself gives evidence of the speaker's attention to the underlying felicity conditions of his request) with the pragmatic function of the question. Many other markers would be likewise excluded were we to view them only as propositional modifiers: as we will see, markers not only have non-referential uses, but such use is sensitive to units of talk which are not definable in propositional terms.

Basing our definition of markers on units of language use is also problematic. Specifying for any speech act the range of utterances through which it can be realized is a notoriously difficult task. Not only are there many speech acts which have neither direct performative verbs nor easily specified felicity conditions, but what is heard as performance of a particular speech act is so sensitive to local conversational context, and so dependent on speaker/hearer shared knowledge, that specifying such a range may be impossible both in practice and in principle. Furthermore, not all units of language use are coterminous: speech acts are sometimes accomplished in less than a sentence, in a single sentence, in a series of sentences; a speech act may occupy more than one turn at talk, just as a turn may contain more than one speech act.[2]

A unit which focuses on how linguistic structure, meaning, and act are phonologically realized in speech might seem to be a more promising basis for our definition of markers. Many efforts to find such a unit have settled on what has been variously referred to as a phonemic clause, tone group, tone unit, or idea unit. Although I am not *defining* markers in relation to such a unit, it is important to discuss some of these efforts simply because my transcription devices are sensitive to their boundaries and thus assign them (at least implicitly) some analytic importance.

The term *utterance* (Harris 1951) was one of the earliest proposed for a unit of speech. In Harris' (1951:14) definition, an utterance is 'any stretch of talk by one person, before and after which there is silence on the part of that person'. According to this definition, an utterance could vary in size (from a single lexical item to a political speech), structural complexity (from a simple to a complex sentence), propositional content, and so on, since the only defining feature was surrounding silence.

More differentiated units of speech have been based on prosodic cues. Boomer (1965: 150) defined the phonemic clause as a 'phonologically marked macrosegment which . . . contains one and only one primary stress and ends in one of the terminal junctures'. Definitions of similar units from other perspectives (e.g. Lieberman 1967: 38–9, Pike 1945: 33) agree on the importance of falling intonation as a mark of finality of such a unit, noting that such intonation is found at the end of declarative sentences. Similarly, Chafe (1980: 14) suggests that 'clause-final rising or falling pitch is the single most consistent signal' of what he calls an idea unit. In addition to characteristic internal prosody, Chafe (1977) has also noted that a pause often precedes the tone unit. Brown and Yule (1983: 160–4) discuss pauses as hesitations which follow tone units, much as punctuation devices follow sentences in written texts.

Units of speech are also said to have syntactic and informational correlates. Laver (1970: 69) suggests that 'the boundaries of the tone-group often, though not always, coincide with those of the syntactic clause', and Chafe (1980:14) notes that 'syntactically there is a tendency for idea units to consist of a single clause'. Halliday (1967), who presents one of the most developed and integrated definitions of a unit of speech, observed that although the tone is a phonological unit, it is also a realization of a unit of information in which a distinction between given and new information is syntactically encoded (see Brown and Yule (1983: 153–79) for critical discussion of Halliday's system).

If prosodic, syntactic, and information characteristics of speech always coincided, identifying units of talk could be quite automatic. But to add to such difficulties, there may be still another feature of tone units. Kreckel (1981: 261) argues that tone units are communicative units such that 'the lexical item within a tone unit which receives phonological prominence (= the nucleus) contributes largely to the semantic weighting of the tone unit, and, thus, to the constitution of a particular tone unit as a particular communicative act'. Although such correlations are quite striking, it would be rare for any single phonologically realized entity to always be a carrier of syntactic, semantic, and pragmatic functions. As Chafe (1980: 14) aptly observes: 'it would be surprising to find that any cognitive entity is consistently manifested in some overt linguistic phenomenon, let alone a conjunction of three such phenomena.' Similarly, Brown and Yule (1983: 167–8) state that we should not be misled into believing that 'there are categorial rules which map information units on to syntactic units which are coterminous with intonationally and pausally defined units'.

Identifying markers in relation to tone units faces the same problems as does identifying them in relation to sentences, propositions, or actions: the words and phrases which I intuitively feel are functioning as markers occur in locations which are not limited by the boundaries of the unit. Although the items that I have listed as markers often do precede units of talk which have the features of tone units, these same items also occur within such units. (1) illustrates both *I mean* and *but* as preface to a tone unit.[3]

(1)   **I mean** I may be wrong, **but** I'm– **I mean** that's what I'm– that's my opinion.

(2) and (3) illustrate *y'know, I mean* and *but* within tone units:

(2)   So **I mean y'know** I just don't know.
(3)   It's not that often **but** I gotta get him together.

Markers also occur at the ends of tone units:

(4)   We have some **y'know**.

Furthermore, some tone units – those that do not coincide with syntactic and information boundaries – can be prosodically filled with the items that I have listed as markers:

(5)   That seems to happen to people a lot, doesn't it? **I mean**...
(6)   Well I think you achieve more in the long run by doing it yourself.
        Y'know.
(7)   Well I guess they will, **but** um... I don't know when.

We are left with the deliberately vague conclusion that markers bracket units of talk. Sometimes those units are sentences, but sometimes they are propositions, speech acts, tone units. As further argument that we should not define those units more precisely, let us briefly look at some additional units which other scholars have shown markers to bracket. Merritt (1984) shows that *okay* displays the speaker's acknowledgement that it is his/her obligation to take the next move in a service encounter, and thus, that it marks stages in service encounters much in the same way as punctuation in written texts. Brown and Yule (1983: 100–5) argue that intonation marks topical units of spoken discourse as paratones, or speech paragraphs. Analysts of American Indian languages (e.g. Bright 1981, Hymes 1981) provide a particularly rich inventory of units of talk defined as to their poetic features, e.g. verses – units which are bracketed by the same sorts of particles I am calling markers. Or consider suprasegmental brackets such as rhythmic shifts or prosodic shifts which segment sections of an interaction (e.g. a job interview) from each other (Erickson 1979). And, finally, nonverbal gestures such as brow raising (Ekman 1979), gaze (Goodwin 1981, Kendon 1967), and posture shifts (Scheflen 1973) mark units (phases) of social interaction. Although these are not all linguistic elements, all of these devices bracket units of talk which are much more broadly defined than sentences, propositions, speech acts, or tone units. Were we to narrowly define the units of talk for our definition of discourse markers, we would miss this similarity – which will turn out to be important for consideration of the more general function of discourse markers (Chapter 10).

In sum, I am being deliberately vague by defining markers in relation to units of talk because this is where they occur – at the boundaries of units as different as tone groups, sentences, actions, verses, and so on. Note that in defining markers in so broad a way, there lies an inevitable temptation to use the presence of a marker as an indicator of some yet undiscovered unit of talk. Given the many gaps in our current knowledge about units of talk (how many are there? do they intersect? are they always marked in initial locations? etc.), this is not always a hopelessly circular procedure. In fact, once we are on firmer ground as to the function(s) of markers, this will become an even more reasonable procedure. Nevertheless, by defining markers in relation to units of talk, I am suggesting that we should try to independently characterize some part of talk as a unit, and then see how (if) the boundaries of those units are marked.

2.1.2 Brackets

The boundaries of units not only of talk, but of social life and social organization in general, are often marked in some way. Partially responsible for the pervasiveness of boundary markers – at least on a social interactional scale – is the fact that they provide frames of understanding through which social life is defined (Goffman 1974: 251–69). Encounters, for example, are bracketed by opening sequences (Goffman 1963, 1971, Schegloff 1972, Schiffrin 1977). Brackets at this level of social organization function in much the same way as do rites of passage at larger ceremonial levels – ratifying participants' identities and establishing the rules and procedures to be followed during an upcoming period of increased access of participants to one another. Encounters are also routinely closed with many of the same ritual meanings being conveyed – except here, a relationship is being marked as solidary despite a pending decrease in participant access (Goffman 1963, 1971; Schegloff and Sacks 1973).

Brackets work not only at different social organizational levels, but at different levels of the organization of talk. Meta-linguistic brackets, for example, can mark a discourse unit as long as a conversation or as short as a word; they can mark units embedded within larger units, e.g. reasons within explanations, or answers within question/answer pairs (Schiffrin 1980). Furthermore, brackets that begin as part of the organizational apparatus of discourse can work their way into the grammar of a language where their bracketing function continues on both a discourse and a sentence level (Sankoff and Brown 1976).

Although brackets may initiate or terminate a spate of activity, initial brackets typically do different kinds of work in discourse than do terminal brackets. Goffman (1974: 255) suggests:

> the bracket initiating a particular kind of activity may carry more significance than the bracket terminating it. For . . . the beginning bracket not only will establish an episode but will also establish a slot for signals which will inform and define what kind of transformation is to be made of the materials within the episode.

And as Hymes (1974: 150) suggests in his discussion of initial modal particles in Wasco Chinook, 'initial position for elements defining mood over the scope of what follows may be widespread, even universal'.

Despite the significance of opening brackets, it is important to note that brackets look **simultaneously** forward and backward – that the beginning of one unit is the end of another and vice versa. It is this anaphoric **and** cataphoric character of discourse markers that I want to capture by including in their definition the property of sequential dependence.

2.1.3 Sequential dependence

I use the term sequential dependence to indicate that markers are devices that work on a discourse level: they are not dependent on the smaller units of talk of which discourse is composed. Several ways of showing the sequential dependence of markers are provided by Stubbs' (1983a: Chapter 4) arguments that elements such as particles, adverbs and connectors cannot be accounted for by explanations which draw solely upon syntactic characteristics of upcoming sentences. Stubbs (1983a: 78) points out, for example, that it has been evident from the days of immediate constituent analysis that sentence grammar cannot fully deal with conjunctions: rather 'they have a sequencing function of relating syntactic units and fitting them into a textual or discourse context'. Furthermore, the distribution of other elements, e.g. the marker *firstly* as well as sentence adverbs such as *frankly*, can be constrained only by discourse and pragmatic facts. Finally, elements such as *well, now, right, you know* make no syntactic predictions (p. 68) although they do allow some predictions about discourse content.

Another way of showing sequential dependence is through combinations and co-occurrences which could not occur were such elements not viewed as part of discourse. In sentences, for example, coordinate conjunctions link items which are members of the same word class or sentence constituent, e.g. nouns can be conjoined with nouns but not with verbs, clauses can be conjoined with clauses but not with nouns. Most sequentially dependent uses of *and* and *but* – coordinate conjunctions in sentence grammar – reflect this restriction in that they link utterances whose syntactic form is that of a declarative sentence. But we also find *and* linking a declarative with an interrogative sentence:

(8)   Debby: I don't ⎡like that.   ⎤
         Zelda: ⎣ I don't like⎦that. **And**, is he accepting it?

just as we find *but* linking a declarative and interrogative:

(9)   Debby: I wanted t'stop the first week I started!
         Zelda: Y'see! That's what I said. **But** who made y'go, your father?

We also find conjunctions linking a declarative sentence with a non-sentence element:

(10)   Zelda: Slim leg. Right. Straight leg.
         Debby: That's right. ⎡Yeh. ⎤
         Zelda: ⎣Yeh. ⎦ **And** I think when my younger son– th–
         there's four years difference between the two: and I think he
         was–it was almost the same.
(11)   Debby: You can ⎡probably sit on the beach. Right. Yeh.   ⎤
         Zelda: ⎣Yeh, *I* go on the beach. Right. **So** I don't⎦ mind.

Another kind of co-occurrence which would be a violation were markers not considered to be sequentially dependent is between the marker and a sentence-internal element. *Now* is a temporal adverb which marks the reference time of a proposition as coterminous with the speaking time. Thus, we would not expect *now* to co-occur with indicators of a reference time prior to speaking time, e.g. the preterit. Yet in (12), we find *now* and the past tense form of *is*:

(12)   Jan: **Now** these boys were Irish. They lived different.

Nor would we expect to find two occurrences of *now* were both adverbs:

(13)   Freda: So I em. . *I* think, for a woman t'work, is entirely up t'*her*.
                  If, she can handle the situation. **Now** I could not now: alone.
(14)   **Now now** don't worry.

Still another co-occurrence violation indicating that *now* has a sequentially dependent role is its use with *then* – a temporal adverb whose reference time contradicts that of *now*:

(15)   **Now** then what's next?

Conjunctions also illustrate co-occurrences which would be violations were their sequential dependence not considered. Two coordinate conjunctions cannot occur together within a sentence, but when their use is sequentially dependent, they receive an appropriate reading:

(16)   Irene: **And** uh. . .**but** they have that– they're– they're so conscious of their um. . .they're always sittin' down and figurin' out their averages.

Other co-occurrences concern the order in which elements combine. In sentences, a coordinate conjunction cannot follow *so*, but in discourse the order can be reversed:

(17)   Irene: They don't even stop. **So: and** they said that they can't even accommodate us.
(18)   Irene: I think it should have been like that from first grade on. **So, but** being they left them all together like this all these years, y'know. . . .

As a final argument that markers are sequentially dependent by definition, we can consider systematic co-occurrences between markers, and features of surrounding discourse. Since Chapters 4–9 provide numerous examples of co-occurrences between particular markers and other discourse devices in specific discourse slots, I will only provide one example here.

(19)   a.   **And** then we lived there for five years,
         b.   **and** we bought– we bought a triplex across the street.
         c.   **And** by that time we had two kids,
         d.   **and** we moved on the first floor,
         e.   **and** rented out the second.
         f.   **And** his brother married then,
         g.   **and** lived on the third.
         h.   **And** we still live together down the shore.

Note that *and* prefaces all of the lines in this example – all of which are separate tone units. The tokens of *and* in (a) (c) (f) and (h), however, follow a slightly longer pause (indicated by the period in the prior line and the capitalization in the new line), and occur with a temporal marker: *then* in (a), *by that time* in (c), *then* in (f), and *still* in (h). But the tokens of *and* prefacing (b), (d), (e), and (g) follow a shorter pause (indicated by the comma in the prior line), and quite strikingly, there are no temporal adverbs used within these units. Thus, (19) is neatly segmented into time periods through the use of a cluster of devices: pauses, temporal adverbs, and *and*. Such co-occurrences provide an argument that use of *and* in (19) is dependent not on the individual clauses, but is sequentially dependent on the structure of the discourse.[4]

2.1.4 Operational versus theoretical definitions

My operational definition leaves many questions unanswered – even questions of a definitional sort. Consider the many different items that I am grouping together as markers: *oh, well, and, but, or, so, because, now, then, I mean, y'know*. Are these items members of a single word class? Are they constituents in a discourse grammar? What methods would we use to discover such membership: co-occurrence restrictions, semantic and/or functional criteria? Are such methods appropriate for discourse? Is it possible to define so disparate a list of items in a way which will let us identify other elements as members of the same class? What of the paralinguistic and nonverbal markers we mentioned in (2.1.1)? Although formally different, they are functionally similar.

Complicating the effort to see these items as members of a single class is the fact that some of them are members of other word classes: *and, but, or, because* are conjunctions; *so* is sometimes conjunction, sometimes adverb; *now* and *then* are adverbs. But what of *I mean*, and *y'know*? Although *y'know* is a clause, *I mean* is not a clause because the verb *mean* requires a second argument. And what of *oh* and *well*? These have been labelled adverb, interjection, filler, particle (Stubbs 1983a, Svartvik 1980); in short, there is little agreement as to the class to which these words belong. But even if we could clearly assign each member of our list to a word class, this would only complicate our efforts to define them as a single class of discourse items, for each word could bring characteristics from its other class membership into the discourse class. And, finally, how do we know that these are the only word classes from which discourse markers could be drawn, or if all the items from such a class are potential discourse markers?

Answers to many of these questions will have to wait until **after** my analysis of markers in Chapters 4–9, because it is then that we will be able to propose a **theoretical definition** of markers. Such a definition will be an **outcome** of my analysis of how markers are used in everyday conversation. This separation of operational from theoretical definition not only allows me to ground my answers to the above definitional questions – as well as my theoretical conclusions about markers – in what speakers and hearers do with these elements, but it also makes a claim about what linguistic classification is supposed to represent: how people use language, and what they use language for. Thus, in Chapter 10, I define markers at a more theoretical level as members of a **functional** class of verbal (and non-verbal) devices which provide contextual coordinates for ongoing talk. It is then that we will see that the many different items which become **used** as markers are so used because of certain characteristics which make them available as sequentially dependent brackets of units of talk.

2.2 Data

My analysis of discourse markers is based on data collected during sociolinguistic interviews. I discuss issues raised by a corpus of sociolinguistic interviews, and describe features of my own corpus in (2.2.1); I then turn to issues concerning speaker identity in (2.2.2).

2.2.1 Sociolinguistic interviews

The main goal in all sociolinguistic interviews is to minimize the effect of the observer's paradox (Labov 1972c) – to observe speakers' everyday use of language without distorting it through the process of observation. In order to accomplish this goal, a variety of interviewing techniques, and more general interactional strategies, are regularly used during the interview itself. In addition, sociolinguistic interviews are often combined with more comprehensive and long range studies of the neighborhoods in which informants live. This not only increases one's familiarity and relationship with informants, but provides opportunities for closer interpretations of norms of language use. The net result of sociolinguistic interviews and neighborhood studies is a data base which compromises some of the deficiencies of other methods of sociolinguistic data collection, such as surveys and participation observation, because it provides both a large body of vernacular speech, and the sort of background knowledge of norms and values needed to interpret the individual, cultural, and social meanings of that speech. (See Labov 1984a for extensive discussion of advantages and disadvantages of different sociolinguistic methods of data collection.)

Note, however, that using sociolinguistic interviews – or indeed, any recorded discourse – in which one has been a participant raises some delicate problems of data control. Being a participant in conversations which later become objects of analysis complicates the observer's paradox: although the goal is to observe everyday language without distorting it through the process of observation, two added risks of distortion develop because of the analyst's participatory status. The first risk develops at the time of the discourse, when the analyst's role in the discourse influences its development. The second risk develops at the time of analysis: what is the analytic role of interpretations and knowledge gained from participatory experience in the discourse? Ideally, one should be able to apply uniform standards of analysis to discourse – regardless of one's own role (or lack of role) in a discourse. But it may be as difficult for linguists to apply uniform standards to discourse analysis as it has been for anthropologists to conduct objective ethnographies (see Agar 1982). And it may turn out to be just as unwise: since social realities are constructed at least in part from individual efforts to make sense, what is one person's definition of what is going on may differ markedly from another's, making a search for consensual (and uniform) definitions a fruitless task.

A corpus resulting from sociolinguistic interviews nevertheless has the potential for being very useful in the analysis of discourse markers. Not only does such a corpus provide a large body of data which allows quantitative as well as qualitative analyses (Chapter 3, 3.4 explains why both are important), but the corpus provides variety in mode of conversational exchange, containing question/answer pairs, story rounds, arguments, clarifications, directions, and so on. It also includes various modes of monologic discourse, e.g. narratives, explanations, descriptions, and a range of speech acts, e.g. requests, challenges, boasts. We will see that this variety is essential for analysis of discourse markers: *well*, for example, is very frequent in question/answer pairs and request/compliance sequences, but *oh* is frequent in repairs, explanations and acknowledgements.

However, given that sociolinguistic interviews have been described as a question/answer format (Wolfson 1976) and as speech situations which inhibit informal talk, why is my corpus useful – or even suitable – for an analysis of discourse? I can isolate four reasons.

First, my interviews were group interviews. The advantages of talking with several informants at a single interview are well documented (e.g. Labov 1984a). During my interviews, people often addressed one another in addition to (or rather than) me, they prompted each other to speak, e.g. to retell a family story or a favorite joke, they sometimes argued with each other and fought for the floor, and sometimes reinforced each other through the joint construction of stories, descriptions, and explanations. In short, the fact that my interviews were two, three and four party interactions meant that a variety of participation frameworks could form and reform.

Second, I shifted my own role within the interviews. Although I at times occupied my more official role as someone who wanted to gather information, I also conveyed distance from that role, sometimes tailoring my conduct according to other role expectations. For example, I routinely told people – about halfway into the interview after they had already expressed their own views on intermarriage – that I was dating someone of a different religion, thus, turning a more abstract topic into one with personal and immediate relevance. Speakers reacted with directives, e.g. 'You have to follow your own heart and your own mind' (Jan), with consolation, e.g. 'You could be very happy honey' (Ira), with pleas, e.g. 'It's your life, but, for God's sake, think about what I told you' (Henry), and with personal questions, e.g. 'Well how will your folks accept it?' (Freda). Thus, after reading a fragment of the transcript from one such conversation, a colleague asked if it was a recorded conversation with my parents. And one of the speakers (Henry) requested that I play our taped conversation for my father; another (Jack) stated that he had taken advantage of his age. The point is that people responded to me through a variety of roles – as I did to them.

A related factor is that I share a Jewish identity with the speakers. Not only did those I interviewed ask me to confirm their own assessments of my religion, but so too, did other Jewish speakers in another neighborhood in which I did further fieldwork; after receiving such confirmation, one woman said that she could then speak freely (although what she spoke about had very little to do with either religious or ethnic identity). Of course, sociolinguistic fieldwork cannot always be limited to those with whom religious, ethnic, or racial identity is shared. But interviewers can always allow informants the leeway to make public their assumptions and questions about interviewer identity – thereby increasing their personal involvement with the interviewer. And interviewers can always work to identify some common ground and shared identity with interviewees.

Another factor which helps account for the usefulness of my data is the ethnic style of the speakers, and more generally, norms for speaking among Jewish Americans. Although we are far from having a full ethnography contextualizing and detailing such norms, beginning work suggests that Jewish conversational style is characterized, among other things, by conversational overlaps, personal topics, and storytelling (e.g. Kirshenblatt-Gimblett 1974, 1975, Tannen 1981). My informants also disagreed with one another in ways which suggested their use of argumentative forms of talk for sociability (Schiffrin 1984a, Simmel 1961, original 1911). For example, they disagreed not only about topics which are inherently disputable, e.g. religion, politics, but questions which had been minimally answered with just the information requested by speakers with different backgrounds prompted sustained disagreement among my informants: questions about the location of a family doctor, belief in fate, educational background, solutions for personal problems, childhood games, location of friends and family, evaluation of local restaurants, who to invite to a party. Topics which speakers themselves developed also led to sustained disagreements: current movies, pets, music, travel. As one speaker, Jack, observed to me toward the end of one evening, 'They should have more interesting questions than this!' Jack's wife Freda disagreed with 'Maybe she didn't get a chance to ask the interesting questions' (implicating that Jack's long-windedness had prevented me from getting to those questions), and Jack came back with 'No, we made it interesting between us...the three of us.' Other speakers, Irene and Henry, argued (according to Irene) 'all the time, all the time'. According to Henry, 'If I want t'get my adrenalin worked up, she comes in' and 'if I say anything, she jumps down my throat!' And as Zelda, Henry's wife, warned one night when next-door neighbor Irene entered their kitchen, 'Oh, you better watch it!'

2.2.2 The speakers

Although I have described several features of my sociolinguistic interviews, what of the speakers themselves? Although one can never be totally sure of locating the most salient speaker characteristics for any linguistic study, discourse studies present two obstacles to analysts' attempts to isolate salient social characteristics. First, unlike other areas of sociolinguistics, discourse analysis does not offer guidelines based on cumulative results from past studies. For example, if one sets out to study phonological variation within a speech community, one often finds prior work showing that in similar communities, certain social attributes have correlated with phonological differences. Thus, one finds a ready-made list by which to categorize individuals in one's own community: age, gender, social class, race, ethnicity, network membership, and so on. But the degree to which discourse analyses incorporate characteristics of speakers varies tremendously. At one end is Labov and Fanshel (1977) in which a body of general propositions derived from knowledge of the speaker's full network of relationships, and social obligations and expectations, is built into the analysis of a single utterance. At the other end is Halliday and Hasan (1976) in which a broad range of texts written by a variety of authors provide data. Ethnomethodological analyses of conversation often reject the view that social status is a static attribute of speakers (Cicourel 1972), and thus draw instead upon data collected from strangers as well as acquaintances. Still another approach to the problem of socially characterizing speakers is to move away from external social attributes to intersubjective qualities of individuals, e.g. their personal styles and strategies (e.g. Tannen 1984). Such an approach can reach an extreme in which only one's own speech can afford sufficient subjectivity for analysis, offsetting the gain in depth of insight by a tremendous loss of generalizability.

Consider, now, that knowledge of social attributes is valuable to linguistics only if the feature being examined is in fact sensitive to social differences. It is here that a second obstacle lies: how do we find out whether particular discourse features are socially distributed? Many features of interest to discourse analysts – strategies, genres, sequential structures – are so tied to social interaction, and to features of an ongoing conversational situation, that it is difficult to isolate more static attributes of speakers (age, social class, etc.) as factors responsible for the appearance of a particular form. Even though some markers are socially evaluated and stigmatized, e.g. *y'know, I mean*, their use is so embedded in their conversational context, and so tied to features of the ongoing and evolving conversation, that one cannot be sure that it is social status differences among speakers that are responsible for different patterns of discourse, and not some fluctuation in the conversational context or in participants' definitions of the situation. In sum, the situated nature of discourse makes it difficult to know to which social differences (if any) discourse features are sensitive.

Characterizing the speakers whose discourse markers we are studying is difficult, then, because we do not know which social features to describe, or even whether discourse markers are linguistic features which are socially distributed within a speech community. With these difficulties in mind, let me introduce the speakers who will speak for themselves in the rest of the study. The Philadelphia neighborhood in which the speakers live is a lower middle class urban area situated between a working class Black neighborhood and an upper middle class White suburb. During the post World War II period when government loans to veterans greatly increased their opportunities to own single family dwellings, the area underwent its greatest period of development: it was then a close-in suburb whose modest brick row houses with lawns in front were considered ideal for young families. Although no longer a suburb, the neighborhood currently maintains much of its initial appeal. Settled there now is a mix of both original residents and more recent residents. Although the neighborhood is mixed ethnically (all White, mostly Italian and Jewish Americans), the speakers on whom I focus here are all Jewish.

I entered the community several years after preliminary interviews had been carried out by students in a sociolinguistics field methods class. Four of the speakers who appear in this study had been interviewed before

(Henry, Zelda, Irene, Freda); two (Ira, Jan) were interviewed because they had been named by others as friends; one (Jack) was interviewed because he is Freda's husband. Establishing the social relationships between speakers on the block was important because my particular interviews were designed not only to learn more about the Philadelphia speech community, but to understand neighborhood communication patterns throughout the city and to establish comparative indices of local communication.

Henry and Zelda are a middle-aged couple with two married sons, three young grandchildren, and one teenage daughter. Both are first generation Americans, their parents having emigrated from the Soviet Union shortly before they were born. Henry is old fashioned ('I come with a different generation') and values tradition ('I don't understand the ways of today'). He talks at length ('Let's get back because she'll never get home', 'Two words! You'll have her here all night!'). Much of his talk can be characterized as soapbox style (Labov 1972c), i.e. he gives opinions without being asked, seeming to address them to audiences wider than those present.

Zelda was the most openly conscious of the tape recorder at our first interview, and in the beginning of the interview, she was relatively quiet ('I'm lettin' you and him talk'). Zelda initially talked more with Irene, a neighbor who was also present during two interviews. During our second interview for which Henry was not present, however, Zelda offered many descriptions of her family, her experiences, and her beliefs; after that interview, she talked more even when Henry was present, sometimes joining Irene's side in disagreements or disagreeing with Henry on her own.

Irene is Zelda and Henry's younger next-door neighbor. Other than a brief time in New York City as an infant (the city where her parents were born and raised), Irene spent her life in Philadelphia neighborhoods close to her present home. She has been married for eighteen years to her high school sweetheart Ken, and they have four children, the oldest of whom is a classmate of Henry and Zelda's teenage daughter. Irene and Zelda share neighborhood life ('Y'know she's been a big help t'me like since I'm workin''). Irene is openly assessed by Henry as a good neighbor ('She's got more sense and nicer than all of them put together') but not a best friend because of their age differences. Although Irene and Henry disagree frequently, Henry is the first to defend Irene ('I feel that she's got a raw deal on things').

Jack and Freda are another middle-aged couple, both born and raised in Philadelphia; like Henry and Zelda, their parents emigrated from the Soviet Union. They have two teenage sons. Jack prides himself on being untraditional ('Well I was a rebel thirty-five, forty years ago'). For example, he sees himself as a Communist ('They're on their way up'), he disapproves of religious loyalties ('The point is religion is a sickening thing with me') and American films ('Tinsel!'). Jack is also a self-taught 'scholar on political science' and classical music, who was once the local committee man and who still plays classical music in his basement.

Freda expresses more traditional views than Jack (on religion and politics, for example). She often disputes not only the positions with which she disagrees, but Jack's right to state a position on which they share a view. But she also openly boasts about Jack ('I think my husband's pretty sensitive'), defends him in neighborhood disputes ('I felt that he was being stepped on'), and turns to him for explanations on issues such as the historical roots of Polish anti-Semitism. Freda initially refused vehemently to talk to me, but she changed her mind almost immediately when Jack (who was eager to talk) began to do so – to the extent that Jack had to admonish her with 'She's *asking me* the questions! *I'm* doin' the answering!'

Ira and Jan are another middle-aged couple who live next door to Jack and Freda. Although their social and cultural backgrounds are similar to those of the other couples, Ira and Jan are slightly more middle class: Ira is a white collar office worker (Henry is a plumber, Jack is a salesman, Irene's husband Ken has a small family business), and their two children are college educated (one is a lawyer). In contrast to Henry's soapbox style, and Jack's self-aggrandizing and didactic style, Ira gives an impression of careful thought and reasoned opinions, giving long explanations, for example, as to why urban neighborhoods change. Jan is characterized by her neighbor Jack as someone who 'knows everything and everybody', or as Freda says, 'Jan is alert.' Ira and Jan were the least argumentative of all the couples interviewed; rather, they often constructed joint stories and descriptions. Jan usually initiated the joint construction of such discourse, claiming that in contrast to Ira ('He's a quiet person and he doesn't socialize a lot'), she is 'the big mouth in the family'.

2.3 Summary

This chapter has operationally defined discourse markers and described the data on which my analysis is based. It is worth noting that some of the same general issues have had to be confronted in both tasks, and that these dilemmas are due to the nature of discourse analysis. As I implied through much of my discussion, deciding which discourse unit to study, how to define that unit, and how to select data are often tasks which do not receive much guidance from previous analyses. Although this is partially because of the vast and ambiguous nature of discourse analysis (Chapter 1, 1.1), I believe that this openness is also an intentional and valuable part of discourse analysis because of the reciprocal relationships that it assumes will hold among theory, analysis, and data. As I stated in (2.1.4), my theoretical definition of discourse markers will follow my analysis. This allows me, first, to ground my answers to definitional questions and my general conclusions about markers in what speakers and hearers do with these elements. Second, and more generally, it allows me to make a claim about what linguistic categories and analyses are supposed to represent: how people use language, and what they use language for. Note, then, that people are necessarily involved in this approach to linguistics – people who are inherently subjective and individual. It is because of these qualities that it is difficult to imagine any *a priori* answers about whose discourse to study, and about which qualities of those speakers will turn out to be important. But, again, this can be a gain, not only because data and analysis can again inform theory in surprising and unexpected ways, but because continual attention to the tremendously rich and varied resources which people draw upon in talk, and the continual search for ways to understand and explain what people say, mean, and do, cannot help but enrich our appreciation of human wisdom and creativity.

3 Questions: Why analyze discourse markers?

The analysis of discourse markers is part of the more general analysis of discourse coherence – how speakers and hearers jointly integrate forms, meanings, and actions to make overall sense out of what is said (see Chapter 1). Within this very general domain of analysis, however, there are several more specific issues which are also addressed through the study of discourse markers. I will illustrate these issues by discussing the markers in several segments of discourse in (3.1) and (3.2), and then summarize them in (3.3). The particular problems raised by markers suggest a method of analysis which builds on the complementary strengths of qualitative and quantitative approaches, and which aims to be both sequentially and distributionally accountable (3.4).

3.1 Markers and the emergence of coherence

The discourse in (1) is a rhetorical argument through which a speaker (Irene) is defending a position – her belief in fate – by presenting personal experiences to serve as evidence, or support, for that position.

(1)   a.   I believe in that. Whatever's gonna happen is **gonna** happen.

       b.   I believe...that...**y'know** it's fate.

       c.   It really is.

       d.   **Because** eh my husband has a brother, that was killed in an automobile accident,

       e.   **and** at the same time there was another fellow, in there, that walked away with not even a *scratch* on him.

       f.   **And** I really fee–

       g.   I don't feel y'can *push* fate,

       h.   **and** I think a lot of people *do*.

       i.   **But** I feel that you were put here for so many, years or whatever the case is,

       j.   **and** that's how it was meant to be.

       k.   **Because** like when *we* got married,

       l.   we were supposed t'get married uh: like about five months later.

m.	My husband got a notice t'go into the service
n.	**and** we moved it up.
o.	**And** my father died the week. . .after we got married.
p.	While we were on our honeymoon.
q.	**And** I just felt, that *move* was meant to be,
r.	**because** if not, he wouldn't have been there.
s.	**So** eh y'know it just s– seems that that's how things work.

For the most part, I will infer the role of the markers in the argument by seeing where in the discourse they occur, and with what they co-occur. This method itself raises certain questions which I also note in later discussion.

Consider, first, that (1) forms an **argument** because it contains two informationally differentiated parts (see also Chapter 1). The main part of an argument is a **position**: a general statement toward whose truth a speaker is committed. Subordinate to the position is support: any information, e.g. personal experience, others' testimony, logical reasoning, which justifies either the truth of the statement or the speaker's commitment toward that truth. Irene's position in (1) is that she believes in fate; she states this in various ways in several locations: lines (a)–(c), (f)–(j) and (s). Support for this position is given through brief description of two experiences in which coincident events had no rational explanation, and are thus interpreted as *meant to be*. This evidence is presented (in lines d–e, k–r) between paraphrases of the position. Thus the position is the main point of the argument, and it brackets the specific experiences serving as support:

(1a)	STRUCTURE OF (1)	
	POSITION	(a–c)
	SUPPORT (experience)	(d–e)
	POSITION	(f–j)
	SUPPORT (experience)	(k–r)
	POSITION	(s)

Several markers in (1) play a role in its formation as an argument. First, we find *because* preceding the support in (d) and (k). *Because* often precedes not just evidence, but other causally related discourse material, e.g. background information in narratives. We find *and* in (f): *and* precedes a self-interrupted restatement of the position. We will see that *and* often precedes material which continues an earlier part of the discourse – especially material which is not subordinate to the overall structure of the discourse (certainly not the case here for the speaker's statement of her position).

Finally, we find *so* in (s), preceding the final paraphrase of the position. We will see that *so* often precedes information understood as resultative (the outcome of connections between reported events) or conclusive (the outcome of inferential connections). Thus, conjunctive markers precede two separate pieces of support, as well as two presentations of the position:

(1b)	POSITION	(a–c)
	Because SUPPORT (experience)	(d–e)
	And POSITION	(f–j)
	Because SUPPORT (experience)	(k–r)
	So POSITION	(s)

(1) thus suggests that the markers *because, and*, and *so* differentiate ideational segments of the discourse, with the subordinate conjunction *because* marking a subordinate part of the discourse (support) and the coordinators *and* and *so* marking a more dominant part of the discourse (the position).

Several questions are raised by these observations. Does the role played by these conjunctions in defining and connecting idea units within an argument parallel their connecting role within sentences? And although we may speak of these elements as marking the idea structure, they do not provide the sole defining features of that structure: certainly the informational segmentation of the argument would remain intact without the markers.

Markers also occur **within** the position and the support. Is their role here also to differentiate ideationally distinct sections of the argument? If so, what would those units be: are there smaller units which combine to form the position and support? (1c) shows the markers which occur within the position and within its support.

(1c)	POSITION: **y'know**	(b)
	SUPPORT: **and**	(e)
	POSITION: **and, but**	(h, i, j)
	SUPPORT: **and, because**	(k, n, o, q, r)
	POSITION: **y'know**	(s)

Look first at the markers *and* and *but* within the position:

f. And I really fee–
g. I don't feel y'can *push* fate
h. **and** I think a lot of people *do*.
i. **But** I feel that you were put here for so many, years or whatever the case is,
j. **and** that's how it was meant to be.

In both (h) and (j), *and* links ideas which seem closely related to just prior ideas. In (h), the speaker is contrasting a feeling of her own (about *pushing fate*) with the actions of others. Note the cohesive devices which help convey this relation: the pro-verb *do*, the use of similar stance verbs *feel*, *think*. In (j), we find *and* continuing a segment which is also both ideationally related to, and cohesive with, the prior discourse. Here the common theme is the speaker's stance toward the proposition *you were put here for so many years*: she feels it (i), and *it was meant to be* (j). (Note the proform *that*.) Thus, within the position, *and* seems to have a role in linking related ideas when the union of those ideas plays a role in the larger ideational structure of the argument: *and* links thematically related material within the position.

   We also find *but* in *i*:

i.   **But** I feel that you were put here for so many, years or whatever the case is

That *but* is an adversative conjunction suggests that what follows *but* is an idea which contrasts with what has preceded. Like *and*, then, it seems that *but* could have a cohesive function within the position.

   But in (i) also poses two further questions. First, how much discourse can be included within the scope of a marker? Two different interpretations of the scope of *but* are possible here. The speaker could be contrasting her position with what was presented in one prior clause – *a lot of people do (push fate)*. Or, she could be contrasting her position with what was presented in two prior clauses – what she feels in contrast to what she doesn't feel. The second question posed by *but* in (i) is this: at what level of discourse can a relationship such as contrast be marked? Instead of interpreting contrast at a local ideational level, we could locate the contrast at a more global level of discourse topic, since the speaker is here returning to the main point of her argument. So *but* could be marking a contrast between the main point and prior discourse which is slightly tangential to that point, i.e. what the speaker believes vs. what she doesn't believe. If all markers have variable scope in discourse, as well as the ability to mark relationships at different discourse levels, then what fixes the range and level of discourse over which they operate?

   Look next at the conjunctive markers within the support sections. In (e), *and* precedes an event whose coincidence with the prior mentioned event establishes the experience as an instance of fate.

d.   Because eh my husband has a brother, that was killed in an automobile accident,
e.   **and** at the same time there was another fellow, in there, that walked away with not even a *scratch* on him.

And in both (n) and (o) is parallel:

m.   My husband got a notice t'go into the service
n.   **and** we moved it up.
o.   **And** my father died the week. . .after we got married.

Here we can argue that *and* has both a cohesive role and a larger structural role. First, *and* has a structural role because it links together events which together function as support for the position. Second, *and* has a cohesive role because interpretation of those events as fateful hinges on their being understood as part of a single, larger situation. In other words, it is the union of the two events that makes them indicative of fate.

What then of *and* in (q):

q.   **And** I just felt, that *move* was meant to be,
r.   because if not, he wouldn't have been there.

Lines (q) and (r) do not actually report fateful events; rather, they present the speaker's interpretation of the situation as one which is due to fate (*meant to be*). Repetition of the phrase *meant to be* from the earlier position statement in (j) provides an important clue to the function of these lines:

i.   But I feel that you were put here for so many, years or whatever the case is,
j.   and that's how it was **meant to be**. [lines k–p]
q.   And I just felt that *move* was **meant to be**.

Meant to be is a formulaic phrase conveying a sense of individual helplessness over life events. Its repetition from (j) into (q) has two effects. First, since it is repeated from the position into the support, it conveys an ideational and cohesive link between these two argument sections. Second, it warrants the speaker's use of this particular experience as evidence for her belief in fate: describing the specific experience and the general belief with the same formula establishes the eligibility of the experience as evidence for the belief. (See Toulmin 1958 for discussion of warrants.) Thus, although the speaker is subjectively assessing the situation – rather than objectively reporting the events (as in k–p) – this interpretation has no less a role in establishing the experience as evidence than did the report. What the interpretation does is justify use of this particular experience as one which counts as an instance of the workings of fate.[1] This switch from reporting to interpreting events, then, is a shift in speaker orientation within the support section of the argument – within a single ideational segment. And it is here that we find *and*.

We also find *because* within the support section in (r):

q.   And I just felt, that *move* was meant to be,
r.   **because** if not, he wouldn't have been there.

Here *because* has a local scope: in contrast to (d) and (k), where *because*
marked a whole section of the discourse as support, *because* in (r) causally
links just the propositions in (q) and (r).

There is one other marker in (1) which I have not yet discussed: *y'know*
within the position.

b.   I believe...that...**y'know** it's fate. [lines c–r]
s.   So eh **y'know** it just s– seems that that's how things work.

Y'know is directed toward gaining hearer involvement in an interaction. In
(b) and (s), *y'know* seems to be marking some kind of appeal from speaker
to hearer for consensus, e.g. for understanding as to the meaning of fate, or
even, for agreement on the position being taken about fate. We will see that
y'know is widely used throughout talk at locations in which discourse tasks
hinge on special cooperative effort between speaker and hearer; I will propose that *y'know* marks speaker/hearer alignment and that it contrasts with
I mean, which marks speaker orientation.

Note that here I am beginning to use information other than co-
occurrence to infer the role of markers: I have tacitly assumed that the
semantic meaning of *y'know* contributes something to its role as discourse
marker. We will return to this general question again and again: is there
some property of the elements used as markers that contributes to their
function?

(1d) summarizes the markers which we have discussed:

(1d)	MARKERS IN ARGUMENT 1	location
	POSITION: **y'know**	(a–c)
	Because SUPPORT	(d–e)
	event **and** event	(e)
	And POSITION	(f–j)
	state **and** contrasting state	(h)
	state **but** contrasting state	(i)
	state **and** interpretation of state	(j)
	Because SUPPORT	(k–r)
	event/event/**and** event	(n)
	event **and** event	(o)
	events **and** state interpreting events	(q)
	event **because** event	(r)
	So y'know POSITION	(s)

3.2 Markers as coherence options

Although the markers in (1) add to its overall structure and interpretation, they are hardly the only devices which either form the argument, or convey its meaning. A brief look at several other arguments shows that their structure and meaning is certainly not dependent on just those markers that we have seen in (1); in fact, the structure and meaning of arguments can be preserved even without markers.

3.2.1 Coherence options: choosing among markers

(2) presents an argument in which the speaker (Zelda) justifies a rule (*you have to start in the beginning*) by presenting specific cases which show that compliance with the rule had a desired effect. The desired effect of the rule is for married children to call their mothers-in-law by some term of address – either 'Mom' or first name. Thus, the rule is Zelda's position; the three cases presented are support for the position. It is important to note that prior to this argument, Zelda had been complaining about her younger daughter-in-law's inability to call her 'Mom': because 'Mom' is an address term which ratifies Zelda's status as a mother – a status that is very important to her – her daughter-in-law's failure to do so is an offense.

(2)	Zelda:	a.	And y'have t'start in the beginning.
		b.	**Now** my daughter in law *did*.
		c.	My older daughter in law from the very beginning she said Mom,
		d.	so she's used to it.
		e.	Mom and Dad.
		f.	See it does m– it's only a name!
		g.	**And** Sam– we told Samuel *too*,
		h.	in the beginning, you call– if you can't say Mom and Dad,
		i.	call 'em by their first name.
		j.	But call 'em *some*thing.
		k.	Not 'uh:::::'
	Debby:		Yeh! And wait for them t'hear ⌈'uh!' ⌉
	Zelda:		⌊Right!⌋
		l.	And she's an intelligent girl
		m.	and she's a *nice* girl.
		n.	She gives us the biggest respect.
		o.	And she's really nice.
		p.	I like her very much.

q.   It's just that she can't say it.
r.   **Now** I remember when I first got married,
s.   and I was in that situation.
t.   And eh the first– like the first. . .few times, I wouldn't
      say anything.
u.   And my husband said to me, 'Now look, it isn't hard,
      just say "Mom"'.
v.   He says, 'And I want you t'do it.'
w.   And I *did* it.
x.   And I got *used* to it.

Although there are many markers within this argument, I will focus only
on those which precede the support so as to contrast them with markers in
parallel positions in argument (1). (I do not examine *and* in the position
because its scope goes beyond the argument.)

Note, first, that (2) has a structure similar to (1) in that multiple
instances of support follow the position. The structure also differs, however, because there is no restatement of the position either between the supporting cases or at the end of the argument. Recall that (2) presents a rule,
which had it been followed would have avoided an offense committed by
Zelda's daughter-in-law. Because Zelda has just complained about that
offense, she now has to strike a somewhat delicate balance between sound-
ing tolerant and intolerant: if she is too tolerant, her hearer may very well
wonder why the offense was an issue in the first place; but if she complains
too much, she can be heard as overly critical of her family to someone who
is a relative outsider. Having to strike this balance affects the structure of
the argument: Zelda either minimizes the offense, or praises the offender
between each piece of support. Both tactics work to convey the closeness of
Zelda's relationship with her family, despite the breach (or in one of
Zelda's prior descriptions, *the sore spot*) caused by her daughter-in-law's
inability to use a term of address which would have ratified Zelda's family
status. The structure of (2) is thus the following:

STRUCTURE OF 2
POSITION   (a)
     Now SUPPORT (experience)   (b–e)
EVALUATION (minimization of offense) (f)
     And SUPPORT (experience)   (g–k)
EVALUATION (praise for offender)   (l–p)
              (minimization of offense) (q)
     Now SUPPORT (experience)   (r–x)

Note, now, that the discourse markers used to bracket the support are *now* (b, r) and *and* (g). Does this mean that these two markers are discourse alternants for *because* – the marker of support in (1)? Certainly they are marking the same informational segment of a similarly structured discourse. Thus, if they are options, why use one marker rather than another? There are also many other discourse slots in which *and* and *because* could not alternate: for example, we have seen *and* marking the position in an argument, clearly a location in which *because* would not occur. And we also find *now* within the support: *And my husband said to me, 'Now look...'.* Are the possible substitutes here the same, e.g. *and, because*? If not, why should *and, now*, and *because* be coherence options in one discourse slot, but not in others? Exactly what is the contribution of the discourse slot, and what is the contribution of the meaning (or other property) of the word itself?

3.2.2 Coherence options: choosing among markers and other devices

Other linguistic devices can accomplish many of the discourse tasks performed by markers. In (3), the speaker (Zelda) is defending her upbringing of her daughter. Her position is that she is strict with her children when it is needed. (The position had been presented earlier in the conversation.) She begins supporting this position with *see*, and then gives reasons for specific actions within the supporting cases with *because*.

(3)   a.   **See**, she is at the point now where she really doesn't run out that much so that there–

        b.   she's not driving a car or anything.

        c.   we *did* have it with the boys, uh: they weren't–they–y–

        d.   when they first started t'drive, they *did* have t'be in by twelve,

        e.   **because** they had a learner's permit.

        f.   We always did tell the boys...

        g.   I always stressed that

        h.   **because** I went through more with the boys than I did with JoAnn.

STRUCTURE OF 3

POSITION /stated earlier/	
See SUPPORT 1 [reason]	(a–b)
SUPPORT 2 [alternative]	(c–f)
event **because** event	(d–e)
SUPPORT 2 [alternative]	(f–h)
because event	(h)

What gives textual structure and cohesion to this argument is lexical repetition (stressed *did*) in (c) and (d), and reiteration of part of the support in (c) (*we did have it with the boys*) and (f) (*we always did tell the boys*). The speaker also maintains thematic continuity on a local, clause by clause basis: topic is continued from the clauses in (a) to (b); a new topic, *the boys*, is introduced in predicate position in (c) and then continued through (e); a new topic, *Well* is introduced in (f) and then maintained through (h). Clearly the speaker could have used markers for the structural and ideational tasks of the argument, e.g. *now, because, y'know* or *but* in (c), *so* or *but* in (f) and (g), and so on.

(4) illustrates still other structural and cohesive devices used in argument. Here, the speaker (Henry) is arguing that there is a difference between two religious groups (his own – Jewish – and others).

(4)
    a.   There is a difference.
    b.   Listen to me.
    c.   There is a big difference.
    d.   **Because** you hear the knocks, when you're in a crowd,
    e.   **and** they'll say you're *different*.
    f.   *This* is the thing you're gonna hear.
    g.   You're *different*.
    h.   My brother heard it in the Marine Corps,
    i.   my younger brother heard it in the Army,
    j.   **and** I heard it in the Army,
    k.   **and** here's my wife here,
    l.   she was in the Navy,
    m.   *she* heard it.
    n.   Everyone of us.
    o.   You got– you could pull out *ten* Jewish guys,
    p.   **and** if they're nice guys everyone of em'll say that somebody said it.

STRUCTURE OF 4
    POSITION   (a–c)
    Because GENERAL SUPPORT (experience)   (d–g)
    SPECIFIC SUPPORT (experience)   (h–n)
    event/event/**and** event **and** event   (j, k)
    GENERAL SUPPORT (experience)   (o–p)
    state **and** event   (p)

Henry presents his position in (a–c) and his support in (d–p). Because his support consists of a generalization (in d–g), which is itself buttressed through more specific support (four experiences in h–m which are summarized in n), Henry's argument is more complex than (1), (2), (3): (4) actually contains an embedded argument in which the support is itself supported. The specific experiences are then reframed as general support in (o–p). What provides textual unity in (4) is a meta-linguistic phrase in (f), syntactic parallels in (h–j), and (m), and repetition in (a) and (c), (e) and (g). Thus ideational structure and cohesion in Henry's argument are provided through a variety of devices other than markers.

If ideational structure and cohesion can be provided through so many different devices, what do discourse markers add to overall coherence? Identifying the contribution of markers to coherence becomes even more difficult when we consider interactional structures and speaker/hearer alignments. In (5), Henry has been arguing with his wife Zelda and their neighbor Irene about women's roles. He has just conceded that having additional children is not a solution to women's boredom. Although there is a rhetorical argument hidden in this interaction (Henry's position about women and his support for that position), we will focus here primarily on the challenges that are presented to Henry's position via attacks on its support.

(5)   Henry: a.   All right maybe that's a foolish statement.

                   b.   **But** let's put it this way.

                   c.   A woman is needed in the house t'clean the house, and t'cook the hou– uh cook the meals, and clean the clothes, there is a tremendous amount of work ⎡for a woman ⎤

    Zelda: d.   ⎣That's off ⎦ Henry.

    Henry: e.   You don't think there's a d– a lot of work for yourself?

    Zelda: f.   You can get– you can get anybody t'come in and clean: the ⎡house.   ⎤

    Henry: g.   ⎣All week?⎦

    Zelda: h.   *That is not the point.*

    Irene: i.   That's not r– no ⎡that's not true.⎤

    Zelda: j.   ⎣That's off.   ⎦ No.

                   k.   That's off ⎡Henry. ⎤

    Henry: l.   ⎣You say ⎦ that's wrong?

    Zelda: m.   Yep. That's not a mother's duty.

                   n.   Just ⎡t'clean and cook and clean.   ⎤

    Henry: o.   ⎣**Well** what would you call a ⎦ mother's duty that– now that you ⎡*are* a ⎤mother?

    Zelda: p.   ⎣When⎦ you supervise the children and ask them, and talk to them,

                   q.   but with the cleaning bit, anybody can do the cleaning bit.

    Henry: r.   **But** ⎡it's still–   ⎤it's still a job regardless=

    Zelda: s.   ⎣Anybody.⎦

    Henry: =of the– it's in that– your house!

But in (b) and (r) precedes Henry's reiteration of his position, and thus, could be said to mark a prominent idea unit in the discourse. *But* also establishes Henry's position as a contrast to Zelda's challenges. Thus, *but* prefaces a particular interactional move: a defense. Similarly, *well* in (o) prefaces a new attack on Zelda from Henry, and thus, a new interactional move: counterattack.

Zelda and Irene are also challenging Henry; in fact, Henry has presented the argument in (5) in response to their earlier challenges (not included here). The opposing moves, however, are not preceded by discourse markers. Rather, the challenges from Zelda and Irene are enacted through added volume, negatives, and meta-talk – *that's off* (d, j), *that is not the point* (h), *that's not a mother's duty* (m), *that's not true* (i), *no* (i,j) – and a semantic generalization opposing Henry's *a woman is needed* (c) with *anybody* (f). Why do discourse markers preface some moves and not others? And would we interpret the same move were a marker to preface Irene's challenge, or were a marker not to preface Henry's challenge? And, finally, which markers are discourse options: *but* and *well* both prefaced adversative moves, but are interactional moves prefaced by *but* really equivalent to those prefaced by *well*?

Thus far, we have begun discussion of each marker with description of its role at a single level of analysis: ideational structure, cohesive meaning, interactional move. But we have ended discussion of so many markers with mention of additional roles that it is time to explicitly address the form/function relationship. Can one form have several functions simultaneously? After distinguishing six functions of language, Jakobson (1960: 353) states:

we could, however, hardly find verbal messages that would fulfill only one function. The diversity lies not in a monopoly of some one of these several functions but in a different hierarchical order of functions. The verbal structure of a message depends primarily on the predominant function.

Jakobson's point suggests not only that a single marker might have multiple functions, but that a marker might have a predominant function: perhaps some markers are specialized for interactional functions, others for ideational functions.

Let us examine (6), an earlier exchange from the disagreement which we just saw as (5). Henry has been arguing that the lack of respect for fathers produced general family and social disorganization. Irene opposes this position by finding a different cause for the agreed-upon disorganization: she argues that standards have changed.

(6)   Irene: a.   The standards though are different today.
       Henry: b.   Heh?
       Irene: c.   The standards are different today.
       Henry: d.   Standards are different.
                 e.   **But** I'm tellin' y' if the father is respected
                       an $\begin{bmatrix} \text{:d eh:} \\ \text{Henry, lemme} \end{bmatrix}$ ask you a question.
       Irene: f.

But in (e) prefaces the meta-linguistic phrase *I'm tellin' you* which intensifies an already disputed position (Schiffrin 1980). Thus, *but* precedes a structurally dominant part of Henry's argument, and could thus be said to have a function in the **ideational structure** of the discourse. Because *but* has an adversative sense, however, it is also a **cohesive** device which adds to our interpretation of the meaning of what Henry is about to say, marking it as a contrast with what Irene has just said. Finally, Henry's remark is a defense against Irene's challenge, and thus, *but* also prefaces a new **interactional move**. Although it would be quite difficult to argue that any one of these roles were predominant within this particular argument, it seems impossible not to argue that *but* is here functioning simultaneously on several planes of discourse. Although it is still an open question as to whether some markers are specialized for particular functions, we can hardly argue either that markers have only one function, or that a single marker has only a single function.

3.3 Why are discourse markers used?

I have illustrated several general questions about markers. Why are discourse markers used? Do they add anything? Or, are they merely redundant features which reflect already existing discourse relationships? If so, what underlying relationships do they reflect? Why use one marker instead of another? And if other devices are alternatives to markers, what conditions delimit the choices among such alternatives?

These general questions are relevant to several additional issues. Consider what happens if we say that markers are cohesive devices. We saw in our discussion of cohesion in Chapter 1, that cohesive devices **reflect** underlying connections between propositions – connections that are inferred by producers and interpreters of a text. But can markers ever **create** cohesion? That is, can they lead a hearer to search for underlying connections that would not otherwise be inferred, or to prefer one reading out of a set of equally plausible readings? We might propose that if any markers were to add cohesion to a discourse, it would be conjunctive markers.

Yet, the literature on *and* is full of conflicting analyses revolving around the very same issue: does *and* have several different distinct senses (in which case *and* could create cohesion), or are its various interpretations (e.g. as a temporal connection, a causal connection) determined only by the meanings of the connected propositions (in which case *and* would reflect cohesion)? As Dik (1968: 250) observes, 'whether particles like prepositions, articles, and connectives have meaning (and if so, what kind of meaning) has been a moot point since antiquity.' Thus, we can hardly turn to traditional scholarship about conjunctions to help answer the question of whether conjunctive markers reflect or create cohesion.

Our initial questions about what discourse markers add also lead to questions concerning markers and discourse structures. Conjunctions either coordinate or subordinate clauses within a sentence grammar. Does this difference apply in discourse as well? Although we hinted that it did – *and* and *so* prefaced the main point of the argument in (1), and *because* prefaced the subordinate part of the argument – it is not at all clear that this distinction either appears in the same way in discourse, or has the same ramifications (e.g. Thompson 1984). Is the way in which conjunctive markers define and connect idea units within argument (and other discourse units) parallel to the way they connect clauses within sentences? Furthermore, is their role in marking connections between smaller units – either units which are syntactically defined such as clauses, or ideationally defined such as events in the support section of an argument – also structural? Although we may speak of these elements as marking structure, we have seen briefly that they do not always provide the sole defining features of the structure. Thus, we have a question analogous to our cohesion question: do markers display structure or create structure?

Other issues to which our initial questions are relevant concern the kind of meaning(s) that markers reflect (or add). Cohesion has to do with semantic meaning, i.e. referential meaning. But linguists commonly distinguish referential meaning from non-referential meaning. Halliday and Hasan (1976), for example, differentiate internal from external meaning; their distinction centers around the location of meaning – in the facts which are being reported (external) or in the speaker's inferences about that report (internal).[2] Non-referential meaning is often viewed as social and/or expressive meaning (see Chapter 1, 1.3.3): this captures its non-representational quality, but focuses more on conventionalized linguistic ways of conveying non-representational aspects of a message, than on either speaker intentions or hearers' inferential procedures designed to infer those intentions (cf. Bach and Harnish 1982).

My brief discussion of *y'know* suggested that *y'know* has expressive meaning, i.e. as a speaker appeal for hearer cooperation in a discourse task. But this expressive meaning may very well include some component, or residue, of referential meaning. We really do not know how – or if – the referential meanings of markers contribute to the way that they are used in discourse. Changes from referential to non-referential meanings are well-documented (see, e.g. Cole (1975), Horn (1984)). Indeed, as Hymes (1974: 149) observes: 'lexical elements and phrases, if they acquire grammatical function in a social or stylistic sense, may lose their earlier lexical force in their new paradigmatic relationships'. But does referential sense or lexical force ever remain to contribute to expressive meaning? Different positions on this question as it bears on the historical present tense, for example, are taken by Schiffrin (1981), Silva-Corvalan (1983), and Wolfson (1979, 1982). Nor is it clear what expressive meanings develop. Clark's (1979, 1980) work on indirect speech acts suggests, for example, that requests are interpreted as more polite (which touches on both expressive and social meanings) the more they contain words and phrases whose lexical meaning makes no contribution. Thus, we have to ask the following question about markers which have referential meaning: does that meaning contribute to their function as discourse markers?

Consider now that my preliminary observations about what markers add to discourse have been based largely on their locations within discourse – where markers occur, and with what markers co-occur. I have just stated, however, that referential meaning may influence discourse function by contributing to expressive and/or social meaning. A broader question stemming out of these observations is this: how do the meanings (or any other properties) of a specific marker combine with its location to produce its discourse function? This question has immediate methodological implications: would we have been as ready to interpret *y'know* as a coordinating structural device as we were to so interpret *and*? Probably not: just as there are features of *y'know* that lead away from such a conclusion, so too, there are features of *and* that contribute to that conclusion. It is here, then, that our questions about markers force us to face one of the most difficult questions in pragmatics: how does context interact with meaning to produce the total communicative force of an expression?

There is still another issue: markers as coherence options. If both referential meaning and context do indeed contribute to the functions of discourse markers, this may greatly reduce the degree to which markers can be coherence options for one another. Although options, or alternative ways of saying the same thing (Labov 1978), are present at all levels of language, defining 'the same thing' is difficult once our level of analysis extends into discourse, and once our notions of same and different go beyond referential meaning. In fact, trying to replace referential equivalence as a requirement for linguistic alternation has been a problem whose lack of easy resolution has greatly hampered efforts to extend the study of linguistic variation beyond phonology (Dines 1980, Labov 1978, Lavandera 1978, Romaine 1981, Schiffrin 1985b).

Often suggested as a replacement for referential equivalence is functional equivalence. Linguistic elements and structures have often been assigned either a cognitive or a communicative function. The assignment of particular functions, however, presupposes knowledge of a larger system, e.g. a cognitive system for processing information, a communication system for transmitting information, within which fulfillment of those functions maintains the system. But functions are often assigned without consideration of the larger system within which any one function has to be located, and with tacit assumption that all functions are fulfilled in some way. It was partially to remedy this unsystemic use of the concept of function that I proposed a model of discourse in Chapter 1: this model can be seen as an outline of the underlying components of talk (exchange, action, ideational, information, and participation) whose systemic interaction with one another produces coherent discourse (see comments on integration of discourse in 1.4).

Even if we can identify functions in a systemic way, there are three additional properties of markers which complicate the search for functional equivalents. First is their apparent multifunctionality. As we have seen, markers may be used in several different discourse capacities simultaneously. This may reduce the degree to which markers are interchangeable, e.g. ideational equivalence may not always mean interactional equivalence. Thus, functionally equivalent options may be found within only one discourse component at a time. Second, markers are never obligatory. What this means is that any utterance preceded by a marker may also have occurred without that marker. But does the absence of a marker also have functions? Third is the syntactic diversity found in the elements used as markers. We do not know, for example, whether syntactic distinctions between adverbs (e.g. *now*) and conjunctions (e.g. *and*) are neutralized at discourse levels, or whether syntactic properties remain to differentiate markers from one another in some way. Although various scholars (e.g. Givón 1979, Sankoff and Brown 1976, Traugott 1979), have argued that syntactic change may originate in discourse structure and communicative processes associated with discourse, the way in which grammatical elements are utilized in the synchronic organization of discourse is largely unknown (but see Thompson 1984).

Talking about markers as coherence options for each other – as alternative ways of saying the same thing – also raises the problem of whether elements as diverse as *and, now,* and *y'know* can form one class of items in a discourse paradigm. In traditional linguistic analysis, items which occur in the same environment and produce a different meaning are in contrast, whereas items which occur in the same environment but do not produce a difference in meaning are in free variation. Are the differences in meaning between markers such as *and, now,* and *y'know* discrete enough to produce contrast? Or, are such markers options which ignore small differences in meaning in the service of larger functional equivalences, such as discourse coherence? Merely having to pose such questions means that even if we could define a paradigm of discourse markers, it is not likely to exhibit the more traditional requirements of some identity of form and some identity of meaning. Rather, it would group together elements with various degrees of functional similarities and partially overlapping distributions.

Thus far, many of our questions have indirectly touched on issues which are important in attempts to define boundaries between subdisciplines within linguistics: syntax and discourse analysis, semantics and pragmatics. Additional questions also touch on these attempts. First, how much discourse beyond a sentence can be included within the scope of a marker? And how is such a range decided? Second, at what level of discourse can a relationship between units be marked? Is it possible to speak of relationships such as contrast, result, and addition not only at a local level of idea structures, but at more global levels? And can we also speak of such relationships on pragmatic planes of talk?

In sum, there are numerous questions which an analysis of discourse markers is forced to address. Since the scope of some questions go well beyond discourse markers *per se*, however, I cannot hope to fully answer each question. Furthermore, some questions are more relevant to particular discourse markers than others, e.g. since *oh* and *well* have no semantic meaning *per se*, my questions about referential meaning have little relevance to their analysis. Nevertheless, the questions posed in this chapter illustrate the general issues which my specific analyses in Chapters 4–9 will address. Chapter 10 will then return to these issues.

3.4 Methodological issues

We have seen that the study of discourse markers is part of the more general study of discourse coherence. In this section, I will discuss how to approach this very broad domain of study. I will be distinguishing between quantitative and qualitative approaches to analysis, but I want to stress before doing so, that these terms represent a somewhat artificial dichotomy. That is, most analyses combine facets of both quantitative and qualitative approaches if not in their actual procedures, in their underlying assumptions. Quantitative analyses, for example, depend on a great deal of qualitative description prior to counting (in order to empirically ground ones' categories) as well as **after** counting (statistical tendencies have to be interpreted as to what they reveal about causal relations). And qualitative approaches often have an implicit belief in the notion that 'more is better', i.e. the more instances of a phenomenon one finds, the more one can trust one's interpretation of an underlying pattern (e.g. Tannen 1984: 37). This is the very same belief which underlies quantitative reasoning and tests of statistical significance.

Furthermore, both qualitative and quantitative analyses often assume that co-occurrences provide supportive evidence. (If one proposes, for example, that the historical present tense in narrative has an evaluative function (Wolfson 1979, Schiffrin 1981), then supportive evidence for this proposal – from either quantitative or qualitative perspectives – would be the discovery of this tense with other evaluative devices.) What underlies this assumption is another assumption: messages are multiply reinforced and internally consistent. Yet, instead of assuming that messages are created through **redundancy**, one can assume that they are created through **complementarism**. That is, it is by no means necessary to assume that all elements in a message contribute in an equal way to the communicative force of that message: not only is it possible that not all parts of a message are multiply conveyed, but it is also possible that the presence of one element which conveys a particular component of a message actually frees other elements from the need to duplicate that component of the message. (Schiffrin 1985b discusses this in relation to the temporal ordering of causal sequences.) My point here is not to justify the validity of either the redundancy or the complementarism assumption. I merely want to note that an implicit belief that co-occurrences are supportive evidence, as well as a deeper assumption about the redundancy of messages, are shared by both qualitative and quantitative approaches.

Qualitative and quantitative analyses make complementary contributions to the study of discourse markers, and more generally, to the study of discourse coherence. We need qualitative analysis, for example, to uncover the idea structures of arguments within which markers have a role, or to interpret speakers' use of evaluation in their argument (as in Zelda's argument about her daughter-in-law in (2)). We also need qualitative analysis to be able to identify particular interactional moves: when does an utterance perform a challenge? But we also need quantitative analysis. Recall that coherence options are neither categorically required nor prohibited (Chapter 1, 1.4). Quantitative analysis of the frequencies with which particular options are used would allow us to show speakers' **preferences** for the use of one option rather than another. Through the use of quantitative analysis, we may also be able to account for why a particular item has a certain function by separating the effect of its referential meaning from the effect of the discourse slot in which it occurs.

Unfortunately, the characteristics of discourse which support one type of analysis are all too often the same characteristics that make it difficult to carry out the other type of analysis – let alone work toward the kind of combined approach that is required to answer the questions raised by discourse markers. For example, one of the features of discourse which hinders quantification is that talk is an ongoing joint creation, in which both forms and meanings are subject to continual negotiation and participant interpretation (see discussion in Chapter 1, 1.4). It is just this quality that can lead an investigator to seat him or herself in the minds of the conversationalists (or even to be a conversationalist) and interpret from the participants' point of view just what is going on. But this quality makes counting exceedingly difficult: for example, even if one wanted to count speaker intentions, how would they be identified with enough objectivity and certainty to do so? Another feature of discourse which hinders quantification is that identification of many conversational regularities depends on a detailed characterization – and interpretation – of their locations in sequential structures. However, one result of such attention to sequential structure is an unwillingness to view the emergent regularities as tokens of the same underlying type. Unfortunately, it is just such a view which would be required for the quantitative analysis of such structures.

On a more general level, qualitative and quantitative analytical approaches are rooted in different theoretical approaches to linguistic inquiry. The former is rooted in a more humanistic, subjective approach in which interpretations of both the observer and the observed so permeate the **particularities** of a description as to defy attempts at generalizations or statements of universals (Becker 1984). The latter is rooted in a more

scientific, objective approach in which particular descriptions are catego-
rized so as to provide a basis for aggregate data and a foundation for
generalizations about shared properties.

The tension between particularity and generalization which differentiates qualitative from quantitative approaches can be seen in the way each
treats the notion of 'typical instance'. Let us assume that one has increased
confidence in the non-randomness of a particular observation if one finds
more than one instance of such an occurrence, for then the observation can
be seen as representative of a more general pattern. Quantitative
approaches can measure the degree to which a pattern is widespread
because they assume that different observations are in some underlying
sense the same – that they share certain objective properties. But for
extreme versions of qualitative approaches, particular observations are so
different from each other that they can be typical instances of widespread
patterns at only the most superficial level of description.

Much of my analysis depends upon the belief that one can find typical
instances of an occurrence which represent more general patterns. Thus,
nothing that I report in the coming chapters is based on only a **single**
occurrence: each observation is backed by multiple examples in my data.
Another way of saying this is that my particular observations are typical
instances of a more widespread pattern.

But at the same time, I will remain aware of the possibility that a **single**
instance of a phenomenon can be as revealing as multiple instances. Hymes
(1972: 35), following Sapir (1916), discusses this point in relation to the
search for cultural patterns. Despite a tendency to place more trust in an
observation that one makes over and over again, a single observation may
be construed as just as real a cultural product: a sonnet, for example, is as
much a cultural product as a kinship system, even though the former is produced only once and the latter is replicated again and again.

A single instance can be revealing for another reason: it can suggest the
need for an explanation which covers a wider variety of phenomena. Schegloff (1972), for example, reports how a single example which did not fit his
explanation of summons/answer sequences forced him to reconsider all of
his other observations, and consequently, to recast his entire description.
The danger with quantitative approaches, of course, is that they would
assign a single instance less significance than repeated instances. And the
danger with qualitative approaches is that each instance would be seen as a
single instance.

Despite these differences (and remembering that the quantitative/
qualitative distinction is a somewhat false dichotomy), it is important to try

to combine both approaches for the analysis of discourse markers. I approach this methodological problem by arguing that discourse analysis can be made accountable to a data base in two different, but complementary ways.

First, by limiting one's analysis to a particular discourse context, e.g. a genre, an episode, an exchange, an analysis can approach **sequential accountability**. As Labov and Fanshel (1977: 354) suggest, an analysis can become 'accountable to an entire body of conversation, attempting to account for the interpretation of all utterances and the coherent sequencing among them'. In such analyses, one's data consist of a limited set of discourses on which attention and interpretation is focused.

Many of the problems raised by discourse markers suggest an approach which aims for sequential accountability. I suggested that form, meaning, and action are interwoven, and jointly negotiated, components of discourse coherence, and thus, that analyzing the contribution of a particular item to coherence should attend to each of these components. Knowledge of these different aspects of discourse may be much easier to acquire in a limited discourse type. Thus, we have one reason to focus a great deal of qualitative description on very limited domains – as we did in this chapter, for example, in our discussion of markers in arguments.

There are equally compelling reasons, however, to aim not for sequential accountability, but for **distributional accountability**. This second approach requires that one's analysis be based on the full range of environments in which a particular item occurs. Note that in analyzing some linguistic elements, we can quite safely restrict our attention to limited discourse types. To understand the historical present tense, for example, we can restrict our attention to narrative since this tense is a feature of that particular genre (although even here we may bring in observations about the present tense in other discourse). But confining an analysis of discourse markers to a limited domain is misleading because markers occur throughout conversation, e.g. in question/answer pairs:

(7)   Freda: How m– long has your mother been teaching?
            Debby: **Well** she hasn't been teaching that long.

in turn-transition spaces:

(8)   Debby: That seems to happen to people a lot, doesn't it?
                       ⎡ **I mean**. . . ⎤
           Jan: ⎣ Quite often. ⎦ Y'never realize it until it happens t'you.

A variety of markers also occurs in direct quotes:

(9)   Jack: Even the teacher admitted it.
                   She says, '**Well** it was– y'shouldn't do it! **But** it was nice!'

in self-repairs:

(10)   Irene: Look at Bob's par– eh father and mo– **well** I don't think his
                   father accepted it, his mother.

in introductions of new discourse topics:

(11)   Henry: **Y'know** I got a cousin– I got a cousin, a girl that speaks eleven
                   languages.

in comparisons:

(12)   Jan: They aren't brought up the same way. **Now** Italian people are
                   very outgoing, they're very generous. When they put a meal on
                   the table it's a meal. **Now** these boys were Irish. They lived
                   different.

    Because discourse markers occur throughout discourse, focusing only on a limited type of talk creates a risk: one can mistakenly equate the general function of a marker with its particular use within a specific discourse type. In other words, one may become so subsumed by the particularities of a discourse whose description is sequentially accountable, that the underlying similarities of that discourse to other forms of talk may be overlooked – as may general functional similarities between the markers in those different discourse types. Thus, a distributionally accountable analysis also requires that one focus less on the particularities of a single discourse than on the categorization of that discourse as a 'typical instance' of a more general type.

    Another reason to consider markers wherever they occur is that context and meaning interact to produce the full communicative force of the expressions used as discourse markers. We saw that markers may have referential meaning that acts in concert with their discourse location. But without considering markers in a variety of discourse locations, we would not be able to tease apart the contribution made by meaning from that made by context, or, to see what meaning and context contribute together. It is here that quantitative analyses become particularly useful, for by comparing the frequencies with which a marker occurs in different discourse slots, we can test different hypotheses about the marker – and the contribution of meaning versus location to its function.

Still another reason to examine markers wherever they occur concerns the fluid and open nature of conversational genres. Although we may define such genres as mutually exclusive types, e.g. narrative versus argument, it is unlikely that everyday conversation contains genres that are totally distinct from each other. Conversational arguments, for example, often resemble descriptions in some respects and explanations in others. Furthermore, arguments and narratives may overlap, as when a story is told to support a position (cf. Irene's two brief experiences in 1). Focusing on markers wherever they occur alleviates the problems that may develop when the discourse which we think of as a closed genre really turns out to be a much more open and fluid combination of diverse types.

How do sequential and distributional accountability intersect? I suggest that they are complementary approaches to discourse analysis. Consider, first, that although distributional accountability is a familiar requirement of quantitative studies of phonological and morphological variation, it has not been applied with the same rigor to the analysis of discourse phenomena. In part, this is due to the nature of such phenomena themselves: although counting all the occurrences of an item requires being able to **identify** all those occurrences as members of a closed set, many phenomena of interest to discourse analysts do not form mutually exclusive sets. Distributional accountability has been hindered in discourse analysis for another reason: discourse analysis does not provide a ready made checklist of what features of discourse are likely to constrain variation within a particular discourse slot (as do, for example, phonological and syntactic analyses). In short, we can identify neither the item, nor its environments, precisely enough to account for constraints on its distribution.

By being sequentially accountable to a particular discourse, however, we can begin to overcome both of these initial obstacles. First, we can understand where a particular item fits within the different components which underlie discourse coherence. This helps in our identification of other members of a set of such items. Second, we can identify the more general features that our particular discourse shares with other discourse. This helps in our identification and categorization of discourse constraints. In short, it is in order to carry out these preliminary but crucial steps in a distributional analysis – to identify an item precisely enough to be able to locate other members of its set, and to categorize its environments – that we are led back to sequential analyses. Thus, distributional and sequential accountability are complementary approaches to discourse analysis.

3.5 Summary

In this chapter, I have presented several sample analyses in order to illustrate the general questions which my analysis of discourse markers will address. The questions are as follows:

What do discourse markers add to coherence?

> Do they create, or display, relationships between units of talk (ideas, actions, turns, etc.)?

Do markers have meanings?

> If so, are those meanings referential and/or social and/or expressive?
>
> If so, how do those meanings interact with the discourse slot to influence the total communicative force of an expression?

Do markers have functions?

> If so, in what component of a discourse system (exchange, action, ideational, information, participation)?
>
> Are markers multi-functional?
>
> Are markers functional equivalents?

These questions are not only important guidelines for my analysis; they also place the study of discourse markers in a broader analytical context, and their answers will lead toward a theoretical definition of discourse markers (cf. Chapter 3). I concluded this chapter by comparing different approaches to the analysis of discourse markers, and suggesting an approach which builds on the complementary strengths of both quantitative and qualitative analyses.

4 *Oh*: Marker of information management

As we saw in Chapter 3, understanding discourse markers requires separating the contribution made by the marker itself, from the contribution made by characteristics of the discourse slot in which the marker occurs. We posed the following questions. Does an item used as a marker have semantic meaning and/or grammatical status which contributes to its discourse function? And how does such meaning interact with the sequential context of the marker to influence production and interpretation?

I examine two discourse markers in this chapter and the next – *oh* and *well* – whose uses are not clearly based on semantic meaning or grammatical status. Beginning our analysis with these markers will force us to pay particularly close attention to the discourse slot itself. This will put us on firmer methodological ground for analysis of markers whose semantic meaning and/or grammatical status interacts with their sequential location to produce their function.

This chapter focuses on *oh*. *Oh* is traditionally viewed as an exclamation or interjection. When used alone, without the syntactic support of a sentence, *oh* is said to indicate strong emotional states, e.g. surprise, fear, or pain (*Oxford English Dictionary* 1971, Fries 1952). (1) and (2) illustrate *oh* as exclamation:

(1)   Jack: Was that a serious picture?
        Freda: **Oh**:! Gosh yes!
(2)   Jack: Like I'd say, 'What d'y'mean you don't like classical music?'
                  '**Oh**! I can't stand it! It's draggy.'

Oh can also initiate utterances, either followed by a brief pause:

(3)   Freda: **Oh**, well they came when they were a year.

or with no pause preceding the rest of the tone unit:[1]

(4)   Jack: Does he like opera? **Oh** maybe he's too young.

We will see, regardless of its syntactic status or intonational contour, that *oh* occurs as speakers shift their orientation to information. (A very similar view of *oh* is Heritage (1984: 299), who views *oh* as a particle 'used to propose that its producer has undergone some kind of change in his or her locally current state of knowledge, information, orientation or awareness'.) We will see that speakers shift orientation during a conversation not only as they respond affectively to what is said (e.g. as they exclaim with surprise as in 1 and 2), but as they replace one information unit with another, as they recognize old information which has become conversationally relevant, and as they receive new information to integrate into an already present knowledge base. All of these are **information management tasks** in which *oh* has a role: *oh* pulls from the flow of information in discourse a temporary focus of attention which is the target of self and/or other management.

I begin with speech activities through which speakers explicitly manage information units. In (4.1), I examine repairs: the replacement of one unit of information with another by either self or other. In (4.2), I examine question–answer–acknowledgement sequences: three-part exchange structures through which a speaker and hearer jointly complete a proposition and then endorse their completion. I then examine *oh* in discourse which is not explicitly structured for information management. In (4.3), we will see that *oh* marks two information-handling tasks – old information recognition and new information receipt – and that these shifts in orientation result not only when information is presented by one speaker to another, but when information is accessed by the speaker's own recall or made available through context changes. I turn then to uses of *oh* which best fit the traditional categories of exclamation and interjection: shifts in subjective orientation (4.4). In conclusion, I consider why internal information management tasks such as those marked by *oh* might be interactionally displayed for pragmatic effect.

4.1 *Oh* in repairs

Repair is a speech activity during which speakers locate and replace a prior information unit. Because they focus on prior information, repairs achieve information transitions anaphorically – forcing speakers to adjust their orientation to what has been said before they respond to it in upcoming talk.

Almost anything that anyone says is a candidate for repair either by the speaker him/herself or by a listener. Once an utterance actually is subjected to repair, however, the method by which it is repaired is more restricted than its initial selection: although both repair initiation and completion can be performed by a listener (other-initiation, other-completion), speakers are more likely to participate in their own repairs either by initiating (self-initiation) or completing (self-completion) the repair. (Schegloff, Jefferson, and Sacks 1977 speak of this tendency as the preference for self-repair; see also Moerman 1977.)

4.1.1 Oh *in repair initiation*

Oh prefaces self-initiated and other-initiated repairs. Examples (5–7) show *oh* at self-initiated repairs. In (5), Freda is answering a question about whether she believes in extra-sensory perception (E.S.P.) by describing her husband Jack's abilities to predict future political events.

(5) I mean . . . he can almost foresee:. . .eh:: for instance with
Nixon. . . . . .He said. . .now he's not in a medical field my husband.
He said coagulating his blood,. . .uh thinning his– Nixon's blood. . .will
not be good for him, if he should be operated on. **Oh** maybe it's just
knowledge. I don't know if that's E.S.P. or not in that c– in this case.

Freda recategorizes a particular description from an instance of E.S.P. to an instance of knowledge: this self-repair is initiated with *oh*.[2]

Another example is (6). Prior to (6), I had just told Henry and Zelda that I went to Girls' High, a local high school.

(6) Henry: Did you go to Olney?
Zelda: Yeh: **Oh** no! ⎡Girls' High:! **Oh** that's right.⎤
Debby: ⎣No Girls' High. Girls' High. ⎦

Despite my having just told Henry and Zelda where I went to high school, Henry asks a question showing that he missed what I said. Zelda begins to answer his question (*yeh:*) – but incorrectly. She realizes her own mistake (*Oh no!*), and replaces her prior answer (with *Girls' High*) – thus initiating and completing her own repair. Her confirmation of this replacement (which I have provided along with Zelda) is confirmed with an additional self-completion: *oh that's right.*

In (7), Jack is explaining the history of Polish prejudice to me and Freda – neither of whom know anything about the subject. He self-initiates a repair (*Oh I'm wrong*) about when Poland was divided by Russia:

(7) Jack: I think it was in seventeen: fifteen, or seventeen fifty five,
I'm not sure when. Eh: **oh** I'm wrong. Seventeen seventeen.

Jack's self-initiation (*oh I'm wrong*) precedes his self-completion (*seventeen seventeen*).

Not all self-initiated repairs are actual replacements of one unit of information with another: in some, speakers search for information to fill a temporary gap in recall. In (8), for example, Jack interrupts a story to provide
background information about his age at the time of the reported experience – which he cannot then remember precisely. *Oh* fills the slot between
his self-interruption and his first attempt at specifying his age.

(8)   There was a whole bunch of oth– I was about– **oh**: younger than Robert.,
        I was about uh. . .maybe Joe's age. Sixteen.

Note that *uh* seems to serve the same general function as *oh* in this example:
both are place-holders for Jack as he searches for information. But *oh* initiates the repair (it is preceded by a self-interruption), whereas *uh* continues the repair.

Examples (9) and (10) illustrate other-initiated repairs.[3] In (9), I am
explaining what I mean by 'ethnic group'.

(9)   Debby: By ethnic group I meant nationality. Okay like um Irish or :–I
               guess there aren't ⎡ too many Irish Jews but ⎤ =
      Jack: ⎣ I see! Yeh yeh. **Oh** yes= ⎦
      Debby: =Italian:
      Jack: =there is!

Jack's *I see* acknowledges my description of ethnic group. His *Oh yes there
is!* is an other-initiated repair to my assertion about Irish Jews.

In (10), Jack and Freda are describing their favourite old movies.

(10)   Jack: How bout uh. . .how bout the one uh. . .uh. . Death of a
                Salesman?
       Freda: Well that was a show, sure.
       Jack: **Oh** that was a movie too.

Both Freda and Jack issue other-repairs. Jack mentions a movie, whose
identification Freda repairs to *show*. Jack then proposes another repair: it
was both movie and show. Although neither Freda nor Jack complete each
others' repair initiations, a later remark of mine shows that I acknowledge
(and, in effect, other-complete) **both** of their repairs: when asked what I
think of the story, I say 'I never saw the play, or the movie. I read it.'

4.1.2 Oh *in repair completion*

Repairs are completed when the repairable is replaced by a new item; additional completion can be provided through confirmation of the replace-

ment. When the replacement is issued by the same speaker who had issued the repairable, we can speak of self completion; when the repairable is replaced by another speaker, of other completion.

Oh prefaces both self and other-completions. Several of our above examples (5–8) contain combinations of self-initiated and self-completed repairs. In (6), for example, Zelda self-initiates and self-completes her replacement of *yeh* with *no* and *Girls' High*, and then further self-completes with *oh that's right*.

(6) Henry: Did you go to Olney?
     Zelda: Yeh: **Oh no!** ⌈ Girls' High:! **Oh** that's right. ⌉
     Debby: ⌊ No Girls' High. Girls' High. ⌋

And examples (9) and (10) showed combinations of other-initiated and other-completed repairs. In (10), for example, Jack other-initiates and other-completes a repair from identification of 'Death of a Salesman' as *show*, to its identification as *movie*.

Oh also occurs when one party completes a repair initiated by the other – when other-initiated repairs are self-completed (11, 12), and when self-initiated repairs are other-completed (13). In (11), Zelda and Henry are answering my questions about who they visit.

(11) Henry: Ah: who can ⌈ answer that, ⌉ the kids. We have nobody=
      Zelda: ⌊ Our kids. ⌋
      Henry: =else.   **Oh** yeh we– my sister=
      Zelda: Yeh, you have a sister.
      Henry: =we see in the summertime a lot.

Henry forgets to mention his sister: thus, Zelda other-initiates a repair to this effect. Henry then self-completes the repair by replacing his earlier answer with one which includes his sister as someone whom he visits.

In (12), Freda and Jack have been describing an accomplishment of their son, but each is describing a different accomplishment.

(12) Freda: They had a nursery school or some such
              thing, ⟋
      Jack: ⟍ and he won something.
      Freda: Before he even started school he went ⌈ s– ⌉
      Jack: ⌊ Not a ⌋
              nursery, he– ha– they were ⌈ working on the far:m= ⌉
      Freda: ⌊ **Oh** that's right= ⌋
      Jack: ⌈ =it was no nursery. An' the– ⌉
      Freda: ⌊ =he was– yes: that's right. He ⌋ was young though.

Jack other-initiates and completes a repair through a *not x, but y* format

(Schegloff, Jefferson, and Sacks 1977): *not a nursery, they were working on a farm.* Freda also self-completes the repair when she acknowledges Jack's replacement.

(13) is an example of a self-initiated, other-completed repair. Rob (Freda's teenage nephew) has just told Freda that he is going skiing at Aspen, where a famous entertainer's wife had recently been indicted for murder.

(13)   Rob: I hope to go to Aspen.
         Freda: Oh you might see um. . .hh what's his name's wife–or she's eh
                  or is she in jail. ⌈   ⌉ A– a–
         Jack: ⌊Who.⌋   ⌈   ⌉
         Rob: ⌊Patty⌋ Hearst?
         Freda: Not Patty Hearst! Aspen's where that fellow was killed.
                  That savage uh. . .killed by uh. . .what's the
                  ⌈entertainer's⌉ ⌈wife? Claudia⌉   Martin–eh ⌈yeh.=⌉
                                                               ⌊yeh. ⌋
         Debby: Oh ⌈I kno–⌉ ⌊   ⌋
         Rob: ⌊Oh! ⌋   ⌊Clau– Claudia⌋ Longet!
         Freda: =You might see her!

Freda cannot remember the wife's name and self-initiates a repair (*um. . .hh what's his name's wife–*) which Rob makes two attempts to other-complete: first, *Patty Hearst?*, and then *Oh! Clau– Claudia Longet!*. (Note, also, my efforts to other-complete: *Oh I kn–*.) Freda repeats Rob's other-completion (using the wife's married name *Claudia Martin*), confirms the other-completion (*eh yeh*), and then incorporates Rob's completion into the utterance previously interrupted by her self-initiation: *You might see her!*

Finally, repairs can be completed more than once – and by more than one party. We have seen several examples of multiple completions: (6), (12), (13).

In sum, that self and other participate in both initiation and completion of repair shows a speaker/hearer division of responsibility for information management. Self-initiation and completion of repair show speakers' sensitivity to their own **production** of discourse: by locating and replacing an item from an outgoing utterance, speakers display their productive efforts. Other-initiation and completion of repair show hearers' sensitivity to their **reception** of discourse: by locating and replacing an item from an incoming utterance, hearers display their pursual of understanding and their effort to interpret what is being said as it is being received. Thus, jointly managed repairs are evidence of a participation framework in which both producer and recipient of talk replace information units and publicly redistribute knowledge about them. In the next section, I examine a repair format which highlights how this division of speaker/hearer effort to manage information influences the use of *oh*.

4.1.3 Oh *in repairs achieved through clarification sequences*

Clarification sequences consist of two moves which are inserted into ongoing discourse (cf. Garvey 1977, 1979, Jefferson 1972, Schegloff 1972). Let us say that Speaker A issues a repairable. A clarification sequence begins when Speaker B **requests** clarification (an other-initiation) of the repairable from Speaker A; the request is complied with through A's **provision** of clarification (a self-completion).

> A: repairable
> B1:   request for clarification
> A2:   provision of clarification

These moves result from very different information-management tasks – and it is these tasks which explain the use of *oh* in clarification sequences.

Let's begin by looking at **clarification requests**. Such requests are used by B to define A's prior utterance as a target for repair. They work by returning the floor to A, whose responsibility it is to provide clarification.

Clarification requests are issued in varying degrees of specificity. The least specified requests, e.g. *what do you mean*, are the products of least work from B, and they delegate the most responsibility back to A to locate and replace the repairable. More specified requests are the results of more work from B because they locate the repairable for A, and may even propose its replacement; consequently, they require less work from A. (14) illustrates a specified request for clarification (B1).

(14)	Val:	Did you know what you were gonna be when you were little?
	Freda:	I should say not.
A	Val:	Did your folks?
B1	Freda:	Know what I was gonna be? What d'y'mean what I was gonna be: what I was gonna do?

In B1, a repairable is twice located (through repetition and *what do you mean*), and a replacement is proposed.

Clarification is also requested when B either repeats or questions a portion of A's prior utterance with rising intonation and contrastive stress on the repairable, as in (15).

(15)   Debby: Is there a rabbi, who's active around here.
        Freda: Yes.
B1   Jack: That *I'm* familiar with?

Not all repetitions with rising intonation (and not all questions) are clarification requests. What differentiates clarification from confirmation requests, or echo questions, is use of contrastive stress on an item which is thus identified as a repairable.

The second move in a clarification sequence, A2, is A's **provision of clarification**. In (14), A2 replaced the prior question:

(14)   Val: Did you know what you were gonna be when you were little?
        Freda: I should say not.
A   Val: Did your folks?
B1   Freda: Know what I was gonna be? What d'y'mean what I was
                 ⌈ gonna be: what I was gonna do? ⌉
A2   Val: ⌊ Did they know what they wanted ⌋ you to be?

Note that this does not conform to the specified options that had been offered through B1. In (15), A2 does select from the options offered in B1:

(15)   Debby: Is there a rabbi, who's active around here.
        Freda: Yes.
B1   Jack: That *I'm* familiar with?
A2   Debby: **Yeh**.

I answer Jack's *That I'm familiar with?* with *yeh* (which reissues my earlier question).

Another example of a replacement which conforms to the specifications of the clarification request is (16). I am asking Jack with whom he discusses problems.

(16) A Debby: Is there anyone you would uh: talk ⌈ about– ⌉
B1   Jack: ⌊   **Oh** ⌋   you mean
                 outside?
A2   Debby: **Yeh** outside the home.
        Jack: *I* wouldn't.

Jack's clarification request *Oh you mean outside?* proposes a specific clarification. My *Yeh outside the home* conforms to this specification.

We might expect *oh* to be used either at the request for clarification (B1), or the provision of clarification (A2) – since each has a role in the replacement of one information unit by another. Table 4.1 confirms that *oh* is used when clarification is requested. But as it also shows, *oh* is never used when clarification is provided.

Table 4.1. Oh *in clarification sequences*

	Request for clarification	Provision of clarification	Total
Oh	11	0	11
Zero	25	36	61
Total	36	36	72

We can explain this difference by comparing the information management tasks undertaken during a clarification sequence. The request for clarification occurs during B's efforts both to interpret, and to respond to, what A has said. Although A provides clarification, it is B who uses the clarification to modify his/her understanding of what À has said, and to build a response. Thus, despite the actual provision of replacement by A, it is B who undergoes the repair process by first **identifying** a repairable, and then **integrating** the repair into discourse as a basis for further response. It is Speaker B, then, for whom the repair is a processing task – and thus B who uses *oh* when requesting clarification.

This division of labor suggests that *oh* might also be used when *B* enters the clarification into discourse. Let us examine, then, what *B* does **after** A provides clarification.

Following A's provision of clarification, B may mark receipt of the clarification either by acknowledging, or using, A's clarification.[4] In (17), B acknowledges the clarification:

(17) Freda: Sometimes he got a notice for staying out past curfew. Recently. In August, that was.
B1 Val: **Oh** curfew? What's curfew?
A2 Freda: A certain time that children have to be in.
  Val: **Oh** your children. **Oh** I see. **Oh** it's personal. **Oh** I–. .I thought there might be police or something.

Other than repetition or paraphrase of the clarification, speakers may acknowledge the clarification with approbation terms – *yeh, right, okay* – which are optionally preceded by *oh*.

(14) was an example in which B uses the clarification in a next utterance: by answering Val's replacement question, Freda incorporates the clarification into her response:

(14) Val: Did you know what you were gonna be when you were little?

	Freda:	I should say not.
A	Val:	Did your folks?
B1	Freda:	Know what I was gonna be? What d'y'mean what I was gonna

be: ⌈ what I was gonna do? ⌉

A2   Val: ⌊ Did they know what they ⌋ wanted you

⌈ to be? ⌉

Freda: ⌊ **Oh** my ⌋ folks knew what I wanted– what they wanted, yes.

Similarly, (16) continued with Jack using my clarification to answer the question which had been posed:

(16) A   Debby: Is there anyone you would uh: talk ⌈ about– ⌉
B1   Jack: ⌊ Oh ⌋

you mean outside?

A2   Debby: Yeh outside the home.

Jack: *I* wouldn't.

Table 4.2. repeats the data from Table 4.1, adding B's use of *oh* in moves which integrate the clarification into discourse. It shows that *oh* is used not only when B requests clarification, but when B enters the clarification into discourse – either acknowledging it (as in 17), or using it in a next utterance (as in 14, 16). In short, these additional data show that because it is B for whom the repair is a processing task, it is this speaker who uses *oh*. A does not use *oh* when providing clarification, because, for A, there has been no clarifying work.

Table 4.2. Oh *at different stages of clarification*

	B's request for clarification	A's provision of clarification	B's entry of clarificaiton	Total
Oh	11 (30%)	0 (0%)	13 (41%)	24
Zero	25	36	19	80
Total	36	36	32	104

There is additional evidence that responsibility for managing information in clarification sequences falls on B – the one who requests, and then uses, clarification. Recall that clarification sequences vary in degree of specificity: some requests merely mark a prior utterance as in need of repair; others query a particular item or suggest a specific replacement. The consequences of specified clarification requests for their producers vary depending upon their recipients' response. We have seen two responses. First, recipients of such requests may provide a clarification which conforms to the specification (as we saw in 16). Another example illustrating A2's selection of clarification in conformity to B1 is (18):

(18) B1 Jack: I don't seem t'understand the question. Y'mean our end
down here don't talk ⌈ to the oth– ⌉
A2 Debby: ⌊ Right. You don't– ⌋
Jack: That's not true. I– I know the people on the other end.

Second, recipients of specified clarification requests may provide a clarification which does **not** conform to the specification (as we saw in 14). (19) is another example of A2's selection of a clarification which does not conform to B1:

(19) Zelda: Y'know, that eh orthopedic doctor? Y'know that took care of
Henry when he had his back?
⌈ Problems? ⌉
B1 Irene: ⌊ Who, that– ⌋ Chinese doctor?
A2 Zelda: No::the Italian. Bonzi!
Irene: Oh yeh.

Whether the clarification provided by A2 selects from the options offered through B1's specified clarification requests affects the use of *oh* upon B's receipt of A's clarification. (Note that $N=28$, the number of specified clarification requests.) Table 4.3 shows that although *oh* is used after 32% of the cases in which A2's clarification did match that anticipated in B1 (as in 16, 18), it is used after 66% of the cases in which A2's clarification did **not** match the clarification anticipated in B1 (as in 14, 19).

Table 4.3. Oh *with B's entry of clarification into discourse*

	A2 matches expected clarification from B1	A2 does not match expected clarification from B1	Total
Oh	6 (32%)	6 (66%)	12
Zero	13	3	16
Total	19	9	28

How can we explain this difference? Recall that specified clarification requests are the product of more work from their producers (from B) than unspecified requests because they locate and possibly replace a repairable. A specified request creates even further work if it turns out to be wrong: if A2 does not select from the options specified in B1, B cannot then use B1 in a next utterance. In effect, then, a wrong guess from B1 creates a second management task for B: first, locate and propose a clarification for the repairable from A; second, replace the proposed clarification from B1.

That B has to undertake a dual management task accounts for B's greater use of *oh* when A2 does not select from B1's specified clarification proposal.

In sum, *oh* occurs when speaker/hearers request clarification during their reception of an incoming utterance, and when they enter that clarification into discourse. The more work involved in this latter task, the more likely it is that *oh* will be used.

4.1.4 Oh *and information managed through repairs*

In sum, *oh* accompanies the information transitions achieved through repairs – specifically, the replacement of, and redistribution of knowledge about, information. Because repairs focus speakers' attention on prior information, forcing them to replace either information that is being currently produced or currently received before they continue conversation, they achieve information transitions anaphorically. In addition, repairs illustrate a participation framework in which both producer and recipient of talk display responsibility for the redistribution of knowledge. However, some repair formats place a heavier burden on one speaker than on another – and it is here that we are more likely to find *oh*.

4.2 Oh **in question/answer/acknowledgement sequences**

Another speech activity which explicitly manages and distributes information is the three-part sequence of question, answer, and acknowledgement. Question/answer pairs complete a proposition, which may then be verbally acknowledged by the questioner – the individual who first opened the proposition for completion. The conditions under which *oh* prefaces questions, answers, and acknowledgements are sensitive to the different information management tasks accomplished in these turns.

4.2.1 Question/answer pairs

Question/answer pairs are adjacency pairs, i.e. sequentially constrained pairs in which the occurrence of a first-pair-part creates a slot for the occurrence of a second-pair-part (a conditional relevance), such that the non-occurrence of that second-pair-part is heard as officially absent (Schegloff and Sacks 1973; see also discussion in Chapter 1). One reason why questions constrain the next conversational slot is semantic: WH-questions are incomplete propositions; yes–no questions are propositions whose polarity is unspecified (e.g. Carlson 1983). Completion of the proposition is up to the recipient of the question, who either fills in the WH-information, or fixes the polarity. This semantic completion allows a speaker/hearer reorientation toward an information unit, i.e. redistribution of knowledge about a proposition.[5]

4.2.1.1 Oh with questions. Question/answer pairs are rarely couplets which are totally disconnected from their containing discourse. In fact, some questions are quite explicitly connected to. immediately prior utterances: for example, we have seen that requests for clarification are often formulated as syntactic questions. Other questions are used to request elaboration of what has just been said. (20) and (21) show that like requests for clarification (4.1.3), requests for elaboration may also be prefaced by *oh*.

(20)   Val: Is it safe?
         Freda: Uh: we found a safe way! But it's the long way!
         Val: **Oh** it's a special way?

(21)   Debby: Does she come here or:
         Jan: No we go out to lunch, mostly, I stop over there.
         Debby: **Oh**, where do you like to go?

Elaboration requests are similar to clarification requests because they, too, focus on prior information. There are two differences, however. First, clarification requests indicate a reception problem which will be resolved through upcoming clarification; elaboration requests acknowledge receipt of information which has been sufficiently interpreted to allow the receiver to prompt its further development. Second, compliance with a clarification request is the amendment of **old** information; compliance with an elaboration request is provision of **new** information.

Despite these differences, both clarification and elaboration requests can be prefaced by *oh* because both display speakers' receipt of information (partial or complete) at the same time that they solicit further information. The only other questions prefaced by *oh* are those which are suddenly remembered by a speaker as previously intended. Prior to (22), for example, I had been checking my interview schedule, when I saw a question that I had not yet asked.

(22)   Debby: **Oh** listen, I forgot to ask you what your father did when
                   you were growing up.

Like requests for clarification and elaboration, the suddenly remembered question in (22) displays the questioner's receipt of information – although here, the just-received information may not be presented by an interlocutor, but may be recalled by the speaker him/herself. In short, questions through which speakers only solicit information are not prefaced by *oh*; it is only questions which are evoked by the reception of information which may be prefaced by *oh*.

4.2.1.2 Oh with answers. Answers to questions are prefaced with *oh* when a question forces an answerer to reorient him/herself to information – that is, when the question makes clear that information presumed to be shared is not so, or that a similar orientation toward information was wrongly assumed. At the same time, answers with *oh* make explicit to the questioner the violation of a prior expectation about information.

Such re-orientations may be caused by a mismatch between the information that the questioner assumed to be shared: the questioner may have assumed too much or too little to be shared, or the questioner may have made a wrong assumption. Consider (23). I have told Irene that I am a student at a local university.

(23)　Irene:　How can I get an appointment t'go down there t'bring my son on a tour?

　　　Debby:　**Oh** I didn't even know they gave tours! I'm not the one t'ask about it.

Irene's son is interested in attending the university, and she assumes that I would know (as a student) that the university gives tours to prospective students. But since I had no knowledge of the tours, Irene's question had assumed more shared information than was warranted: my *oh* shows both my receipt of this new information (see 4.3.2) and alerts Irene to her misguided expectation as to what information we had shared.

(24) illustrates a question/answer pair in which the questioner assumes too little shared information. Zelda and I are discussing low-interest college loans for her daughter, and I question Zelda's knowledge about a particular government loan.

(24)　Debby:　You must know about P.H.E.A.A.?

　　　Zelda:　**Oh** I'm gonna apply for all that. Yes I do. I went to the counselor, yes. And she told me there are three forms to fill out. And we do it next year. So, I know all about that.

Note that my question strongly assumes a positive answer (because of the modal *must*, and the declarative form). But Zelda knows still more about the loan than my question had anticipated. Thus, the question had assumed less shared information than was actually warranted.

An example of a questioner making a wrong assumption is (25). Henry had been telling me about a person with a Ph.D. employed as a ticket seller at a summer resort.

(25) Henry: I saw a guy workin' on the beach with a Ph.D.! Couldn't get a job!
      Zelda: He ⌈ was sellin' beach tickets! ⌉
      Debby: ⌊ Don't tell me nowhhhhh. ⌋ Ugh.
      Henry: That's right!
      Debby: What did he have his Ph.D. in?
      Henry: **Oh** I wasn't talkin' to him, a woman was tellin' me.

Like many Ph.D. candidates (and recipients) I was concerned about future employment. Because I had assumed that Henry had spoken to this person, I ask for further information about him. But Henry cannot answer my question because I had made a faulty assumption.

In sum, answers to questions are prefaced with *oh* when the answerer re-orients him/herself to the information under question – a re-orientation caused by the questioner's misjudgement of what information the answerer shares.

4.2.2 Oh *with acknowledgement of answers*

Question/answer pairs are often followed by the questioner's response to the informational content of the answer which has been elicited. Such responses may vary from evaluations of the answer (endorsements, challenges) to re-solicitations of the answer (as accomplished through requests for clarification).[6] Another possible response is acknowledgement of the answer, i.e. the questioner's display of receipt of the answer.

Consider, however, that exactly **what** is acknowledged varies depending upon whether the questioner finds that the answer to his/her question contains anticipated information. Although it is not always possible to know – as analysts – what questioners expect answers to contain, we can find several hints in the linguistic form of the question. Because yes–no questions provide answerers with a choice between two possibilities – positive or negative – they suggest that questioners expect a binary choice to be sufficient. Disjunctive questions are like yes–no questions because they show the questioner leading the answerer toward a choice from a limited set of options (often a binary set). In WH-questions, adverbials (*who, what, where, when,* etc.) suggest questioners' anticipation of a broad range of answer options. With other question forms, questioners do not so much present answerers with a choice between (or among) options, as they seek confirmation for their own choice. Tag questions, for example, are declarative statements with postposed tags through which questioners seek agreement with the content of the statement. Similarly, declarative statements presented in a rising intonation (and transcribed with a question mark as in *You want to come?*) also provide a proposition for which agreement is sought.

Although we cannot know with certainty whether answers do conform to questioners' expectations, we can see whether they conform to the linguistically encoded expectations just described. Three kinds of non-conforming answers can be identified. First, answerers may not conform with the question-encoded options because they lack the requisite knowledge:

(26)   Debby: Is there a coffee clique on this block?
         Zelda: I don't know.

Second, if the circumstances being questioned are themselves equivocal, even the range of options offered through a WH-question may be insufficiently broad to allow conformity with the question-encoded options:

(27)   Sally: How does it work around here when somebody gets married
                    t'somebody from a different group, like, ⌈   ⌉ Yeh.
                    Or...yeh, =
         Zelda: religion?
         Sally: ⌈ =or nationality, ⌉ or something.
         Zelda: ⌊ Well....it–it   ⌋   all depends on
                    um...now my husband...believes in eh marrying eh in his
                    own religion.

Third, respondents may find the question inapplicable because of an inaccurate speaker-assumption. (It is this condition that we discussed in 4.2.1.2.) In asking a WH-question, for example, the questioner assumes not only a set of options, but the truth of the proposition being questioned. In (28), my question shows my assumption that Henry and Zelda have friends – an assumption they deny.

(28)   Debby: Who has more friends. Between you.
         Zelda: ⌈ No::we don't see:: our=   ⌉
         Henry: ⌊ We really don't have that many friends. ⌋
         Zelda: =old friends.

In asking a yes–no question, the questioner assumes a binary choice. In (29), however, Zelda's assumption that Sally is, or is not, from Philadelphia is not exactly accurate. Thus, neither question-encoded option provides a sufficient basis from which to choose an answer.

(29) Zelda: Are you from Philadelphia?
      Sally: Well I grew up uh out in the suburbs. And then I lived for
              about seven years up in upstate New York. And then I came
              back here t'go to college.

Consider, now, that what the questioner acknowledges upon receipt of an answer varies depending upon whether the answer conforms to his or her expectations. When answers are selected from the question-encoded options, what questioners acknowledge is **receipt of anticipated information**. In (30), for example, Ira asks me a WH-question, and marks his acknowledgement of my answer with *yeh*, followed by another question:

(30) Ira: How long you been going with this guy?
      Debby: Um six years.
      Ira: Yeh wha'did your mother say anything?

On the other hand, if answers are not selected from the question-encoded options, what questioners acknowledge is **receipt of unanticipated information**. In (31), for example, Irene's answer does not conform to the expectations encoded through my question:

(31) Debby: So what, you have *three* kids?
      Irene: I have *four*. ⎡ Three boys ⎤ and a girl.
      Debby: ⎣ *Four* kids. ⎦   **Oh** I didn't know that.

Note that I am not distinguishing old from new information: both anticipated and unanticipated answers provide **new** information. But new information which has been anticipated creates less of a reorientation than does new information which has not been anticipated. Given my discussion about *oh* thus far, we would expect *oh* to be used more after unanticipated answers. Table 4.4 compares *oh* to other acknowledgement markers (approbation terms) and to zero-acknowledgement.[7]

Table 4.4 shows that *oh* is not likely to mark questioners' receipt of anticipated answers. In contrast, other acknowledgement markers (*yeah*, *right*, *uhhuh*) and zero-markers are used mostly when answerers have selected from the question-encoded options (compare across the rows). *Oh* thus marks a reorientation toward a proposition whose completion had been differently anticipated. This kind of reorientation is similar to that achieved by a repair: both focus on a prior unit of information and anaphorically adjust the speaker's representation of that information. And the processing task which is marked by the acknowledgement is analogous to the replace-

Table 4.4. Oh *and answer-acknowledgements*

	After answers which do select from question-encoded options	After answers which do not select from question-encoded options	Total
Oh	10 (7%)	18 (56%)	28
Other markers	34	6	40
Zero	99	8	107
Total	143	32	175

ment task marked by a speaker's use of an other-provided clarification (4.1.3).

These results are not meant to suggest that *oh* does not display other kinds of reorientations toward the just-completed proposition presented in an answer. In (32), for example, I ask Henry a question whose answer makes me realize that I hadn't needed to solicit that information. Thus, after his answer, *oh* displays my recalculation as to what was shared.

(32)   Debby: Where'd y'grow up? You were talking about
                 ⌈ the old neighborhood. ⌉ **Oh** sure. I knew that.
        Henry: ⌊ Strawberry Mansion.   ⌋

We see in the next section that *oh* often marks the recognition of familiar information. In (33), my acknowledgement of Zelda's answer precedes my further use of that information as a basis for an additional inference which functions as a request for elaboration (4.2.1.1).

(33)   Debby: Where d'your cousins live? You said they come
                 ⌈ down: from somewhere. ⌉
        Zelda: ⌊ They live in the   ⌋   Northeast.
        Debby: **Oh**, okay. So you have a lot of family up in the Northeast.

We see in the next section that *oh* often marks the receipt of new information.

4.3 *Oh* and the status of information

Thus far we have focused on speech activities whose goal is the management of information and whose exchange structure helps accomplish that goal. We have seen that *oh* marks different tasks involved in this management: the production and reception of information, the replacement and redistribution of information, the receipt of solicited, but unanticipated, information. *Oh* is more likely to be used when locally provided information does not correspond to a speaker's prior expectations: in repairs, questions, answers, and acknowledgements, *oh* marks a shift in speaker's orientation to information.

Use of *oh* is hardly confined to speech activities whose exchange structure is focused on information management. In this section, I examine *oh* first, as a marker of recognition of familiar information – more specifically, old information which has become newly relevant – and second, as a marker of new information receipt.[8]

4.3.1 Oh *as recognition display*

Recognition of familiar information is often conversationally triggered. In the following examples, one speaker prompts another into recall, which is then explicitly marked not only with *oh*, but with confirmation of the correctness of the prompt, and/or provision of information testifying to the speaker's prior knowledge.

In (34), I prompt Zelda and Henry through use of *do you know X?* (Chapter 9 discusses the role of *y'know* in introducing topics.)

(34)   Debby: No this is–d'you–d'you know um: I was talkin' to the
                         Kramers, down, 4500.
         Zelda: **Oh** yeh, Freda?
         Debby: ⎡ Yeh. ⎤
         Henry: ⎣ **Oh** ⎦ yeh. Jack?

Both Zelda and Henry mark their recognition with *oh* and with elaboration of the topic which I have evoked (the Kramers' first names). (35) and (36) are similar: the prompting speaker uses a try-marker (Sacks 1971) to identify a topic and the prompted speaker responds with *oh* and the addition of information:

(35)   Zelda: We ate at the– we ate at the: eh that Shanty? Seafood Shanty?
         Debby: **Oh** yeh, I've heard that's good.

(36)   Jack: I was supposed t'play elegy on the violin. Do you remember
                  then?   All kids would=
         Freda: **Oh,** yes!
         Jack: ⎡ =play that. ⎤
         Freda: ⎣ **Oh,** that's ⎦ the first!

Recognition of familiar information may also result from the speaker's own cognitive search for a particular piece of known information. In (37), for example, Zelda and Henry are telling me about their favorite restaurants;

Henry has just said that they have been eating out more than ever.

(37)   Zelda: And uh– **Oh**! We– when we go to the kids, we always eat out.
                    We eat at the F1– Blue Fountain.

It sounds as if Zelda is about to add another restaurant to her list of favorites (because of her initial *and*; see Chapter 6). But she switches to a reason for the frequency with which they have been dining out (*when we go to the kids, we always eat out*), and then mentions another restaurant (*Blue Fountain*). The reason seems to be a sudden recall, and it is the reason that is marked by *oh*.

In (38), Rob asks Jack to provide the identity of *my boyfriend*.

(38)   Jack: I hate to admit this but he has much more talent than
                   ⎡ uh. . . *my* boyfriend. ⎤   ⎡ Glickman.   ⎤
         Rob: ⎣ Yeh. I think so too. ⎦ Who? **Oh.**⎣ Joey Brenner? ⎦

After asking *who?*, however, Rob seems to realize the identity of Jack's boyfriend himself, and requests confirmation from Jack just as Jack is supplying him with the information. (Note that these two names refer to the same individual: the former is a stage name.)[9]

Finally, progressive stages of information recognition can be marked by *oh* – regardless of whether those stages have been conversationally or cognitively triggered. A previous example illustrates. In (17), Freda triggered Val's recognition of the meaning of 'curfew' with her *a certain time that children have to be in*. Each component of Val's recognition is marked with *oh*.

(17)   Freda: Sometimes he got a notice for staying out past curfew.
                   Recently. In August, that was.
         Val: Oh curfew? What's curfew?
         Freda: A certain time that children have to be in.
         Val: **Oh** your children. **Oh** I see. **Oh** it's personal. **Oh** I–. .I
                   thought there might be police or something.

Another example is (39). Here, the recognition of familiar information is both cognitively and conversationally triggered.

(39)   Henry: She: s– missed out on a good man.
         Debby: Hmmthis isn't the guy who was *here*, is it?
         Henry: Last week.
         Debby: **Oh** I didn't– **oh oh**. ⎡ The car ⎤ dealer.
         Henry: ⎢ I didn't–⎢
         Zelda: ⎣ The one ⎦ that was flirting with you.
         Debby: **Oh** hhhhh. Now I know which one you mean!

Three pieces of information contribute to my recognition of the referent of *a good man* in Henry's initial utterance. The first two (*the guy who was here, the car dealer*) are cognitively triggered in that I am the one who locates the identificatory information. The last (*the one that was flirting with you*) is conversationally triggered because it was provided by Zelda.

4.3.2 Oh *as information receipt*

Oh also marks a speaker's receipt of new information. In (40), for example, Zelda doesn't know prior to Irene's telling her that Irene's husband Ken had been fixing their back door. Note how Irene prompts Zelda's realization by introducing the new discourse topic with *y'know*.

(40) Irene: You know who was bangin' out there for twenty minutes.
                Ken.   He didn't know where I was.=
      Zelda: **Oh**
      Irene: [=He was fixin' the back]   door.
      Zelda: [**Oh** I didn't hear him!]

Speakers also introduce new discourse topics by tying them to information they assume their hearers will find familiar. Henry and Zelda know that my parents own a house near their summer home. In (41), they are trying to find a location with which I am familiar in order to locate their summer home for me.

(41) Debby: Where are you? Which– [which street?]
      Henry: [We're on] Arkansas. Right
              from– across from the bank.
      Zelda.   D'y'know where the Montclair is? And the Sea View?
              D'you ever ride down the:– [uh   ]   The=
      Debby: [The] motels? There?
      Zelda: =motels. On the boardwalk. [D'you go bike riding?   ]
      Henry: [Do you know where Abe's]
              is?   ] Right across the=
      Debby: Yeh I know where Abe's is.]
      Henry: =street.
      Debby: **Oh** it's that way.

When I finally do acknowledge a familiar location (*where Abe's is*), Henry locates his home in relation to that place. I then acknowledge receipt of this new piece of information.

My examples thus far suggest that the receipt of new information may occupy several turns at talk – with one speaker gradually prompting into a new information state. (42) is another such example. Irene and Zelda are discussing Henry's upcoming dental extraction.

(42)   Irene: You have Blue Cross and Blue Shield?
        Zelda: That doesn't cover it.
        Irene: Yes it *does*! You tell him you have Blue Cross and Blue Shield.
                  It paid for Jesse's.
        Zelda: Did it? **Oh** I'm gonna go in there, I have the card.

Irene uses a brief personal experience (*It paid for Jesse's*) to lead Zelda toward the new information. After confirming the new information, Zelda acknowledges its receipt.

Of course not all newly received information is explicitly prompted by an interlocutor. Consider (43). Irene has been telling a story about how local politicians do not serve their constituents' needs.

(43)   Irene: Years ago, my husband's family were all in the laundry
                  business. And that's the business that his father was in, and
                  that's how he worked, his way up
                  ⌈t'become– t'go through law school.⌉
        Zelda: ⌊**Oh** is *that* his business? I didn't ⌋ know that.

That the politician's father was in the laundry business is background information for Irene's story. Yet, it is this piece of information whose receipt Zelda marks – hardly information whose transfer is explicitly prompted.[10]

Note, also, that new information need not be prompted through verbal means at all: context changes create new information which may be marked with *oh*. In (44), I am talking to Zelda in her kitchen when she hears Henry coming downstairs and approaching the kitchen:

(44)   Zelda: Uh:: when I was a child, I lived in Glendale. It was lovely, it
                  was beau– **oh** here he is! Wanna talk t'him too?
        Debby: **Oh** I'll say hello.
        Zelda: Hey, Henry, you girlfriend's here!
        Henry: [from living room] **Oh** yeh?
                  [enters kitchen]   **Oh** how y'doin'? How are y'hh?

And, finally, because *oh* marks information recognition, and new information receipt, it can be used as a back-channel signal that alternates with other signals of hearer attention (*yeh, mmhmm*) or occurs in conjunction with them. Such signals often occur at turn-transition spaces. (45) shows the back-channel use of *oh* upon recognition of two pieces of familiar information. I have told Zelda that two features of the street on which my

parents live (a street with which she is familiar) cause my parents to complain: first, the street is noisy, and second, the street it big.

(45)   Debby: The one thing my parents complain about is that the s– uh
                  the street is noisy. ⌜Y'know=   ⌝
        Zelda: ⌞ **Oh** yeh. Right.   ⌟
        Debby: =cause it's a big street.
        Zelda: **Oh** yeh. =
        Henry: ⌜It's a highway!   ⌝
        Zelda: =Yeh, and it's goin' up– and that–⌞the bridge is there!⌟

In sum, *oh* marks two changes in information status: the recognition of
familiar information and the receipt of new information. Either change
may be conversationally triggered by something that an interlocutor says
(although that contribution need not be something that explicitly prompts
the change), cognitively triggered by the speaker's own processing of information, or contextually triggered by an event.

4.4 *Oh* and shifts in subjective orientation

Speaker orientation to information is not just a matter of recognition and
receipt of the informational content of ongoing discourse. Orientation also
involves the **evaluation** of information: speakers respond affectively and
subjectively to what is said, what they are thinking of, and what happens
around them. Just as speakers display shifts in objective orientation, so too,
do they display shifts in subjective orientation. And not surprisingly, *oh*
can be used when speakers display shifts in expressive orientation.

One such subjective orientation is **intensity**: a speaker is so committed
to the truth of a proposition that future estimates of his or her character
hinge on that truth (Labov 1984b). In (46), for example, I have unintentionally provoked a disagreement between Freda and Jack about something
for which they both display strong feelings: girls' high schools. Note
Freda's repetition, meta-talk, and contrastive stress on *do* – all expressions
of intensity commonly used in argument (Schiffrin 1982b: Chapter 8).

(46a)   Debby: Well I think there's a lot of competition between girls.
                  In an *all* girls school. More than well– more academically
                  ⌜ anyway. ⌝
        Freda: ⌞ **Oh**   ⌟ yes. **Oh** yes. They're better students I *do* believe
                  that.

Later in the argument, Freda responds to Jack's accusation that the girls'
high school which she and I both attended is no longer academically

respected. Her defense intensifies when Jack adds to his accusation the demise of the local boys' high school.

(46b)   Jack: In fact it had lost its popularity, didn't it.
                  Girls' High. ⌈   ⌉ And Central High.
         Freda: ⌊ No. ⌋   **Oh** no.

She later solicits endorsement of her position from me. Note her use of *oh yes* upon receipt of my endorsement, and, as preface to her response to Jack's question — a response which intensifies her position about the academic quality of Girls' High still further.

(46c)   Freda: You went there more recently
                  than ⌈ I. ⌉
         Debby: ⌊ Yeh.⌋⌈Um...it's—⌉
         Jack: ⌊Doesn't   ⌋
                  hold the:.. like it *used* to.
         Debby: It still has a reputation. ⌈   ⌉ In some ways.
         Freda: ⌊ **Oh** yes.⌋
         Jack: But, like it did?
         Freda: **Oh** yes. Girls' High is still rated. Y'know Girls' High is rated
                  higher than Central. I just read recently that Girls' High is *still*
                  rated the highest.

Thus, in (46), *oh* accompanies Freda's increasingly intensive orientation toward her position. The cumulative interactional effect of these progressive shifts in Freda's own commitment to her position is increased distance from Jack's position.

Intensification occurs not only in argument: it occurs whenever speakers strengthen their reactions to what is being said. In fact, many cases of *oh* which might be traditionally classified as exclamatory can be seen as speaker intensification. In (47), for example, I have reached the end of a story about my parents' encounter with the local police following the robbery of their home. Henry's strong emotional reaction is a shift in his expressive orientation because it is a shift in his evaluative involvement.

(47)   Debby: He found out that um the kid had been killed in a gang fight
                 ⌈ the nighthhbefore.   ⌉ So=
        Henry: ⌊ [sharp intake of breath] **Oh** Go:d. ⌋
        Debby: =it just ended like ⌈ that. ⌉
        Henry: ⌊ Tsk. ⌋ Tsk.   Pshew.

Another example is (48): I am surprised at Irene's description of her job (it turns out that she is not being literal).

(48)   Irene: I'm an N.T.A. ın ⌈ school. ⌉   Uh: really a cop.=
        Debby: ⌊ What's ⌋ that?

```
Irene:  ⌈ =See that the   Yeh.  See that the  ⌉ kids behave.
Debby:  ⌊ Oh real:  ly?          No kidding?! ⌋
```

Reorientations to information are also occasioned when speakers discover a discrepancy between their own and another's evaluation of a piece of information, e.g. their level of commitment to a proposition. In (49), for example, Freda and Jack have been comparing the housecleaning efforts of their new neighbor to the lack of such efforts from their previous neighbor. After Freda defends the old neighbor, Jack counters the relevance of Freda's defense by building his point into a general truth. Note the various devices which achieve this: *y'know* (see Chapter 9), a rhetorical question and answer, and *c'mon*.

```
(49)    Jack:   Yeh, she never did ⌈any  ⌉thing. ⌈Rose never did⌉
                anything.          ⌊Huh?⌋        ⌊No she didn't ⌋
        Freda:  but she had that girl.
        Jack:   Oh! Help don't do these things! C'mon. Y'know they just
                wipe this off, and wipe that off, and underneath it's dirty.
                Y'know it's help! And why should they? It's your house, not
                theirs.
```

Thus, *oh* prefaces a reorientation occasioned by Jack's realization that Freda's level of commitment toward a particular proposition does not match his own: the degree to which Freda was expected to believe a certain proposition was misjudged.

Subjective reorientations are also created when one speaker's display of over-commitment to a proposition causes the other to re-evaluate the propriety of that commitment. In such cases, *oh* may work to propose the speaker's reorientation toward that proposition, and thus, to propose a new speaker/hearer alignment. In (50), Henry asserts that Irene should be closer with her family. Both Zelda and Irene dispute his assertion: Zelda says that Irene's family situation does not parallel Henry's (who had siblings close in age), and Irene says that she is talking about different family members.

```
(50)    Irene:  I'm not that family orientated. ⌈ Like they are. ⌉
        Henry:                                  ⌊ She should be. ⌋
                She's got a nice family.        ⌈ She's got lovely=⌉
        Zelda:                          Well, ⌊ she really– wait=⌋
        Henry:  ⌈ =children. ⌉
        Zelda:  ⌊ =a minute  ⌋ she doesn't have any ⌈ sisters,  ⌉
        Irene:                                      ⌊ I'm not   ⌋ talkin' about
                my children.
        Henry:  Well you should make it so, it's good.
        Zelda:  Oh, c'mon!
```

Note that despite (because of?) Zelda's and Irene's disputation of his position, Henry persists in his assertion. It is this further display of commitment that occasions Zelda's *Oh, c'mon!*: Henry has gone too far and should know that he is now obliged to take a different course of action.

This sense that one has pursued a commitment beyond reasonable expectations appears again in (51). Henry and Irene have been arguing about parents' ability to prevent children's intermarriages. Henry's position is that parents can prevent intermarriages; Irene's is that they cannot.

(51)   Henry: But if it's my own children, where I could have direct saying in
                       the fact, then I'll say it.
        Irene: But you can't have direct saying if some– if the
                       ⌈ kid comes home ⌉ and says 'I'm in love ⌈ with so and= ⌉
        Henry: ⌊ *Who* can't have ⌋   ⌊   *Who* can't= ⌋
        Irene: ⌈ =so', what're you gonna do? ⌉
        Henry: ⌊ =say it? *You* can't say it. ⌋   *I* could say it.
        Irene: **Oh** ⌈ Henry c'mon. ⌉
        Henry: ⌊ He's my dau– ⌋ it's my daughter.

Irene poses a hypothetical situation with an inevitable outcome (*what're you gonna do*) to which Henry does not verbally attend. Irene's *Oh Henry c'mon* then conveys that Henry has pursued his position beyond reasonable expectations of intensity.

In sum, speaker orientation is not just objective recognition and receipt of information: it is also evaluation of the content of one's own talk, as well as the content of another's talk. Just as shifts in objective orientation are marked by *oh*, so too, are shifts in subjective orientation.

4.5 Why *oh*?

We have seen that *oh* marks different tasks of information management in discourse. These productive and receptive tasks, however, are hardly dependent on *oh*: speakers are certainly able to replace, recognize, receive, and re-evaluate information without verbalization through *oh*. Why, then, does *oh* occur?

Since the overall role of *oh* is in information state transitions, let us begin with this component of talk (discussed in Chapter 1, 1.5). One of the basic goals of talk is the exchange of information. This goal can be realized because speakers and hearers redistribute knowledge about entities, events, states, situations, and so on – whatever real world knowledge is being represented through talk. Furthermore, because discourse involves the **exchange** of information, knowledge and meta-knowledge are constantly in flux, as are degrees of certainty about, and salience of, information. Another way of saying this is that information states are constantly evolving over the course of a conversation: what speakers and hearers can reasonably expect one another to know, what they can expect about the other's knowledge of what they know, how certain they can expect one another to be about that knowledge, and how salient they can expect the other to find that knowledge are all constantly changing. In short, information states are dynamic processes which change as each one of their contributing factors changes.

Oh has a role in information state transitions because *oh* marks a focus of speaker's attention which then also becomes a candidate for hearer's attention. This creation of a joint focus of attention not only allows transitions in information state, but it marks information as more salient with a possible increase in speaker/hearer certainty as to shared knowledge and meta-knowledge. So it is by verbally marking a cognitive task, and opening an individual processing task to a hearer, that *oh* initiates an information state transition.

But suggesting that *oh* has a pragmatic effect – the creation of a joint focus – does not really answer the question of **why** *oh* has this pragmatic effect. To try to answer this question, let us consider in more detail how *oh* is situated in social interaction.

First, *oh* makes evident a very general and pervasive property of participation frameworks: the division of conversational labor between speaker and hearer. Back-channel *oh*, for example, ratifies the current participation structure of the conversation: speaker remains speaker, and hearer remains hearer. Thus, *oh* as back-channel not only marks information receipt, and marks an individual as an occupant of a specific participation status (active recipient), but it also ratifies the current division of turn-taking responsibilities in the exchange structure.

Second, *oh* displays individuals in specific participation statuses and frameworks. Because *oh* displays one's own ongoing management of information, its user is temporarily displayed as an individual active in the role of utterance reception. Recall that *oh* is used not only as a back-channel response, but to incorporate requested clarifications and unanticipated answers into talk. These uses display a hearer as an active recipient of information who acknowledges and integrates information as it is provided. This functional capacity is complementary to the speaker's capacity as animator (Goffman 1981b: 144): both display individuals as occupants of mechanically defined nodes in a system of information transmission.

Oh displays still another aspect of participation frameworks: speaker/ hearer alignment toward each other. We have seen that individuals evaluate each other's orientations: what one defines as an appropriate level of commitment to a proposition, another may define as inappropriate. Different speaker/hearer alignments can be characterized in part by whether individuals share subjective orientations toward a proposition. For example, we might characterize an argument as an alignment in which Speaker A is committed to the truth of a proposition to which B is not similarly committed, and Speaker B is committed to the truth of another proposition to which A is not similarly committed. When *oh* marks a speaker's realization of the other's unshared commitment, then, it may serve as a signal of a potentially argumentative stance. Thus, it is because *oh* makes accessible speaker/hearer assumptions about each others' subjective orientations toward information, that it can display speaker/hearer alignments toward each other.

And, finally, consider that conversation requires a delicate balance between the satisfaction of one's own needs and the satisfaction of others' needs. Included is not only an individual cognitive need – individuals need time (no matter how short) to transform the content that they have in mind into talk – but a reciprocal social need: individuals need to receive appreciation for self and show deference to others (Goffman 1967, Lakoff 1973a, Tannen 1984). *Oh* may help service individuals' cognitive needs by providing time to focus on informational tasks – while still displaying one's interactional presence in deference to the satisfaction of social needs.

In sum, although *oh* is a marker of information management tasks which are essentially cognitive, the fact that it verbalizes speakers' handling of those tasks has interactional consequences. Thus, use of *oh* may very well be cognitively motivated. But once an expression makes cognitive work accessible to another during the course of a conversation, it is open for pragmatic interpretation and effect – and such interpretations may become conventionally associated with the markers of that work. Intended interactional effects and meanings may thus account for the use of *oh* as readily as the initial cognitive motivation. Such conventionalized effects may further explain why speakers verbally mark information management tasks with *oh*.

4.6 Summary

Oh is a marker of information management: it marks shifts in speaker orientation (objective and subjective) to information which occur as speakers and hearers manage the flow of information produced and received during discourse. Orientation shifts affect the overall information state of a conversation: the distribution of knowledge about entities, events, and situations. Although *oh* is a marker of cognitive tasks, its use may have pragmatic effects in interaction.

5 *Well*: Marker of response

Like *oh*, use of *well* is not based on semantic meaning or grammatical status. Although *well* sometimes is a noun, an adverb, or a degree word, its use in utterance initial position is difficult to characterize in terms based on any of these classes.[1] Rather, it has been labelled interjection, filler, particle, hesitator, and initiator (Svartvik 1980).

Sacks, Schegloff and Jefferson (1974) observe that *well* often begins turns. Like other turn-initiators, *well* reveals little about the construction of the upcoming turn – an important feature as turn-beginnings may overlap prior turns and thus be partially unanalyzable by those to whom the turn is addressed. At more global levels of conversational organization, *well* (along with *okay* and *so*) is used as a pre-closing devise, offering its recipient a chance to reinstate an earlier or unexpanded topic, or to open another round of talk, prior to conversational closure (Schlegloff and Sacks 1973). Labov and Fanshel (1977: 156) suggest that *well* can also shift talk toward already shared topics of mutual concern, not just during pre-closings, but throughout conversation.

Well also figures in particular conversational moves. Lakoff (1973b) observes that *well* prefaces responses that are insufficient answers to questions. Pomerantz (1984) finds that *well* prefaces disagreements, alternating in this environment with *yes but* and silence. Owen (1983) adds that *well* can precede an answer in which a presupposition of a prior question is cancelled, as well as non-compliance with a request, or rejection of an offer. Wootton (1981) shows that *well* precedes parents' responses to their children's requests more often when those responses reject, rather than grant, the requests. Thus, *well* signals moves that are in some way dispreferred (Pomerantz 1984).

Many of the specific results of my analysis parallel previous analyses of *well*. I will propose, in addition, that *well* functions in the **participation framework** of discourse, as opposed, for example, to *oh* which functions to organize the **information state**. More specifically, I will argue that *well* is a **response** marker which anchors its user in an interaction when an upcoming contribution is not fully consonant with prior coherence options. It is because this function displays a speaker in a particular participation status – **respondent** – that it functions in the participation framework.

Recall that, in Chapter 1, I stated that one of the central tasks of everyday talk is the accomplishment of conversational coherence: how can what one speaker says be heard to follow sensibly from what another has said? I proposed that responsibility for coherence is divided between speaker and hearer, such that a speaker is expected to formulate an utterance so that its message is accessible to a hearer, who is then expected to demonstrate through a next utterance attention to that message.

I begin my analysis of *well* by maintaining one of the idealized assumptions of my model in Chapter 1 (1.5): conversational coherence proceeds in a pairwise (local) fashion, such that one speaker's utterance (turn, idea or act) gains coherence through its relation to the immediately prior utterance (turn, idea or act) of the other speaker. Sacks (1973, Lecture 4, pages 11–12) describes the importance of 'next-position':

> There is one generic place where you need not include information as to which utterance you're intending to relate an utterance to ... and that is if you are in Next Position to an utterance. Which is to say that for adjacently placed utterances, where a next intends to relate to a last, no other means than positioning are necessary in order to locate which utterance you're intending to deal with...[2]

Maintaining the assumption that conversational coherence proceeds in a pairwise fashion, whereby an initial utterance sets up an expectation of a coherent response in the next available conversational slot, provides for the use of *well* in question/answer exchange pairs and request/compliance action pairs (5.1). I then examine occurrences of *well* which cannot be explained by a pairwise view of coherence (5.2). My conclusion synthesizes the analysis of *well* through discussion of coherence options and the participant role of respondent (5.3).

5.1 *Well* and local coherence

5.1.1 *Question/answer pairs*

As we discussed in Chapter 4, question/answer pairs are adjacency pairs, i.e. sequentially constrained pairs in which the occurrence of a first-pair-part creates a slot for the occurrence of a second-pair-part (a conditional relevance), such that the non-occurrence of that second-pair-part is heard as officially absent (Schegloff and Sacks 1973). We also noted that questions constrain the next conversational slot for both semantic and pragmatic reasons: questions are incomplete propositions, or propositions whose polarity is unspecified (e.g. Carlson 1983); questions are among the linguistic means of enacting requests for information and actions, and thus impose – through their underlying appropriateness conditions (Gordon and Lakoff 1971, Labov and Fanshel 1977: Chapter 3) – an expectation of fulfillment. Thus, both completion of a proposition, and compliance with a request, can be enacted through the second-pair-part of answer.

Consider, now, how satisfaction of the constraint to answer a question is shaped by the linguistic form of the question. Individuals asking questions can make clear through the design of their questions what information will suffice as a minimally coherent answer. Yes–no questions provide respondents with a choice between two possibilities – positive or negative. Thus, the constraint to find an answer to a yes–no question which is propositionally sufficient can be easily met by a respondent: confirm or deny a proposition. In WH-questions, adverbials (*who*, *what*, *where*, *when*, etc.) target what information will be needed to complete an unfinished proposition, and thus what information will provide a propositionally sufficient answer. But WH-questions differ from yes–no questions because they open up a set of choices for the speaker, allowing for selection among a range of options. Finding an answer to a WH-question, then, may require more work from a respondent: select one member from a set of options. Thus, questions impose the same conversational constraint: they are to be answered. But the linguistic form of questions creates different possibilities for the satisfaction of the constraint, i.e. different ideational options for those answers.

5.1.1.1 Questions, ideational options, and well *with answers.* Use of *well* with answers is sensitive to the linguistic form of the prior question. Table 5.1 shows that answers were marked with *well* more frequently after WH-questions than after yes–no questions. This difference (which fully parallels Svartvik's 1980 results in his corpus) suggests that when the conditions for propositional sufficiency of an answer have been relatively delimited by the form of the prior question, *well* is not as useful for marking the answer as a coherent response.

We might expect, then, that *well* would be relatively infrequent with whatever other question forms also limit respondents' options. Disjunctive questions, for example, are like yes–no questions because they allow the respondent a choice from a limited set of options (often a binary set). Other question forms do not so much present a choice between options, as assume

Table 5.1. *Yes–no questions, WH–questions, and* well*–marked answers*

	Yes–no questions	WH–questions	Total
well precedes answer	37 (10%)	56 (21%)	93
well does not precede answer	343	211	554
Total	380	267	647

that a choice has already been made for which confirmation is sought. Tag questions, for example, are declarative statements with postposed tags through which speakers seek agreement with the content of the statement. Similarly, declarative statements presented in a rising intonation (and often transcribed with a question mark as in *You want to come?*) also provide a proposition for which agreement is sought. Table 5.2 shows that *well* rarely preceded answers following any of these questions forms.

Table 5.2. *Limited option questions and answers with* well

	Tag questions	Intonationally marked declarative statements	Disjunctive questions	Total
well precedes answer	1 (3%)	3 (5%)	2 (6%)	6
well does not precede answer	32	56	32	120
Total	33	59	34	126

My data thus far have shown that use of *well* with answers is influenced by question form: *well* is more frequent when a larger set of answer options is encoded through the form of the question.[3] What happens, however, when respondents do not select an answer from the options encoded by the linguistic form of the question? Although a question guarantees a conversational slot for an answer (because it is an initial part of an adjacency pair), it does not guarantee that the **ideational content** of that answer will be selected from whatever options are offered through the question's form. Asking a yes–no question, for example, only **proposes** two options: it hardly insures that respondents will confirm or negate the proposition being questioned.

In Chapter 4, I isolated three conditions which might cause a respondent to diverge from the options offered by a prior question. I review these conditions (and their examples) here. First, respondents may be unable to choose an option because they lack the requisite knowledge:

(1)   Debby: Is there a coffee clique on this block?
         Zelda: I don't know.

(2)   Debby: Where d'y'think they're coming from?
         Irene: I don't know. I really have no idea!

Second, respondents may find the question inapplicable because of an inaccurate speaker-assumption. In asking a WH-question, for example, the questioner assumes not only a set of options, but the truth of the proposition being questioned. In (3), my question shows an assumption that Henry and Zelda have friends – an assumption they deny.

(3)   Debby: Who has more friends. Between you.
         Zelda: ⎡No::we don't see:: our=   ⎤
         Henry: ⎣We really don't have that many friends.⎦
         Zelda: =old friends.

In asking a yes–no question, the questioner assumes a binary choice. In (4), however, the questioner's assumption that the respondent is, or is not, from Philadelphia is not exactly accurate. Thus, neither option offered by the question provides a sufficient basis from which to choose an answer.

(4)   Zelda: Are you from Philadelphia?
         Sally: **Well** I grew up uh out in the suburbs. And then I lived for
                   about seven years up in upstate New York. And then I came
                   back here t'go to college.

Third, if the circumstances being questioned are themselves equivocal, even the range of options offered through a WH-question may be insufficiently broad to allow an expected answer:

(5)   Sally: How does it work around here when somebody gets
                   married t'somebody from a different group,
                   like, ⎡   ⎤ Yeh. Or...yeh,=
         Zelda: ⎣ religion? ⎦
         Sally: ⎡=or nationality, or something. ⎤
         Zelda: ⎣**Well**....it–it   ⎦ all depends on um ... now
                   my husband...believes in eh marrying eh in his own religion.

(6) is a particularly useful example of this condition.

(6)   Debby: You can...tell somebody's from South Philly?
         Zelda: Sometimes y'can.
         Henry: *I* can. **Well**:, if one– if they *use* it, then I can, if they *don't* use
                   it, then I *don't*!
         Irene: I– I don't really know.

In response to my question about whether Zelda, Henry, and Irene can identify Philadelphians by the neighborhood in which they live, I receive three responses: Zelda expresses the equivocality of the situation being questioned, Irene conveys her lack of knowledge, and Henry retreats from an affirmative answer, to *well* and an expression of equivocality which parallels Zelda's answer. Thus, three conditions might cause respondents to diverge from the options offered them by a prior question: lack of adequate information or knowledge, an inaccurate assumption by the questioner, a complication of the situation being questioned.

When respondents do not take the ideational options offered by the form of a prior question – for any of the above reasons – *well* is frequently used to mark the answer. Table 5.3 shows that when respondents answer yes–no questions with something other than confirmation or negation, they are more likely to preface that response with *well*. And Table 5.4 shows that when respondents answer WH-questions with something other than one of the choices proposed through the question, they are more likely to preface that response with *well*. Thus, *well* is used when respondents diverge from the options for coherence offered them by a prior question.

Table 5.3. *Answers to yes–no questions and* well

	Confirmation	Negation	Other	Total
well precedes answer	7 (4%)	2 (1%)	28 (48%)	37
well does not precede answer	161	152	30	343
Total	168	154	58	380

Table 5.4. *Answers to WH–questions and* well

	WH-information given	WH-information not given	Total
well precedes answer	32 (14%)	24 (56%)	56
well does not precede answer	192	19	211
Total	224	43	267

The data in Tables 5.3 and 5.4 predict that minimal answers to questions would not be prefaced by *well*. That is, *well* is used when respondents do not match questioners' assumptions as to what constitutes the ideational

content of an answer – when they do not fulfill the question options. Therefore, we would expect that *well* would not be used in the opposite circumstances – when answers strictly adhere to question options.

Indeed, when yes–no questions were answered minimally with either *yes*
or *no*, the questions were never prefaced by *well*. When WH-questions
were answered with single lexical items which represented familiar knowledge (e.g. name, age), the answers were rarely prefaced by *well*. The few
exceptions to the restriction of *well* from minimal answers actually demonstrate its near categorical nature. In (7), for example, Zelda has forgotten
her childhood address – information normally assumed to be easily retriev-
able; *well* accompanies her information search.

(7)　　Sally:　　But otherwise, you lived in West Philly. Whereabouts?
　　　　Zelda:　　**Well**, I was born at Fifty second and em. . . . . . .tsk. . .oh I
　　　　　　　　　forgo–**well**. . . . . . . .I think it's Fifty second and Chew.

And in (8), *well* prefaces an answer that is clearly outside of the questioner's expectations, i.e. at least in mainstream adult expectations, gym
does not usually count as a school topic:[4]

(8)　　Sally:　　Are there any topics that you like in particular about school, or
　　　　　　　　　none.
　　　　Lon:　　**Well**. . . . . . . .gym!

That *well* does not typically precede minimal answers, however, does
not mean that it cannot **follow** such answers. In fact, when respondents
begin their answers with minimal tokens of question acknowledgement,
and then add more information, we often find *well* prefacing the addition.
In (9), I ask a tag question, a form that severely restricts hearers' response
options:

(9)　　Debby:　　That's quite a neighborhood, isn't it?
　　　　Irene:　　Yeh **well** I don't really have too much trouble.

After minimally acknowledging my tagged assertion with *yeh*, and thus fulfilling the ideational expectations encoded by the question form, Irene
modifies her acknowledgement. She prefaces that second part of her
response with *well*. Other examples show that even when questions do not
so severely delimit respondents' options, expansions of answers after minimal tokens can be prefaced by *well*. In (10), Irene's answer to Sally's
question consists of a narrative describing an instance of the sort of experience about which Sally asked: the narrative follows an affirmative answer
to the yes–no question.

(10)   Sally: Have you ever been frightened by something that happened?
                  Y'know like with one of your kids . . . at night or
                  something?   Y'know=
        Irene: Yeh w–
        Sally: =when they're dreaming or something?
        Irene: Yeh, **well** I had a bad experience with Alan.

In (11), Zelda seems to be unsure of what to answer, switching from *no* to
well to *no*.

(11)   Sally: Do you think you get more common sense as you grow
                  older, ⎡ or–   ⎤
        Zelda: ⎣ No: ⎦ **well**, no. Uh: if you have it, you have it.

Well may also follow a turn-initial minimal token when the affirmation or
negation provided through the acknowledgement token needs repair.

(12)   Debby: Do you ever go down in the winter?
        Zelda: No:. **Well** we go down but our house is closed.

(We see more examples of *well* with repairs, as well as other modifiers of
prior content, in 5.1.2, 5.2.3.)

   We have seen that speakers use *well* more frequently when the ideational
options offered by questions are not precisely followed in the content of
answers. Speakers may also use *well* when they expand an answer following
a minimal token of acknowledgement to the question. But speakers are not
likely to use *well* when they do no more than strictly adhere to the response
options encoded by the form of the question. Thus, one feature of
question/answer pairs which constrains the use of *well* concerns the match
between ideational options offered by questions and the idea provided in
answers.

5.1.1.2 Ideational structure of answers. Another feature of question/
answer pairs which constrains the use of *well* is the idea structure of the
answer. In one possible structure, respondents delay the main portion of
the answer – the ideational core of the response – with introductory
phrases. *Well* can preface either the introductory phrase or the main
portion of the answer. Let us consider the former possibility first.

   In (13), I request particular information from Zelda, who defers provision of that information with the opening phrase *well that's a sore spot*.

(13)   Debby: What does your daughter in law call you?
        Zelda: **Well** that's a sore spot.
                  My older daughter in law does call me Mom.
                  My younger daughter in law right now is a– to nothing.

Other examples in which *well* occurs with introductory phrases include
(14), in which *well* prefaces a meta-linguistic introduction:

(14)   Debby: Suppose you were having a problem though like with your
                    kids or something you just didn't know what to do? Who
                    would you go to talk to? Y'mean y'wouldn't. . .
         Henry: **Well**, I figure this way.
                    Why can't I– why can't I talk to my own family [continues]

and (15), in which *well* prefaces a disclaimer (Hewitt and Stokes 1975):

(15)   Debby: What does a house rent for around here?
                    [Jack answers, and discussion between Jack and Freda over the accuracy
                    of his answer follows]
         Freda: **Well** we don't know. But I would say. . .more than two fifty.

One of the more complex answer deferrals involves the use of a story to
respond to a question: a story defers a response by contextualizing it in a
personally evaluated report of a prior experience (cf. Labov and Fanshel
1977: 106). This means that hearers may have to interpret evaluative
devices (Labov 1972a) to understand the point of the story in order to find
the answer to the question – a task even further complicated by the multiple
levels of meaning conveyed through stories (Polanyi 1979, Schiffrin
1984b). Thus, we find that *well* may accompany narrative abstracts
(Labov 1972a) when they function simultaneously as introductory brackets to answers:

(16)   Debby: What happened?
         Zelda: **Well**. . .at one time he was a very fine doctor. And he had two
                    terrible tragedies. [story follows]

When respondents defer the ideational core of their answers – either with
introductory brackets or through contextualization in a narrative – they are
imposing extra work on their hearers: they are, in effect, requesting that
their hearers temporarily suspend their expectations for propositional completion of the question. *Well* figures in this request because it shows the
speaker's orientation to the conversational demand for an answer, despite
the fact that the answer has not been immediately forthcoming. Thus, we
find that speakers may defer the content of their response with *well* itself,
especially when it is lengthened or accompanied with filled or unfilled
pauses:

(17)   Debby: How much education do you think a young man needs
                    nowadays, to get a job

Irene: Uh:. . . .**well** I think there're for the profession– like
            something that my husband is in now [continues]
(18)   Sally: What does it mean:. . .if somebody has common sense.
            D'you have any idea ⎡i– ⎤
Zelda: ⎣**We**⎦**ll**:. . .I think if they have common
            sense um. . .[continues]

Note, however, that precisely because *well* displays speakers' aliveness
to the conversational demand for an answer, it provides speakers with
increased flexibility and a certain measure of looseness in complying with
other conversational demands. In other words, because beginning an
answer with *well* anchors a speaker in the conversational exchange by displaying an aliveness to conversational demands, it actually allows a temporary suspension of other conversational expectations – especially the
expectation for propositional completion of the answer through an immediately forthcoming answer.

A complementary technique for answer deferral is to insert *well* between
whatever portion of talk is responsible for the response delay (e.g. an introductory bracket or even an exchange of turns), and the portion through
which the ideational core of the response will be provided. The role of *well*
in these answer deferrals is to reinvoke the relevance of the temporarily
bypassed question, and to dispel any relevance of the just-prior talk for the
main conversational task of providing an answer. This use of *well* allows
respondents to manage multiple involvements and concerns without reneg-
ing on the conversational demand for an answer. Consider (19).

(19)   Zelda: They get just two years. But she hasn't gotten anything yet
            cause they don't know if they want to approve it.
Debby: Why not?
Zelda: They did last year. [decreased volume]
            Well cause they say that more than likely she'll go back to
            work in September.

In (19), for example, Zelda continues to develop what she had been saying
prior to my question *why not*. She then prefaces her answer to that question
with *well*. Note how Zelda's renewed volume and use of the conjunction
cause also mark her *well*-prefaced utterance as the ideational core of her
answer to my question.

Well also allows speakers to show over-involvement with a question, and
to propose its continuing relevance even after the questioner's expectations
of an answer have been satisfied. In (20), for example, I have asked Ira why
he decided to live in a particular neighborhood:

(20)   Debby: What made you decide t'come out here? Do y'remember?
        Ira: What made us decide t'come out here. **Well** uh we were
                    looking in different neighborhoods and then uh this was a
                    Jewish community and we decided t'come out here.
                    [continues with two more reasons]
        Debby: Yeh. Yeh it's about fifteen minutes from West Philadelphia.
        Ira: **Well** uh a– another th– thing that I took in consideration I was
                    working at the Navy Yard at the time [continues]

Ira provides three reasons for his decision (not all reproduced in 20). I
endorse one of the reasons, but then Ira attends not to that endorsement,
but to the continuation of his own explanation with still a fourth reason. Ira
marks his continued answer with *another thing* and with *well*.

Note, also, that respondents can use *well* to help manage joint involvements with their questioners which may delay the adjacency of an answer.
For example, speakers sometimes cannot answer a question without clarification of that question, so they must themselves *ask* a question before
beginning their own answer (see 4.1.3). What is created, then, is an embedded question/answer pair (Schegloff 1972) in which Question 2/Answer 2
makes possible Answer 1:

        Speaker A: ⌈ Question 1
        Speaker B: | ⌈ Question 2
        Speaker A: | ⌊ Answer 2
        Speaker B: ⌊ Answer 1

Speakers often reinvoke the relevance of the initial question by marking its
answer (*Answer 1*) with *well*, in effect, subordinating the question/answer
pair which had delayed that response:

(21)   Debby: ⌈ [Q1] Do you think there'll ever be a time when color doesn't
                | make a difference?
        Jack: | ⌈ [Q2] In this country?
        Debby: | ⌊ [A2] Yeh.
        Jack: ⌊ [A1] **Well** of course there will.

Not all exchanges embedded between a question and its answer are relevant to the eventual provision of the answer. In fact, when exchanges or
remarks have little to do with the question *per se, well* works as an interactional resource through which speakers manage some of the complex participation frameworks created by multi-party conversations. In (22), Jack
has been asking his teenage son Lon if he remembers the movie *The Ten*

Commandments.

(22)   Freda: ⌈Is em: ⌉ Lonnie.
          Jack: ⌊Did you like⌋ it?
          Lon: Was ⌈allright. I saw it four ⌉ times ⌈though. ⌉
          Freda: ⌊He can't remember it.⌋   ⌊Lonnie.⌋
          Jack: Do you like it eh: eh: still like it?
          Freda: Lonnie.
          Lon: It's all right.
          Jack: Or did it wear off: or what.
          Lon: It's all right.
          Freda: **Well** it sure didn't stick.
                      Lonnie. Upstairs in the bathroom [continues]

During Jack's interrogation, Freda is also bidding for her son's attention.
She finally answers the question addressed to Lon, prefacing her response
with *well*. By marking her remark as an answer to Jack's question (despite
Lon's prior answers), Freda establishes a dual stance in the conversation:
she is openly addressing Jack, but her response is also directed to her son
whose inattentiveness to her prior bids justifies the factual content of her
answer that the ten commandments (or at least the one commanding honor
for father and mother) *sure didn't stick.*

    Finally, the ideational organization of talk into main and subordinate
topics creates a similar structure in which *well* marks a response to the
dominant topic. In (23), Zelda and I are talking about kin terms.

(23)   Zelda: Sometimes Jo when she calls on the phone, will say,
                 'Hello Mommy.' But I guess that's just eh: an
                 endearment.⌈   ⌉ Yeh.
          Debby: ⌊ Yeh. Probably. ⌋
                 Well I used t'do the same thing with– with Dad. Y'know,
                 I'd say t'my mother, 'Is Daddy home yet?' or something
                 ⌈ like that.   ⌉
          Zelda: ⌊ Right. Right. ⌋ **Well** our kids too. 'Hi Dad' an– or 'Where's
                 Daddy?'

After each new piece of information about this topic is offered, the recipient of that information acknowledges it. Although each acknowledgement
marks acceptance of the information as part of the overall topic, it is subordinate to the main conversational concern. Each return to the main topic –
each provision of a new example of how a kin term is used – is prefaced by
well.

5.1.1.3 Well, questions, and answers. I began this section by showing that
well is used more often when the range of answer options encoded through

the linguistic form of a question is relatively broad. I also found *well* to be more frequent when answers diverge from the ideational options offered by a prior question – regardless of the linguistic form of that question. Finally, I examined how *well* is used in question/answer pairs in which the main portion of the answer is preceded by other material, showing that *well* could preface either the introductory or main portion of the answer.

My results thus far suggest that *well* is more likely to be used when a respondent cannot easily meet a conversational demand for a response because the idea content of his or her answer will not fit the options just opened by a prior question. This explanation for *well* is based on an assumption that individuals will search first for coherence in adjacent utterances, more specifically, that an utterance in an answer slot will be searched for its relationship to an immediately prior question before it is searched for a coherence relation with some earlier part of talk.

Although such an assumption has been a useful point from which to begin to locate *well* in conversation, we will find uses of *well* which have little to do with pairwise coherence. Before we turn to uses of *well* which have little to do with the local coherence accompanying adjacent units of talk, however, let us examine another conversational pair in which *well* is used – request/compliance action pairs.

5.1.2 Request/compliance pairs

I suggested earlier that one reason why questions constrain the next conversational slot is that they often enact requests with which the addressee is expected to comply.[5] It is not surprising, then, to find that requests enacted through other syntactic forms also receive responses marked with *well*. Although it is not always easy to identify requests – because of the variety of interactional goods that they solicit (including appreciation) – I will argue that non-compliance with a request is more likely to be marked with *well* than is compliance. Again, the argument will be that the options which a first part (a question, a request) have opened for a second part (an answer, a compliance) have not been actualized.

Let us start with requests for action. In (24), Irene issues a request for action to Henry and Zelda, who have been talking about topics other than those on my previously announced conversational agenda (see Chapter 2, 2.2.1).

(24)   Irene: Let's get back because she'll never get home.
               Debby: **Well**, actually we don't have that much more.

Various conditions underlie the appropriateness of Irene's request. One condition is an assumption of need: without the directive, Henry and Zelda would continue diverting attention from the conversational agenda: I have more on my agenda, I want to be home by a reasonable hour, and so on. If any of these (or other) conditions do not hold, the request would become irrelevant, and compliance unnecessary. This is exactly what my response conveys: because there is not much more to talk about, there is no need to request a return to the agenda.

Requests for confirmation are a bit harder to identify (but see Chapter 8, 8.2.3.2). Such requests are often identifiable because of the information state assumed to hold at the time of speaking, that is, speaker/hearer knowledge and meta-knowledge (see Chapter 1, 1.5). That is, if a speaker makes a statement about an event about which a hearer is expected to have knowledge, that statement is heard as a request for confirmation from its hearer (cf. Labov and Fanshel 1977: Chapter 3). Included as requests for confirmation, then, are statements about the hearer's past life, abilities, likes and dislikes, knowledge, and so on. In (25), for example, I request Ira's confirmation of an inference that I have drawn about Ira from his prior statement:

(25)   Ira: And I've been working for the federal government ever since. Thir–thirty six yearshhhh.
        Debby: So you must like them as an employer then.
        Ira: **Well** I like my job, now.

Ira does not confirm my inference; rather, he implicates through his restriction of the statement to *now* that he did not previously like them as an employer. Another example shows a speaker combining minimal acknowledgement of an inference (*yeh*:) with expression of a lack of knowledge (*I don't know*) and, finally, denial of the inference prefaced by *well*.

(26)   Debby: Yeh I bet that there would be a lot more competition also if it's a boy and a girl.
        Zelda: Uh:. . .yeh:. I don't know. **Well** right now they're okay.

Still another example shows a third party making explicit why an inference could not be confirmed as requested, i.e. the inference was too vague:

(27)   Debby: What language did your parents speak?
        Ira: Uh Jewish.
        Debby: Yeh. But you didn't learn it.
        Ira: **Well** I understand 'em but I couldn't– I ⌈ hhhhh ⌉
        Jan: ⌊ He ⌋ never
                  learned to speak it he could understand 'em.

A final example comes from a three-party conversation in which one party makes a claim about a third party to the second party: because the target of that claim is present, he may treat it as a request for confirmation. In (28), Freda is boasting to me about Jack's musical talent:

(28)   Freda: He can usually tell you not only what the piece is, but who it
                  was written by.
        Jack: **Well** that's no big deal!

Jack deflates the boast, thereby failing to supply confirmation for Freda's statement about his talent. Thus, these four examples show different ways of failing to supply requested confirmation – and marking that failure with *well*.

Other requests are identifiable because they are statements about inherently disputable issues, e.g. opinions (Atelsek 1981, Schiffrin 1985c; see also Chapter 8, 8.1.2 of this book). Here we might speak of requests for evaluation. In (29), for example, I indicate the disputability of the proposition for which evaluation is requested by my introductory *some people say*:

(29)   Debby: Well some people say that y'know just talking to a good friend
                  or: somebody in the family, is just as good as talking to a
                  psychiatrist.
        Irene: **Well** it depends on your problem, y'know how much your
                  problem is. [continues]

Irene's response – prefaced with *well* – focuses on the difficulty of supplying the requested evaluation.

I stated earlier, however, that it is difficult to specify the conditions under which utterances are understood as requests for goods which are interactionally valued – goods such as confirmation and evaluation. In fact, Goffman (1974: 546) suggests that almost anything that one person says can be treated as a request for **appreciation**: 'the response we often seek is not an answer to a question or a compliance with a request but an appreciation of a show put on'. Goffman's point is relevant for our purposes because it suggests that responses that do not supply appreciation are marked by *well* more often than responses that do supply appreciation. Indeed, this is exactly what previous research has shown: *well* is used with disagreements, denials, and insufficient answers – all responses which fail to show appreciation (Lakoff 1973b, Owen 1983, Pomerantz 1984, Wootton 1981). My data also provide many such examples:

(30)   Henry: I don't go out of my way eh: because eh:
        Zelda: **Well** you would go out of your way!

(31)   Henry: She should be. She's got a nice family.
        Zelda: **Well** she really– wait a minute. She doesn't have any sisters–

(32)   Jack: This is not a rooted nation anymore.
        Debby: **Well** y'still find that ⌈ sometimes in– ⌉
        Jack: ⌊ We're mobile! ⌋

(33)   Debby: How much education do you think a young man needs
                  nowadays to get a job?
        Henry: College. Definitely.
        Zelda: **Well**, I think even more than the four years.

Thus, *well* does seem to occur when responses fail to supply appreciation –
even though we may not have *a priori* definitions of each preceding
utterance as appreciation-seeking.

It is difficult to support quantitatively the argument that *well* marks non-
appreciative responses, simply because we cannot identify all of the
utterances for which speakers expected (or hoped) to receive appreciation.
But we can compare *well* to other turn-initial markers which can be independently characterized as appreciative or non-appreciative.

Consider the relationship between turn-initial markers and the location
of turn-transition. Since Sacks, Schegloff and Jefferson's (1974) initial observations on turn-taking, a great deal of work has shown the many factors
that are important in defining, and assigning evaluative meaning to, particular types of turn-transition. Analysts have pointed out the role of syntactic (Zimmerman and West 1975), prosodic (French and Local 1983),
nonverbal (Goodwin 1981), multi-channelled (Duncan 1972), cultural and
stylistic (Tannen 1983, 1984), and interpretive (Bennett 1978) factors in
defining locations for, and types of, turn-transition. A common distinction
is between turn-transitions at syntactic junctures or junctures otherwise
marked as possible completion points, and turn-transitions at junctures
which are not possible completion points. (34a) and (b) illustrate the
former; (35), the latter.

(34a)   Henry: So doctors are– well they're not God either.
        Zelda: He said that they didn't think he saw it.

(34b)   Ira: When it was hot, y'slept with the doors and windows open.
                  Not one w– there wasn't anything like this. But today uh:. . .
        Jan: It's these kids that are out for money for drugs.

(35)   Irene: But ⌈ I could never– ⌉
        Henry: ⌊ But you still   ⌋ have a family structure.

Table 5.5 compares the turn-transition location of *well* with the locations of three other markers: *and, so,* and *but.* (We will see in Chapter 6 that *and* and *so* are markers of speaker continuation, and *but* is a marker of contrast.) Thus, when speakers begin turns with *and* or *so* – markers of continuation and development – they are more likely to do so at a point in their interlocutor's talk which is a possible completion point. This trend is reversed with *but* – a turn-initial marker of contrast which often initiates disagreement. *Well,* however, falls only slightly below *and* and *so*: 85% (185) of 218 tokens of turn-initial *well* were at cooperatively timed turn-entry locations. This suggests that *well* marks only slightly less appreciation than either *and* or *so* – balancing, perhaps, the lack of appreciation to be shown through the uncooperative content of the turn, with display of appreciation through the timing of the turn. Thus, turn-entry location suggests that *well* marks considerably more appreciation than *but*.

Table 5.5. *Turn-transition location and initial markers*

	Possible completion	Not possible completion	Total
and	38 (95%)	2	40
so	38 (100%)	0	38
but	25 (52%)	23	48
well	185 (85%)	33	218
Total	286	58	344

Sequences in which speakers switch between *but* and *well* also show the difference between these markers. In (36), *well* marks a more conciliatory move than *but*. Henry and Irene are arguing about mothers' responsibilities; Irene has just disputed Henry's position that mothers' diminished responsibilities are caused by current desires for upward mobility by pointing out that mothers always had responsibility for childrearing.

(36)   Irene: Because the mother is the one that raises and *makes* the child
                 go to Hebrew, or go ⌈ t'church or=   ⌉
        Henry: ⌊ Yeh but– but–= ⌋
        Irene: ⌈ =go here or go there.   ⌉
        Henry: ⌊ =**well** this is because ⌋ she's home t'see that the child does
                 it.
        Irene: Right!
        Henry: But the child– the mother's not there, so the child plays
                 hooky!

It is when Henry begins to concede to Irene that he switches from *yeh but* to *well*, and then when Irene begins to use Henry's concession as a basis from which to infer further agreement (*Right!*) that Henry switches to *but*.[6]

A final example illustrating the difference between *but* and *well* comes from a television talk show – the type in which advocates of two sides of a controversial issue are invited on the air to expose viewers to all sides of that issue. The host of the show had not been successful in eliciting the expected controversy and the following exchange occurred:

(37)   Interviewer: But?
           Interviewee   **Well** there is no but.

By asking *but?*, the interviewer clearly expected to elicit the expected point of controversy; by responding *well there is no but*, the interviewee clearly marked his inability to comply with the request for disagreement.

I have argued again in this section that *well* is used when the options opened by an initial member of a two-part pair for completion by the second member of that pair are not fulfilled. Whereas 5.1.1 showed this use in question/answer exchange pairs, this section has shown the same use in request/compliance action pairs. Note, then, that I am moving closer to the view expressed in Chapter 1, in which the overall coherence of discourse requires an integrated view of all its components: coherence is not just a conversational accomplishment to be met through the location, content, and structure of an answer, but an interactional accomplishment to be met through the actions and displays performed through locally situated moves.

Yet, I have still been maintaining our idealized assumption that conversational coherence proceeds in a pairwise fashion – that one speaker's utterance, regardless of whether we see it as a sequentially relevant idea or act, gains and provides coherence through its relation to the immediately prior utterance. Let us turn to occurrences of *well* which have little to do with pairwise coherence.

5.2 *Well* and non-local coherence

Although our discussion thus far has focused on *well* in response to an adjacent utterance from another, there are other occurrences: with requests (5.2.1), with contingent responses (5.2.2) and with self-responses (5.2.3).

5.2.1 Requests

Because requests typically seek, rather than provide, a response, we would not expect *well* to precede requests. But the need to both seek and provide response coincides under several circumstances and *well* can preface a request under just such conditions.

First are requests for clarification and elaboration (see Chapter 4, 4.1.3, 4.2.1.1). Such contingent queries (Garvey 1977) display the speaker's receipt of information at the same time that they solicit further information. (38) illustrates a request for clarification:

(38) Debby: How did you get the name of the doctor you're using now? Where'd y'find him?
       Zelda: **Well** y'mean our family doctor?

(39) illustrates a request for elaboration:

(39) Jack: Then I worked for the fruit store. Yeh, I was selling eggs. I think I was fifteen, then.
       Debby: **Well** was that a full time job, or like a...

Both requests for clarification and for elaboration can be prefaced by *well*.

Second are requests that are organized relative to each other, such that each request is a response to a prior question and its answer. Such requests fall into a series, with the next member of the series an effort to elicit information in response to the failures of earlier efforts. The clearest illustration is the re-presentation of an initial request after completion of a clarification sequence. Examine, then, how (38) continues:

(38) Debby: How did you get the name of the doctor you're using now? Where'd y'find him?
       Zelda: Well y'mean our family doctor?
       Debby: Yeh. **Well** how did y'find him?

After I provide clarification for Zelda (with *yeh*), I reissue the question. The dependency of the question on the clarification is marked with *well*. (39) shows the same dependency after Jack elaborates in response to my request:

(39) Jack: Then I worked for the fruit store. Yeh, I was selling eggs. I think I was fifteen, then.
       Debby: Well was that a full time job, or like $\begin{bmatrix} \text{a...} \\ \text{Oh I} \end{bmatrix}$
       Jack:
       was a chi– a kid, doin' it.
       Debby: Oh. Oh. **Well** what about your first full time job?

After Jack elaborates, I acknowledge that information with *Oh. Oh.* (see 4.2.2), and then reissue the question, with its dependency on the contingent sequence marked with *well*.

A series of requests marked with *well* can also occur when questions on one speaker's agenda are not answered because of changes in the conversational topic. Recall that one of my goals was to learn about neighborhood communication patterns, and to this end, I had a specific series of questions to ask (see 2.2.1). When the topic of talk diverged from that agenda, I often prefaced a return to its questions by *well*:

(40)   Jack: hhhhhyou're probably gonna walk very d– hhhvery
               depressed! By the time y'walk outa here! Don't take it
               ⎡ t'heart! hhhhh ⎤
       Debby: ⎣ It doesn't   ⎦ really bother me that much. I've thought
               about a lot of these things anyway. Um......**Well** how–
               how is the neighborhood different, y'know from when y'first
               moved here?

Similarly, when a response did not satisfy the particular need for information underlying a request, I often rephrased the request and marked it with *well*. In (41), I was seeking names of confidants:

(41)   Debby: **Well** some people say that y'know just talking to a good friend
               or: somebody in the family is just as good as talking to a
               psychiatrist.
       [response not included]
               Well d'you– d'you know anyone who you could talk to, like
               that?
       [response not included]
               Well who– who are some of the people that you would want to
               confide in? If you were having. .
       Henry: If I would, I would go to a rabbi.

Finally, requests were reissued with *well* when a respondent conveyed reluctance to comply. Consider (42). Irene has been telling me about her childhood friends.

(42)   Irene: I don't see them that often. One lives in Jersey and one lives in
               the Northeast.
       Debby: Umhmm.
       Henry: Tell 'em about the ⎡ girl ⎤ you were real close:=
       Irene: ⎣ But– ⎦
       Henry: =you were raised, an' they got money, and they don't know y'.
       Irene: Who? Diane? Oh. Well:. . .
       Henry: **Well** she wants t'know!

Henry requests that Irene tell me about a particular friend who has become snobbish. When Irene does not comply (see discussion in Schiffrin 1985c), Henry reissues the requests by naming me as its co-maker, prefacing it with *well*.

Note, now, that reissued questions and requests are not always neutral in key. In fact, in (42), the reissued request is an indirect challenge that implicates Irene's unwillingness to comply with a request whose reasonableness had been assumed (Labov and Fanshel 1977: 95). *Well* adds to our interpretation of the second request as challenging precisely because it marks it as a response to the failure of the prior exchange to meet Henry's expectations.

The last environment in which *well* is used with requests is when a request is based on the speaker's use of information from prior talk to draw an inference for which confirmation is requested. In such cases, the request displays the speaker's understanding of a prior utterance (and is thus a response) at the same time as it seeks confirmation for that understanding. (See also Chapter 7 on *so* and Chapter 8 on *then*.) In (43), for example, I mark a question with both *well* and *then*, establishing it both as a response to Henry's prior utterance (his announced intention to leave the room to watch television), and as an action which seeks further response:

(43)   Debby: **Well** when can I talk to you then?

I began this section by noting that requests typically seek rather than provide response. But we have found several locations in which requests are simultaneously information-seeking and information-providing, and it is in such locations that *well* occurs with requests.

5.2.2 Contingent answers

Well is also used in exchange structures in which a speaker responds not to an initial question, but to a question/answer pair. (44) illustrates.

(44)   Zelda: a.   D'y'know where the cemetery is,   [Question 1]
                         where Smithville I: Inn is?
         Debby: b.   Yeh.   [Answer 1]
                                                                  [PAIR A]
         Zelda: c.   **Well**, when y'get to the cemetery,
                         y'make a right.   [CONTINGENT RESPONSE A]

The directions which Zelda provides in (c) depend on both (a) and (b) as a completed question/answer pair, i.e. on my acknowledgement of the location in Zelda's question. Thus, Question 1 and Answer 1 together constitute a pair upon which (c) is contingent. It is this pair to which *well* marks a response.

Such pairs are often treated by speakers as a means to an end – the ratification of the initial speaker's right to continue talking (see Chapter 9, pp. 285–90). In (45), for example, Henry requests and gains from me a license to make an assertion through the creation of just such a structure:

(45)   Henry: Because I eh :– I passed– like you s– remember we were talking
                   when you pass judgement on people when y– like y- p–pass an
                   opinion?
        Debby: Umhmm.
        Henry: **Well** I pa :–passed an opinion before I moved in here.

In sum, *well* can mark responses not just to a single part of an exchange pair, but to both parts upon whose completion a next utterance is contingent.

5.2.3 Self-responses

Speakers respond not only to their interlocutor's talk, but to their own talk. When they do so, they are shifting their **orientation** toward what is being said. Such shifts may consist of adjustments to the ideational content of talk (self-repair; see 4.1 in Chapter 4), changes in the deictic center of talk (reported speech), and alterations in the objectivity of talk (reflexive frame breaks). I briefly discuss each of these shifts.

First, *well* occurs with self-repairs, e.g. category replacements:

(46)   Look at Bob's par– eh father an' mo– **well** I don't think his father
        accepted it–his mother.

Well also marks background repairs (see Chapter 9, pp. 300–1), after which speakers return to the development of what they had been talking about prior to the addition of background material:

(47)   **Well** like I say the only thing different I think may be with– **well** in our
        area, it isn't because of the school. But the only difference I would think
        would be maybe the better schools out there.

In these examples, speakers are treating their own prior talk as something to be responded to – to be modified, corrected, replaced – and they display that talk as a propositional object to be monitored and attended to as carefully as an interlocutor's talk.

Some examples even suggest that speakers' monitoring of their own talk is more finely attuned than their monitoring of others' talk. In (48–49), speakers engage in self-repairs without glottalized self-interruptions and without hearers' realizations that a modification was in order.

(48)   So we decided since he was living in West Philadelphia, **well** *both* my
        mother and father, we decided to come out here.

(49)   And you have land, and uh. . .**well** in fact, you don't have t'o– uh have
        land, as long as you have serfs.

Second, *well* marks the orientation shifts created by reported speech, i.e. talk whose original time, place, and possibly author is not concurrent with the ongoing conversation. Not surprisingly, many cases of reported speech marked with *well* are reported responses. In (48), for example, Jan is reporting a prior interaction with her daughter as an illustration of why she should date boys only of her own religion.

(50)   a.   One was a–. . .his father was a friend of my husband's.
        b.   And when I heard she was goin' out with him, I said, 'You're
              goin' out with a Gentile boy?'
        c.   She says, '**Well** Daddy knows his father.'
        d.   I said, '*I* don't care.'
        e.   So she introduced him,
        f.   and they went out,
        g.   and she came home early,
        h.   and I said, '**Well**, y'goin' out with him again?'

Jan reports her own request for information in (b); her daughter's reported response is in (c), prefaced by *well*. Later in the story, Jan marks her response to her daughter's date with *well* (in h), thus showing her role as an evaluative audience to a reported event (the date itself).

(51) shows that other functions of *well* are also replicated in reported speech. Zelda is telling a story about how she and Henry decided to have a third child seven years after their second child was born. A string of reported dialogue ends with Henry's answer to Zelda's question prefaced by *well*: his response is that he doesn't know (see Section 5.1.1.1), and it follows a contingent pair.

(51)   And I said em 'Would you like to have another baby?' He says, 'Now?!' I
        said, 'Yeh:!' And he says, '**Well** *I* don't know.'

One of the functions of reported speech is to allow the speaker to perform a prior utterance in its original form (or at least to create the fiction of originality, cf. Tannen, forthcoming), and thus to present it as if it were occurring at the present moment. This performance is accomplished through various structural and deictic changes, e.g. in tense, person, mood. Since *well* is a response marker that anchors its user in a conversation, its use within a direct quote furthers the shift in frame and the reproduction of a prior utterance. In fact, the use of *well* after a quotative verb actually helps to define the upcoming talk as reported speech, even if it is **indirectly** reported:

(52)   And uh now that the– her father's not a twin, and his mother's not a twin. But the twins in the family say **well** they were so surprised that of all the people, that she had the twins.

The third orientation shift marked by *well* occurs with reflexive frame breaks. In these shifts, speakers treat their own just-completed discourse as talk open to their own evaluation, displacing it as if it were already prior experience available for reflection and commentary (Goffman 1974). In (53), *well* displays Henry's shift in orientation from description to evaluation of events.

(53)   a.   I've heard people say about other people, 'He hates Jews!'
        b.   Now what did we ever do to 'em that they hate 'em.
        c.   So y'laugh it off **well** he's ignorant!
        d.   **Well** how many times d'y'have t'hear it in a lifetime?
        e.   I heard it a lot.

In (c), Henry reports a response *well he's ignorant* to a just-described experience. He follows this with a reflexive frame break in (d): a rhetorical question/answer pair. Both responses are prefaced by *well*.

A similar shift from description to evaluation occurs in (54).

(54)   a.   I– I could show y–
        b.   they talk about the Negroes, they want a certain percentage of the big– big companies.
        c.   **Well** I could show you a lot– I'll show you a lot of Jews that are not. . .in the big companies.
        d.   I'll show you there ain't a half a per cent in them.

Henry shifts from a description of what others say about the special treatment accorded Blacks (in b) to his evaluation of the treatment accorded Jews (c, d). Note how prior to the description in (b), he had begun his evaluation without *well* (in a). He adds *well* only after that evaluation could be heard as a response to the just-completed description; as he continues his evaluation in (d), *well* is dropped.

I argued earlier that *well* is a response marker which anchors the speaker in an exchange and/or action pair when options proposed by the first part of such a pair (for idea completion, for compliance with a request) are not actualized by the second part of the pair. Now we have seen that *well* occurs in several locations that have little to do with the local expectations created by pairs in talk. In order to fit these uses into our analysis, I will explicitly abandon the idealized assumption that conversational coherence proceeds in a pairwise fashion.

5.3 *Well* and coherence options

In the beginning of this chapter, I repeated an observation from Chapter 1: one of the central tasks of everyday talk is the accomplishment of conversational coherence, i.e. the joint creation and display of connections between utterances such that what one speaker says can be heard to follow sensibly from what the other has said. In Chapter 1, I had proposed several points about coherence which are relevant to my analysis of *well*. First, I had argued that structures, meanings, and actions function in an integrated manner as jointly managed resources for the production and interpretation of coherence. I also proposed that both language-users and language-analysts construct models of the relations between units (sentences, propositions, actions) based not only on how such units pattern relative to other units of the **same** type, but on how they pattern relative to units of **other** types. In other words, both users' and analysts' models are based on a patterned integration of units from different levels of analysis. Finally, I observed that any such model faces a difficulty: multiple options for coherence are always available for both speakers and hearers.

Well is one device used by speakers in their attempts to build coherence in the face of multiple options: *well* anchors the speaker into a conversation precisely at those points where upcoming coherence is not guaranteed. Since coherence is based on what is said, what is meant, and what is done, as well as relationships among saying, meaning, and doing at both local and non-local locations in talk, it is not surprising that what can temporarily upset the expectation of upcoming coherence is tremendously variable: an answer whose propositional content is not presupposed by a prior question, non-compliance with a request, disagreement or lack of appreciation, a question which both seeks and provides reponse, a shift in orientation, and so on. *Well* shows the speaker's aliveness to the **need** to accomplish coherence despite a temporary inability to contribute to the satisfaction of that need in a way fully consonant with the coherence options provided through the prior discourse. Thus, speakers who flagrantly violate one aspect of discourse coherence – and are diagnosed as schizophrenic – may nevertheless locate one aspect of their selves in the world of conversation through use of *well*:

(55)　　Doctor:　　　What is your name?
　　　　Patient:　　　**Well**, let's say you might have thought you had
　　　　　　　　　　　something from before, but you haven't got it anymore.
　　　　　　(from Laffal 1965, quoted in Labov and Fanshel 1977: 2)

Although the patient may very well be schizophrenic, he has used *well* in response to a WH-question for which he may not have a ready answer, and thus marks his interactional presence in talk, if not his full informational presence.

5.4 Summary

We have seen in this chapter that *well* is a response marker: *well* anchors its user in a conversational exchange when the options offered through a prior utterance for the coherence of an upcoming response are not precisely followed. More generally, *well* is possible wherever the coherence options offered by one component of talk differ from those of another: *well* locates a speaker as a respondent to one level of discourse and allows a temporary release from attention to others.

Well can be used for so general a discourse function because it has no inherent semantic meaning. *Well* is thus similar to *oh* (Chapter 4): both *well* and *oh* are available for a general discourse function because of their lack of referential meaning. The main difference is that *well* marks responses at an interactional level, and *oh* marks responses at a cognitive level.[7] In the next chapters, I turn to markers which have both semantic meaning and grammatical status as conjunctions: *and, but, or, so, because*. We will see that their function as markers is somewhat delimited by their semantic and grammatical status.

6 Discourse connectives: *and, but, or*

In my discussion so far, I have focused on expressions (*oh, well*) whose linguistic contribution to their discourse function as markers is minimal. I now shift to a very different set of markers: *and, but,* and *or*. Because these elements have a role in the grammatical system of English, their analysis as markers has to proceed somewhat differently: in addition to characterizing the discourse slot(s) in which they occur, we need to consider the possibility that grammatical properties of the items themselves contribute to their discourse function. Thus, after my description of their discourse function, I will consider possible relationships between these functions and the syntactic, semantic, and pragmatic properties of conjunctions. We will also see that these markers form a set of discourse connectives, and that they have both ideational and pragmatic functions in talk (i.e. in exchange and action structures, and in participation frameworks).

6.1 *And*

And has two roles in talk: it coordinates idea units and it continues a speaker's action. Although *and* has these roles simultaneously, it will be easier to demonstrate them by describing them separately.

6.1.1 Building a text

I begin by observing that *and* is the most frequently used mode of connection at a local level of idea structure: 1002 clause-sized idea units in my corpus were prefaced by *and*, compared to 440 by *but*, 206 by *so*, and only 53 by *or*. Skewed frequency of a form often implies its distribution in a relatively less restricted set of environments and indeed, *and* does occur in environments shared by other modes of connection. (1) shows the use of *and* in a contrastive environment.

(1)   a.   See this is what every country does.

     b.   **But** we lost,

     c.   and we were serious,

     d.   and we tried to win.

     e.   **And** we lost.

Jack is explaining that every country tries to win the wars it fights (a, c, d); the United States, however, lost the Vietnam war (b, e). The contrast between the efforts to win and the unintended loss is marked, first, with *but* (in b), and then with *and* in (e). *And* thus occurs in an environment shared by *but*.

   (2) and (3) show that *and* also occurs in an environment shared by *so*. In (2), Jack is explaining why his neighborhood has been residentially stable: he prefaces the reason (b) with *cause* and its outcome with *so* (c):

(2)   a.   It's in the last four years that people are not moving in and out so much.

     b.   Cause the– the mortgages went up, y'see.

     c.   **So**, people are not moving that often.

In (3), on the other hand, Zelda prefaces an outcome of a reason with *and*. She is explaining why she remembers a particular childhood game; note, again, preface of the reason with *because*.

(3)   a.   That's one game I remember

     b.   because we had a driveway:

     c.   and, like we would hide,

     d.   and they would walk around the driveway?

     e.   Y'know?

     f.   **And** I– I remember it so distinctly.

After explaining why she remembers the game (b–e), Zelda again mentions that memory (f). Her paraphrase of that outcome is prefaced with *and* rather than *so*. Thus, (2)–(3) show that *and* can occur where *so* can occur.

   And also shows some similarities to 'zero', i.e. to asyndetic connection. First, *and* acts like 'zero' as a variable constraint on some elements internal to the clause. In a previous study (Schiffrin 1981), I found that *and* behaved much like 'zero' in terms of its relationship with tense switching in everyday oral narratives: although temporal connectives (*so, then, all of a sudden*) in narrative favored switching between the historical present and the preterit tenses, neither *and* nor 'zero' favored switching. The contrast between temporal connectives, on the one hand, and *and* and 'zero', on the other hand, suggests the similarity between *and* and 'zero'.

   Second, *and* and 'zero' can be sequential options for one another within a text. That is, *and* and 'zero' can create a syntagmatic contrast which differentiates the idea segments of a text: if either *and* or 'zero' becomes a textual norm, speakers may then bracket a new idea segment by deviating from that norm to use the other mode of connection (cf. Labov 1972a, Polanyi 1979, Wolfson 1979). Such shifts often accompany a functionally based transition in idea structure. In both (4) and (5), for example, *and* separates a general conclusion from a list of specific events which are asyndetically connected. In (4), Ira is describing his open-mindedness toward Blacks:

(4) a.   I uh I go on trips with 'em,
     b.   I bring 'em here,
     c.   we have supper, or dinner here,
     d.   **and** I don't see any problem
     e.   because I'm workin' with college graduates.

The three events in (a), (b), and (c) form a description of Ira's specific activities – activities which provide grounds for his general attitude statement in (d). In (5), Henry similarly separates specific events from a generalization. Henry is listing the attempts of anti-Semites to destroy the Jewish tradition (a–d), and summarizes their failure (e).

(5) a.   They threw us in the fire,
     b.   they shot us,
     c.   they killed us,
     d.   they put us in the gas chambers,
     e.   **and** they couldn't do it.

The summary in (e) conveys the failed attempts of anti-Semites – despite their collective acts aimed toward destruction of Judaism. Thus, (e) is a conclusion about the prior string of events as a collective unit.

However, there is nothing inherent in either *and* or 'zero' which makes one more suitable as a marker of a particular idea unit: the same textual segmentation could just as easily have been marked through the opposite pattern of switching. Thus, had the distribution in (4) been reversed, as in (4'), the sequence would still be segmented through the switch between *and* and 'zero'.

(4') a.   I uh I go on trips with 'em,
      b.   **and** I bring 'em here,
      c.   **and** we have supper, or dinner here,
      d.   I don't see any problem
      e.   because I'm workin' with college graduates.

(6) is an actual example whose connective pattern is similar to the constructed example in (4'). Henry is talking about the old days:

(6)   a.   What changed the whole way of living is the automobile.
       b.   You couldn't go anywhere,
       c.   so you congregated together,
       d.   **and** y'got in one big truck, or something
       e.   **and** you went– went on a picnic,
       f.   **and** you had a good time.
       g.   Today, you could care less!

The events from (c) to (f) are conjoined by *and*. These events collectively describe the *whole way of living* prior to automobiles when people *couldn't go anywhere* (b), and they form a collective contrast with the situation of *today* (g). Thus, in this example, it is *and* which groups specific events together in service of a more general point – whereas in (4) and (5), it was *and* which prefaced the more general point.

As I suggested above, the more general principle underlying this flexibility between *and* and 'zero' concerns the creation of syntagmatic contrasts: once a textual regularity has been developed – even if it is developed for only a short sequence – a new idea unit can be introduced by a change from that textual norm. The participation of *and* in this syntagmatic pattern suggests that *and* conveys no more referential information than 'zero'.[1]

Consider, now, that switching between different modes of connection has a potentially important consequence for the idea structure of a text: it displays units at a higher level of discourse structure. Our prior examples have already illustrated this point. In (4)–(6), idea units are grouped into a larger segment of 'support' which stands in a functional relation to another segment of 'position'. In short, switching between *and* and other modes of connection can display global relations between higher-level units of discourse.

(7) illustrates this general principle in a text more complex than those considered thus far: *and* works at a local level to link clauses into sections of a story, and 'zero' works at a global level to separate segments of a story. In (7), Irene is responding to my question about her acquaintance with a local politician (a–c). She then gives her opinion of the politician (d), and supports that opinion with a story about his lack of interest in his constituents (e–m).

(7)   [How do you know him?]
       a.   I know him because years ago, my husband's family were all in the laundry business.
       b.   **And** that's the business that his father was in,
       c.   **and** that's how he worked his way up t' become– t'go through law school.
       d.   But uh I don't think too highly of him

e.	because a couple years ago, when the ki– the teachers were out on strike,
f.	**and** the schools were closed,
g.	**and** we went over there,
h.	**and** we asked him y'know to see if he could do something about it,
i.	gettin' 'em t'go back at least.
j.	He came t'the door, all dressed in an ascot, and a bathrobe
k.	**and** he said, 'I didn't *ask* you people t'vote for me,'
l.	**and** I thought, 'Sure, now that you're in office. . .' he didn't ask us t'vote for him.
m.	So I really lost a lot of respect for him.

Irene links (a) through (c) with *and*: the utterances on these lines explain her acquaintance with the politician, and thus, answer my question about her relationship. In (d), she offers her opinion, and then justifies her opinion through her story (beginning in e).

If we focus attention just on the story itself, we see that it is divided into two main segments. The first segment (e–i) provides descriptive and temporal background. *And* links these functionally similar clauses (in e–i). The second segment of the story (j–l) reports the face-to-face encounter with the politician. But compare (j) to (k) and (l): the first event reported in this section (*he came t' the door* in j) is **not** prefaced by *and*, although both of the following events in (k) and (l) **are** prefaced by *and*. Thus, the story is divided into two segments through *and* (which connects the clauses within each segment), and through 'zero' (which connects the two sets of clauses). In other words, *and* works in (7) at a local level, and 'zero' at a global level to differentiate background and foreground sections in the story:

> BACKGROUND   (e–i)
>   event
>   **and** event. . .
> FOREGROUND   (j–l)
>   event
>   **and** event. . .

It is not only switching between *and* and 'zero' which allows global idea structures to emerge from smaller sets of idea units. Examine, again, the last part of Irene's story:

(7)	j.	He came t'the door, all dressed in an ascot, and a bathrobe
	k.	**and** he said, 'I didn't *ask* you people t'vote for me,'
	l.	**and** I thought, 'Sure, now that you're in office. . .' he didn't ask us t'vote for him.
	m.	**So** I really lost a lot of respect for him.

Irene's switch from *and* in (k–l) to *so* in (m) helps to establish her story as support for her opinion from (d) *I don't think too highly of him*. Thus, Irene's discourse has a more complex structure than previously suggested:

POSITION	(d)
Because SUPPORT (=STORY)	(e–l)
BACKGROUND	(e–i)
event	
and event...	
FOREGROUND	(j–l)
event	
and event...	
So POSITION	(m)

And thus works within the story frame, whereas *so* in (m) – *So I really lost a lot of respect for him* – moves out of the story frame and embeds the story as support for a position.

Many other stories similarly suggest that when *and* becomes the textual norm (as it has in (7)), *so* creates a sequential contrast with that norm. Consider (8) – a story from Zelda (which I don't quote in full). Zelda had been telling me about some friends that she has had for 30 years. She recalls that her friend's third pregnancy spurred her and Henry to have their third child. (8) is the end of her story:

(8) a. **And** I said, em, 'Would you like t'have another baby?'
  b. He says, 'Now?!'
  c. I said, 'Yeh:!'
  d. **And**, he says, 'Well *I* don't know.'
  e. **And** we did.
  f. We had JoAnn, and it was becau–
  g. **and** now, whenever she sees us, she says you have to thank *me*.
  h. That you have your daughter.
  i. So...yeh. They're very good friends of ours.

Although lines (a–h) are within the story, (i) shifts out of the story frame back to the point Zelda had made prior to the story: *they're very good friends of ours*. Zelda thus shifts from *and* within the story to *so* for her exit from the story (see also Chapter 7).

In the last two examples, I have used narratives to show how switching between *and* and other modes of connection can display the idea structure of a text. I turn now to explanatory sequences (explanations, arguments) to show how *and* works at different levels of embedding in idea structures.

Observe, first, that *and* can connect ideas locally within both of the functionally differentiated sections of an argument – the position and the support. In (9), Jack and Freda have disagreed about which religion is the most prejudiced. Jack claims that Catholics are less prejudiced than Jews because Catholic prejudice differs by nationality. His position is in (a–e); his support for this position is in (f–j).

(9)   Freda: I don't know whether it's the Jew:, or the Catholic.
                       Cause they're pretty ⌈ well prejudiced.   ⌉
       Jack: ⌊ No the Catholic is– ⌋ now hold
                       it.
       a.   It varies.
       b.   Among the Catholic you'll find a very staunch pre–
             prejudiced person,
       c.   **and** yet, you'll go to another state, and another area,
       d.   **and** it's entirely different.
       e.   **And**, country by country it's different with the
             Catholics.
       f.   I keep thinking of the French Catholic.
       g.   It's entirely different than the Spaniard Catholic.
       h.   **And** the Spaniard Catholic is entirely different from the
             Italian Catholic.
       i.   **and** the Italian Catholic is different from the
             Hungarian Catholic.
       Freda: In other words–
       Jack: j.   As far as their prejudice goes.

Jack first establishes the general position that Catholic prejudice varies (a) by the state, area (b–c) and country (e). *And* connects the locations in which Catholic prejudice varies. Jack then supports his position through specific examples: French vs. Spanish (f–g) vs. Italian (h) vs. Hungarian (i). *And* also connects these specific examples. Thus, *and* works locally within both the position and the support.

   (10) is another example of *and* working locally within the support. Jack and Freda have been arguing about the value of coeducation. Freda had attended Girls' High (a school with a reputation for academic excellence) many years before, and feels that its lack of male students encouraged too much competition among its females. Jack disagrees and (10) supports his position:

(10)   a.   Y'see. . .if a– a bunch of girls are in the class,
        b.   **and** one girl is not so bright,
        c.   she may not feel too good about it,
        d.   but is she m– m– couldn't– couldn't care less what you thought
              of her,

e.	because you're a girl
f.	**and** she's a girl.
g.	But see you're in a class...
h.	**and** you feel you're not...*up* t'the rest of the class,
i.	**and** there's boys *and* girls in the class,
j.	**and** you're a girl *or* a boy,
k.	you'd feel a little...impish.

Jack's overall strategy is to compare the reactions of less intelligent students in a class with only girls, to the reactions of those in a class with girls and boys. He separates these two hypothetical scenarios with *see* (a, g) and *but* (g), and he connects the events and states within each scenario with *and* (b, f, h–j). (*But* in d also works within the first scenario.) Thus, Jack's support consists of a comparison: *and* links the events within each part of the comparison, and *but* and *see* separate the two parts of the comparison.

In (9) and (10), we have seen *and* at the most local level of idea structure – connecting events within the position, and events within the support.

> POSITION
>   EVENT
>   **and** EVENT
> SUPPORT
>   EVENT
>   **and** EVENT

(11) shows *and* at a higher level of idea structure. Zelda is explaining why she did not send her children to Girls' High (the same school discussed by Jack in 10). She links two different reasons with *and*.

(11)	a.	See when our kids were ready t'go to high school, they could've gone t'Girls' High, also.
	b.	But number one, they had already started the school here,
	c.	**and** number two, we said, 'Why go, and subject yourself to the eh the Els, and all that!'

In (11), *and* connects the two reasons – not the events within a single reason. Thus, *and* is connecting two pieces of support at a higher level of idea structure.

> POSITION
>   SUPPORT 1
>   **and** SUPPORT 2

And can work at still a higher level of discourse structure to connect presentations of the position. In (12), Irene is explaining why she is sorry that her parents spoiled her as a child.

(12)   [Were your parents pretty strict or: . . .]
    a.   Not at all.
    b.   **And** not t'my disadvantage. I mean not to my advantage as I–
               I see it now.
    c.   Cause there's a lot of things that are harder for me to adjust to
               now,
    d.   because I got everything I wanted then.
    e.   **And** now I don't think it's a healthy situation at all.

Irene's position is in (b): spoiling a child creates problems for the adult.
She presents one reason to support her position, and another reason to support her first reason. That is, the first reason (c) supports the position of
(b): because it is now difficult to adjust to limitations (c), Irene now sees
her spoiled childhood as a problem (b). The second reason (d) supports
not the position, but the first reason: because everything was given to her
(d), it is now difficult for Irene to adjust to limitations (c). Following the
two reasons, Irene restates her position from (b) in (e): a spoiled childhood
is problematic. The restated position is prefaced by *and*. Thus, the structure of Irene's explanation is as follows:

        POSITION
           REASON
              because REASON
        and POSITION

I have used different examples of discourse to illustrate the use of *and* at
progressively higher levels of idea structure. (13) shows that *and* can work
at different levels even within the same discourse. Ira is explaining why he
is against intermarriage.

(13)   a.   Well I– I think y'run into a problem if eh. . .if you ever have
               an argument,
    b.   y'know you're not– you're not stabilized when you start
               t'argue.
    c.   **And** you could let words slip that you could be very sorry for.
    d.   For example, eh. . .eh. . . let's assume the husband's a w– a–
               a– a– the husband's Jewish
    e.   **and** the girl's, say, Catholic,
    f.   **and** they have an argument
    g.   **and** she says 'You goddamn Jew!'
    h.   Now she wouldn't say something like that, if she was rational.
    i.   **And**, maybe it don't mean anything,
    j.   but it still hurts.
    k.   Uh **and** I– I think when the children come I think eh how
               d'y'raise the kids?

Ira's position (presented elsewhere in our conversation) is that intermarriage causes problems. In (13), he defends his position by describing two problems: the use of ethnic insults during arguments (a–j), raising children (k). The first problem is summarized in (a–c), and we find *and* working at a local level within this summary. Ira then illustrates this problem in (d–i). Again, we find *and* at a local level within this illustration: *and* links the specific events in (d–g), and links the interpretation of those events in (h–i). The second problem with intermarriage is given in (k). It, too, is initiated with *and*. Thus, the structure of Ira's explanation is as follows:

```
POSITION
     GENERAL SUPPORT 1          (a–c)
          EVENT
        and EVENT
            SPECIFIC SUPPORT     (d–j)
            EVENT
          and EVENT
    and GENERAL SUPPORT 2        (k)
```

In sum, (13) shows that *and* can link different levels of idea units within the same discourse: local units (events within the general support, and within the specific support) and global units (two pieces of general support).

We have now found *and* at several different levels of idea structure in explanatory discourse, ranging from the most local level of events within support, to the most global level of position. We have also found sequences in which *and* functions at more than one level of idea structure at once. But we have not found sequences in which *and* functions at **all** levels at once – to connect events, support, and position. The use of *and* in such sequences would be somewhat dysfunctional – since the organizational advantage of switching between different modes of connection would be lost. When speakers do use *and* at several different levels, then, they often accompany it with more explicit indicators of overall structure. (14), for example, is a continuation of (9): Jack has continued his argument that Catholic prejudice varies nationally, to an explanation of such differences. But he then returns to the initial conversational motivation for his arguments and answers my question about which people are the most prejudiced. (14) presents the end of his arguments.

(14)   a.   The Pole for centuries was divided
        b.   then put upon by other nations.

   c.   **and** so therefore sh– sh– she held on to her Catholicism with
such a tenacity,

   d.   that– that– that's fanatics– fanaticism.

   e.   **And** uh: that's– that's the answer.

   f.   That's why I say they're the most prejudiced.

In (c), Jack closes his argument about why Polish Catholics are prejudiced;
he marks that closure with both *so* and *therefore* in addition to *and*. In (e),
Jack closes his answer to my much earlier question with a meta-linguistic
marker *that's the answer* and an explicit marker of the status of his just-
completed discourse as reason for his answer (*that's why I say*). Thus,
even though *and* occurs at these two very different levels of idea structure,
it is accompanied by other devices which differentiate these levels and explicitly mark their location within the overall structure.

    Rather than use explicit markers and meta-language as a structural sub-
stitute for connective switches, speakers can use prosody to segment their
discourse. In (15), Zelda is describing some of her prior homes.

(15)   a.   **And** then we lived there for five years,

        b.   **and** we bought– *we* bought a triplex across the street.

        c.   **And** by that time we had two kids,

        d.   **and** we moved on the first floor,

        e.   **and** rented out the second.

        f.   **And** his brother married then,

        g.   **and** lived on the third.

        h.   **And** we still live together down the shore.

And prefaces all of the lines in this example. The tokens of *and* prefacing
(a), (c), (f) and (h), however, occur after a longer pause with falling intonation (indicated by the period in the prior line), and with a temporal expression: *then* in (a), *by that time* in (c), *then* in (f), and *still* in (h). But the
tokens of *and* prefacing (b), (d), (e), and (g) occur after a shorter pause
and less of a fall in intonation (indicated by the comma in the prior line),
and quite strikingly, there are no temporal expressions used. Thus, (15) is
segmented into time periods through prosody and temporal expressions.

    So far, I have been considering *and* as a marker of functionally differen-
tiated idea units: background and foreground in narratives, support and
position in arguments and explanations. Referential units are also marked
by *and* – again, at both local and global levels. Examples (16) to (18) contain two discourse topics each; that is, each contains two referential topics
at a discourse level. *And* is used locally in (16), globally in (17), and at both
levels in (18).

    In (16), I have asked Zelda which restaurants she and Henry like. She answers by explaining why they have been eating out so frequently.

(16)   [Where d'y'go in Philly if y'wanna go out t'eat?]
        a.   Well, uh: we have a cousin club.
        b.   **And**, we meet once a month.
        c.   **And**, what we do with our once a month is we go out for
                  dinner, on a Saturday night.

Zelda's explanation contains the first discourse topic: the recurrent activities of the cousin club. These activities are conjoined with *and*. Zelda then goes on to the second discourse topic – which provides the answer to my question about where she eats out:

        d.   So, we've gone t'the Tavern:..
        e.   **and** we've gone– every month we go to another place.
        f.   Eh:...**and** we go eh: we went t'the Riverfront twice.

The second topic is a list of restaurants that she and Henry have visited: like the recurrent activities in the first topic, these past activities are conjoined with *and*. Thus, the parts of each topic are locally connected by *and*. Note, however, that what *and* does not mark is the transition from the first to the second discourse topic. Rather, we find *so* in (d): *So, we've gone t'the Tavern*. The topic segments of (16) are:

        TOPIC 1
            EVENT
            and EVENT
            and EVENT
        so TOPIC 2
            EVENT
            and EVENT
            and EVENT

In (16), then, *and* is used to link events within a discourse topic. The events are locally connected by *and*, but they also become globally differentiated from each other through the switch between *and* and *so*.

And can also differentiate discourse topics at a global level. In other words, *and* can also mark the following topic segments:

        TOPIC 1
            EVENT
            EVENT...
        and TOPIC 2
            EVENT
            EVENT...

(17) illustrates. Irene is explaining her recent interest in sports.

(17)   [What sports, particularly?]
         a.   Really football and baseball.
         b.   Cause two of 'em play on little league teams.
         c.   So I hadda learn to. . .understand the game,
         d.   or I was sitting on the bench like three days a week not
                     knowing what was goin' on.
         e.   **And** with the football, they're very big on football.
         f.   So I've been trying t'watch it on Sunday,
         g.   and trying t'understand it a little bit more.

Irene introduces the two sports of interest in (a): football and baseball.
These two sports are her two discourse topics. She then gives reasons for
her interest in each sport, first baseball (b–d) and then football (e–g). Her
explanation thus begins by delineating what topics are to be expanded, and
then branches into those two topics. Because *and* (in e) helps to segment
the explanation into the two prefigured topics, it is differentiating the
discourse at a global level of discourse topic.

(18) shows that *and* can be used as both local and global levels of
discourse topic. Zelda and I have been discussing how working women
manage childcare. I ask about her family.

(18)   [Do either one of your daughter in laws work?]
         a.   No but they did.
         b.   Both my daughters in laws worked.
         c.   Uh: my older daughter in law worked for four years while my
                     son was in school.
         d.   **And** she didn't become uh pregnant until he graduated.
         e.   **And** uh: she feels that once her children are in school, she'd
                     like to go back.
         f.   **And** my younger daughter in law, uh: they got married when
                     she was eighteen.
         g.   **And** she uh: was just starting Beaver.
         h.   She took up that pre nursery school?
         i.   For two years?
         j.   Y'know that get set program?
         [continues with discussion of school program]

In (b), Zelda establishes her two daughters-in-law as her two discourse
topics. She then describes the experience of each: the elder (c–e), the
younger (f–j). Thus, the topic structure of (18) parallels that of (17): two
topics are first introduced, and then each is expanded. Like (17), *and* segments the two discourse topics: *my younger daughter in law* is prefaced

with *and* in (f). But like (16), *and* also works within each topic. Thus, *and* works at both global and local levels.[2]

In this section, I have shown that *and* is used in contrast with other means of connection (as either textual norm or textual deviation) as a source of structure in particular sequences. I have also shown that discovering which textual segments are bracketed by *and* has required looking into the discourse content and structure for different idea units. Thus, it is the containing discourse which tells us what units are being marked by *and* (or by any other mode of connection): since the constituent.ideas in a discourse themselves convey information, *and* cannot work independently of that information.

What I have not yet addressed is the structural role of *and* itself. I suggest that *and* is a discourse coordinator: the presence of *and* signals the speakers' identification of an upcoming unit which is coordinate in structure to some prior unit. But because texts contain units which are both locally and globally related, through either functional or referential means, *and* marks different kinds of units at different levels of discourse structure. Thus, wherever we find *and*, we know we have a unit that is connected to a structurally equivalent unit somewhere in the prior discourse – but the identification of those units depends on the use of textual information beyond *and* itself.

6.1.2 Continuing an action

When considered just as a marker in idea structures, *and* seems to be free of meaning. But if we consider the role of *and* in interaction, *and* does seem to have a pragmatic effect. I show in this section that *and* is a marker of speaker-continuation.[3]

Consider, first, that the information presented in talk is often packaged into interactional units: the experience reported in a narrative, for example, occupies a turn at talk, or an answer in an adjacency pair. Speakers often work to fit their talk into an interactional slot (e.g. Jefferson 1979) and particular linguistic devices are often designed to ease that task (e.g. Ochs 1979a). The use of *and* is one such device.

Let us start by examining a familiar example. We discussed (16) for its topic structures. (16) also shows how information can be interactionally packaged through the use of *and*. Recall that (16) is Zelda's answer to my question about where she and Henry go out to eat.

(16)   [Where d'y'go in Philly if y'wanna go out t'eat?]

a.   Well, uh: we have a cousin club.

b.   **And**, we meet once a month.

c.   **And**, what we do with our once a month is we go out for dinner, on a Saturday night.

d.   So, we've gone t'the Tavern:..

e.   **and** we've gone– every month we go to another place.

f.   Eh:....**and** we go eh: we went t'the Riverfront twice.

I defined two parts of Zelda's answer according to discourse topic: (a–c) explains the cousin club and (d–f) lists restaurants. Note now that these two parts are also defined by their different functions within the answer: (a–c) is information which had not been requested (note *well*; see Chapter 5); (d–f) is information which had been requested. Switching between *and* and *so* in (16), then, does organize the discourse topic. But because the two discourse topics themselves have different functions within the answer, the connective switching also differentiates the discourse in terms of its informational requirements as an answer, that is, as a unit of talk which is tailored to a particular conversational slot.

Let us look at another example. (19) provides Zelda's answer to a question from Sally (a sociolinguistics student):

(19)   Sally: You lived in West Philly? Whereabouts?

        Zelda: a.   Well, I was born at 52nd and em...tsk...oh: I forgo– well .... I think its 52nd and Chew.

                b.   **And** um...and uh I grew up really in the section called Logan.

                c.   **And** then, I went into the service, for the two years,

                d.   **and** then when I came back, I married...I– I– I got married.

                e.   **And** I– then I lived at uh 49th and Blair.

                      Which is ⌈ West Ph–   ⌉

        Sally: ⌊ Where's that ⌋

        Zelda: f.   It's right off of 49th and ⌈ Main. ⌉

        Sally: ⌊ Oh. ⌋ Oh yeh. Yeh.

        Zelda: That's where I lived.

                g.   **And** then we moved here.

Observe first that Zelda joins each locational transition from (a–e) with *and*: 52nd and Chew, Logan, the service, back to Logan, 49th and Blair. When Sally asks for more information about the last-mentioned location, Zelda answers that question, and then returns to her prior answer with *and* (in g). Thus, *and* links the ideas within Zelda's answer; it helps define the boundaries of this interactional slot and delimit the conversational location of information relevant to the question.

Let us look again at the last part of (19):

Sally:	Where's that
Zelda:	It's right off of 49th and ⌈ Main. ⌉
Sally:	⌊ Oh. ⌋ Oh yeh. Yeh.
Zelda:	That's where I lived.
g.	**And** then we moved here.

I noted above that in (g), Zelda reopens an interactional unit (her answer) whose completion had been interrupted by Sally's request for locational information. Use of *and* in such circumstances is typical: *and* often displays an upcoming utterance as part of a not yet completed interactional unit.

(20) illustrates how *and* can be used in repeated attempts to continue an interactional unit when it has been threatened by alternative talk. Jack has been arguing that neither Russians nor Americans live in systems which are true to their ideologies. He compares the use of the word 'communism' to the use of the word 'irregardless': his claim is that people use both words even though the words do not really mean what people think they do.

(20) Jack: But over here, we use that– wor:d so: . . . just like we use the word here *ir*regardless, which there is no such word, right?

Freda: Um but not with most pe– I just use it and everytime I use it I know I'm wrong.

Jack: No but *I* use it. I– I– ⌈ I– irregardless. ⌉
Freda: ⌊ You use it too? ⌋

Debby: ⌈ I use it.   ⌉
Jack: ⌊ **And** there's ⌋ no such word.

Freda: *I* think there may have been a word like that at one ⌈ point in time cause I ⌉ use it all the time.
Jack: ⌊ No. No there wasn't. ⌋

No. There wasn't.

And. . .that's the way we use the word 'communism.'

Two comments from Freda threaten to change the course of Jack's projected argument, and Jack twice reclaims his right to complete what he had begun. First, Freda asks me if I use 'irregardless': Jack overlaps my answer to reiterate that there is no such word – precisely the point on which his comparison is based. Second, Freda explains her use of 'irregardless' by suggesting that it may have existed previously: after twice responding that there was no such word, Jack completes his comparison. Both of Jack's efforts to regain control over the topic of talk – and thus, over his argument – are initiated with *and*.

A similar example is (21). Jack has been boasting about a childhood friend who became a well-known comedian. Just prior to (21), he has been comparing this friend to other members of their childhood clique; his claim that this friend had little talent is a way of establishing their especially close relationship.[4]

(21)   He was very ambitious, but lacked talent. He really didn't have too much. But he had guts!hhh He had– and he had dedication. I will say that.

What happens next creates a potential intrusion into the course of Jack's description. Jack has been holding a glass of water and begins to look around for a place to put the glass. Freda, who is standing near him, asks in a non-serious key:

Would you like me to hold it for you?

Jack responds (also non-seriously):

Just don't move!

As Freda starts to jokingly sit on the floor, I say:

Why don't you sit at his feethhh?

Freda turns to her nephew Rob, as Jack tries to regain his turn to talk with *and*:

Freda: [Would you please] put this on the floor for him?=
Jack: [**And** uh:]
Freda: =On the floor you can put it!
Rob: All right.

Following the interchange between Freda and Rob, Jack again continues with *and*:

Jack: **And** uh: I was just eh:
          we had a friend in our group uh: named Dash.
          A much more talented– *now* if [he–]
Freda: [He] had more talent.

Thus, again we see that speakers use *and* to convey that they have more to say – regardless of another's alternatively proposed activity.

Of course hearers do not always recognize their own remarks as peripheral to the development of a speaker's discourse. In (22), for example, Zelda has been telling me that her younger daughter-in-law does not call her 'Mom'. I ask whether she faces similar problems with Zelda's husband.

(22)   Debby: What does she call your husband? The same problem?
        Zelda: Yeh. I don't think she says anything [yet.]
        Debby: [Yeh] it's hard I imagine.

Zelda: I imagine it is.
           And you have t'start in the beginning. Now my daughter in
           law did. My older daughter in law from the very beginning
           [discourse continues; see (2) in Chapter 3]

Although Zelda responds to my question, and then to my expression of
empathy, the topics which I have introduced seem not to have been her
main involvement. Rather, Zelda has a general opinion about how the
naming problem should be solved (*you have t'start in the beginning*) and
she has specific evidence to support her position (see (2) in Chapter 3):
people have to start using kin-based address terms as soon as they marry
into a family, and this strategy worked for three other people who faced the
same dilemma. In short, Zelda has an argument to present: her use of *and*
allows it to be heard as a continued involvement with a prior topic of her
own interest. At the same time, it defines my remarks as peripheral to her
involvement with that topic.

Recall now my earlier point about idea structures: the identification of
specific idea units bracketed by *and* depends on discourse content and
structure. Identifying the interactional unit bracketed by *and* is similarly
dependent on discourse – although here we are talking not about idea content and structure, but about interactional content and exchange and action
structures. So far, we have been examining the following kind of sequence:

A: DISCOURSE UNIT
B: ASIDE
A: RESPONSE TO ASIDE
          and DISCOURSE UNIT

A's discourse unit is one whose ending may have been projected to occupy a
single turn at talk. Examples of such units are stories, explanations, and
arguments – the same discourse units whose idea structures were examined
in 6.1.1. B's remark is a side remark in relation to A's projected unit:
examples are requests for clarification, endorsements, disagreements, and
so on (see Jefferson 1972).

My interpretation of speakers as 'continuing' prior discourse has depended upon my analytic ability to understand information about the
exchanges and actions which comprise interactional structures. The task
for actual interlocutors is the same: speakers and hearers would not be able
to recognize such things as 'continuations' without an ability to interpret
such information.

Let us examine *and* in other interactional sequences – since *and* is hardly limited to discourse units whose projected endings have been threatened. *And* can be used to link questions in a question agenda, i.e. a pre-arranged set of questions through which speakers plan to proceed in a fixed order:

A:	QUESTION 1
B:	ANSWER 1
A:	**and** QUESTION 2 (...n)

(23) illustrates:

(23)	Sally:	a.	Could I have both of y our names, first. T'start with.
	Zelda:		Okay. Go ahead.
	Irene:		Irene Bloom.
	Sally :	b.	**An:d**...
	Zelda:		Zelda Freed.
	Sally:		Okay.
		c.	**And** your address is: what?

Sally's questions in (a) and (c) request demographic information – name, address – from both Irene and Zelda. (Note Zelda's *Go ahead* to Irene, showing her awareness that both are expected to answer.) Gaining demographic information is part of Sally's question agenda: sociolinguistic interviews routinely start with requests for such information. Sally's *An:d* in (b) functions as part of this same question agenda; it is an elided request for Zelda to provide the same information just given by Irene.

Another interactional structure in which *and* can mark a continuation is the following:

A:	QUESTION 1
B:	ANSWER 1
A:	**and** QUESTION 1'

The key part of this structure is QUESTION 1' – a request for elaboration of ANSWER 1 (see Chapter 4). Compliance with this request will have the effect of expanding information from ANSWER 1, that is, continuing the general content of ANSWER 1. (24) illustrates:

(24)	Sally:	a.	What was the first job that you had, when you got out of school.
	Zelda:		I worked in a: um coffee em.....eh coffee manufacturing. They used to eh buy the coffee green, and uh– and I worked as the: eh billing clerk.
	Sally:		Uhhuh.
		b.	**And** when was that?
	Zelda:		Eh: I gradu– nineteen:– nineteen forty.

Sally's question in (b) is QUESTION 1': it addresses the information just provided in Zelda's answer (ANSWER 1) to QUESTION 1 (from a). *And* is used because QUESTION 1' continues the relevance of ANSWER 1.

We have seen in this section that *and* marks a speaker's definition of what is being said as a continuation of his/her own prior talk. It is in this sense that *and* has a pragmatic effect as a discourse marker: this effect is due to the speaker's definition of his/her own upcoming utterance as a continuation of the developing content and structure of an interaction. Thus, *and* marks an utterance as a speaker-defined continuation in an interaction.

Since *and* does have this pragmatic effect, we should not be surprised to find that *and* can be used to negotiate a continuation even when it is not structurally warranted by the prior interaction. (25) illustrates. Prior to (25), Jack had been telling a funny story about a childhood friend who became a well-known comedian. (21 preceded the story.) In (25), Jack has reached the end of the story events (the experience reported in the narrative). He does not end the storytelling, however; in fact, he bypasses two opportunities to do so, choosing instead to re-enter the story events. *And* marks this re-entry – thus imposing a continuative effect on a discourse whose structure had actually warranted otherwise. Let us examine (25).

(25) Jack: a. He knew how t'get the– he knew the whole audience'd laugh.

   b. So he must've had something [to him.

Freda: [Even the] teachers, huh?

Jack: c. Even this teacher, this one that– she laughed.

   d. She couldn't help it!

   e. **And** I'm playin' [hums melody]

   f. and I'm playin', y'know!

Line (a) closes the complicating action of Jack's story by internally evaluating the experience (Labov 1972a). Line (b) reiterates the point of the story. Since speakers often repeat the point of their story as a way of ending its conversational relevance, (b) is a potential closure for the storytelling. Freda's question (*Even the teachers, huh?*) provides another potential story closure for it provides Jack a reason to insert additional evaluation. Although Jack does add such evaluation (c–d), he then returns in (e) to an event which had been deeply embedded in the story experience: playing a particular melody (hummed in e) was a central event in the experience, and one deeply embedded within the narrative action. This return to the narrative action is prefaced by *and*. *And* thus imposes a continuative effect: Jack is continuing the story even though it already had been structurally completed, and even though an end to its period of conversational relevance had been proposed.[5]

Consider, now, that since *and* is used to mark a speaker's continuation, we would not expect to find it used as a turn-transition device – as a way of showing a speaker's readiness to relinquish the floor. This can be examined by finding exchange structures with the following turn-transition shapes: either an incoming speaker begins to talk during, or immediately after, a current speaker's utterance of *and uh:* or *and...* If the current speaker then **returns** to the floor to talk about the prior topic, I will interpret that speaker as not having been ready to relinquish his or her turn. (26) illustrates.

(26)   Irene: It's unusual, I feel, when y'have three boys, and then the last
                    one's a girl.
                    And uh:....   it's unusual.=
         Zelda: That's right.
         Irene: =Cause she'ld really be a spoiled little brat if she wanted to.

I found 13 examples of this turn-transition shape, and in all but one, the current speaker did return to the floor to talk about the prior topic. First, the exception. In (27), Sally has inferred from Irene's prior remark that the reason she stopped working was because she got married.

(27)   Irene: I didn't work anymorehhh.
         Sally: You got married **an:d** . . .
         Irene: I *was* married when I started to work.

In (27), Sally is using *and* as she is requesting Irene's confirmation of her inference (*you got married*). It is not surprising that *and* is here a turn-transition device: in fact, it reinforces Sally's request for confirmation by soliciting **Irene's** continuation.

The examples which conform to my expectation suggest that incoming talk which occurs either in overlap, or in tandem, with a current speaker's *and* is interpreted in one of two ways: a shared turn, an interruption. To a certain degree, how such talk is heard depends on its content: shared turns are more likely interpretations when incoming content endorses (as in (26)) or adds to what is said; interruptions are more likely when incoming content is off the topic or disagrees with prior talk.

Examine, first, the use of *and* when speakers share a turn space to add ideas. In (28), Ira and Jan are describing the difficulties in a relative's adjustment to full time motherhood.

(28)   Ira: a.   She was a very active girl. . . .
                  b.   and this: this: staying home,

	c.	and drinking coffee with other girls
	d.	**and**...⌈ ⌉ keep going to a mall, =
Jan:	e.	⌊ It's not for her. ⌋
Ira:	f.	**and**... wheeling a kid, sort of...
	g.	this wa:s
Jan:	h.	It's not challenging enough for her.
Ira:	i.	*That*. Plus another incident that happened eight. . seven. . . how many years ago?

Ira first continues his own description past Jan's contribution (d). He then seems to be inviting Jan's continuation (f) for when his use of *and* does not prompt Jan, he tries different devices, hedging (f) and vowel elongation (g). And after Jan's coda-like remark (h), which Ira acknowledges (*that* in i), he begins to describe another problem faced by the same relative, again, opening the turn space for Jan with *how many years ago?*

Even if such sharing is not as explicitly invited as in (28), other uses of *and* are still interpretable as turn-sharing if the incoming content completes the current speaker's conjunct. In (29), Jan and Ira are describing their hospitality toward their son's girlfriends:

(29)	Jan:	a.	We've had many stay here.
		b.	And I've always ⌈ been very ⌉ nice t'them.
	Ira:	c.	⌊ He brings– ⌋
		d.	he'd bring 'em home from Pittsburgh,
		e.	**an:** ⌈ ⌉ Penn State,
	Jan:	f.	⌊ wants you t'meet 'em. ⌋
	Ira:	g.	**an:**⌉
	Jan:	h.	⌟all over the place.

Note that Ira does not stop his own description after *an:* in (e); even though Jan completes the conjunct (f), so does Ira with *Penn State*. Jan's second completion (h) then continues Ira's formation of the list of where their son's girlfriends have come from (although Ira does not then continue his own description or repeat Jan's).

Compare (30) to (28) and (29). In (30), Zelda is answering my question about the location of the nicest houses in Philadelphia.

(30)	Zelda:	a.	Well I'm not too familiar with up in the
		b.	Northeast, but we have Upper Merion:
		c.	**and**...⌈ Woodside.
	Henry:	d.	⌊ Nicest house is the happiest house. Honest
		e.	t'God. ⌈ I swear t'God. ⌉ But the=
	Zelda:	f.	⌊ But she don't mean ⌋ that though.
	Henry:	g.	=nicest house is the happiest house.
	Zelda:	h.	Parkland.

Henry's remark in (d) clearly does not address the topic of Zelda's answer. Instead of shifting her answer to accommodate Henry's remark, Zelda continues her list (c, h), even after commenting (f) on the irrelevance of Henry's remark. Thus, I interpret Henry's incoming talk as an interruption to Zelda's continuation.

Consider, now, that both the shared turns (of 26, 28, 29) and the interruption (of 30) support my expectation that *and* is not used as a turn-transition device. The difference between these two outcomes is in the sort of realignment created: shared turns are a cooperative realignment of turn-taking responsibilities which does not require **either** party to relinquish a bid for the floor; interruptions are an uncooperative realignment. But the fact that either type results when incoming talk overlaps, or is in tandem, with *and* shows that *and* is a marker of current speaker's continuation.

In this section, I have shown that *and* is a marker of speaker continuation: *and* marks a speaker's definition of what is being said as a continuation of what had preceded. But *and* does not provide information about **what** is being continued: rather, that information is provided from other cues in the content and structure of interaction. Thus, we can no more use *and* to identify the interactional unit that is being continued, than we can use *and* to identify the idea that is being coordinated. All *and* displays is continuation and/or coordination: more precise identifications depend on discourse content and structure.[6]

6.1.3 Ideas and actions

Although I have discussed the interactional meaning of *and* separately from its coordinating role in idea structures, it should be obvious that the boundary between these two roles is merely analytical: *and* has both ideational and interactional roles simultaneously. I have already implied this through my use of a single example (16) to illustrate both functions. To be more explicit about the simultaneous functions of *and*, let us examine how speakers continue explanations within interactions. The first example (31) is of a speaker continuing his own explanation; the next two (32, 33) are of speakers continuing others' explanations.

In (31), Ira and Jan are answering my question about why they chose their neighborhood.

(31)   Debby: What made you decide t'come out here? Do
                    y'remember?

        Ira: a.   What made us decide t'come out here.

b. Well uh we were looking in different neighborhoods,
c. **and** then uh this was a Jewish community
d. **and** we decided t'come out here.
e. Uh the– several of the communities we looked uh they weren't– they weren't Jewish
f. **and** we didn't wanna live there.
g. Then we decided on Glenmore.

Ira is providing several reasons for the decision to move to Glenmore. He prefaces both his reasons with *and* (c, f) and his mention of the decision (d). Important also is the repetition in Ira's answer: he opens his answer in (a) by repeating my question, and he repeats *we decided* (d, g) after both reasons. This repetition establishes the relevance of the answer to the question (which asks *what made you decide to come out here?*). More importantly for my current point, the repetition also has a boundary function: it proposes the closure of the answer (Schiffrin 1982a). Indeed, after Ira's repetition in (g), I comment on the history of the community.

> Debby: I didn't realize this had been a Jewish community for twenty years. I didn't really. . .

My comment is an indirect request for Ira's confirmation (see Chapter 8, 8.2.3.2) which he partially provides in (h).

> Ira: h. Well it's been like this ever since *we've* been here.

Ira then provides another reason why he and Jan chose Glenmore – a reason Jan identifies as *the best part* – even though his explanation has been previously closed through the repetition in (g).

> Ira: i. **And** the price was right ⌈ hhhh. ⌉
> Jan: ⌊ That ⌋ was the best part.

And the price was right thus reinstates the conversational relevance of a previously closed topic – the decision to move to Glenmore. It does so because it provides a new reason for the decision. Since I had questioned the decision in my initial question (*What made you decide t'come out here?*), Ira's provision of another reason continues to fill the conversational slot of 'answer'. In short, because *the price is right* is both ideationally and interactionally situated, *and* marks its location in both structures.

In (32) and (33), speakers use *and* to continue explanations initiated by others. In (32), Zelda and I are wondering why families don't get together as often as they used to.

(32)   Debby: I don't know what it is. Maybe– maybe you're forced– y'know
                   there's so many ⌈ pressures, like to make ⌉ a living.
          Zelda: ⌊ **And** you have your– ⌋
                   And you have your– **and** you have your wi:ves, your
                   husband's family, it's too many.

Zelda's turn-initial **and** – repeated with each successive attempt to state her
point – displays her point as a continuation of my prior remarks. But it does
more: it marks her point as an additional reason in what becomes a jointly
constructed explanation as to why families are not as close as they used to
be. In short, it creates a participation framework in which both parties
share responsibility for building a single text. That one speaker's continuation of another's ideas through *and* changes the participation framework
of talk is possible only because *and* serves both ideational and interactional
functions simultaneously.

    (33) is similar. Zelda has been explaining why her daughter is spoiled.

(33)   Zelda: My older son was eh– was al– was twelve when she was born.
                   And Samuel was s- seven. So that eh: . . .y'd know it–
                            ⌈ it's– it's different.   ⌉
          Irene: ⌊ **And** being a change ⌋ of sex makes a difference too.

Irene adds a reason just as Zelda is concluding her explanation (note
Zelda's *so* and *y'know*; see Chapters 7 and 9 respectively). *And* adds Irene's
reason to the explanation, thereby continuing its development as an idea
structure, and creating a joint text. But, again, *and* is both ideational and
interactional marker: *and* continues another's ideas and transforms talk
into a product of mutual effort whose idea structure is jointly constructed.[7]

6.1.4 And: *coordination and continuation*

I have proposed that *and* is a structural coordinator of ideas which has
pragmatic effect as a marker of speaker continuation. But discovering
which ideas are coordinated by *and*, and which actions are continued, has
required looking into the content and structure of ideas and interactions.
Thus, it is the containing discourse which tells us what idea units, and what
interactional units, are being marked by *and*.

6.2 *But*

Although *but* is a discourse coordinator (like *and*), it has a very different
pragmatic effect: *but* marks an upcoming unit as a **contrasting** action.

Because this effect is based on its contrastive meaning, the range of ideational uses of *but* is considerably narrower than that of *and*. We saw, for example, that *and* alternates with 'zero' to produce syntagmatic contrasts which organize both the referential and functional units of an idea structure, at both local and global levels. Not only does *but* not alternate with 'zero', but it does not coordinate functional units unless there is some contrastive relationship in either their ideational or interactional content.

Although the contrastive meaning of *but* gives it a narrower range of uses than *and*, its range is still fairly wide for the simple reason that contrastive relationships themselves are tremendously variable. Sometimes such relationships are transparent enough to be found in the semantic content of propositions, but others are buried within speakers' and hearers' culturally based world knowledge, or implicit in their expectations about each other and each other's conduct.

6.2.1 Contrasting ideas

Let us start by examining (34), an argument from Henry. Some background knowledge will help in understanding this argument (see also Chapter 2, 2.2.2). Henry (who is Jewish) does not like the idea of marriage between people of different religions. He also feels that the Jewish people have been subjected to a great deal of discrimination and intolerance and provides both historical and personal testimony to support this (e.g. (5) in this chapter). Although such intolerance is morally wrong, it is also unfair because of the tolerance shown by Jews toward others: Henry states that Jews are the most liberal, generous and compassionate people in the world. These three points are important not only because they are recurring themes in much of what Henry says, but because they are related in a particular way in the argument in (34).

The position which Henry is supporting in (34) is that intermarriage is wrong. Prior to this, Irene has stated that although she doesn't like the idea of intermarriage, she feels that eventually there will be only one religion in the world. Thus, she is not as opposed to it as Henry. (34) is Henry's rebuttal to Irene.

(34) a.   You're not livin' in a world where you have equality completely.
      b.   You put *that* in this world, *I'll* go along with it.
      c.   If it stays that way,
      d.   and where it does not make any difference, . . .
      e.   *yes*. I'll go with that in a second.

f.   I won't disagree with anything.
g.   **But** the– the Arabs call us infidels. . .
h.   the Christians call us pagans. . .
i.   It's true.
j.   We're nothing.
k.   And yet we started everything.
l.   We started everything,
m.   and we're– we're infidels? We're pagans?
n.   Where does that come off?
o.   That don't add up!

Henry's position is that intermarriage is wrong. The reason (support) for
this position is the existence of anti-Semitism. In (a–f), Henry argues that
if this were non-existent – if Jews were treated as equals – then he would
accept intermarriage. In (g–o), Henry provides evidence that Jews are not
treated as equals. Thus, because anti-Semitism does exist, Henry cannot
accept intermarriage. *But* in (g) – *But the– the Arabs call us infidels. . .* –
marks the contrast between the hypothetical situation (that would force
him to disavow his position) and the actual situation (that allows him to
maintain his position). So far, then, we have the following argument:

POSITION 1: I'm against intermarriage
   SUPPORT 1: Jews face intolerance
      IF NOT [SUPPORT] THEN NOT [POSITION]   (b–f)
      If Jews faced tolerance,
      then I would not be against intermarriage.
but SUPPORT 1: Jews face intolerance   (a, g–o)

Henry then contrasts the intolerance faced by Jews with the tolerance
provided by Jews. This contrast becomes a new position, and evidence is
presented to support his position.

p.   *But,* in my father's house, we were not taught hate.
q.   Never did we ever say this damned Catholic, or that damned
            Protestant, or that damned nigger or– or anything–
r.   It was proven for a fact that my father took a colored man off
            the street,
s.   and he didn't have a place t'sleep,
t.   he put him in his own *house*.
u.   He took an old Jewish man
v.   and put him on the sofa in the Depression.
w.   And he took a– he took a uh– a– a– Catholic, who gave him a
            job,
x.   his sister was a *nun*, kissed my father on the forehead!
y.   So we were not *hate*.

After contrasting the intolerance faced by Jews with the tolerance provided by Jews, Henry provides personal evidence for that tolerance (q–x). Henry's initial argument against intermarriage thus contains an embedded argument in which a new position (Jews provide tolerance) is supported. Because this new position is an idea which contrasts with the support from the main argument (Jews face intolerance), it is prefaced by *but*. Henry then repeats his position about Jewish tolerance from (p) in (y) – *we were not taught hate, so we were not hate*.

but SUPPORT 1: Jews face intolerance	(a, g–o)
but POSITION 2: Jews provide tolerance	(p)
SUPPORT 2: We were kind to all	(q–w)
so POSITION 2: Jews provide tolerance	(y)

After closing his embedded argument (in y), Henry refers to his personal experience in the army:

z.	**But**, I went into the army
aa.	and I– I felt the hostility in some people.

The hostility which Henry faced contrasts with the tolerance provided by his family. Thus, (z) – (aa) contrasts with the content of POSITION 2 (Jews provide tolerance). This contrast explains the use of *but* in (z). The mention of hostility also has a broader structural role in the argument: it provides an instance of SUPPORT 1 (Jews face intolerance), and thus provides evidence for the main position of the argument (I'm against intermarriage). In sum, the overall structure of the argument is:

POSITION 1: I'm against intermarriage	
SUPPORT 1: Jews face intolerance	
IF NOT [SUPPORT] THEN NOT [POSITION]	(b–f)
If Jews faced tolerance,	
then I would not be against intermarriage.	
but SUPPORT 1: Jews face intolerance	(a, g–o)
but POSITION 2: Jews provide tolerance	(p)
SUPPORT 2: We were kind to all	(q–w)
so POSITION 2: Jews provide tolerance	(y)
but SUPPORT 1: Jews face intolerance	(z–aa)

We have seen that *but* marks both position and support in Henry's argument. But it does so only when the content of those units contrast with prior ideas: *but* in (g) contrasts an actual situation with a hypothetical situation; *but* in (p) contrasts the tolerance faced by one group with the tolerance provided by that group; *but* in (z) marks both of these contrasts (because of its dual role in the argument as a contrast with POSITION 2, and as SUPPORT 1). In sum, although *but* marks idea units which are functionally related – support, position – their functional relationship is less important than their contrastive content in explaining the use of *but*.

Consider, now, that semantic content does not always explain why two units stand in a contrastive relationship (see, also, discussion in 6.4). Many contrasts are inferrable only because a particular proposition violates speaker/hearer expectations – expectations which are grounded not in prior propositions in the discourse, but more deeply grounded in background knowledge about the world (Tannen 1979). Consider (35). Jan, Ira, and I have been discussing summers at the seashore. We had commented on how nice one particular resort used to be.

(35)   Ira: Yeh it was very nice when we were kids. You had
                        ⌈ two ⌉ weeks there when you were pregnant=
      Jan: ⌊ I st–⌋
      Ira: =there, right?
      Jan: I used t'go every summer. My mother'd send me down with
                 relatives. **But** I used t'cry I wanted to go home. I didn't like it.
      Debby: When you got *home*. You liked the summer there. No?!
      Jan: I'm not one for staying too long down there.

Jan reports that she spent parts of her childhood summers at the seashore. However, contrary to cultural expectations about children enjoying the seashore, and contrary to our prior remarks about the seashore being a nice place, Jan did not enjoy her time there. Thus, she reports her reaction with *but*. I misunderstand the connection, however: because of my expectations about the seashore based on my own enjoyment, I mistakenly infer that Jan liked the seashore so much that she cried when she had to leave. Jan's message is actually quite clear; my misunderstanding is grounded in my different expectations about the seashore.

The content of upcoming talk can also contrast with speakers' expectations about the proper way to present themselves to their hearers. A frequent topic for my informants, for example, was intermarriage and, more generally, relations between members of different religions, ethnic groups, and races. Individuals often went to great lengths to balance the sometimes polarizing views which they presented with a more integrationist image of themselves. Ira, for example, interrupted another topic under discussion to tell me that he had been invited to the wedding of a Black co-worker. Jan volunteered her opinion about her son's relationship with a Puerto Rican girl:

(36)   Jan: I don't agree with it. I don't– I don't say it's– it's. . .because of
                  color, I think it's eh the way you're brought up. Too much
                  difference.

Jack refused to answer questions about ethnic stereotypes and solidarity, saying instead that he judges everyone individually regardless of group membership. Jack also stated that he hoped his sons would not marry Black women – but not because of race *per se*:

(37)   Jack: I would. . .probably feel hurt. Not because he married a
                  Black girl, because what he'd have to face. . .in this country,
                  because of the racial situation as it is. So polarized now.

Jan's *I don't say it's because of color* in (36), and Jack's *not because he married a Black girl* in (37), suggest that they expect their remarks to be interpreted as implicating precisely what they are denying. By explicitly presenting the conclusions that they expect their hearers to infer – the very conclusions they want to avoid – they are able to partially cancel their saliency. As Goffman (1974: 521) states: 'Anyone who identifies himself with the standards against which the culprit is being judged (and is found wanting) can't himself be all that bad – and isn't, and in the very degree that he himself feelingly believes he is.'

Indeed, after cancelling the potency of unflattering conclusions about themselves, individuals often go on to present fairly polarizing statements.[8] Prior to Henry's argument against intermarriage in (34), for example, he stated:

(38)   Henry: Now I don't want you to think that I'm biased, **but** this is the
                  way I was brought up.

(38), then, is Henry's effort to prevent me from thinking the wrong thing about him: he contrasts an unflattering conclusion about his motivation which I might infer from his position against intermarriage, with a preferred conclusion more in line with a favorable image of himself. The first conjunct dispels the unflattering conclusion; the second conjunct substitutes a less damaging conclusion.

(39) prefaces a story from Zelda about how an Italian family in her neighborhood bothered a Jewish family. It is clear from Zelda's story preface (and her story) that she blames the Italian family for the neighborhood trouble.

(39)   Zelda: a.   They did terrible– the Italian family, did–
                  b.   it's not because they're Italian,
                  c.   because there are– some Italians are lovely–

> d.   **but** this one Italian family did terrible things t' the
>   Jewish family.
> e.   Terrible.

In (39), the first conjunct in (c) presents the potentially unflattering conclusion: Zelda thinks that Italians are inherently bad. The second conjunct
in (d) repeats the remark which could have led a hearer to infer that damaging conclusion about Zelda's beliefs.

Two linguistic devices in the phrases in (36)–(39) work together to have
the effect I have described: negation and *but*. Negatives are used in more
restricted environments than their corresponding affirmatives, for
example, when the affirmative has been explicitly stated or is somehow expected (e.g. Givón 1978). Thus the fact that the initial clauses contain
negatives provides a clue that the speaker expects a certain conclusion to be
inferrable. *But* (which is optional in the second clause – it was absent in
(36) and (37), and present in (38) and (39)) contrasts the conclusion being
denied (the conclusion that prior or upcoming talk could implicate) with a
preferred conclusion. Thus, *but* is used when the content of what is said
contrasts with speakers' perceptions about how their talk will be taken as a
portrayal of self – and when those perceptions clash with their sense of what
would constitute a suitable self for presentation to their hearers.

Just as individuals bring their expectations about the world and about
themselves into a conversation, so too, do they bring their expectations
about what will happen during an interaction. For example, a speaker may
expect to **receive** certain information from another. Such an expectation is
not necessarily made overt: friends, for example, routinely expect to be
'filled in' on what happened to the other during time apart. Or, a speaker
may expect to provide certain information to another. Sometimes the provision of that information is thwarted. If a friend exhausts a conversation
with tales of her own experiences, for example, then one's own story
attempts may not even get started, or, once started, may not get completed.
Interactional knowledge combines with knowledge about the real world
(the world whose objects and events are semantically represented) and with
knowledge about self and other, to produce a wide range of speaker/hearer
expectations – any of which may be contrasted by upcoming talk. And any
of these contrasted expectations can occasion the use of *but*.

In order to show how interactional expectations occasion the use of *but*, I
focus on *but* in question/answer pairs. This is a convenient focus because
answers are formed in response to multiple expectations created by a prior
question. Not only are respondents expected to provide certain infor-

mation which will complete a questioned proposition, but (because questions are requests for information) they are also expected to comply with a request. Another expectation – at least for my informants – was to provide more than the information which would propositionally complete the prior question. In fact, virtually none of the questions which I asked during my interviews were answered with only the information required: very few yes–no questions, for example, received only a *yes* or *no* response.[9] Expansion beyond the minimal information required in an answer suggests that individuals expect answers not only to complete a proposition, but to elaborate a proposition – perhaps to satisfy other interactional demands (e.g. for conversational involvement, Tannen 1984).

The interactional expectations for an answer change somewhat when the information requested by the question can not be provided. Questions are like other requests in this regard: failure to comply with a request requires efforts to save the face of both requestor (who may be seen as having been inopportune or intrusive) and requestee (who may be seen as disrespectful or inconsiderate of the other's needs). Thus, non-compliances with requests are accompanied by some form of mitigation or remedial work (an apology, account, explanation, excuse, and so on, Brown and Levinson 1978, Goffman 1971, Owen 1983) which readjusts the speaker/hearer relationship in the face of its unexpected challenge (cf. *well* in Chapter 5).

Since answering a question requires respondents to satisfy different expectations, it is not surprising to find that an answer may contain portions which are differently geared toward satisfying those expectations.[10] We will see that individuals may differentiate the following portions of their responses by *but*. What *but* contrasts in such answers is the **functional** relation of material in the response to the different expectations created by a prior question.

Let's start with answers in which *but* marks a referential contrast in addition to a functional contrast. In (40), whose structure is seen as 6.1a below, I assume that Ira was born in North Philadelphia. My statement of that assumption requests his confirmation (Labov and Fanshel 1977: 100).

(40)   Debby: And you were born in *North* Philadelphia.
       Ira: a.   No. I was born in uh in– in *South* Philadelphia,
            b.   **but** I moved to North Philadelphia when I was a year old.

Both (a) and (b) in Ira's response are tailored to my request: (a) corrects my faulty inference about where he was born; (b) clarifies Ira's connection

Figure 6.1. *Functional contrasts marked in answers by* but

	A:		request for information (X)	
6.1a	B:		information (X)	
		but	information (Y)	in (40), (41)
6.1b	B:		information (X)	
			information (Y)	
		but	information (X)	in (42)
6.1c	B:		information (Y)	
		but	information (X)	in (43)
6.1d	B:		inability to comply	
			information (Y)	
		but	inability to comply	in (44), (45)
6.1e	B:		information (X)	
			disclaimer of (X)	
		but	information (X)	in (46)

to North Philadelphia. *But* prefaces (b) because of its referential contrast with (a): North vs. South Philadelphia; being born vs. being a year old. However, *but* also differentiates two parts of the response: one part provides the requested information; the other part minimizes the extent of my faulty inference by finding some connection with the location to which I had referred. Thus, we might see (b) as Ira's efforts to mitigate his inability to confirm my request precisely as I had stated it – in other words, a face-saving effort which is socially, as well as informationally, cooperative.

(41) illustrates another answer with a sequential contrast which is both referentially and functionally based. Again, (41) shows the structure in 6.1a. Like (40), *but* prefaces the part of the answer which, although extraneous to the actual information requested, provides a more socially cooperative response.

(41) Sally: Did you ever have a dream, where you woke up and you found yourself like on the floor: or. . .sleepwalking or anything like that?

Zelda: No I didn't. **But** my eh   yeh. My older boy
Sally: kids?
Zelda: uh: eh: he: –especially s– he– he used t'talk, in his sleep, before he married,

It is interesting to note that Sally anticipates how Zelda will provide a fuller response – through a story about her children. This suggests that questioners and respondents share expectations about what information counts as a possible accessory to, or replacement for, the requested information.

(42) also contains two functionally differentiated response portions. In contrast to (40) and (41), however, *but* prefaces the portion which informationally completes the questioned proposition, rather than the portion which is more socially cooperative. Thus, (42) shows the structure in 6.1b. Sally has asked Zelda if she is interested in sports.

(42)   Zelda: a.   Ump um. I'm not interested in it.
                    b.   My family is.
                    c.   JoAnn is.
                    d.   She knows more than the boys do.
                    e.   **But** not me.

Zelda states that she is not interested in sports (twice in (a), once in (e)), thus informationally satisfying the expectations of the question. She also adds information about who in her family is interested in sports. This information is both a referential contrast (Zelda vs. her family) and a functional contrast (what was requested vs. what was not requested). Her return to the strictly informational segment of her answer in (e) – both a referential and functional contrast – is marked with *but*.

(43) differs from (42) only because the informational portion of the answer (X) is presented just once. Thus, (43) shows the structure in 6.1c. But like (40)–(42), this portion is both functionally and referentially contrastive with a prior utterance, and it is marked by *but*.

(43)   Debby: Okay do either of you speak any language besides English?
         Jan: I can read Latin,
                    but I can't speak it.
         Debby: How bout you? ⌈ Can you– ⌉
         Ira: ⌊ I– I   ⌋   could uh speak Hebrew
                    years ago, **but** uh no longer.

In responding to my question about their ability to speak a second language, Jan and Ira both provide me with more information than I have requested: Jan can read Latin, Ira used to speak Hebrew. After providing this extra information, each makes their answer relevant to the focus of my question: Jan cannot speak Latin, Ira can no longer speak Hebrew.

Recall, now, that when individuals cannot provide requested information, it may be seen as non-compliance with a request, and it may occasion as much remedial work as do other non-compliances. I also mentioned that among my informants, it seemed to be socially cooperative to provide more than the information requested. Thus, individuals continued to talk after they had fulfilled the informational requirements of the answer, often by contrasting others' reactions with their own, or by addressing the topic under question in a more general fashion.

Similar strategies are available for the performance of remedial work in answers which do not provide the requested information at all. Consider (44), which shows the structure in 6.1d. Sally has asked Zelda if she thinks there will ever be a time when color doesn't matter. Such a question is understood as a request for an opinion, which Zelda does not provide.

(44)   Zelda: a.   I don't know.
                     b.   It's a very– a lot of people do think so.
                     c.   That at one time it's just gonna be one.
                     d.   **But**, I really don't know.

Zelda first responds that she doesn't know (a) – that she has no opinion. After she presents others' opinions (b, c), she restates her own lack of opinion (d) as both a referential contrast with others' opinions, and a functional contrast within the response. Note that (44) shows the same sequencing and location of *but* as (41) and (42) – it is the identity of the contrastive units which differs.

(45) is a similar example from Jack: although Jack does begin to provide the requested information in (b), he changes direction.

(45)   Debby: Do you think the synagogue brings people closer?
          Jack: a.   I wouldn't know how to answer that, really. Uh=
          Freda: It may–
          Jack: b.   =It might socially uh:. . . .
                     c.   **but** jeez I wouldn't really know.
                     d.   Cause I–⎡ I ⎤
          Freda: ⎣ If ⎦ we were connected, we might
                            ⎡ be able t'answer. ⎤
          Jack: e.   ⎣ *Might* have an ⎦   answer for y',
                     f.   **but** *I* have no answer.

Jack starts by saying that he can't answer (*I wouldn't know how to answer* in a), but then begins to do so (b). He then restates that he can't answer (c), prefacing that disclaimer with *but*. Freda mentions the circumstances which would give them the requisite knowledge (if they were part of the local synagogue), which Jack repeats in (e). Jack then paraphrases his inability to answer (f), again, prefacing it with *but*.

Now consider (46). This illustrates the structure in 6.1e: a structure in which *but* prefaces the actual provision of information which accompanies a disclaimer. In (46), Jack first complies with a request for information, and then mitigates his ability to do so.

(46)   Debby: Would you say this is a friendly block?
        Jack: a.   Fairly friendly.
                 b.   Wouldn't you say?
                 c.   We're a little bit prejudiced, I think.
                 d.   Ah: because uh: we've been here so long that we don't
                        even remember the original groups that were here.
                 e.   So we're bad to judge.
                 f.   We're not the one to judge.
                 g.   **But** I would say fairly, fairly friendly.

Jack complies informationally with my request first in (a). After addressing Freda in (b), Jack explains why his answer might not be objective (c–f),
thereby mitigating its force. He then restates the informational content of
his response (g). The second provision of the requested information contrasts with its disclaimer, and it is prefaced by *but*.

The examples thus far have suggested that *but* can display only one contrastive segment per answer, and that such a contrast is both referential and
functional. But (47) shows that *but* can mark several functionally contrastive segments of an answer.

(47)   Debby: How much education do you think a young man needs
                        nowadays?
        Jack: a.   I don't know how to answer that really.
                 b.   Everyone I've met that went to college don't seem too
                        educated to me,
                 c.   **but** then again I shouldn't judge
                 d.   I'm not an– I'm not what y'call formally really formally
                        educated,
                 e.   so I can't judge.
                 f.   **But** I :– I find boys that're– that go to college don't
                        know: how many oceans there are in this world even.
                 g.   I don't know if– if you think I'm exaggerating,
                          ⎡ or not. ⎤
        Debby: ⎣ No, I ⎦ don't. I don't. I think that's ⎡ right. ⎤
        Jack: h.   ⎣ So: ⎦
                        I : g– I think. . .they should go to four colleges before
                        they get a job,
                 i.   because they don't learn much in one college.

Jack provides five pieces of information in his answer: (1) he doesn't know
how to answer my question (a); (2) he thinks college education is worth
little (b, f, i); (3) he should not really judge the value of college (c, e); (4)
he is not educated (d); (5) young men should attend four colleges (h). This
information is presented in the following sequential configuration. (In line
with the above diagrams, I designate the requested information by X, and
the extra information by Y.)

```
A:   REQUEST FOR INFORMATION (X)
B:   INABILITY TO COMPLY        'I don't know'                 (a)
     INFORMATION (Y)            'college is not worth much'(b)
     but DISCLAIMER OF (Y)      'I shouldn't judge'           (c)
         REASON                 'I'm not educated'            (d)
     so DISCLAIMER OF (Y)       'I shouldn't judge'           (e)
     but INFORMATION (Y)        'college is not worth much'(f)
     so INFORMATION (X)         'go to four colleges'         (h)
     because INFORMATION (Y)    'college is not worth much'(i)
```

Thus, in (47), *but* prefaces both the additional information (Y) and its disclaimer. And although these idea units are functionally contrastive within the answer, they are not referentially contrastive.

In sum, I have suggested that answers can contain portions which are referentially and/or functionally contrastive, the latter because they have different roles in relation to the expectations established by a prior question. *But* can mark any of these portions.

Consider, now, that in many of the answers examined above (37, 39–42) what was marked by *but* was a **repeated** portion of the answer. Consider, also, that those repetitions were always of material which **preceded** the immediately prior, adjacent material. Thus, we might interpret such uses of *but* as speakers' efforts to return to a prior concern – to return to the fulfillment of a prior expectation imposed upon them by the question.

The use of *but* to preface repetitions (or paraphrases) of non-adjacent text – text which contrasts functionally with prior adjacent text – is hardly limited to answers. In the next section, I examine other sequences in which *but* marks a speaker's return to a prior concern as part of my more general shift from contrasting ideas to contrasting actions.

6.2.2 Contrasting actions

I begin by describing *but* as a marker of speaker-return under several interactional circumstances. I then suggest that this function allows *but* to be a point-making device with additional expressive and interactional corollaries.

The best way to differentiate speaker-return from referential contrast is to consider two discourse markers which are more specialized than *but* for these functions: *anyway* and *however*. *But* is interchangeable with both of these markers, although they are not interchangeable with each other – replacing one for the other produces a meaning change in the discourse.[11]

Let us examine a discourse in which both *however* and *anyway* are used. In (48), I have asked Freda how she found the doctor who is treating her sprained foot.

(48) a. Well it so happens I have. . .first of all. . .
   b. you want the history of this?
   c. I have boys that went through many a break.
   d. Falls:, etcetera, falls. . .
   e. So I do know of an orthopedist, that's connected with the
     nearest hospital.
   f. **However** when this happened, I went to the emergency.
   g. And from the emergency they suggested that I use this doctor
     that I always knew from the past who's a– who's a
     um. . .wha'd'y'call it, bone man, what'd'y'call him.
   h. **Anyway**, that's how I got ahold of *him*.
   i. **But** the average doctor that I've needed in the past?

However in (f) prefaces a referential contrast: Freda contrasts the doctor she is currently using for her sprained foot (f) to her usual doctor (c–e). But suppose Freda had used *anyway* instead of *however*: *anyway* would mark the prior discourse as tangential to the main point. We can see this by looking at *anyway* in (h). During her description of how she found her current doctor, Freda forgets the word 'orthopedist' (g). Her efforts to self-repair are tangential to her main point (how she found her current doctor) and she returns to that point with *anyway*. *Anyway* also implicates that what Freda is saying has been presented before; note that *that's how* in (h) is anaphoric – referring back to the description in (f) and (g).

Even though *however* and *anyway* are not themselves interchangeable, *but* can be used instead of either. In fact, *but* sometimes conveys both the referential contrast marked by *however* and the functional contrast marked by *anyway*. Let us look at the end of (48):

  (h) Anyway, that's how I got ahold of *him*.
  (i) **But** the average doctor that I've needed in the past?

But in (i) marks a referential contrast between the specialist doctors described in (e–h) and an average doctor. It also marks a functional contrast because (i) acts as a request for clarification of my much earlier question. Thus, Freda is about to make a renewed effort to satisfy the informational requirements of my question – thereby implicating that even though her prior talk did not fulfill that expectation, she is aware of that need. So *but* creates an anaphoric tie – as did *anyway* in (h).

As further evidence that *but* is functionally similar to *anyway* in (48), let us examine (49). (49) is another answer from Freda which faces the same informational predicament. The predicament in (44) is resolved with *but*, *anyway*, and a meta-linguistic reference to *the point*. Freda has been asked if she believes in socialized medicine, and if she would be willing to pay higher taxes to receive that service. She responds by talking about how expensive her medical bills are without socialized medicine. In (49), she is giving an example of the fees paid when her son broke his arm.

(49) a. Now I hadda y– he broke his arm recently.
      b. Em. . . . . .he was an outpatient.
      c. And it only took twenty minutes.
      d. I mean he went three times.
      e. The first time they hadda t– wait for the swelling t'go down,
      f. the second time somethin' else–
      g. third time, he hadda– he hadda shape it out.
      h. Twenty minutes.
      i. Outpatient.
      j. He had a choice, he could've stayed overnight.
      k. Eh: since then he has eh messed it up,
      l. he will have t'have that taken care of, uh when he's fully grown.
      m. **But** anyway, the point is, twenty minutes of service, w– from the doctor, cost one hundred and forty five dollars.

Freda's point is that she paid a lot of money for very little service: she conveys this initially (b, c) and after describing the service (h, i). Because she diverges from this point (to describe what has happened to her son's arm since the initial treatment (k–l)), she has to re-establish it as the most salient message of her discourse. She thus returns to her point with *but anyway*, and prefaces it with *the point is*.

Consider, now, that we have already seen *but* as a marker of speaker-return in some of our question/answer examples (37, 39–42). We can also observe it following self-repairs. Self-repairs are usually not made a topic of overt interactional concern, instead remaining tangential to a speaker's overall pursual of a point; indeed, even when they do become a focus of conversation, they are often treated as side sequences (e.g. Jefferson 1972).[12] In (50), Jack is describing the economic policies of the Soviet Union; he refers to a particular policy of the 1920s which he misnames:

(50) a. It was called N.E.P.
      b. It was a little before R.N.– N.R.A.
      c. **But** they called it N.E.P.

In (b) he self-repairs from R.N. to N.R.A; in (c), he returns to his description of N.E.P. with *but*. In (51), Irene is contrasting urban with suburban neighborhoods:

(51) a.   The only difference I think may be with–
      b.   well in our area, it isn't because of the school.
      c.   **But** the only difference I would think would be the schools.

In (a), Irene begins to describe urban/suburban differences in general. She self-repairs in (b): her own urban neighborhood has an excellent public school so her generalization will not apply in this particular case. In (c), she returns to her general description with *but*.

Because question/answer pairs and self-repairs are easily identifiable forms of talk, they are useful discourse units in which to show the speaker-return effect of *but*. Yet, *but* occurs throughout conversation in discourse which is not as clearly bounded and discrete as these two units. I suggest that *but* has the same pragmatic effect even when what is being returned to is not part of a full fledged discourse unit – just as *and* has an effect of speaker-continuation even when the idea and/or interactional structure of talk warrants otherwise (as in 25).

Consider, first, that speakers may have certain points that they want to make. For example, I spoke of Freda's 'point' in (49): doctors charge too much money. Sometimes points are presented as answers to questions or emerge because they are topically related to a questioned proposition. The latter was the case in (49): Freda had been asked whether she was willing to spend more money for socialized medicine, and responded by complaining about how much she already spends for medical services.

Other points emerge through their contextualization in a narrative or as a supported position in an argument (see Chapter 1, 1.4). However, although both narratives and arguments have to be interactionally situated – fit into a conversation in terms of topicality, turn space, and so on – arguments are more difficult than stories to present intact. This is because the position supported in an argument is often disputable, perhaps culturally defined as such (politics, religion) and/or interpersonally defined as such (whether Henry should have a sandwich at 9.00 p.m.). The disputability of the position means that arguments are challenged and interrupted during the process of their construction, such that they do not always emerge as an intact sequence of position and support.[13] And this means that the point of an argument often gets lost in the scuffle.

When other conversational concerns take precedence over a speaker's efforts to make a point (by supporting a position) a return to the point may be marked by *but*. Consider a point made by Jack at various times during our conversations: Jack does not like religion. The first indication that I had of this point was Jack and Freda's response to my question about their feelings on intermarriage. Jack paraphrases Freda's response that although she would never object to intermarriage with another religion, she would object to intermarriage with a very religious person.

(52a)   Freda: However, I *would* object strenuously, if it was. . .
                   ⎡ *any* kind   ⎤ of religious– very religious per ⎡ son. ⎤
         Jack: ⎣ A religious– ⎦   ⎣ in   ⎦
                   other words, extremely ⎡ religious. ⎤
         Freda: ⎣ Jewish   ⎦ or otherwise,
                   I would eh. . .eh– ⎡ I would cry.   ⎤
         Jack: ⎣ In other words, ⎦ fanatically
                   religious, whether it was Jewish, or non-Jewish,
                   if it's fanatically ⎡ religious, = ⎤
         Freda: ⎣ That   ⎦ would upset me.
         Jack: = we would be upset. Y'know.

Jack returns to this point twice during the ensuing conversation. The first return follows a general discussion of religious fanatics (*Now there's where I'm prejudiced*; see Chapter 8 on *now*). Then, after a range of other topics (including my family background, Jack's family background, race relations, the United States vs. the Soviet Union, capitalism vs. socialism) the discussion turns toward the prejudice of Poles. Jack begins explaining why he himself is *prejudiced against the Pole, very much* by describing Poland's political mistakes during World War II. He then returns to his general point about religion:

(52b)   Jack: And then in the end Hungary took these two countries in the
                  end anyhow. So I mean it shows you. **But** that isn't the point.
                  The point is. . .religion is a sickening thing with me. I want to
                  throw up when I see a very religious Jew, or a very religious
                  Catholic, or a very religious Protestant.

With *but that isn't the point, the point is* Jack contrasts the conversational salience of two topics: he subordinates the salience of his prior descriptions of Poland's mistakes to the conversational salience (and subjective importance) of his point about religion. He does so despite the various topics that separate his most salient point from its initial presentation. And as Jack continues, Freda ties Jack's point to the context of its initial presentation as an answer to my question about intermarriage:

(52c)   Jack: I– I– I think I'm very contemptuous. Very hateful. Cause
                  I feel they separate the world. They keep people ⎡ apart.   ⎤
         Freda: ⎣ I guess ⎦

you realize now why we could accept a daughter in law who is *not* Jewish. But we wouldn't want a religous one.

In sum, *but* marks Jack's return to his point about religion amidst various different topics and exchanges. Note, also, that no **referential** contrasts are being marked. Rather, the contrast is between a point which the speaker defines as important enough to bear restating, and other conversational concerns which become subjectively defined as subordinate to that point.

Another source of intrusion upon a point is an interlocutor who **agrees** with what is being said and competes for the right to present the same, or a similar, point to a third party. (All of my informants did this at times. Jack at one point stated, 'She's asking *me* the questions! *I'm* doin' the answering!') (53) illustrates how two people, both trying to use the same material to make a point for a third, use *but* to return to their points.

In (53), Freda and Jack are describing to me a young woman (both Jewish and Italian) they recently met who has coined a term for herself: 'Jewop'. ('Wop' is an ethnic slur for Italians.) Their description is related to their previous point about religion: since they do not like religious extremes, they are pleased to have met someone who so casually defies them through her own upbringing and her invention of the term 'Jewop'. (In addition to *but* as a marker of speaker-return, the sequence contains several referential uses of *but* which I summarize following the example.)

(53)   Freda: a.   How bout that little girl that's in– that's visiting with Mae?

                       b.   I can't think of her name, nor do I remember what she said.

                       c.   **But** she was half. . .Italian, half Jewish–

                       d.   what did she call herself?

    Jack: e.   Oh: yeh. She called herself–. . .a Jewop!

    Freda: f.   A Jewop!

    Jack: g.   That was cute!

                       h.   ⌈ She was. . . ⌉ ver:y, very interesting ⌈ t'listen to!   ⌉

    Freda: i.   ⌊ A Jewop! ⌋   ⌊ she's a Jewop! ⌋

                          ⌈ Jewop! ⌉   ⌈ **But** she was raised, as ⌈ a– = ⌉

    Jack: j.   ⌊ Her   ⌋ father was. . . ⌊   ⌊ Wait a= ⌋

    Freda: ⌈ =Catholic.   ⌉

    Jack: k.   ⌊ =minute her ⌋ father was Italian, and her mother was Jewish? Or ⌈ was ⌉ it the other way around.

    Freda: l.   ⌊ Yes. ⌋   She eh:

                       her father was ⌈ Italian, she was raised– ⌉ =

    Jack: m.   ⌊ And she was a great ⌋ product of these two.

Freda: n.   =**But** she was raised by the Jewish grandmother,

    ⌈ and ⌉ sent to the Jew– eh to the ⌈ Catholic school!=⌉

Jack: o.   ⌊ **But–**⌋   ⌊ **but** lived=⌋

Freda: p.   ⌈ =She was raised ⌉ as a Catholic,=

Jack: =at ⌊ home with a Jew.⌋

Freda: q.   ⌈ =**but** who lived at home with a Jew. ⌉

Jack: r.   ⌊ And she wound up marrying an Italian ⌋ boy!=

Freda: s.   ⌈ And she said she really is a Jewop! ⌉

Jack: t.   ⌊ =Isn't that somethin'? ⌋

    u.   **But** she ⌈ is tremendous. ⌉

Freda: v.   ⌊ **But** she was ⌋ very aware of *both*.

Jack: w.   And she was very interesting.

    x.   And she was a pleasure t' just listen to.

The first *but* in (c) separates material which is tangential to the point (the girl's name, what she said) from material central to the point (she was half Italian and half Jewish). Referential uses of *but* are in (o) and (q). In (o), Jack contrasts two parts of the girl's background: going to a Catholic school (mentioned by Freda) and living with a Jew. Freda makes the same contrast in (p) and (q).

But has both a referential and a speaker-return function in (n): Freda begins (l) to describe the girl's upbringing. She presents the two contrasting parts of that upbringing first without *but*:

Freda: l.   Yes. She eh: her father was Italian, she was raised–

But as Jack continues (and overlaps) her description (in m), Freda restates the latter part of that description in (n) – this time prefacing the contrast with *but*:

Freda: n.   **But** she was raised by the Jewish grandmother, and sent to the Jew– eh to the Catholic school!

But in (n) marks not only the referential contrast initiated in (l), but reclaims the floor for Freda – and her right to make her point.

Freda and Jack continue their descriptions in different ways:

Jack: r.   And she wound up marrying an Italian boy!

Freda: s.   And she said she really is a Jewop!

Then each makes a general point about the girl. Jack's point is that the girl profited from her dual upbringing:

Jack: u.   **But** she is tremendous.

This point reinforces Jack's earlier point (discussed in (47)) about over-attachment to any one religion. Freda's point is slightly different:

Freda: v.   **But** she was very aware of *both*.

Freda's point reinforces her earlier position that she approves of intermarriage. This approval is similar to Jack's position against religious differences, but her reason for it differs: it is because intermarriage allows children to learn about more than one tradition.

Thus, both Freda and Jack compete to describe a situation which allows them to reinforce their own previous points. *But* is used throughout their presentations not only to show referential contrasts, but to mark their competing claims for the floor and to allow them to return to the points which their presentations have supported.

Another interactional circumstance under which a speaker can return to a point with *but* is when that point is being defended against a challenge. Prior to (54), for example, Henry has been describing his weekly card games, and I ask what Zelda does during Henry's time with his friends. Henry answers for Zelda, saying that she is not bored, she likes to read, and she feels content when all is well with her family. Henry also feels that Zelda deserves some time away from the kitchen:

(54)   Henry: She likes to be served, because she's always
                              workin' ⌈ hard and she– ⌉   I think=
        Zelda: ⌊ Yeh. I like ⌋ to go out and eat.
        Henry: ⌈ =that's quite natural. She's entitled to it. ⌉
        Zelda: a. ⌊ I like it. ⌈   ⌉ **But** I don't lead a=⌋
        Debby: ⌊ I like it too. ⌋
        Zelda: =very exciting life.
        Debby: b. ⌈ Yeh **but** you're happy. ⌉
        Henry: c. ⌊ Oh **but** you lead a ⌋ good life!
        Zelda: d. Well, it's not exciting.
        Henry: e. Wha– what d'y'call exciting? ⌈ D'y' ⌉ want your=
        Zelda: f.   ⌊ Oh– ⌋
        Henry: g. =adrenalin t'work up?   ⌈ D'you think= ⌉
        Zelda: h.   No, **but** I really ⌊ don't= ⌋
        Henry: i. ⌈ =that's exciting? ⌉ You think that's good ⌈ Zelda? ⌉
        Zelda: j. ⌊ =think my life– ⌋   ⌊ No. ⌋
               k. **But** I don't do anyth–
        Henry: l.   Every body prays– everybody
                     prays– y'know y'can't win in this world.

Zelda says that although she likes to go out, she does not lead an exciting life (a); *but* marks this contrast in expectations (e.g. going out is expected to be exciting). I respond that Zelda is happy; again, *but* marks a contrast in expectations (e.g. lack of excitement means unhappiness).[14] Henry responds similarly that Zelda's life is good (c). These remarks implicate that Zelda should be satisfied with being happy and should realize that she has a good life – in other words, that Zelda should not complain. But Zelda restates her point, retreating somewhat by shifting from *but* to *well* (see Chapter 5, pp. 117–19). Henry then responds by challenging the notion that excitement is valuable (e); Zelda begins to repeat what seems to be her same point (*No, but I really don't think my life* (h, j)) as Henry continues to challenge the value of excitement (i). Despite Zelda's agreement with Henry's specific challenge (*no* in j), she does not give up her point (*But I don't do anyth–* in k) until she is finally interrupted again.

Another example of the repeated use of *but* is (55). What is particularly striking about this example is the accumulation of point-making devices with each successive try to make the point. Freda has said that intermarriages produce healthy attitudes in children. Jack misunderstands her point: he responds as if she had said that Jews generally approve of intermarriage. He then makes the very same point that Freda had made. (55) begins as Freda tries to reclaim her point.

(55) Jack: a.   The child is healthy.   ⌈ I mean physio⌉ logically.
      Freda: b.   **But** ⌊I s:– physi– ⌋
              c.   Why not when it comes to a Jew?
      Jack: d.   The Jew is still the *last* one t'want t'intermarry.
              e.   Read it anywhere.   ⌈The⌉ Jew is the one who=
      Freda: f.   **But** I ⌊sa: ⌋
      Jack: g.   =will not accept. ⌈The rabbis⌉ preach, ⌈'Don't=⌉
      Freda: h.   **But** I did–⌋   ⌊**But** I=⌋
      Jack: ⌈=intermarry.'⌉
      Freda: i.   ⌊=*did* say ⌋ those intermarriages that we have
                   in this country are healthy.
              j.   That's all I said.

Freda's efforts to reclaim both the floor and her point go from *but I s:–* to *but I sa:* to *but I did–* to *but I did say*. Each effort thus adds more point-making devices: the meta-linguistic verb *say* (Schiffrin 1980), the pro-verb *do* (here emphatic in function), and contrastive stress on *do*.

The repeated use of *but* is also striking in (55) for it is not the norm. That is, only 26% of the seventy-three recycled turn-entries in my corpus repeated the turn-initial markers which had been present on the first attempt at turn-entry. Distribution of the twelve cases of *but* in this environment was hardly different from other markers: 33% were repeated. Thus, Freda's repetition of *but* is itself a point-making device which indicates her efforts to correct Jack's misrepresentation of her point, and thereby, to defend that point.

My examples thus far suggest that because *but* is a marker of speaker-return, it can gain an additional expressive function as a point-making device which indicates the speakers' orientation (e.g. of commitment, intensity) to a particular assertion.[15] Uses of *but* as a point-making device with expressive overlays are particularly sensitive to the way a remark is interactionally situated: speakers switch between *but* and other markers as the interactional status of their remarks is redefined through hearer responses.

(56) illustrates Henry switching from *and* to *but*. Henry begins to make the point that fathers receive less respect than they used to, and that this is related to middle class economic values. When Irene disagrees (note, with *but*), his point becomes a defense.

(56) Henry. a. **And** not— ⌈   ⌉ and there is less=
      Irene: b.   ⌊ **But** it's not a ⌋ matter of– even–=
      Henry: ⌈ =respect– ⌉
      Irene: c.   ⌊ =Henry if ⌋ they have more money– even if they don't
                   have the ⌈ money– ⌉
      Henry: d.   ⌊ **But** ⌋ today there is less respect
                   [Henry continues]

Henry begins his point in (a) with *and* as a continuation of a prior argument. After Irene's challenge (c), he returns to that point – which is now a defense – with *but*.

Consider (57). Freda and Jack are responding to my question about the average cost of a house in their neighborhood.

(57) Jack: a. Now this is an end house, ⌈ so this would get more. ⌉
      Freda: b.   ⌊ No I don't know. It   ⌋
              c. depends– **but** don't t– don't talk about this one.

Freda switches from an expression of doubt (*No I don't know*) to a stronger disagreement (*don't talk about this one*). *But* accompanies the latter.

Finally, in (58), Henry switches from *but* to *well* (a more concessive marker; see Chapter 5, pp. 117–19) as he starts to see Zelda's viewpoint. Henry has been accusing Zelda of not being equally close with all her cousins. Zelda admits a difference in feeling, but maintains that this is how it should be.

(58) Zelda: a. And I like   my cousins, one of them=

       Henry: b.   You have–

       Zelda: c. =better than the ⎡ others! ⎤   And that's how=

       Henry: d.   ⎣ You do–⎦ you do–

       Zelda: e. ⎡ =it is:! ⎤ Yeh! Yeh because you feel– you ⎡relate=⎤

       Henry: f. ⎣ You do? ⎦   ⎣ **But**–⎦

       Zelda: g. =to one more than the ⎡other. That's silly=⎤

       Henry: h.   **Well**:⎣What you have in=⎦

       Zelda: i. ⎡=to say ⎤ why should they all   be the same.

       Henry: j. ⎣=common.⎦   ·   Nah I mean–

                no no no no no.

Henry continues his challenge of Zelda through (f) and his use of **but**. He then drops his challenge to concede that individual feelings about relatives might differ (h, j) and to begin an explanation of what he had meant.

We have seen now that speakers use *but* to present points which have been interrupted, misunderstood, and/or challenged. Speakers' interactional need to present a point in such circumstances may be so strongly felt that it overrides other more cooperative interactional practices – such as cooperative turn-taking. We can see if this is so by comparing the turn-entry location of *but* to other turn-initial markers.

I define turn-entry location as the location *vis-à-vis* a current speaker's turn at which a next speaker begins. I will distinguish two such locations: transition space entry, and non-transition space.[16] (59) gives examples of the former, and (60) of the latter. To clarify the examples, I identify where each second speaker begins talking relative to the prior speaker's turn.

(59)   clause-final position

       Henry: So doctors are– well they're not God either.

       Zelda: He said that they didn't think he saw it.

       turn-transition device

       Ira: There wasn't anything like this. But today uh. . .

       Jan: It's these kids that are out for money for drugs.

(60)   mid-clause entry

       Irene: But ⎡ I could never–⎤

       Henry: ⎣ But you still ⎦ have a family structure.

Because transition space entries are informationally cooperative – they allow the current speaker to reach a possible completion point – I will refer to them as cooperative transitions; similarly, I refer to non-transition space entries as uncooperative.[17]

Table 6.1 compares the turn entry locations of the most common turn-initial markers in my corpus: *oh, well, and, so* and *but*. The contrast between *but* and the other turn-initial markers is striking: whereas all of the others are used predominantly when speakers cooperatively initiate a turn, *but* is used in only half of such locations.

Table 6.1. *Turn-entry location and turn-initial markers*

	Cooperative turn entry	Uncooperative turn entry	Total
oh	92 (90%)	10	102
well	185 (85%)	33	218
and	38 (95%)	2	40
so	38 (100%)	0	38
but	25 (52%)	23	48
Total	378	68	446

Recall that I am defining uncooperative turn-entries on an informational basis: they are entries which do not allow a prior speaker to reach a possible completion point. So the uncooperative placement of turns initiated with *but* shows speakers' placement of their own utterances in the conversation taking precedence over their interactional consideration of others' utterances. This supports my suggestion that the use of *but* reflects the interactional precedence of making one's own point – when such a point has been interrupted, misunderstood and/or challenged, and when such a point is the object of a speaker commitment, i.e. a marked expressive stance.

Given these observations, it should not be surprising that *but* is used not only when speakers defend their points against challenges, but when they actually issue those challenges, that is, when they initially disagree. (61) illustrates. Henry is saying that wealthy suburban life (*across the way*) makes people snobs.

(61)   Henry: Y'see you move across the way, you live in a big house;
                  and, you belong to eh maybe a country club
                  ⌈ eh: it's a different phase of living! ⌉
        Zelda: ⌊ **But** it doesn't necessarily mean you have ⌋ to!

The important point here is that *but* prefaces a remark which disagrees with the prior remark – although it is not a defense of a previously challenged point.

(62) illustrates the use of *but* for both challenge and defense. Henry has been arguing that anti-Semitism will always exist.

(62)   Henry: a.   Lemme tell y', ⎡ these things are gonna happen. ⎤
        Irene: b.   ⎣ Right **but** as the generations ⎦
                       go on they won't know of it,
                 c.   and they won't *see* it.
        Henry: d.   **But** ⎡ they know it in Israel! ⎤
        Zelda: e.   ⎣ **But** see that's it– ⎦ Irene, that's why Israel
                       has all ⎡ the pictures. ⎤
        Henry: f.   ⎣ They show ⎦ you everyday t'remind the
                       children.
        Irene: g.   What? Oh Israel, yeh.
                 h.   **But** you don't live in Israel.

Irene agrees that anti-Semitism did exist (*right*) but disagrees on its perma-
nence (b, c). Henry and Zelda counter that the generations of Jews in Israel
will always be aware of anti-Semitism (d, e). Irene concedes this (*Oh
Israel, yeh*). Her rebuttal (h) both challenges Henry and Irene, and pre-
serves her initial position.

Finally, an example from Chapter 5 illustrates how strongly individuals
expect *but* to preface disagreements – whether they are disagreements
which challenge, defend, or both. The example comes from a television
talk show in which advocates of two sides of a controversial issue are invited
on the air to expose viewers to all sides of that issue. The host of the show
had not elicited the expected controversy and finally asked his interviewee
but? This was the host's final effort to elicit the expected controversy, and it
was understood as a request for disagreement simply because of *but*. However, since the interviewee did not, in fact, disagree with the other guest, he
responded *well there is no but*.

6.2.3 But: *a contrastive marker*

We have seen that *but* marks an upcoming unit as a contrast with a prior
unit and that this meaning is part of every use of *but*. (Although most
linguists agree that *but* does have meaning, there is disagreement about
whether it is semantic or pragmatic meaning; see 6.4.) Although the contrastive meaning of *but* gives it a narrower range of uses than *and*, its range
is still fairly wide for the simple reason that contrastive relationships themselves are knowledge-based and context-based, as well as proposition-
based.

We have also seen that *but* marks functionally differentiated portions of
answers – portions which fulfill different expectations of a prior question.

In many such answers, what is marked by *but* is a repeated portion of the answer – a portion which had preceded the immediately prior, adjacent material. I suggested that, in this role, *but* is similar to *anyway*, whereas in a more purely referential role, it is similar to *however*.

We went on to see that many uses of *but* (not only in question/answers and self-repairs) could be interpreted as speakers' efforts to return to a prior concern of making a point. I suggested that the use of *but* in point-making has an expressive relevance, in that a repeated point displays a committed orientation toward a proposition, and an interactional corollary, in that stating one's point can take precedence over other interactional goals. Given these two relevancies, it is not surprising that *but* is also used to issue disagreements. I grouped all such efforts together as contrastive actions – as speakers' efforts to make a point in reaction to interruptions, distractions, challenges and disagreements.

Finally, I have treated the different uses of *but* in different sections, but as I stated with *and*, this is for analytical convenience only. There are many examples in which simultaneous functions are being fulfilled by *but* – where *but* marks referential contrast, functional contrast, and contrastive actions simultaneously (e.g. 53).

6.3 *Or*

Or (a coordinator like *and* and *but*) is used as an option marker in discourse. It differs from *and* and *but* not only in meaning, but because it is more hearer-directed: whereas *and* marks a **speaker's** continuation, and *but* a **speaker's** return to a point, *or* marks a speaker's provision of options to a **hearer**. More specifically, I will suggest that *or* offers inclusive options to a hearer: *or* provides hearers a two-way choice between accepting only one member of a disjunct, or both members of a disjunct.

I begin by describing how *or* provides idea options in arguments – a mode of discourse whose organization has also revealed the use of *and* and *but*. *Or* is used in arguments primarily to mark different pieces of support as multiple evidence for a position. In (63), for example, Jack is arguing that American movies never present a realistic view of life. He presents two examples to support his generalization about the lack of realism.

(63) Jack: a. I'm – I'm speaking how kind everybody is on the movie.
      b. **Or** uh . . . how a poor working girl is out looking for a
          job, with a hundred and ninety dollar suit on her back!

There are two potential ways to interpret *or* in (63). First, we could say that

Jack is directing his hearers to choose one example – either example, but only one. This would mean that *or* is **exclusive**: only one member of the disjunct can hold. Second, we could say that Jack is directing his hearers to choose (a), (b) or both. This would mean that *or* is **inclusive**: either one member, or both members of the disjunct, can hold. (Note that the inclusive interpretation of *or* includes the exclusive, because it allows it as one possible interpretation.)

Consider, now, that if we allow *or* to mark inclusive options, we can account for interactional advantages gained through the use of multiple evidence. That is, inclusive *or* creates more of an evidential choice than exclusive *or*: a hearer can choose to accept the first disjunct, the second disjunct, or both. Creating an evidential choice increases the chance that one's point will be accepted because it minimizes the cost that rejection of any single piece of evidence might have. And the possibility that both pieces of evidence will be accepted as cumulative support is itself a means of strengthening a position. These advantages can be accounted for only if we allow *or* to mark inclusive options.

Let us examine another example with this issue in mind. In (64), Jack is stating that power elites will always use social differences to justify economic inequities (e.g. 'they're poor because they're . . .').

(64)   Jack: a.   It's when there's an economic situation
                   b.   then they use race.
                   c.   **Or** they use nationality,
                   d.   **or** anti Semitism,
                   e.   **or** what have you.

The selection of a single disjunct would certainly provide support for Jack's position. Furthermore, it would make sense since only one feature of social identity is likely to be used by a particular power elite at a time. But note that Jack is listing examples which support a generalization: note the tag *what have you* as well as the indefinite *they*. This suggests that the selection of all of the disjuncts is also a possibility: all of these examples together would provide support for his general position. Thus like (63), (64) suggests an interactional advantage to allowing *or* to be inclusive.

That *or* offers the wide evidential choice associated with its inclusive reading is explicit in (65). Jack is arguing that there is no American culture (he means culture as 'classics') because the country is too young. He prompts his nephew Ron to try to think of examples of American culture. If Ron fails (as Jack expects him to), then Jack's point will be supported.

(65)   Jack: a.   We have no culture yet.

	b.	We have no stable – each state has its own:
	c.	see, would you – what would you call American
	d.	culture. . . . I'm talkin' now, about=
Freda:	e.	Stupid.
Jack:	f.	=classical lines. I'm talkin' about the classics.
	g.	Like, mention some good symphonies.
	h.	**Or** some good uh: . . . very good literature.

Ron is explicitly prodded to provide examples of American culture (g, h), and an example either of a symphony, or a literary work, will suffice. But then when Ron can find no examples, Jack himself names European musicians and writers (Tennyson, Goethe, Beethoven) as a way of comparing America's lack of culture with European culture. Because Jack himself chooses examples from both categories, I interpret *or* in (h) as inclusive: although one option would suffice, both are possible.

The same interpretive possibilities are illustrated in (66). Freda is explaining why she prefers going to restaurants without other couples.

(66)	Freda:	a.	We prefer eating alone.
		b.	Cause: what we like– what we like, most other people either don't want t'go: for it,
		c.	**or**, um . . . you feel responsible if you suggest a place.
		d.	I eh eh– eh I prefer eh I *do* prefer eating alone.

Either (b) or (c) alone is sufficient reason for Freda's preference. But the two reasons also have a joint effect: they allow Freda to commit herself to her claim about her preference with a greater degree of certainty.

Thus far, I have suggested that multiple evidence creates two possible advantages for a speaker. First, it reduces the dependency of a position on any single piece of evidence, thus correcting for the possibility that hearers will reject a piece of evidence and thus reject the position. Second, the very fact that the speaker has more than one piece of support for a position can itself be evidence of its value. Both these advantages can be derived only if we interpret *or* as inclusive.

Consider, now, that *or* is also used to offer inclusive options to hearers in disagreement (67), clarification (68), and response to questions (69). In (67), Zelda uses *or* to challenge Henry's position that marriages between people of different religions never work.

(67)	Zelda:	a.	Yeh. But wait: it doesn't mean because they're not of the same religion that they're – they're eh gonna be terrible.
		b.	**Or** if they *are* of your religion that things are gonna work out well,

c.   it's the person. . . . *too*.
d.   So it takes *both*.

The two disjuncts together challenge Henry's position: not only is it the case that intermarriages always fail, but it is also the case that other marriages do not always succeed.

In (68), Freda announces that she would never send a daughter to the all girls' high school that both she and I had attended.

(68)   Freda: a.   If I had– had a youn– if I had a daughter,
                  b.   I'd never send her t'Girls' High.
        Debby: c.   Y'think its too uh . . .
        Freda: d.   I would never send her t–
                  e.   no no no it's a very good school.
                  f.   But I– **or** eh for that matter I would never send a boy, to an all boys' school, either.
                  g.   So it's not that I mean Girls' High or Central are gonna be– I just don't– I think it's an unhealthy– it's an unhealthy situation.
                  h.   I think boys and girls should be together.

Freda responds to my partially completed request for her reasoning as if I had already misunderstood that reasoning: *no no no it's a very good school.* The disjunct in (f) clarifies her position by providing an analogous claim about an all boys' school.

In (69) Irene is answering my question about where she would like to live.

(69)   Irene: a.   I'd like t'live in Huntingdon ⌈ hhhhhhh ⌉
        Debby: b.   ⌊ Oh! Who ⌋
                        wouldn't ⌈ hhhh   ⌉
        Irene: c.   ⌊ hhhhI ⌋ was up there with my husband last
                  d.   week. There are some beautiful homes ⌈ up ⌉ there.
        Debby: e.   ⌊ Yeh. ⌋
                  f.   They are really nice.
        Irene: g.   **Or** I have cousins that live up in eh: Holland Pennsylvania, up past State Road?
                  h.   Up there are you familiar?
        Debby: i.   No I've never gone up that far.
        Irene: j.   So, they're *big* houses. They're– they're nice houses. Real nice.

Compare what *or* does in (69) to what *and* or *but* would do in the same position. Whereas *and* would continue Irene's response, and *but* would mark her renewed compliance to a request for information, *or* marks the choice between the two locations mentioned in the answer. Note that because

Irene can only live in one place – and either Huntingdon or Holland would do – *or* seems to have an exclusive reading here. But on the international level of question and answer (or request for information and provision of information), *or* is inclusive: Irene is offering her questioner the option of taking either Huntingdon (a), Holland (g), or both, as her response.

I began this section by focusing on evidential choices in arguments, and suggesting that such a choice may be interactionally beneficial to its maker. Consider, now, that a similar benefit is provided when *or* is used in questions. That is, questioners increase their chances of gaining an answer when they convert yes–no questions into open-ended disjunctions with one or more *or* tags.[18] Such an increase is created when the *or* tag changes the range of answer possibilities either by adding more specific response options, as in (70):

(70)   Debby: Do you go down the shore? Like Atlantic City **or** Wildwood, **or** Cape May?.

or by generalizing the response options so that the respondent can select her own, as in (71):

(71)   Debby: Are y– are these people around, from the block, from the neighborhood . . . **or** where.

But there is not much interactional advantage to the *or* tag in (72), since it merely specifies the binary choice already provided in the prior question:

(72)   Debby: Were you here in the United States, **or** did you go overseas?

Again, the interactional advantage of *or* tags can be derived only if we interpret *or* as inclusive.

In sum, I have proposed that *or* is an inclusive option marker in discourse: it provides hearers with a choice between accepting only one member of a disjunct, or both members of a disjunct.[19] Thus, *or* is fundamentally different from *and* and *but* because it is not a marker of a speaker's action toward his own talk, but of a speaker's desire for a hearer to take action. More specifically, *or* represents a speaker's effort to elicit from a hearer a stance toward an idea unit, or to gain a response of some kind. *Or* thus prompts the exchange of responsibility for the maintenance of conversation, whereas *and* maintains the status quo, and *but* returns it to a prior state. (I discuss this contrast in more detail in Chapter 10, after we see it reappear in slightly different form for other markers.)

6.4 Conjunctions as discourse markers

Before closing this chapter, it might be useful to briefly compare my analysis of *and*, *but* and *or* to other analyses, for it is possible that an analysis of these conjunctions as discourse markers can provide a new (and useful) perspective on some of the issues that have been noted (6.4.1). At the same time, I want to be able to consider the possibility that the discourse functions of conjunctions are based in their grammatical properties (6.4.2).

6.4.1 Syntax, semantics, and pragmatics of conjunctions

Sentence grammars define *and*, *but*, and *or* syntactically as coordinating conjunctions (e.g. Gleitman 1965, Quirk *et al.* 1972). For example, *and*, *but* and *or* all prohibit backwards pronominalization:

(73)   *He$_i$ isn't coming to the party
         and/but/or John$_i$ went to the movies.

Subordinate conjunctions, on the other hand, allow backwards pronominalization:

(74)   Because/although/since he$_i$ isn't coming to the party, John$_i$ went to
         the movies.

Although *so* falls with the coordinate conjunctions by this test, *so* does not group with the coordinate conjunctions by another test – that only one coordinate conjunction is possible in a compound sentence (Dik 1968). Compare (75a) and (b).

(75)   (a)   *John isn't coming to the party and but he went to the show.
         (b)   John isn't coming to the party and so he went to the show.

The semantic properties of conjunctions are less well defined than their syntactic properties. In fact, the attempt to assign meaning to conjunctions has long plagued both linguists and logicians: whether 'connectives have meaning (and if so, what kind of meaning) has been a moot point since antiquity' (Dik 1968: 25).[20]

Even a structural definition of coordination allows for the possibility that coordinators have meaning: 'a construction consisting of two or more members which are equivalent as to grammatical function, and bound together at the same level of structural hierarchy by means of a linking device' (Dik 1968: 25). That is, the linking devices – coordinators – may have meaning in addition to their binding role.

Posner (1980) isolates two broad perspectives on the question of which semantic value (or how many values) is to be assigned to a coordinator: the meaning-minimalist and the meaning-maximalist. One difference between these views reflects more general uncertainty about the relative contribution of semantic and pragmatic meaning to the total communicative force of an utterance. The minimalist view places less of the signalling load on the referential meaning of a particular form, and more on pragmatic principles governing use of that form in context-bound utterances; the maximalist view reverses that division of labor. The two views also differ on the role assigned to context. For the minimalist, context is a source of inferences which interacts with the minimal meaning contributed by the coordinator; for the maximalist, context provides information which is propositionally compatible with the referential information conveyed by a conjunction – if not actually conveyed by the conjunction itself.

The same questions which underlie the meaning-minimalist/maximalist controversy pervade my analysis of discourse markers. Recall that in Chapter 3, I asked how the functions of markers are a product of both their own properties and their contexts. This question reflects the same uncertainty about the relative contribution of semantic and pragmatic meaning to the total communicative force of an utterance as does the meaning minimalist/ maximalist controversy. But by moving the uncertainty to a discourse level, the question claims that it is not only the semantics and pragmatics of particular items and utterances which create communicative meaning: it is also the discourse context of an utterance which contributes to the total communicative force of that utterance.[21]

The minimalist view is currently popular among semanticists and pragmaticists who identify natural language conjunctions with logical connectives. Both *and* and *but* would be semantically identical to the truth-functional connective '&' (e.g. Gazdar 1979, Kempson 1975) and *or* would be semantically identical to logical disjunction 'v' (e.g. Borowski 1976, Hurford 1974). Such accounts propose that principles of pragmatic interpretation (primarily Grice's maxims) are used by speakers and hearers to supply additional inferences about speaker-meaning (but see Lakoff 1971, Leech 1983, Schmerling 1975). Posner's (1980: 116) conclusion is representative of this approach. He concludes that all sentence connectives have meanings equivalent to logical connectives but that

corresponding to the special purpose and circumstances of communication further content elements can be acquired by a sentence connective on the basis of the formulations, the meaning and the facts described in the connected sentences. These content elements occur as **conversational suggestions**, more specifically, as **connexity-suggestions**.

However, neither the actual derivation of such inferences, nor the discourse and contextual constraints on their derivation, have been described in detail.

In contrast to the minimalist view, the meaning-maximalist view is that coordinators have specific meanings which contribute to coordinate constructions. Take *and* again. The maximalist view of *and* would define it as either polysemous (multiple senses housed in one lexeme) or ambiguous (multiple lexemes housed in one phonological form).[22] *And* would thus be used in specific contexts because its meaning is compatible with the semantics of the compound proposition.

One immediately notes that *and* forms coordinate sentences in which a tremendous variety of semantic relations between clauses is possible. Consider the sentences in (76) (from Posner 1980):

(76)   a.   Annie is in the kitchen and (there) she is making doughnuts.
       b.   Annie fell into a deep sleep and (during this time) her facial
               color returned.
       c.   The window was open and (coming from it) there was a draft.
       d.   Peter married Anne and (after that) she had a baby.
       e.   Paul pounded on the stone and (thereby) he shattered it.
       f.   Give me your picture and I'll give you mine. (If you give me
               your picture, I'll give you mine.)
       g.   The number 5 is a prime number and (therefore) it is divisible
               only by 1 and itself.

Were one to view *and* as a means of conveying relations of location (a), simultaneity (b), source (c), succession (d), cause (e), conditionality (f), and conclusion (g), one would have a very large set of synonyms for *and*, and an equally large set of homonyms housed in one lexeme – and a set which could quickly multiply. Note, also, that any of these relations can be inferred **without** *and*. Thus, what is to stop one from considering a speaker's pause between verbal utterances as a synonym for *and* (Posner 1980: 105), and even worse, saying that pausing has the same multiplicity of interclausal meanings?[23]

One striking difference between the minimalist and maximalist views of *and* concerns the treatment of symmetric and asymmetric *and*. Maximalist views would identify these as two different (polysemous or ambiguous) senses. Lakoff (1971), for example, takes the view that although one sense of *and* **is** parallel to & (in its symmetry), the other cannot be parallel because it is both asymmetrical and presuppositional of the first conjunct. The minimalist view of *and* as truth-functional accounts for asymmetric *and* in terms of pragmatic maxims. Kempson (1975), for example, argues that because time sequence between propositions can be interpreted without *and* (cf. 76a), it is not *and* which contributes an inference of temporal order. Kempson (1975: 198) proposes instead that such an inference results from a maxim such as 'Unless you explicitly mark the time relation, make your narration of events reflect their sequence.' Kempson (1975) also argues that the temporally asymmetric interpretation of *and* cannot result from presupposition, since the denial of any single conjunct can render an entire sequence false – just as the truth-functional properties of & would predict. Schmerling (1975), however, criticizes minimalist approaches such as Kempson's by pointing out that not all asymmetric conjunction involves temporal sequence: asymmetric conjunction includes aspectually related verbs whose underlying form is not two independent clauses (and thus cannot be represented as logical conjunction between two propositions).

Although disagreement about *but* is also focused on a meaning-minimalist/maximalist controversy, the disagreement takes a different form. That is, it is generally agreed that *but* has a contrastive meaning: the controversy is whether this meaning is semantic or pragmatic. If semantics is restricted to truth-conditional meaning, *but* and *and* are defined semantically as truth-functional equivalents. But this provides no way of accounting for the contrastive meaning of *but*. For example, (77a) and (b) have the same truth-conditional meaning: both are true if and only if both conjuncts are true.

(77)   a.   I went to the store and the store was closed.
         b.   I went to the store but the store was closed.

Although (a) and (b) are truth-functionally equivalent, they differ in their overall communicative meaning because of a difference between *and* and *but*: expressed in (77b) is a contrast between the propositions expressed in the two conjuncts. However, it is not possible to account for such a difference semantically within a truth-conditional semantics.

Another difficulty in semantically accounting for the contrastive meaning of *but* lies in the source of the contrast. In (77b), for example, the two conjuncts are in contrast only because we (as speakers and hearers) expect a normal course of events: one does not go to a store unless one knows (or expects) it to be open. (78a–b) exemplify this still further.

(78a)   Liz did not get the job but she is happy.

Understanding the contrast conveyed by *but* in (78a) requires the background knowledge that people want to get jobs, and thus, they are likely to be unhappy when they do not. (78a) thus contrasts an expected outcome (Liz will be unhappy if she does not get the job) to an actual outcome (Liz is happy). Very different knowledge would be required to understand the contrast in (78b):

(78b)   Liz got the job but she is happy.

Here we would still assume that the fact that Liz is happy counters expectations. But our expectations would have to differ: we would have to assume that Liz did not want the job. Thus, the contrast between the two conjuncts remains the same; what differs is the background knowledge which explains the contrast.

Van Dijk (1977a, 1977b) accounts for the intuition that *but* marks an exception to a normal course of events by proposing that the underlying logical structure of a compound *but* proposition contains a conditional and a negative. Thus, the truth conditions of *but* would be identical to those of *and* with 'the proviso that the consequent be false in most alternative possible worlds which can be reached from the antecedent' (van Dijk 1977a: 81). Lakoff (1971), on the other hand, accounts for the same intuition by positing two different sources of contrastive knowledge. First is a semantic contrast between two lexical items, e.g. *John is tall but Bill is short*. Second is a pragmatic contrast between speaker/hearer expectations and actuality, e.g. *Mary is poor but happy* (that is, there is no lexical contrast between *poor* and *happy*: but one would not expect poor people to be happy).

Kempson (1975) claims, however, that *but* cannot be accounted for at all in a semantic analysis since reliance on speaker/hearer expectations (Lakoff's pragmatic knowledge) makes it impossible to predict what contrasts would be a prerequisite for *but*. She follows Grice's (1975) suggestion that the contrastive meaning is a result of a conventional implicature: it 'appears not to be part of the word's meaning ... but it seems in some sense always a consequence of the word's use' (Kempson 1975: 175). Two common tests for conventional implicature support Kempson's proposal (see Grice 1975, 1978; Kartunnen and Peters 1979). First, the contrastive meaning of *but* is detachable: it is not implicated in truth-functionally equivalent ways of stating the same thing. We saw this in (77a) and (b) above: *and* does not evoke a contrast. Second, the contrastive meaning of *but* cannot be cancelled. Thus, it seems contradictory to say:

(79)   Although Mary is poor but happy, there is no contrast between these
          two states.

The conventionally implicated meaning of *but* is defined by truth-conditional semanticists (such as Kempson) as a pragmatic meaning.[24]

Or presents a quandary to semanticists and pragmaticists similar to that of *but*: which part of its meaning is semantic (truth-functional) and which is pragmatic (implicated by use in context)? Gazdar (1979: 81) summarizes: 'One theory claims that it is ambiguous between inclusive and exclusive disjunction ... The other theory maintains that the expression is unambiguous, having only the inclusive reading: the exclusive 'reading' which it appears to have in certain cases is explained by reference to implicature.' The former view is the maximalist position; the latter, the minimalist. (See also Barrett and Stenner (1971), Borowski (1976), Hurford (1974), Pelletier (1977).)

Meaning-minimalist and maximalist views are by no means restricted to sentence level analyses of conjunctions. Van Dijk (1977a, 1977b) analyzes both sentence-forming and sequence-forming connectives in a single minimalist framework. Unlike the truth-functional analysis, however, he differentiates coordinative connectives from logical connectives by basing the interpretation of the former on a relevance logic which considers the intensional meanings of connected propositions. For example, *and* in both sentences and sequences would connect propositions whose own meanings – not those of *and per se* – are what evoke more specific interpretations of connectedness, e.g. of location, simultaneity, sequence, cause, consequence.

Or take Halliday and Hasan's (1976) view of *and*: their analysis of *and* as a cohesive tie equivocates between minimalist and maximalist views. As a cohesive tie, *and* is a texture-creating device which contributes additive meaning by tying an upcoming proposition to a prior proposition and marking its dependency upon that prior proposition for interpretation. But like other cohesive devices, *and* **reflects** the semantic content of a text. It is this reflective quality that leads them (perhaps unintentionally) toward what sounds like a multiple-meaning view of *and*: they categorize *and* not only as additive, but as **adversative**, more specifically, contrastive (along with *but* and *on the other hand*), simply because it can preface an upcoming proposition whose content contrasts with that of the prior proposition.[25]

Attempts to assign meaning to conjunctions at both sentence and discourse levels are further complicated by their openness to both external and internal meanings (Halliday and Hasan 1976) – a distinction which differs slightly from the semantics/pragmatics distinction. External meaning is 'inherent in the phenomena that language is used to talk about' (p. 241); it is analogous to referential meaning (usually considered as part of semantics). Internal meaning, on the other hand, is 'inherent in the communication process' (p. 241), the speaker's own '"stamp" on the situation – his choice of speech role and rhetorical channel, his attitudes, his judgements and the like' (p. 240). In short, internal meaning encompasses expressive and social meanings, the non-referential information usually included in the domain of pragmatics.

The external/internal distinction, however, reformulates the relationship between semantics and pragmatics. Semantic properties are often seen as different in kind from pragmatic factors: for example, referential meaning may be said to be rule-governed, whereas communicative meaning is principle-governed (Leech 1983), or semantic knowledge may be said to be part of competence and pragmatic knowledge part of performance (Kempson 1977, but see Gumperz 1981, 1984 and Hymes 1972). In contrast to the discontinuity between semantics and pragmatics, Halliday and Hasan (1976: 267) suggest a continuity from external to internal relations: 'internal relations may be regarded as an extension of the underlying patterns of conjunction into the communication situation itself, treating it, and thereby also the text – the linguistic component of the communication process – as having by analogy the same structure as "reality"'. Thus, one is led to search for ways in which the internal meanings of conjunctions (their pragmatic uses) are extensions of their external meanings (their semantic values).

In sum, conjunctions mark structural relationships between constituent parts of a sentence. Conjunctions also have semantic values which partially restrict what can be connected; such values interact with the meanings of the propositions being connected in ways which are governed not only by semantic rules of connectivity, but by pragmatic principles through which external and internal meanings are created. The meaning-minimalist and maximalist views reverse the division of labor inherent in the communication of utterance meaning: the minimalist view reduces the signalling load of a particular form, and increases the role of pragmatic principles and contextual information; the latter reverses that division of labor.

An overall advantage of any minimalist position is a simplified dictionary entry. But the effect of so simple a semantic description is the need to account for the contribution of context to the interpretation of speaker meaning, and to incorporate pragmatic analyses of context (including surrounding discourse, speaker/hearer background assumptions and knowledge, and so on) into one's analysis of when a conjunction is appropriately used. In short, such an effort would have to explain how context augments inferences about intersentential connections, and how such inferencing leads to the pairing of conjunctions with certain speaker-meanings in particular contexts.

An analysis of the discourse functions of conjunctions has the general advantage of offering a more systematic view of context.[26] Such a view is needed for either minimalist or maximalist views of semantic meaning. But there is also a peril: although a discourse perspective provides an increased range of contexts, it is doubtful that all of the context-bound uses of conjunctions found in discourse would be relevant (or should be) to sentence internal uses.

A discourse analysis of conjunctions also has specific advantages. My analysis has shown the following. First, *and* has two uses: (1) *and* is a structural device for building text which can enter into syntagmatic contrasts with asyndetic connection, (2) *and* has pragmatic effect as a marker of continuation in interaction. These uses of *and* both support the minimalist position that *and* has little semantic meaning, as well as the minimalist view of context. (They say nothing, however, about whether the minimal meaning of *and* is truth-functional.) Thus, *and* is a structural device only because of its relation to its containing text. Similarly, the continuative effect of *and* is a consequence of a speaker's situated context-bound use, which can, however, be used to impose a continuative effect even if it is not structurally warranted. In short, the content of ideas and actions are not themselves part of the meaning of *and*; rather, they are contextual parameters which work with *and* to organize ideas and perform actions.

Second, my analysis of *but* has confirmed its contrastive meaning. It supports prior observations that the source of an inferrable contrast is tremendously variable, including referential, functional, and interactional knowledge and expectations. In viewing *but* as a marker of speaker-return – which gains expressive overlays as a point-making device – I have also implied that *but* has a pragmatic effect which depends on this contrastive meaning.

Third, my analysis of *or* shows that it is used to mark inclusive options. The fact that such options are marked by *or* (but not by *and* or *but*) suggests that there is a residue of logical meaning underlying the use of *or* in discourse. And the fact that I have found inclusive *or* in very specific discourse locations suggests that perhaps the inclusive interpretation is strongly context-dependent, and that so too is an interpretation of **exclusive** choice, e.g. compare an airline hostess asking *coffee, tea, or milk* (exclusive *or*), and then *cream or sugar?* (inclusive *or*). But these suggestions say little about whether the expression *or* itself is ambiguous or unambiguous between the two readings.

6.4.2 Conjunctions: between sentence and discourse

Figure 6.2 summarizes my findings concerning the use of *and*, *but*, and *or* as discourse markers. It suggests that the discourse roles of *and*, *but* and *or* parallel their grammatical roles. The coordinative role of these conjunctions can also be thought of as their function in idea structures, their semantic role as their textual meaning, and their pragmatic role as their interactional effect. These parallels differentiate conjunctive markers from the others considered thus far (*or* and *well*) whose linguistic contribution to their use as markers was minimal. Rather, the linguistic properties of *and*, *but* and *or* interact with the discourse slot(s) in which they occur to produce their discourse functions.

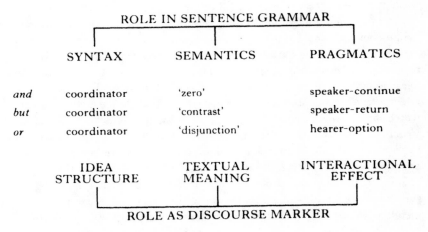

Figure 6.2. *Conjunctions as discourse markers*

7 *So* and *because*: Markers of cause and result

I consider *so* and *because*[1] together because they are complements both structurally (7.1) and semantically (7.2). Like *and*, *but* and *or*, *so* and *because* have grammatical properties which contribute to their discourse use. When *so* and *because* mark idea units, information states, and actions, their functions are straightforward realizations of these properties. But when *so* has a pragmatic use in participation structures, its grammatical properties are less directly realized (7.3).

7.1 Structure: main and subordinate units

So and *because* are grammatical signals of main and subordinate clauses respectively, and this grammatical difference is reflected in their discourse use: *because* is a marker of subordinate idea units, and *so* is a complementary marker of main idea units. Before I show this, however, it is important to define 'subordinate' and 'main' in discourse. Such designations depend on both the functional and referential organization of talk. From a functional perspective, subordinate material is that which has a secondary role in relation to a more encompassing focus of joint attention and activity. From a referential perspective, subordinate material is that which is not as relevant in and of itself, as it is to a more global topic of talk. I also assume that material which is functionally and/or referentially dependent is likely to be structurally dependent on a larger textual unit of talk, and thus, subordinate in this sense.

One reason it is difficult to identify subordinate and dominant units in discourse, however, is that what is subordinate in one particular structure need not be subordinate within another. Within a narrative, for example, the orientation (descriptive background material) is secondary to the complicating action (telling what happened) and it is relevant to the content of that section of the discourse, rather than as a description in and of itself. But identical descriptive content in other discourse contexts need not be subordinate: descriptions can be given as ends unto themselves rather than as preludes to narrative events.

Nor is subordinate material always unimportant in a discourse. Consider (1): the orientation to a story told by Henry about a practical joke played on his brother when the two were young.

(1)   Henry   a.   We went to clean the drain in the sn– in the snowstorm.
                    b.   This was right after the war.
                    c.   **So,** w– we– it was– my feet were wet.
                    d.   We were riding in the truck. In a car.
                    e.   I say, 'Hey Joe.' I said–
                    f.   I took my stockin's off, and my shoes.
                    g.   **So** we get t'29th and Green,
                    h.   we live on 41st and Green,
                    i.   **so** we g– get t'29th and Green.

Orientation material is presented in (a) and (b); after an aborted entry into the complicating action in (c), Henry inserts additional orientation in (c) and (d); (e), (g) and (i) also initiate the complicating action (note the use of the historical present tense as an indicator of narrative events, Schiffrin 1981), but (e) and (g) are again interrupted by orientation in (f) and (h).

Although each piece of embedded orientation is subordinate to the story events, each is important for the interpretation of those events and for the point of the story. Henry reports later that he asked his brother if he would carry him into their house. But we understand the motivation for this (and hence its significance) only because we know that Henry's shoes and socks were off (f) – and this, because his feet had been wet (c). Still later in the story, Henry's brother refuses to carry him, Henry punches him, and then throws him into the snow (see 18). This is significant only because we know that Henry and his brother *live on 41st and Green* (h), and thus, that Henry's brother has to walk twelve blocks home. In (1), then, Henry presents background information about removing his shoes, and his childhood residence, well before that information is actually needed for interpretation of later story events and for the story point. Thus, although the orientation is subordinate to the story events, it is an important prerequisite for understanding those main events, and for understanding the overall point of the story (also see 18).

Let us now consider the structural role of *so* and *because*. I begin with discourse in which there is a fairly clear differentiation of main from subordinate material: explanatory discourse (see Chapter 1). In (2), Zelda uses both *so* and *because* to mark main and subordinate levels of explanatory structure. She is explaining why she and Henry are not going to see their son that evening.

(2)   Zelda: a.   Well we were going up t'see uh. . .my– our son tonight,
                     b.   but we're not
                     c.   **cause** the younger one's gonna come for dinner
                     d.   **cause** he's working in the neighborhood.
                     e.   So that's out.

The event being explained is in (b): *we're not*. The first reason is in (c), and a reason for that reason is in (d). Thus, Zelda uses *cause* to progressively embed reasons in her explanation. What is marked by *so* in (e) is the thwarted plan: *that* refers to the initial plan described in (a). Thus, *so* has the widest possible discourse scope in this example: Zelda returns to the point at which she began her explanation. But note that she could have returned to any of the intermediate levels with *so*:

(2')   a.   Well we were going up t'see uh. . .my– our son tonight,
          b.   but we're not
          c.   **cause** the younger one's gonna come for dinner
          d.   **cause** he's working in the neighborhood.
                          so he's gonna come for dinner.
                     so we're not.
          e.   So that's out.

Zelda does mark intermediate levels of structure with *so* in (3). I have asked Zelda what her grandchildren call Henry.

(3)   a.   Well they– they get a little mixed up right now,
         b.   **so** they– **so** eh: **so** my husband said,
                 'Well call me Henry.'
         c.   And they do!
         d.   And they holler Henry!!!
         e.   **Cause** they really don't know!
         f.   They don't know what a name is!
         g.   A name is a name.
         h.   **So** they really don't know.
         i.   **So** what will happen with that situation, I don't know.

After explaining why her four-year-old grandchildren call Henry by his first name (a–b), and describing their use of his name (c–d), Zelda explains why the name can be used (e–h). Note that although Zelda initiates and closes this explanation with the same idea unit (*they really don't know*), she initiates it with *cause* and closes it with *so*. Use of both *cause* and *so* marks the idea unit, first, as a subordinate reason, and, second, as a main unit in relation to a more embedded reason (g). Zelda next returns to the most superordinate portion of her explanation with *so* in (i): she does not know what will happen with *that situation*. In short, *so* marks two levels of structure in (3).

In (4), Jack uses *so* to return only to an intermediate level of explanatory structure. He is responding to my query about the friendliness of his block:

(4)   a.   Fairly friendly.
         b.   Wouldn't you say?
         c.   We're a little bit prejudiced, I think.
         d.   Ah **because** uh: we've been here so long that
                          we don't even remember the original groups
                          that were here.
         e.   **So** we're bad to judge.
         f.   We're not the one to judge.
         g.   But I would say fairly, fairly friendly.

Jack complies informationally with my query in (a). After checking with Freda in (b), Jack explains the equivocation in his response by stating that he and Freda are prejudiced (c). He then gives a reason for that prejudice (d) and restates the prejudice (e–f): Jack returns to that intermediate level of structure in his answer with *so*. (See (46) in Chapter 6 for discussion of *but* in g.)

Just as *so* can have a narrow or wide scope in explanatory discourse (marking intermediate or higher levels of structure), so too can *because*: *because* can open a slot for one reason (narrow scope, as in 2) or several reasons (wide scope). In (5), for example, Irene is explaining why her neighborhood is agitated at the impending opening of a take-out seafood house (to be managed by Blacks):

(5)   Irene: a.   And the people are all up in: eh: y'know, arms,
                   b.   **because** these guys have applied for a liquor license.
                   c.   And it *is* like a half a block away from the school.
                   d.   And it *will* tend probably t'bring people up into this
                         neighborhood. Y'know.
                   e.   And, y'know, they're afraid.

Because is used only once in Irene's explanation. But once *because* initiates the explanatory unit of 'reason', Irene can use *and* to continue to provide reasons, and to mark them as structural coordinates with each other (see Chapter 6 on *and*). Thus, *because* has a wide scope in (5): it marks Irene's string of reasons as a single subordinate unit in her explanation for her neighbors' agitation (a).

We have seen so far that *so* and *because* can be used at different levels of structure in explanations. The same observations apply to *so* and *because* in narratives. Consider, first, that stories can themselves be subordinated to larger discourse units: stories can be told not just to report a specific experience, but to warrant a general point being made by the speaker. The entry to such a story can be marked with *because*, and the return to the main point marked with *so*. We have seen such a story in Chapter 6 (example 7): in Irene's story about her disappointment with a local politician, she first stated her opinion of the politician, then prefaced a story justifying that opinion with *because*, and then left the story by restating the opinion with *so*.

A similar example is (6). I have asked Henry if he talks to anyone prior to going to a doctor. He answers with a story (not all presented here) about a friend who received medical advice from relatives and neighbors which was superior to that received from a series of medical specialists:

(6)   Henry: Sometimes it works. **Because** there's this guy Louie Gelman, he went to a big specialist. [story] **So** doctors are– well they're not God either!

In short, when stories are told to support opinions, they are subordinate parts of a larger discourse unit.

Consider, next, that information within a story can also be divided into subordinate and main units. The subordination of orienting information (time, place, persons) to narrative events is clearest when such information is embedded within the narrative action. Embedding an orientation with *because* is complementary to returning to the complicating action with *so* (see 1). In (7), Zelda interrupts a story about where she and Henry have lived to provide background information about a landlady:

(7)   a.   We lived there for two weeks without water, or gas.
           b.   We had electricity.
           c.   And it was wonderful that we could wake up in the morning, and play the radio, and do what we want.
           d.   **Because** this landlord–landlady was terrible!
           e.   And then we lived there for five years,
              [continues]

Zelda interrupts her story to explain why a place with severe shortcomings (no water or gas) but freedom to *play the radio* was wonderful. This embedded orientation is prefaced with *because*. *And* then continues Zelda's story about her different homes.

Thus far, I have shown that *because* is a marker of subordination and *so* a marker of main units by focusing on two discourse units (explanations and narratives) within which chunks of information are differentiated. I have suggested that both markers can have narrow or wide scope within these discourse units. Another way of expressing this difference in scope is to say that *so* and *because* can function either locally (narrow scope) or globally (wide scope).

Consider, now, still another indicator of a local structural difference between *because* and *so*: *because* tends to introduce sentence topics which play a subordinate role in the discourse. In order to demonstrate this, I need to first define the two ordering options made available through *so* and *because*. In the first option, a causal antecedent X precedes a consequent Y; I refer to this as *X so Y*. In the second option, a consequent Y precedes an antecedent X; I refer to this as *Y because X*.[2]

I focus on the subjects of three sentences: X, Y, and the NEXT sentence. Compare (8), a sequence in which a NEXT subject (*we*) first appears in X in an *X so Y* sequence:

(8)   (X)   And **we** didn't know what to do!
        (Y)   So **Henry's oldest brother, he** always believed in that.
                  'Let's go to a rabbi.'
        NEXT   But **we** never did get to the rabbi.

to (8'), an ordering reversal of (8) in which the NEXT subject first appears in X in a *Y because X* sequence:

(8')   (Y)   **Henry's oldest brother, he** always believed in that.
                  'Let's go to a rabbi.'
        (X)   Because **we** didn't know what to do!
        NEXT   But **we** never did get to the rabbi.

My expectation is that a subject of X which is continued into a NEXT sentence is more likely to have appeared previously in a position which is not marked as syntactically subordinate (in *X so Y* as in (8)) than in a position which is marked as syntactically subordinate (in *Y because X* as in 8').

Table 7.1 confirms this expectation: when the subject of X is continued after a causal sequence, it is more likely to be a subject which previously appeared in X in an *X so Y* sequence, than in X in a *Y because X* sequence. In sum, subjects in X in *Y because X* sequences are more likely to have short discourse lives than subjects presented in X in *X so Y* sequences. I interpret this as a reflection of their referential subordination in discourse, and therefore, as an indirect reflection of *because* as a marker of local subordination.

We have seen thus far that *because* is a marker of a subordinate discourse unit, and *so* is a marker of a main unit. But because discourse is an ongoing, joint construction of multiple structures (Chapter 1), units of talk may be

Table 7.1. *Subject continuity and previous subordination*

	X so Y	*Y because X*	Total
Subject of X is continued	24 (50%)	12 (20%)	36
Subject of X is not continued	24	48	72
Total	48	60	108

defined as subordinate or main in more than one structure at once. What this means is that what is subordinate in one structure may or may not be subordinate in another.

First, let us focus on structures in which more than one subordinate unit converges: answers to questions whose idea structure consists of an explanation. The parts of such answers which are functionally subordinate in the question/answer structure often coincide with ideationally subordinate parts of an explanation. In (9), for example, I have asked Jack with whom from his neighborhood he and Freda go out.

(9)   Jack: a.   Well d– we didn't go out with too many from this block, did we.
       b.   Bowman:, who else.
       c.   Not too many.
       d.   **Because** we got too many of our old friends, y'know, that uh. . .
       e.   These are just neighbors, we see them everyday.

I have requested information about Jack's neighbors, and this initial information (a–c) is the main portion (the ideational core) of his answer. After explaining his answer (d), Jack refocuses it on the neighbors (e). *Because* in (d) thus prefaces the subordinate unit of the answer and of the explanation.

In (10), both *because* and *so* are used to mark convergent portions of an explanation and an answer. I have asked Zelda with whom she shops.

(10)   Zelda: a.   She [= Irene] goes with me a lot,
        b.   **cause** she has more patience. . .with my daughter than I do.
        c.   **So**, sometimes we go shopping together with my daughter.

The information in Zelda's answer is that she shops with Irene (a) and her daughter (c). Zelda also explains why she goes with Irene (b), prefacing that subordinate information with *because*. She closes her answer by repeating its main information with *so* (c).

Or reconsider Zelda's explanation about her grandchildren's naming practices (3). This explanation was given in response to my question to Zelda about what her grandchildren call Henry.

(3)	a.	Well they– they get a little mixed up right now,
	b.	so they– so eh: so my husband said, 'Well call me Henry.'
	c.	And they do!
	d.	And they holler Henry!!!
	e.	**Cause** they really don't know!
	f.	They don't know what a name is!
	g.	A name is a name.
	h.	**So** they really don't know.
	i.	**So** what will happen with that situation, I don't know.

Zelda returns to an intermediate point with *so* in (h) and to the main portion of her discourse with *so* (i). Since Zelda is answering my question about terms of address, her return to this topic (*what will happen with that situation, I don't know* in i) is not only the closing part of her explanation but also the main informational portion of her answer.

Let us consider the second possibility: what is defined as subordinate in one discourse structure may not be subordinate in another. (11) illustrates how a reason in an explanation (subordinate) can be a jointly endorsed discourse topic (main). In (11), Zelda is describing a recent day on the beach with her grandchildren. She reports that her daughter-in-law took the children off the beach for their nap early in the afternoon.

(11)	Zelda:	a.	And then she took 'em off for their nap.
		b.	Which I was just as glad,
		c.	**cause** it's quite strenuous!
		d.	Y'know?hhhhhh
	Debby:		I'm sure it is!
	Zelda:	e.	I wen– I ran t'get them the wa:ter, and the buckets, and washed their hands, and then washed their feet to put the sneaks on!
		f.	It's a lot of work!
		g.	And it was really hot and humid that one Saturday.
		h.	Sweat was just pouring down my m–
		i.	boy was I glad theyhhhwent off at one thirty!

Zelda offers a reason for (b) *I was just as glad* in (c): *cause it's quite strenuous*. With *y'know* in (d), Zelda proposes (c) as a joint topic of attention (see Chapter 9); my response (*I'm sure it is!*) endorses that proposal. It is at this point that Zelda's subordinate reason gains a second definition as a main discourse topic. Zelda then specifies what made her day strenuous (e–g) and intensifies her description of the difficulty (h). Both the specifications and the intensification are relevant to the *strenuous day*; thus, they are themselves subordinate to the main discourse topic opened in (c).

Zelda then restates in (i) the idea which prompted her explanation:

(11)   a.   And then she took 'em off for their nap.
        b.   Which I was just as glad,
        c.   **cause** it's quite strenuous!
                [description of strenuous day]
        i.   boy was I glad theyhhhwent off at one thirty!

Was I glad repeats (b); *they went off at one thirty!* paraphrases (a). In short, (i) repeats the outcome of the *strenuous day* (described in c–h). Thus, (i) closes Zelda's description of her strenuous day by defining that description as something which is not only the main (albeit temporary) conversational topic, but a subordinate unit in an explanation.

Question/answer pairs demonstrate how a single utterance may be subordinate within one discourse structure, but not in another. (12) shows that the main portion of an answer may be marked with *so* even when it is not the main portion of an explanation.

(12)   Sally: You said your teachers were old fashioned. Did they
                            ever hit kids, or:
        Irene: a.   Yeh. I had one teacher, her name was Frank,
                  b.   we used t'call her Frankenstein.
                  c.   **So**, yeh, she would hit kids with a ruler.

Irene first answers Sally's yes–no question (a) and then diverts for a moment to mention the teacher's nickname. Although her tangent in (b) is certainly a subordinate part of her answer, this tangent is not a subordinate part of an explanation: not only can it not be prefaced with *because*, but we do not understand that the teacher's name was 'Frank' because the students used to call her 'Frankenstein'. Irene then returns to her answer – even restating *yes* and expanding her reply – with *so*. Although this is the main portion of her answer, the teacher's corporeal methods of punishment are not semantically understood as a result (either fact-based, inference-based, or action-based; see 7.2) of her nickname. Thus, *so* marks the main portion of the answer – but not of an explanation. (I consider further pragmatic uses of *so* in 7.3.)

The use of *because* in interpersonal arguments – disputes – shows more strikingly how information which is marked as ideationally subordinate (as

a reason) can have a central interactional role (as a challenge). In (13),
Irene and Henry are arguing about parental response to intermarriage.
Henry is defending an Orthodox Jewish practice in which parents ritually
mourn for a child who marries a Gentile as if that child had died. Irene
challenges him.

(13)   Irene: a.   They are the only ones that are losing out.
                  b.   They'll cover a mirror, throw the pictures outa the
                        house, do all–   .
                  c.   *That's* asinine, Henry.
        Henry: d.   **Because** you don't understand,
                  e.   see, **because** ith– it was $\begin{bmatrix} \text{done that way–=} \\ \textit{I don't understand WHAT?} \end{bmatrix}$
        Irene: f.
        Henry: g.   =*You* don't understand *why* it was done that way.

After Irene disputes the wisdom of the Orthodox practice (a–c), Henry
challenges Irene by implicating that her opinion is due to her lack of understanding (d–g). Defining Irene's disputation as the result of her lack of understanding protects the validity of Henry's own belief in the wisdom of the
practice: it moves the disputation from the realm of factual disagreement to
a realm of speaker understanding, thus shifting the blame from the Orthodox practice itself to Irene's knowledge of the practice. *Because* thus
figures centrally in the strategy underlying Henry's challenge – even
though it marks information which is ideationally subordinate.

   (14) illustrates how a reason can move into a still more prominent role in
an argument to figure not only in a challenge, but to be the actual focus of
dispute. Henry and Irene are arguing about women working outside the
home. Irene's position is that women should work (for a variety of reasons
including self-fulfillment), but Henry thinks that family responsibilities
(especially children) should preclude outside work. Irene describes her
own situation as a way of showing that family and work can be combined.

(14)   Irene: a.   But I could never go back to the point wh– where I
                        didn't work.
                  b.   Give it up now that I have been exposed to it for a year
                        and a half, and feel=
        Henry: c.   **Because** the– the
        Irene: d. $\begin{bmatrix} =\text{being home} \\ =\text{goodies are there!} \end{bmatrix}$ and just
        Henry: e.   **Because** the goodies
                        are $\begin{bmatrix} \text{there!} & \text{But if=} \\ \text{Money– Not so much the goodies y–} \end{bmatrix}$
        Irene: f.
        Henry: g.   =Ken made a livin', d'you think it would be *right* for
                        you to work?
                  h.   Would you– would your fam–$\begin{bmatrix} \text{NO. } \textit{Absolutely not.} \\ \text{YES. Y'know why?} \end{bmatrix}$
        Irene: i.

	j.	**Because I** $\begin{bmatrix} \text{don't think a woman today} \\ \text{I'm dea– dead against it.} \end{bmatrix}$ is content=
Henry:	k.	
Irene:		=to be the stagnant housewife of cooking, and cleaning, and you feel like your brain, is– gets to a point, and it stops.

In (14), Henry begins by proposing a financial explanation for why Irene likes to work (c, e). Irene begins to dispute this explanation (f), thus elevating the status of an ideationally subordinate part of the argument into a main conversational topic. As Henry attempts to return the argument to its initial point of disputation – it is wrong for women to work (g–h) – Irene incorporates her disputation from (f) into a challenge to Henry's just-stated position:

(14)	Irene:	i.	YES. Y'know why?
		j.	**Because** I don't think a woman today is content=
	Henry:	k.	I'm dea– dead against it.
	Irene:		=to be the stagnant housewife of cooking, and cleaning, and you feel like your brain, is– gets to point, and it stops.

In other words, Irene works because she is not content to be a housewife – not *because the goodies are there* – and this is a valid reason even without financial need. Irene's explanation in (j) thus refutes Henry's *because the goodies are there*, at the same time that it defends her own position about women's right to work. In sum, although Irene is not successful in convincing Henry of her main position, she is successful in elevating the status of 'women's reason for work' to the main point of contention – for it is this to which Henry next responds:

(14)	Henry:	Then have more babies. That'll keep you busy.

Irene then challenges this response and the argument continues.

In this section, I have shown that *because* marks subordinate idea units, and that *so* marks main units of discourse, at both local and global levels. Thus, *so* and *because* mark transitions between main and subordinate levels of structure in discourse. Because discourse is multi-structured, however, what is marked as subordinate in one structure need not be subordinate in another.

7.2 'Cause' and 'result' in discourse

Because and *so* have semantic meanings which are realized at both sentence and discourse levels: *because* conveys a meaning of 'cause', and *so* conveys a meaning of 'result'. These meanings appear on three planes of discourse: ideational structure, information state, and actions; I will speak of them in different terms depending upon on which plane of talk I focus.[3] Figure 7.1 shows which terms will be associated with each plane. A **fact-based** causal relation between **cause** and **result** holds between idea units, more precisely, between the events, states, and so on, which they encode. A **knowledge-based** causal relation holds when a speaker uses some piece(s) of information as a warrant for an **inference** (a speaker-inference), or when a speaker intends a hearer to do so (a hearer-inference). An **action-based** causal relation holds when a speaker presents a motive for an action being performed through talk – either his/her own action or an interlocutor's action.

Figure 7.1. *Semantic realization of* so *and* because *in discourse*

	Discourse plane		
	Ideational structure fact-based	Information state knowledge-based	Action structure action-based
because	'cause'	'warrant'	'motive'
so	'result'	'inference'	'action'

(15a–c) illustrate the differences among these relations (cf. van Dijk 1977a: 68–76).

(15) a.   John is home because he is sick.
      b.   John is home because the lights are burning.
      c.   Is John home? Because the lights are burning.

In (15a), the event 'John is home' is a result of the event 'John is sick'. In (15b), however, 'John is home' is a conclusion inferred by the speaker on the basis of evidence – the burning lights. 'John is home' in (15b) can also be considered the final step of an underlying syllogism:

(16) a.   If John's lights are burning, John is home.
      b.   John's lights are burning.
      c.   So/therefore, John is home.

(15a), however, would not be the result of a syllogism. Not only do different concepts of causation underlie (15a) and (b), but so, too, do different states of affairs: only the fact-based causal relation (of 15a) assumes a change of state over time (von Glaserfeld 1974). And in (15c), the speaker is questioning the proposition 'John is home', i.e. requesting information about its truth. Neither a syllogism, nor a change of state over time, is assumed in (15c); rather, the *because* clause gives the motive for the request. (But see discussion in 7.2.4.)

I turn now to the use of *so* and *because* to mark fact-based (7.2.1), knowledge-based (7.2.2) and action-based (7.2.3) causal relations in my corpus. Although I begin with examples in which only'one causal relation is marked, I end with examples in which more than one relation is simultaneously marked (7.2.4).

7.2.1 'Cause' and 'result' in idea structures

Because and *so* can mark fact-based cause and result relations at both local and global levels of discourse. (17) illustrates *so* at both levels. Zelda is explaining why her daughter-in-law stopped work: she had been verbally abused and frightened by a group of teenagers she had been counselling. (17) follows a narrative (not included).

(17) a.   **So**, my son wouldn't let her go back there anymore.
      b.   And she tried to get other jobs and she couldn't.
      c.   **So** what she did, she got a job as a uh bookkeeper in an office.

The event in (a) resulted from the prior story events: thus, *so* functions globally over a wide range of talk. The daughter-in-law's work as a bookkeeper (c) was a result of her inability to find *other jobs* (which she had been trained for). This too is a fact-based relation, but since only one event is being causally related to (c), *so* is here functioning locally.

Another local fact-based use of *so* is in resolutions for narratives. (18) is the last part of a story told by Henry (discussed as (1) also): the story reports a practical joke which he played on his brother when the two were younger. The concluding events in Henry's story are his reaction to his brother's refusal to carry him in the snow. The final event within this conclusion is when Henry punches his brother in the nose:

(18) n.   I said, 'When we get home, Joe,' I says, 'you'll carry me in the house!'
      o.   I say, 'I ain't got no shoe:s, or no stockin's on.'
      p.   He said, 'Carry yourself in the house! I ain't carryin' y'in!'
      q.   **So** I went BOOM!

Although one might argue that a resolution is the result of an entire complicating action – not just the prior event – in (18) this does not seem to be the
case: the event in (p) is clearly the immediate provocation for the event in
(q).

Let us contrast *so* in Henry's coda from the same narrative. After reporting further actions – Henry throws his brother into the snow – Henry evaluates the narrative events through a coda:

(18)   w.   **So**, he laughed about it for years,
         x.   he says it was worth it!

Henry's coda draws the story to a close by relating all of the past story
events to the present. The coda also evaluates the entire experience as
funny (and as something which his brother did not regret). Because the
coda reports the brother's laughter as a reaction to the entire experience, *so*
has a global function here.

Many of my examples in (7.1) also illustrate a fact-based relation marked
by *so* and *because*. Reconsider (2).

(2)   Zelda: a.   Well we were going up t'see uh. . .my– our son tonight,
                     b.   but we're not
                     c.   **cause** the younger one's gonna come for dinner
                     d.   **cause** he's working in the neighborhood.
                     e.   **So** that's out.

Zelda's reason in (c) is a fact-based cause of the changed plan (b); the same
relation holds between (d) and (c). Similarly, Zelda's summary of the
changed plans (e) is a fact-based result of the just-reported reasons (c, d).

7.2.2 'Warrant' and 'inference' in information states

Like the cause/result relation, the warrant/inference relation also concerns
idea units. However, what is marked by *because* and *so* is not a relationship
between ideas *per se*, but the use (by either the speaker or the hearer) of
idea units as a basis for additional knowledge. Because speaker/hearer
knowledge is involved, the warrant/inference relation concerns the plane of
discourse I have called 'information state' (Chapter 1).

Consider, first, that speakers do not come into a conversation with a full
supply of knowledge and meta-knowledge about shared information:
rather, information states evolve as different domains of knowledge
become relevant to current topics, and as listener reactions display the current status of a particular piece of information. In other words, even

though speakers may enter a conversation with initial **assumptions** about what information is shared, their knowledge and meta-knowledge about what information is **actually** shared continually evolves throughout a conversation.

Now suppose a speaker wants a hearer to be able to draw upon a particular piece of information as a background aid to interpretation of what else is said. If a speaker assumes a hearer shares knowledge of that information, and is correct in that assumption, then that information does not have to be explicitly presented whenever it is relevant to interpretation of adjacent discourse. But if a speaker cannot assume such knowledge, then that information may have to be explicitly presented whenever it is relevant for adjacent interpretations – even if it is intended for use only as background material for more topical talk.

I suggest that background knowledge be considered 'warrants', and interpretations which use background knowledge 'inferences'.[4] Let us briefly reconsider an earlier example of the 'warrant' and 'inference' relationship: a syllogistic argument.

(16)   a.   If John's lights are burning, John is home.
        b.   John's lights are burning.
        c.   So/therefore, John is home.

I consider (16a) and (b) as background information which warrants the deductive inference in (c); without such information, the event 'John is home' might very well correspond to fact (and thus be true), but it would not have been openly warranted by the presentation of background evidence. Thus, the deductive inference in (c) is an interpretation warranted by the background knowledge of (a) and (b).

Once we consider background knowledge as 'warrants', and interpretations which use background knowledge as 'inferences', we can see that the warrant/inference relation creates two shifts in information state. The first is when a warrant is presented, i.e. when unshared background information becomes shared. This is when *because* may be used: *because* prefaces unshared information when the speaker intends the hearer to use that information as background knowledge for the interpretation of more topical talk. The second information state transition is when newly shared information is used as a basis for interpretation of topical talk; this is when *so* may be used. *So* thus prefaces a change not in knowledge, but in meta-knowledge (since an inference which has just been openly warranted is one to whose knowledge both speaker and hearer can attest).

One location in which warrants and inferences create information state transitions is when narratives are used as evidence for general conclusions. In an earlier sequence (6), for example, Henry warrants his conclusion that 'doctors are not God' with a story about a neighbor who was wrongly diagnosed by three physicians but correctly diagnosed by a next-door neighbor:

(6)   Henry: Sometimes it works. **Because** there's this guy Louie Gelman,
                       he went to a big specialist. [story] He said it would've been a
                       little bit more, he would've strangled to death! **So** doctors are—
                       well they're not God either!

(19) is similar. Zelda has just completed a story about her adult son's reunion with childhood friends.

(19)   Zelda: And she says, 'We have lots of room,' she said, 'even for—' Gary
                       has a big dog, she said, 'even for the dog!' **So**, it's really nice
                       eh: y'know t'renew friendship.

In both (18) and (19), the story events (not all included here) do not factually cause the states reported at the story's end; rather, they are specific events which serve as background evidence to warrant speakers' general conclusions.

   Another example of a warrant/inference relationship is (20). Freda is describing the efforts of her new neighbors at housekeeping.

(20)   Freda: a.   I don't even know them t'talk to them.
                       b.   And they scrub.
                       c.   I mean they're scrubbin', and rubbin', and polishin'. . .
                       d.   **so** that they really mean business.

The activities Freda describes in (b) and (c) do not cause the neighbors to *mean business* (d). Rather, they list specific activities which warrant Freda's generalization about her neighbors.

   In each of the examples thus far, the background information was conveyed in an entire discourse unit: both Henry's and Zelda's conclusions are warranted by stories, Freda's conclusion is warranted by a list of events. In addition, what is warranted is a single idea unit: Henry's conclusion about doctors, Zelda's conclusion about childhood friendships, Freda's conclusion about her neighbor's intensity.

   The next example illustrates that both warrants and inferences can be conveyed as single idea units. (21) is an extract from Zelda's story about her day on the beach with her twin grandsons. Zelda states that she gave her twin grandsons toy buckets of the same size.

(21)   Zelda: a.   So I figured, 'Well, I'll give them both the same size.
                       b.   **Cause**, y'know, one looks at the other.
                       c.   And eh: my s— started t'cry.

Zelda cannot assume that I shared knowledge about sibling rivalry between twins: thus, she interrupts her narrative to provide this background information. (Note that this newly shared information is prefaced with *y'know* (see Chapter 9).) In (21), then, the provision of background information in a single idea unit allows remedial interpretation of a prior idea: it retrospectively alters the information state.

In sum, *because* can be used to preface information when the status of that information as shared background knowledge is uncertain and when that information is important for understanding adjacent talk. This use marks an information state transition because it is a shift from unshared to shared knowledge. And *so* can be used to preface information whose understanding is supplemented by information which has just become shared background. This, too, marks an information state transition because it is a shift in meta-knowledge: an inference which has just been openly warranted is one with a different degree of speaker/hearer meta-knowledge than one which is only implicitly warranted.

7.2.3 'Motive' and 'action' in discourse

I turn now to the third plane of discourse on which causal relations are realized: **motive** and **action**. I illustrate three action/motive pairs: request and account, compliance and justification, claim and grounds.

The first set of examples show *because* prefacing accounts for requests (22)–(24) and then *so* prefacing a request which has just been accounted for (25). In (22), Irene echoes Zelda's appeal to Henry to stay on the topic.

(22)   Zelda: Hen, we're off the subject.
         Irene: Yeh, let's get back, **because** she'll never get home.

Irene accounts for her request by saying that if it is not complied with, I will *never get home*. In (23), Zelda is indirectly requesting that I continue with some of my interview questions – even though Irene has just left for a few minutes.

(23)   Zelda: Can you work any of this with just the two of us, or y'have
                    t'wait for Irene.
                    Cause I don't know how long she'll be.

Zelda's request is accounted for by her uncertainty about the length of Irene's absense. In (24), Freda requests clarification following a question that I have asked about who she and Jack go out with:

(24)   Freda: D'you mean 'did' or 'do'. **Cause** we don't go out with anybody
                   much anymore.

Her request is motivated by her realization that the question cannot be
answered if I mean *do*.

Next, in (25), *so* prefaces a request which has just been accounted for by
prior talk. Henry and Irene have been arguing about the ability of a current
Presidential candidate to capture the Catholic vote. Irene mentions that
her Catholic neighbor Al does not plan to vote for the candidate.

(25)   Irene: a.   And if he doesn't get the Catholic vote, that he can't
                         become President.
        Henry: b.   He'll *get* the Catholic vote.
        Irene: c.   *This guy says* NO.
                   d.   You take somebody like Al says, I– he don't know
                         anything about him.
                   e.   Why should he vote for him?
        Zelda: f.   He'll–
        Irene: g.   *There are a lot of people that* [*feel that way*=
        Zelda: h.   [Wait a minute=
        Irene: [=*Henry!*
        Zelda: [=**so** who] would Al vote for?

Irene supports her position that Catholics will not vote for the candidate by
describing her Catholic neighbor's reaction to the candidate (d, e) and then
generalizing from her example (g). Zelda (in h) then wants to know who Al
would vote for; her request for this information is motivated by Irene's description of Al's indecision.

Consider, now, that compliance with a request can also be motivated:
speakers can justify their particular way of agreeing to do what has been
requested. Prior to (26), for example, I had requested that Henry and
Zelda draw the boundaries of their neighborhood on a map. Zelda justifies
the way she and Henry comply with my request:

(26)   Henry: Right in here, isn't it?
        Zelda: Yeah. Right where I drew the circle. **Cause** that's down the
                   hill, all this.

Note, also, that since questions are requests for information, the provision
of that information in an answer is another level of compliance with a
request. Thus, in (26), Zelda is actually justifying **two** actions: her drawing on the map, and her answer to Henry's question about the accuracy of
his sketch. (27) also illustrates the compliance/justification pair:

(27)   Debby: What was your father's job?
         Zelda: Eh:......Well, I'm gonna say my uncle. **Cause** that's who
                   I was raised by.

Zelda justifies her answer (which provides information about her uncle) to
my question (which requested information about her father).

Still another motive/action pair in which *because* and *so* are used is claim
and grounds. A **claim** is a speaker's effort to maintain access to valued
goods that have been contested in some way; by goods, I include not only
information (the domain of verbal claims) but rights, privileges, and pos-
sessions.[5] **Grounds** are whatever a speaker uses to insure access to such
goods. Verbal grounds (what Toulmin 1958 calls backing) are either
specific or general: they may be either specific events drawn from the
speaker's biography which instantiate the claim, or generalizations which
validate the claim by showing it to be part of a wider truth. (See Chapter 1,
1.4 on argument.)

An example of the claim/grounds relationship is (28). Irene is claiming
that Jews are not taught to be as prejudiced as are Gentiles. She grounds
this claim by instantiating it: a Gentile neighbor has told her stories of her
own anti-Semitic upbringing.

(28)   Irene: a.   I don't feel that the Jewish people were– were taught,
                         like you said, to *hate*, as strongly as the Catholic people
                         were, taught, in their church.
                   b.   **Cause** my neighbor we've discussed it many times.

Henry and Zelda then argue that Protestants were as anti-Semitic as Catholics (not included in (28)), but this does not affect Irene's claim because
she has no knowledge of Protestants, and thus, no grounds by which to re-
assess her claim.

         Irene: j.   I don't know any of them.
                   k.   But I know like my one friend– like Rita said,
                   l.   years ago, they were forbidden t'come up the hill!

(The use of *I know* reveals that the grounds in (k) are simultaneously a warrant for an inference; see 7.2.4.)

In sum, *because* can mark the motive for an action, and *so* can mark an
action which has just been motivated: request and account, compliance
and justification, claim and grounds.

7.2.4 *Facts, inferences, and actions*

I have suggested thus far that *because* and *so* mark not only the idea structures of texts, but the relationships between ideas and speaker/hearer
inferences based on those ideas, as well as the relationships between
speakers' stated motives and actions. But as I stated in Chapter 1, discourse
is coherent not only because of relationships between the ideas that are conveyed, and because of how speakers use knowledge to draw inferences, and
because of the actions they perform – although each one of these certainly
makes a contribution. Rather, discourse is coherent because of systematic
relationships among different components of talk – such as idea structures,
information states, and action structures.

Given this integrative view of discourse, it should not be surprising to
find that a causal relationship may be realized on more than one plane of
talk at once. Let me return to my initial examples: although I have suggested that (15a) and (15b) invoke only one reading each, both statements do
allow either reading in an appropriate context. If we imagine (15a) in the
context of (29a), its fact-based reading is replaced by (or, more weakly,
supplemented by) a knowledge-based reading:

(29a)   A: Where's John today?
         B: I don't think he was feeling well yesterday.
         A: Maybe John is home because he is sick.

In (29a), 'John is home' is a conclusion inferred by A based on A's use of B's
information that 'John is sick' – whether or not it is a factually based cause/
result relation. (Thus, we might find probability markers (*maybe, must*)
here.) And if we imagine (15b) in the context of (29b), its inferential reading is replaced by a fact-based reading:

(29b)   A: Where's John today?
         B: John likes to leave the lights burning in his house. But there's a
                  problem with his electric system and he's afraid the lights will
                  short circuit and start a fire. So he called the electrician, but
                  now he has to wait at home to let him in. So, John is home
                  because his lights are burning.

In (29b), we could infer that 'John is home' is a factual result of the burning
lights – not a speaker's warranted inference about John's location.

Consider further that both (15a) and (15b) can be considered as claims
(suppose two people are arguing about whether John is at home or at
work). In such cases, 'he is sick' and 'his lights are burning' are motives
(grounds) for the claim.

Similarly, the question/answer pair from (15c) can be seen as knowledge-based and fact-based:

(15)   c.   Is John home? Because the lights are burning.

Although *Is John home?* is a request for information which is motivated by the observation of John's lights, *his lights are burning* is also a background warrant from which the speaker infers the possibility of John's being home (cf. the syllogism in 16). And, finally, a factual 'cause' and 'result' relation can be shown: the context suggested in (29b) could lead to the questioned proposition in (15c).

The same multiple realizations of fact-based, knowledge-based, and action-based relations is possible when the propositional order of our examples is reversed and the connective is *so*.[6]

(30)   a.   John is sick, so he is home.
        b.   John's lights are burning, so he is home.
        c.   John's lights are burning. So is he home?

It is also important to note that multiple readings are possible even when no causal conjunction is present to link two clauses. Compare (31a) to (31b–c):

(31)   a.   Rain wet the terrace.
        b.   The terrace is wet because it rained.
        c.   It rained, so the terrace is wet.

Certain verbs invoke vague readings: Cattell (1978) discusses the relationship between *why* questions and verbs of volunteered stance, such that the question *why do the police believe Sue killed Harry?* has a dual reading, but substituting response stance verbs, e.g. *admit*, or non-stance verbs, e.g. *mention*, produces only one reading. (Compare *The police believed/ admitted Sue killed Harry because he had a large life insurance policy*.)

What I am suggesting, then, is that the multiple realization of 'cause' and 'result' relations is not a product of *because* or *so*. Rather, it is due to our understandings of causality. Although full consideration of how causal relations are actually worked out (either in scientific or everyday reasoning) is not important for discussion of causal connectives, it does seem that most conclusions which we draw about cause and effect are not based on observations which empirically warrant them: events are not usually observed both before and after a stimulus, as well as compared to a control event to which the stimulus has not applied. Rather, most conclusions are based on our interpretations of causal relations according to our own (culturally relative) schemata for making such interpretations. Since we assume that others are following parallel procedures – basing their inferences on their own schemata – we interpret many statements from others as conclusions warranted by the speaker's own perspective.

Consider, now, how multiple relations are realized at a discourse level – and thus how *so* and *because* mark relations between 'cause' and 'result', 'warrant' and 'inference', and 'motive' and 'action' simultaneously.

(32) shows the marking of factual and inferential relations by *because*. Irene is describing how confused personal relationships can become when one's family, friends, and co-workers are all acquainted.

(32)   Irene: a.   Well I think a lot of the confusion, happened really,
                 b.   **because** of the family relationship.
                 c.   **Because** the– the– there were friends that went with
                      them, that remained friends with.
                 d.   It's very hard t'remain friends with both sides.
                 e.   **Cause** you're afraid t'say something, or this or that.

There are three causal pairs in (32): *a because b*, *ab because c*, and *d because e*. But both cause/result and warrant/inference readings are possible in each pair. For example, (b) can be interpreted as the cause of the confusion reported in (a) and as the evidence which warrants Irene's opinion about the confusion. The same duality is possible for (ab) and (c): (c) is the cause of the difficult situation reported in (ab) and the evidence which allows Irene to conclude that such a situation exists. Thus, both factual and inferential relationships hold.

(33) shows the marking of factual and inferential relations by *so*. Zelda has been telling me about her teenage daughter JoAnn's growing independence: JoAnn is spending her first summer away from home.

(33)   Zelda: a.   She just got a job:
                 b.   Oh I didn't tell you!
        Debby: c.   Oh no!
        Zelda: d.   She got– she– she had applied eh: for a job at uh the
                      drugstore, as a counter girl?
                 e.   Y'know luncheonette? As a waitress?
                 f.   And they called her Sunday.
                 g.   **So** she's workin',   she's been working, =
        Debby: h.   Oh great!
        Zelda: i.   = and she says, 'I'm so tired!'

As Zelda begins a story about how JoAnn's new job is making her too tired for evenings with her friends, she realizes that I know nothing about JoAnn's new job (note Zelda's *oh* and my *oh*; see Chapter 4). In (d), Zelda thus provides background information about JoAnn's job: note how she checks my receipt of this information with rising terminal intonation (and *y'know*; see Chapter 9). After Zelda completes her background description, she returns to the main story with *so*. *So* thus marks not only an information state transition, but a fact-based result: *she's workin'* is a factual result of *they called her Sunday*.

The next example shows all three realizations: fact-based, knowledge-based, and action-based. Henry is stating that the Jewish people are generous:

(34)   Henry: a.   We *give*.
                  b.   **Cause** it's in the Bible t'give.
                  c.   It's in our Bible t'give.
                  d.   My mother had a nickel in the house,
                  e.   she used t'give a beggar two cents!
                  f.   And this is no lie!
                  g.   I seen it myself.
                  h.   I saw it with my own eyes.

We give (a) has both a factual and inferential role. Henry first mentions the factual cause of generosity: religious doctrine (b–c). He then reports a specific event which warrants his more general conclusion about generosity: he himself has seen his mother share her money with those less fortunate (d–h). *We give* is also a claim about Henry's own generosity which is grounded through an instantiation (*my mother had a nickel*). Thus, the utterance *we give* (a) is not inherently defined either as a result of the causes in (b–c), or as a conclusion warranted by the evidence in (d–h), or as a claim grounded by an instantiation (d–h). Rather, it gains these roles through its relations with upcoming utterances.

We give also figures in a grounds/claim relationship at a larger scale: it grounds Henry's claim that he is not bigoted.[7] Just prior to (34), Henry had been talking about how his two sons, who had both married within their religion, were pleased that their father (Henry) had forbidden them to do otherwise. This description leads to the following claim and grounds.

(34')   a.   Now *that* doesn't mean I *hate*.
         b.   **Because** the Jewish people are the most liberal minded people in the *world*.
         c.   There ain't nobody more compassionate, and more generous, and more eh–
         d.   we give more money– we give more money for donations, than any other nationality in the world!
         e.   D'you know that?

> f.   We're very compatible– we're compassionate people.
> g.   we *give*.

Henry's claim is that he is not bigoted (a). He grounds this claim through a generalization – the general generosity of the Jews (b–g). *We give* (in g) is part of the generalization. Thus, *we give* has multiple functions in Henry's argument: it is a motivated claim, a factual result, and a warranted conclusion, as well as grounds for the larger claim that Henry is not bigoted.

(35) is another example of a grounds/claim relationship in which fact-based and knowledge-based relations are also realized. Zelda has stated that she is strict with her children, but Irene playfully contests Zelda's efforts at discipline by citing her liberalness toward her daughter. Zelda claims that she was strict with her two older sons, but that her daughter does not require discipline.

(35)   Zelda: a.   We *did* have it with the boys,
                  b.   uh: they weren't– they– y– when they first started
                        t'drive, they *did* have t'be in by twelve,
                  c.   **because** they had a learner's permit.
                  d.   We always did tell the boys . . .
                  e.   I always stressed that
                  f.   **because** I went through more with the boys than I did
                        with JoAnn.

Zelda's claim is that she was strict with her sons. She first presents this claim in (a): note *did* as a marker of its contested status. She grounds this claim with an example and an embedded reason (b–c). Zelda then makes the claim again (d–e). This time she provides the fact-based reason for its content: the boys required discipline (f).

(36) shows how simultaneous causal relations may be interactionally emergent. Irene and Zelda are arguing about the problems of adolescence. Irene claims that teenagers will have fewer sexual problems than she did:

(36)   Irene: a.   But eh I mean, I feel like, even with the sexual . . .
                        situation,
                  b.   I don't feel that tha– *I* had hangups when I got married.
                  c.   My neighbor, we've discussed it ⌈ many times. ⌉
         Zelda: d.   ⌊ They'll have ⌋
                        them too!
         Irene: e.   They won't have em' as much.
         Zelda: f.   ⌈ Maybe not as much but they will have– ⌉   *But* =
         Irene: g.   ⌊ **Because** they'll be more aware of things ⌋
         Zelda: h.   = *they will have some!*

Irene's claim (a–b) is grounded with a personal experience (c) but then interrupted by Zelda (d). After modifying her claim (e), Irene backs it with a reason: *because they'll be more aware of things* (g). Irene's reason works as a defense in her argument because it shows that her claim is motivated – that her conclusion is warranted. Thus, the reason is a background warrant for the main conclusion of Irene's argument.

It is important to note that the multiple realization of fact-based, knowledge-based and action-based causal relations is not limited to claims and grounds. (37) illustrates this overlap as a speaker justifies compliance with a request. Prior to (37), I had asked Irene which relative she sees most often. She answers that although she sees her mother very often, she cannot really say that she sees her **more** than her mother-in-law.

(37)   Irene: a.   I can't say really that I visit my mother anymore than
                               my mother in law,
                 b.   **cause** they live in the same apartment house.

The clause in (b) justifies Irene's response as a compliance with my request (action-based), provides a reason for why Irene visits both relatives equally frequently (fact-based), and warrants Irene's conclusion that she sees neither relative more frequently (knowledge-based).

Finally, let us consider how knowledge-based relations may actually figure in the definition of actions. I illustrate with requests for confirmation. We have already seen that newly shared information may serve hearer's needs: a speaker may present background information so that a hearer can use that information as warrants for further inferences (7.2.2). Consider, now, that material not intended to be used as a basis for hearers' inferences may be so used. In (38), for example, Zelda has been telling me where her relatives live.

(38)   Zelda: They live in the Northeast.
            Debby: Oh okay. **So** you have a lot of family up in the Northeast.

After Zelda reports that her cousins *live in the Northeast*, I mark my receipt of that information (with *oh*, see Chapter 4) and then state my inference that that is where many of her relatives live.

It is the fact that my inference is drawn from what Zelda has said which creates a request for confirmation.[8] By marking a response as an inference warranted by one's interlocutor, a respondent assigns to the initial speaker partial responsibility for the accuracy of his/her own inference. However, the division of responsibility for interpretation does not then end: such requests return the floor to the speaker who first warranted the inference – so that the inference may be confirmed. In (38), for example, Zelda con-

tinues with *right* and then a description of all her relatives who live in the
Northeast. In short, responsibility for the **next** move is shifted back to the
one who provided the initial warrant.

   The division of responsibility created by a joint warrant/inference pair
often buttresses challenges in interpersonal arguments. Prior to (39), for
example, Freda and Jack have been arguing about the merit of the all girls'
high school attended by Freda (and myself). Freda has argued that there is
less competition in such schools; hence, girls are better educated. But she
then describes what happens when her school hosted male visitors:

(39)   Freda: a.   See we had no men teachers in there.
                     b.   We had somebody come in the– in the assembly,
                     c.   and y'just eh he wore a pair of pants.
                     d.   Everybody was so excited.
          Jack: e.   Well nobody paid attention t'what was *said* then.
          Freda: f.   Maybe not! ⌈ hhhhh ⌉
          Jack: g.   ⌊ **So** aca ⌋ demically wasn't so hot, was it?
          Freda: h.   No.
          Jack: i.   Their mind wasn't on what uh . . . it was all about,
                           then.
                     j.   I mean *this* is the point *I* was tryin' t'make.

Freda's description in (b–d) allows Jack to gain agreement from Freda on a
point preliminary to his main point: note in (e) the use of *well* as a response
marker (Chapter 5) and *then* as a marker of succession (Chapter 8). Freda's
agreement (f) is then used by Jack as a warrant for the very point he had
been trying to make during their prior argument. Note that Jack not only
marks his point as having been warranted by Freda's own statements (with
so): he returns the floor to Freda in a way which strongly delimits her
answer options (the tag *was it?*). Thus, Jack makes it very difficult for
Freda to maintain her initial position without admitting a self-
contradiction; thus her concession follows in (h). In sum, the division of
responsibility created by a joint warrant/inference pair can strengthen a
challenge by forcing one's opponent either to admit a self-contradiction or
concede a point.

   I have described in this section how a causal relationship may be realized
on more than one plane of talk at once. This has meant that *because* and *so*
may simultaneously mark the idea structures of texts, the information state
transitions resulting from relationships between warrants and inferences,
and the relationships between speakers' stated motives and actions.

7.2.5 Semantic meaning of so and because in discourse

I have suggested that *because* and *so* mark causal relations which are fact-based, knowledge-based and action-based. Although facts, knowledge and actions are very different entities, my suggestion is that the same semantic meaning – the same causal relation – is being realized in all three cases. Thus, *because* and *so* mark relations not only between idea units, but between ideas and speakers' inferences which figure in the conversational evolution of information states, and between speakers' stated motives and actions. What greatly complicates efforts to describe this relation is the fact that the cause of a result, the warrant for an inference, and the motive for an action are often presented simultaneously: a single pair of utterances can invoke all three relationships without necessarily differentiating them linguistically.

Recall, now, my conclusions about the meanings of *and*, *but* and *or* (Chapter 6). First, I concluded that although *and* has no semantic meaning at a textual level (it is comparable to 'zero'), the semantic meanings of *but* and *or* ('contrast' and 'disjunction' respectively) can be realized at a textual level. Second, I concluded that *and*, *but* and *or* have pragmatic effects in interaction: they mark 'speaker-continue', 'speaker-return' and 'hearer-option' respectively. Third, such effects are dependent on a combination of discourse context and semantic meaning.

So far, my proposal for *because* and *so* is very similar: the semantic meanings of *because* and *so* are realized at a textual level. But I have not yet considered the pragmatic effects of these markers. I turn to this in (7.3).

7.3 *So* and participation structures[9]

So functions in the organization of transitions in participation framework. Such transitions occur when speaker and hearer adjust the allocation of responsibility for the achievement of particular conversational tasks, e.g. taking a turn at talk, completing the parts of an adjacency pair, organizing and maintaining discourse topics. Although transitions occur on various planes of talk, e.g. the shifts between the main and subordinate parts of an explanation are ideational transitions (7.1), participation transitions have two characteristics which differentiate them from the others. First, the transition itself is one in which speaker shifts responsibility to hearer; second, the shift from speaker to hearer is centered around the accomplishment of a particular interactional task.

It is important to point out that transitions in participation framework are only **potential** loci for shifting responsibility from speaker to hearer: if a hearer does not take an offered turn, for example, the speaker may him/herself continue (cf. Sacks, Schegloff and Jefferson 1974). The fact that participation transitions are only potentially transitional means not only that they are open to negotiation, but that a marker which is used in such locations must have a dual role: to show that a hearer has an option to take a next move, and to allow a speaker to continue if such an option is not taken. In other words, if a hearer does not take the opportunity to bring about a proffered transition, then a speaker may continue. I will suggest that this is precisely what *so* marks.

I begin to show the function of *so* in participation transitions by focusing on turn exchange. In Chapter 6, I described the role of *and* in turn exchange by finding sequences in which an incoming speaker began to talk either during, or immediately after, a current speaker's *and uh: or and . . .* If the current speaker then returned to the floor to talk about the prior topic, I interpreted that speaker as not having been ready to relinquish his or her turn. I also interpreted the incoming talk as either a shared turn, or an interruption, with either interpretation showing that *and* is not used as a turn-transition device.

Examining *so* in the same environment shows a striking difference. Out of the 15 sequences in which a next speaker's turn-initiation followed or overlapped a current speaker's *so uh:, so . . .,* or *so:,* 10 were sequences in which the incoming talk of the next speaker was sustained as a new turn – rather than becoming part of a shared turn or an interruption. This contrasts with 1 such outcome out of 13 identical environments with *and*. Thus, in contrast to *and* – which marks a speaker's continued turn – *so* is a turn-transition device which marks a speaker's readiness to relinquish a turn.

Since *so* is a turn-transition device, it should not be surprising to find it followed by explicit turn-transition phrases if a next speaker does not avail him/herself of the opened turn space. Such phrases explicitly open a participation slot to a hearer. Prior to (40), for example, Jack has been describing the changing role of America in the world.

(40)   Jack: We're considered the . . . more or less: the oppressors. **So** eh
                    . . . take it from there.

After *so*, Jack indicates his willingness to end his current turn and open the conversation to others' initiatives with *take it from there*. (41) is similar. I have been asking Irene about her participation in school and synagogue groups; as Irene is explaining that she finds such groups cliquish, Henry reinvokes an earlier theme of their conversations to charge that *people are people* (i.e. people should not be prejudiced). As Irene rebuffs Henry, Henry complains that he is *not allowed to say anything*. Irene then turns to me with:

(41)   Yeh.   **So**? What else you want t'know?

Explicit turnover phrases such as those in (40) and (41) cancel the speaker's own opportunity to continue (unless, of course, the speaker follows with equally explicit phrases which reclaim that opportunity). Turn transitions proposed by *so* without explicit turnover phrases, however, do allow a speaker to continue if no turn exchange occurs, i.e. they are potential rather than actual turn transitions. In (42), Henry has been describing to me how he and his poker partners pool their winnings for trips to the race track.

(42)   Henry: a.   And we'll bet on the horses . . . which is very good.
         Debby: b.   So y'do that once a year? With the–⌈all the men?   ⌉
         Henry: c.   ⌊Oh. No maybe a⌋
                           couple times a year!
         Debby: d.   Oh great! Yeh. Why spend it all at once?! ⌈   ⌉
         Henry: e.   Yeh. ⌊Get eight⌋
                           hundred dollars every year or something like that.
                    f.   A thousand dollars a year.
                    g.   **So**: eh. . . . . . but we buy beer and . . . cake and
                           that's– we spend it out of our own money.
                    h.   **So**: eh:
         Debby: i.   **So**, when Henry's gone, what do you do?

I continue the conversation twice (b, d) with requests for confirmation (see pp. 254–7). After Henry elaborates his confirmation (e, f), he marks a potential transition location with *so* (g). I do not begin talking, however, and so Henry maintains the floor by linking the current topic (money) with an earlier topic (food served at card games); note that he uses *but* after *so* to return to that earlier topic (Chapter 6). He then marks another potential transition with *so* (h) and this time I do take the floor: since my question in (i) is directed to Zelda, my use of *so* here marks not only a topic transition, but a participant transition.

So also marks turn transitions at the completion of adjacency pairs, e.g. question/answer pairs.[10] An example from Chapter 6 (#8) is relevant here. Zelda told a story about how a close friend's pregnancy encouraged her to have a third child. Her story had been introduced as she was answering my questions about her friends. After Zelda closed the story, she marked its reievance to my earlier question with *So . . . yeh. They're very good friends of ours*. By so doing, she established the topicality of her story to my preceding question – thus completing the adjacency pair – and she closed her turn. (12) from the current chapter also illustrates. Sally had asked Irene whether her primary school teachers ever hit the students.

(12)   Irene: a.   Yeh. I had one teacher, her name was Frank,
                    b.   We used t'call her Frankenstein.
                    c.   **So**, yeh, she would hit kids with a ruler.

After Irene answers Sally's yes–no question (a), she mentions the teacher's nickname. She then returns in (c) to answer the question, marking with *so* her completion of the adjacency pair, and thus, a turn-transition location.

Does *so* have meaning when it is used in participation transitions? In many of my examples, *so* seems to be marking a 'result' in an explanation as well as a potential participation transition. Consider (43). Zelda has been justifying the fact that her highest academic degree is from high school.

(43)   Zelda: a.   When I graduated high school, it was very good,
                    b.   because there were a lot of kids that didn't graduate.
         Irene: c.   Really. A lot of the ⌈ kids were ⌉ forced t'go to=
         Zelda: d.   ⌊ **So em**: ⌋
         Irene: =work, and stuff.
         Zelda: e.   Right!
                    f.   And so that *I* felt that I was . . . one of the lucky ones!

Zelda explains why she values her high school degree in (a) and (b). Zelda's *so* in (d) is similar to her use of *so* in other explanations (e.g. 2, 3) in which she states an outcome, presents a reason, and then restates an outcome. Thus, it is reasonable to assume that she may be about to restate her evaluation; in fact, she does precisely this in (f) after Irene's endorsement (c). But because Zelda's *so* overlaps with Irene's endorsement, it can also be functioning to mark the participation transition.

Or consider (44). Henry and Zelda have been explaining to me why they don't mind being in their summer seashore home in the rain, for then they just adopt their ordinary household routine rather than go on the beach. Henry then suggests that my circumstances when visiting my parents at their seashore home is similar.

(44)   Henry: a.   We listen to the radio, or read a book.
                    b.   I mean it wouldn't bother y'!
                    c.   Y'fall right in as if you're home.
         Debby: d.   Sure.
         Henry: e.   Y'got your parents there and everything.

Debby:	f.	Sure.
Henry:	g.	**So**: eh: it's not– you have any sisters or brothers?
Debby:	h.	I have a brother.

Henry seems about to state a conclusion in (g). Thus, *so* could be functioning ideationally in an explanation. No one takes the floor during or after *so*, however, and Henry then continues his own turn. But note that he shifts the topic of the conversation and asks me a question – moves which do create a turn exchange despite their temporary hold on the floor.

There are other examples where the meaning of *so* as 'result' seems to be conveyed elliptically at participation transitions. In (45), for example, Irene has been describing a high school fight to Sally.

(45) Irene: a. And there was all kinds of cops around the school.
              b. Y'know.
              c. **Cause** we were afraid t'be in school.
              d. But uh: that was really like uh we were in eleventh, twelfth grade.

Sally: e. What school was ⌈ that? ⌉   Uh huh.   So=
Irene: f.   ⌊ North ⌋ Philly.   **So** uh:
Sally: g. =that– there were already lots of black kids going t'that school ⌈ by ⌉ the time–
Irene: h.   ⌊ Yeh. ⌋

Irene explains that cops were around the school (a) because the students not involved in the fighting (the White students) were afraid (c) to be around those who were (the Black students). (Irene's *but* in (d) contrasts the time of the fight (high school days) with the time period Sally had originally asked about (primary school days).) Sally's question in (e) continues the overall discourse topic: Sally requests, and gains, the name of the school. Irene's *so* in (f) marks her willingness to transfer the floor back to Sally – if Sally has more to say. Sally does: she requests confirmation for her inference about the racial composition of the school. Thus, Irene's *so* marks a participation transition, but because Irene had been presenting an explanation, it is also possible to interpret it as an elided preface to a conclusion.

(46) is similar to (45) with one crucial difference: the participation transition is not actualized after *so*. Irene is explaining why she prefers city to suburban life.

(46) Debby: Y'think it's isolated, or what?
      Irene: a. Yeh. **Cause** I– I like t'know that in case I need something, like, with Zelda,

	b.	or : y'know, she's been a big help t'me
	c.	like since I'm workin' the kids– kids always here,
	d.	or, in an emergency she's here t– t'get them or whatever until I can get there.
Debby:	e.	Yeh. Yeh, that's ⌈ important. ⌉
Irene:	f.	⌊ So : I ⌋ know I have a girlfriend that lives in Havertown,
	g.	and she doesn't know her neighbor on either side.

Again, Irene is explaining something: she presents several reasons for her urban preference in (a–d). And again, Irene's hearer adds a comment which maintains the overall discourse topic: I agree that Irene's reasons are important (e). Irene overlaps my endorsement with *so* again indicating that she will relinquish the floor if her hearer has more to say. But since I have no more to say at that point, Irene continues her explanation in (f). Thus, Irene's *so* marks a potential participation transition: because I do not take the floor, Irene herself continues to talk. But again, it is possible to consider Irene's *so* not only as a potential transition marker, but as an elided preface to a conclusion. (I return to the fact that what follows *so* in (46) is another reason for Irene's conclusion in discussion of 48 and 49.)

(47) is another example. Prior to (47), Jack and Freda had been explaining that they would not want their children to marry religious fanatics. Following my introduction of a new (but related) topic – a well-known religious fanatic who was facing legal difficulties – the discussion shifted still further away from Jack and Freda's personal feelings. My shift in topic had also been a shift in participation structure – for I had taken control of the topic away from Jack and Freda. In (47), Jack closes the topic that I had introduced and returns to his own topic, thus, creating a topic-centered shift in participation structure.

(47)	Jack:	a.	People who are religious, don't eh : e– are emotional,
		b.	and when y'deal with emotion, you're not dealing with eh rationality
		c.	a : and y'know factual– y'know you have to *watch* what y'say t'people who're emotionally involved with religion.
		d.	Y'know ⌈ people. . . ⌉ **So**, but eh eh=
	Debby:	e.	⌊ Yeh, yeh it is uh. . . ⌋
	Jack:	f.	=speaking for my*self*, I couldn't care *less*, eh for Moon, or eh :. . . . . . or eh : who's the new ra– who's the new ra– or Billy Graham, or– or : ⌈ the Pope, or : ⌉ that's
	Freda:	g.	⌊ That's not– ⌋ not even a religion, it's : : [phone rings]

In (d), Jack moves the discussion from generalizations about religion to a
description of his own feelings. His *so* closes the topic which I had introduced, but because it follows closely my agreement (e) with his point (from
d), it also marks Jack's willingness to allow me to say more if I so desire.
Thus *so* in (47) does the same participation work as it did in (46): it marks
the speaker's willingness to allow the hearer to take the floor. Also like (46),
so allows the speaker to continue if the hearer does not do so, and this is
what Jack does – using *but* to return to his own topic. Again, *so* marks a
potential shift in participation framework which could also be referentially
meaningful.

Let us now consider more fully the question of whether *so* has referential
meaning when it is used in participation transitions. I suggest that *so* in
(45), (46) and (47) does convey a 'result' meaning even if no result follows.
Its use in these examples is elliptical: *so* instructs the hearer to recover a
conclusion (an inference, a claim) which has already been presented, or
which is otherwise mutually known because of e.g. just-presented reasons
and/or support.

This elliptical meaning of *so* helps to account for its use at potential participation transitions. That is, *so* indicates that a speaker has reached a
point in the presentation of his/her ideas at which a hearer can infer what
would come next even if it is not explicitly stated. The joint accessibility of
unstated information creates a point of potential closure for a discourse
topic: once both speaker and hearer know the likely conclusion of what has
just been said, it is possible for either speaker or hearer to move on to a new
topic of talk. Hence, a potential participation transition.[11]

To complicate matters again, however, speakers do use *so* in ways which
seem to **conflict** with any 'result' meaning. A striking illustration of this is
provided by comparing two of Irene's arguments. In (48), Irene is arguing
that Jewish children are not raised to be as prejudiced as Catholic children
(also discussed as 28). She supports her position by reporting a conversation with her Catholic neighbor Rita.

(48)   Irene: a.   I don't feel that the Jewish people were– were taught,
                            like *you* said, to *hate*, as strongly as the Catholic people
                            were, taught, in their church.
                  b.   **Cause** my neighbor, we've discussed it many times.

Irene begins her support (in b) with *cause* – thus displaying it as a warrant
for her generalization, as well as the grounds for her claim (both in a). Now
compare (49), in which Irene supports her tolerance toward intermarriage,
again by reporting a conversation with her Catholic neighbor:

(49)   Irene: a.   *I* feel that my children should marry within their
                        religion.
                  b.   But, if they chose . . . *not* to, it wouldn't be the worst
                        thing in the world for me.
                  c.   **So** we had a long discussion, my neighbor's Italian.
                  d.   We had a long discussion a couple weeks ago,
                  e.   all the kids and I were sittin' . . . and *her*,
                  f.   we were sitting on the patio.

In (49), Irene begins her support with *so*. But *so* and *because* are semantic
converses. Thus, if *so* is prefacing a unit whose semantic meaning would
warrant the use of *because*, how can *so* have any referential meaning at all?
That is, if *so* had referential meaning here, it would mark the position,
rather than the support.

Note now, that one could argue that the same interpretive dilemma arose
in the elliptical *so* of (46). After I had agreed with Irene's reasons for liking
the city, Irene compared her closeness with Zelda to a suburban friend's
alienation from her neighbors as a way of further supporting her preference
for city living.

(46)   Debby: e.   Yeh. Yeh, that's ⎡ important. ⎤
        Irene: f.   ⎣ **So**: I ⎦ know I have a
                        girlfriend that lives in Havertown,
                  g.   and she doesn't know her neighbor on either side.

Since this comparison is further support for Irene's preference for urban
life, the location of *so* in the ideational structure of Irene's explanation in
(46) is similar to that in (49): *so* prefaces not Irene's position, but her support.

(46)   POSITION: Urban living is isolating.
            because SUPPORT: My neighbor is helpful.
            She helps with the children.
            She helps in emergencies.
        so SUPPORT: My suburban friend does not know her neighbors.

Again, if *so* were functioning referentially (even elliptically to instruct a
hearer to recover a mutually known conclusion), we would not expect to
see it prior to the support.

The only way I can reconcile these examples is to go a bit deeper into the
meaning of 'result'. A 'result' is a change in circumstance which is brought
about by a prior cause – a transition of some kind. Marking textual transitions from fact-based, knowledge-based and/or action-based causes to re-

sults is certainly the most transparent use of the meaning of *so*. But perhaps it is not the only use of that meaning: perhaps marking a transition in participation framework is one step further from the direct meaning of 'result', and marking a transition in an argument from position to support is still one step further in the breach between referential meaning and pragmatic use – but not yet completely dissociated. Thus, when *so* prefaces the functional transition from one idea segment to another, even when that transition is to the support rather than position segment of an argument, its use may still reflect its 'result' meaning – but only the 'transition' component of that meaning.

In sum, *so* is used at potential transition locations in talk – when speakers offer hearers a turn at talk, a chance to complete an incomplete proposition by answering a question, an opportunity to change topic. Such transitions are potential shifts in participation framework because they are opportunities to adjust the allocation of responsibility for the achievement of particular conversational tasks, e.g. taking a turn at talk, completing an adjacency pair, organizing and maintaining discourse topics. Because such locations are **potential** loci for shifting responsibility from speaker to hearer, *so* has a built-in flexibility when it is used to mark such shifts: if a hearer does not take the option (does not take a turn, answer a question, introduce a topic), the speaker may him/herself continue. And finally, the meaning of *so* is a basis for its function in participation transitions in two ways: *so* may convey an elliptical meaning of 'result', or *so* may extract from 'result' a meaning of 'transition'.

7.3.1 So *and* and

Before closing this section, it is important to note that although *so* and *and* share some properties, they also differ in very specific ways. First, *so* and *and* share a pragmatic effect of speaker-continuation, but *so* differs because of its function in participation transitions. *So* marks speaker-continuation as an **alternative** to participant change in potentital transition locations in talk. This function contrasts sharply with that of *and*, which is used when continuing is the **preferred** option.

In addition, because *so* marks invited transitions in participation, it is similar to *or*, which also allocates interactional responsibility to the hearer (Chapter 6). We will see other markers (*then* in Chapter 8 and *y'know* in Chapter 9) which share with *so* and *or* a focus on the hearer as opposed to the speaker (cf. *and* and *but* in Chapter 6, *I mean* in Chapter 9).

Another reason why *so* and *and* differ has to do with those linguistic properties of *so* which differentiate its discourse use from *and*. *So* has semantic meaning (its 'result' meaning) which restricts its use. For example, although both *and* and *so* can connect events in a narrative, only *and* can connect reasons in an explanation, or pieces of support in an argument – for the semantic role of these idea units would conflict with the 'result' meaning of *so*. (Although see discussion of (49).)

Furthermore, events which are understood as 'causes' are asymmetrically ordered (both temporally and logically) with events understood as 'results'. This asymmetry further differentiates *so* from *and*: although *and* is a symmetric marker in discourse (with asymmetric understanding a result of textual relations between idea units; see discussion in 6.4.1), *so* is asymmetric. Consider (50), a simplification of an argument which I considered as (34) in Chapter 6:

(50)   SUPPORT   (1) My father helped X.
                      (2) My father helped Y.
                      (3) My father helped Z.
         POSITION   We were not prejudiced.

If each piece of support were connected with *and*, their order could be rearranged without changing our understanding of their discourse role. Thus, supportive events which are joined by *and* in an argument can be rearranged among themselves because of the symmetry of *and*. But compare prefacing each such event with *so*: not only would one event then be interpreted as a result of the prior event(s), but rearranging their order would produce a very different understanding of which is antecedent and which is consequent.

Similarly, compare prefacing the position by *so*, and the support by *because*: reversing the order of support and position in an argument would change their functional identity (without an accompanying shift to *because*).

(50')   a.   We were not prejudiced.
         b.   **So** my father helped X.

As soon as a piece of support is prefaced with *so*, a change in order alters its discourse role: thus, in (50'), we understand (b) not as support, but as a specific consequence of the general lack of prejudice in (a).

Finally, whereas *and* is a coordinate marker, *so* is a superordinate marker. This means that if both markers are used in a single discourse unit, *and* coordinates units which play a collective role in relation to a dominant unit marked by *so* (although, of course, *and* can also coordinate units within the dominant unit marked by *so*). Reconsider a narrative from Irene ((7) in Chapter 6), whose structure can be simplified as (51):

(51)   Background
                      and background
              So main narrative event
              and main narrative event

We would not find structures such as (51'):

(51')   Background
                        so background
              And main narrative event
              so main narrative event

Nor would we find *and* marking a narrative resolution, and *so* the events leading to that resolution (cf. Henry's story in (18)), or *so* marking subordinate discourse topics and *and* marking the main discourse topic (cf. (16) in Chapter 6).

7.4 Summary

I have shown in this chapter that *so* and *because* convey meanings of 'result' and 'cause' which may be realized as fact-based, knowledge-based, and/or action-based relations between units of talk. Like the other markers considered thus far, *so* and *because* work at both local and global levels of talk. At a local level, *so* and *because* allow two ordering options which are thematically constrained by surrounding discourse. Like *and*, *but* and *or*, *so* and *because* are used in discourse in ways which reflect their linguistic properties. Finally, although *so* has a pragmatic use in participation structures – as a marker of potential transition – *because* has no such analogous function.

8 Temporal adverbs: *now* and *then*

Thus far, we have examined markers which either have no lexical meaning (*oh, well*) or whose semantic meaning influences their use on non-ideational discourse planes (*and, but, or, so, because*). I turn now to two markers whose deictic meaning influences their use on several different discourse planes.

Deictic elements relate an utterance to its person, space, and time coordinates. *Now* and *then* are time deictics because they convey a relationship between the time at which a proposition is assumed to be true, and the time at which it is presented in an utterance. In other words, *now* and *then* are deictic because their meaning depends on a parameter of the speech situation (time of speaking).

I will use the term **reference time** to refer to the deictic relationship between a proposition and its speaking time, i.e. the time of its utterance (Jakobson 1957). For example, (1a) and (1b) present the same propositional content:

(1)   a.   Sue teaches linguistics now.
        b.   Sue taught linguistics then.

They have different reference times, however, because they establish different time periods, relative to the speaking time, during which Sue's *teaching linguistics* is assumed to be true: in (1a), it is true during a period overlapping with the speaking time; in (1b), it is true during a period prior to the speaking time. This difference is indicated not only by the shift from present to preterit tense, but by the time adverbs *now* and *then*. It is this shift in reference time which indicates that *now* and *then* are time deictics.

We will see that the deictic properties of *now* and *then* have an impact on their use as discourse markers.[1] One such property is their differentiation on a proximal/distal axis. This axis contrasts not only time deictics (present versus preterit tense, *now* versus *then*), but person deictics (*I* versus *you*) and place deictics (*here* versus *there*, *come* versus *go*). Elements on the proximal end are ego-centered: they are located closer to the speaker and to the speaker's space and time.

The deictic center of an utterance usually shifts from one proximal (ego-centered) location to another as individuals exchange speaking roles during an interaction. However, deictic center is also subjectively influenced depending upon the point of view, and the frame of reference, being taken by a speaker. One such subjective influence is the speaker's personal evaluation of a state of affairs; compare expressions such as *he went* (distal) *through a hard time last year* with *he came* (proximal) *through a hard time last year* (Clark 1974). Clark suggests that ego-centered, proximal elements are used by a speaker to convey a positive personal orientation toward a particular state of affairs.

In addition to the deictic concepts of reference time and proximal/distal axis, there are two time relationships which are important for understanding the discourse functions of *now* and *then*: event time and discourse time. **Event time** differs from reference time because it is not a deictic relationship: rather than indicate the temporal relationship between a proposition and its presentation in an utterance, event time indicates the temporal relationship between propositions themselves. It is because event time shows a relationship between linguistic events internal to a discourse, rather than between a linguistic event and a situational parameter, that it is not deictic. Consider (2):

(2)   Sue wrote a book.
        She was teaching linguistics then.

The reference time of both propositions in (2) is past (prior to speaking time). The event time is the relationship between the two propositions: as indicated by the progressive, and by *then*, the two overlap in time. I discuss the use of *then* as an indicator of event time in (8.2.2).

Discourse time refers to the temporal relationships between utterances in a discourse, i.e. the order in which a speaker presents utterances in a discourse (see 8.3 for discussion). (3) suggests the influence that discourse time may have on the demonstratives *this* and *that*.

(3)   Question: How do you feel about X
        Answer: I'll answer **this** way.
                      [answer]
                      That's the way I feel.

As (3) suggests, some elements (*this*) look forward in discourse time and some elements (*that*) look backward in discourse time.[2] We will see that *now* and *then* are one such set of elements.

In sum, three temporal concepts (reference time, event time, and discourse time) influence the discourse function of *now* and *then*. So, too, does the proximal/distal opposition between *now* and *then*, and the evaluative quality of the proximal *now*.

8.1 *Now*: Speaker progression

We will see in this section that the discourse function of *now* reflects its status as the proximal member of the pair *now* and *then*: *now* marks a speaker's progression through discourse time by displaying attention to an upcoming idea unit, orientation, and/or participation framework. Before we do so, however, it is important to distinguish adverbial from marker *now*.

8.1.1 Now: *adverb or marker*

Although the categories of adverbs and discourse markers are clearly different, it is not always easy to decide in which category a particular token of *now* is functioning. One method is to find combinations which would be co-occurrence violations for one category, but not the other. For example, we would not expect the two time adverbs *now* and *then* to co-occur – because when *now* is temporal, it contrasts with *then*. Yet speakers can use *now then* to mark transitions in topic, argument, activity and so on (e.g. *now then, what should we do next*). Nor would we expect two tokens of adverbial *now* to co-occur. This restriction means that initial *now* is a marker in cases like (4):

(4)   So I em. . .I think, for a woman t'work, is entirely up t'her. If, she can handle the situation. **Now** I could not now: alone.

But when *now* is not a time adverb, it **can** be repeated in the formulaic expression *now now* (an expression of comfort).

The identification of *now* as either adverb or marker is also influenced by discourse context. Indeed, the distinction may even be neutralized by a context: if *now* is in a discourse whose topic structure allows a temporal reading, it may not be possible to assign it an interpetation as either adverbial or marker. Consider *now* in comparisons. In comparisons, a speaker first introduces (either explicitly or implicitly) a main topic; the topic then branches into two subtopics; the difference between the two subtopics is the focus of the discourse.[3] Yet, comparisons can be between two different times, and it is in such comparisons that *now* seems to have a temporal reading. In (5), for example, Freda's topic is the ethnic composition of her neighborhood; the subtopics are two different times for which ethnicity is described.

(5)   Freda: a.   It was at one time all: almost all Jewish.

              b.   **Now** it's I would say $\begin{bmatrix} \text{si–} \\ \text{six} \end{bmatrix}$ ty Jewish, forty Italian.

    Jack: c.

Now in (b) seems to be a time adverb not only because of its co-occurrence with the present tense (this is a necessary but not sufficient condition) but because the comparison in the discourse is between time periods (*at one time* versus *now*). But *now* is routinely used in all sorts of comparisons, and this complicates our identification of *now* in (5). In (6), for example, Zelda is comparing the street where my parents have a summer home (a) to the street on which her own summer home is located (b).

(6)   a.   It's nice there.

       b.   **Now** our street isn't that nice.

Here we would not identify initial *now* as a time adverb (despite the present tense) simply because the comparison in the discourse is between locations rather than times. (Compare the interpretation had Zelda said *At one time our street was nice* in a.) But in temporal comparisons such as (5), the time difference is the subtopic differentiation; thus, we cannot be absolutely sure which contrast is being marked by *now* (or indeed if the time and subtopic contrasts should even be considered different). Thus, I suggest that the discourse structure of temporal comparisons neutralizes the distinction between *now* as a time adverb and *now* as a marker.

In addition to discourse context, intonation influences our identification of *now*. Although I have not transcribed it in my examples, *now* receives tonic stress and high pitch as a time adverb in (5). But *now* receives neither prosodic feature as a marker in (6): rather it is the focus of the comparison (*our*) which is stressed and higher pitched. Another prosodic feature is also important. Consider (7) without the distinctive prosodic features noted. Freda is explaining that the tree in front of her house has become an expensive nuisance.

(7)   a.   No I like the tree,

       b.   it's gotten too big.

       c.   They used t'keep them trimmed.

       d.   **Now** for us t'do that

       e.   oh it's gotta be a hundred dollar bill!

Depending upon stress and pitch, (7) can be interpreted as a time comparison (what *used to* happen vs. what *now* happens) or a person comparison (what *they* do and what *we* do). Suppose, however, that one of our adverbial cues (stress on *now*) is coupled with slight falling intonation on *now* followed by a pause:

(7')   c.   They used t'keep them trimmed.
            d.   ***Now***, for us t' do that
            e.   oh it's gotta be a hundred dollar bill!

In such cases, *now* is a marker rather than an adverb: the pause after *now* intonationally separates it from the rest of the utterance, thus allowing *us* to be stressed in a separate tone unit. And stress on *us* creates a person comparison (*they/we*) rather than a time comparison.

By examining *now* in comparisons, we have been able to see how a combination of features differentiates adverbial from marker functions of *now*: reference time of the proposition, the topical centrality of time in the discourse, and intonation. But now let us see what can be learned about the discourse function of *now* by building upon our preliminary observations about its use in comparisons.

8.1.2 Now *and the progression of ideas*

Now occurs in discourse in which the speaker progresses through a cumulative series of subordinate units. Although we have already seen *now* in one such type of discourse – comparisons – others include lists and arguments. (8) shows where *now* can occur within such discourse.

(8)   (explicit identification of unit 1)
            (**now**) subordinate unit 1a
            ((**now**) subordinate unit 1b)

(8) shows, first, that the explicit introduction of the discourse unit is optional. In other words, the discourse in which *now* occurs need not be **explicitly** structured or identified as having two subordinate units. We will see that, in comparisons, *now* occurs not only when the comparison is explicitly identified as having two clearly introduced subtopics, but also when the subtopics under comparison are only **implicit**. (8) also shows that *now* is optional before either subpart of the discourse, and that the second subordinate unit is also optional.

Let us begin with comparisons in which the identity of the unit is explicitly introduced, and *now* occurs before both subunits. In (9), Jan is comparing the childrearing practices of Italians and Irish. This comparison is explicitly introduced in (a):

(9)   a.   They aren't brought up the same way.
        b.   **Now** Italian people are very outgoing,
        c.   they're very generous.
        d.   When they put a meal on the table it's a meal.
        e.   **Now** these boys were Irish.
        f.   They lived different.

Following the introduction of the comparison, Jan uses *now* to introduce both subtopics: Italians (b) and Irish (e).

In (10), a comparison is also prefigured (in a, *it depends*). The following description (c–d) is then understood as a subtopic, and *now* is used with the first subtopic. I have asked Jack the price of houses on his block.

(10)   Jack: a.   It depends.
                 b.   Uh: what it has inside.
                 c.   **Now** this is an end house,
                 d.   so this would get more.

Although the branching of the topic (value of houses) is not developed by Jack, note what Freda does:

(10)   Jack: d.   ⌈so this would get more.   ⌉
          Freda: e.   ⌊No I don't know. It depends–⌋
                 f.   but don't t– don't talk about *this* one.
                 g.   We just know of one, that was sold.
                 h.   So that was sold for close t'twenty seven.

Not only does Freda begin the same comparison as Jack (*it depends* in (e)), but she does develop the two subtopics: she compares her own house (*this one*; note the proximal *this*) with another house (in (h); note the distal *that*). Thus, in (10), two different speakers indicate a comparison in two different ways: Jack prefigures the comparison and marks its branching into one subtopic with *now*; Freda prefigures the comparison and differentiates two subtopics without *now*.

Not all comparisons are as explicitly identified as those in (9) and (10): some are presented without a prior statement of their more general unifying topic (11–12), some are interpretable as comparisons because of tacit agreement that the topic being spoken about is disputable (16–17), and still others are heard as implicit comparisons because they are presented as personal opinions (18–19).

First consider comparisons which branch into two subtopics, but have no introductory identifying statement. In (11), Jack uses *now* to differen-

tiate two subtopics: my parents' opinion on intermarriage from my boyfriend's parents' opinion.

(11)   Jack: How does mother feel about this. About ⌈ your= ⌉
        Debby: ⌊ About. . .⌋
        Jack: =situation.   Yeh.
        Debby: Uh– with my boyfriend?   She's
                   adjusted. Y'know I think– like I said before, she likes him
                   very ⌈ much. ⌉
        Jack: ⌊ In   ⌋ other words, she's in the tolerating stage.
                   Now how about his parents?

Jack then goes on to use the answers which his comparative questions have
elicited from me as a basis for a generalization about the tolerance of different religions.

   In (12), Irene is describing the educational system at the local school.

(12)   a.   They have an open classroom at Lansdon.
        b.   **Now** there's lots of the mothers in that room are very upset
                about it.
        c.   I'm not.

Although Irene does not introduce her comparison with a topic statement
(e.g. 'people have very different reactions to the classroom'), it is clear that
the fact that *lots of the mothers* are upset (b) is a contrast with Irene's own
reaction (c). *Now* marks the assessment in (b) as a comparison. (12 also
provides an example in which only the first subpart of the comparison is
marked with *now*.)

   Consider, next, that some topics are tacitly defined as disputable, such
that the mere introduction of the topic into a conversation raises the possibility of disagreement. Disagreement is a particular mode of comparison
because it juxtaposes what the speaker claims with what the hearer claims.
Thus, topics which raise the possibility of disagreement simply because
they are understood as inherently disputable are, by definition, a focus of
comparison.

   One inherently disputable topic for my informants was intermarriage.
Here is Irene's reaction when Zelda tells her (as she enters the room) that
we have been talking about intermarriage:

(13)   Oh you: wanna start a fight here.

Later, when Zelda has not presented her own opinion, Irene accuses Zelda
of not saying anything because of the interpersonal disputability of the
topic (*he* refers to Henry):

(14)   You haven't even *said* anything, cause you're afraid he's gonna *kill* y'!

Or consider Freda's reaction when I brought up intermarriage:

(15)   It's a hot one whoa ho : ho :!

The disputability of intermarriage for my informants meant that statements of opinion on the topic were likely to be compared to others' opinions. And it is for this reason that *now* prefaced many opinions about
intermarriage. In (16), for example, Sally has asked Zelda how she feels
about intermarriage.

(16)   a.   Well,. . .it– it all depends on um. . .
        b.   **Now** my husband believes in eh marrying in his own religion.
        c.   And he tried to stress it with the boys.

After introducing a comparison (again with *it depends*), Zelda prefaces her
husband Henry's position with *now*. She then continues with her own opinion. In (17), Jan, Ira and I are discussing problems of intermarriage. Right
after Ira had stated his opinion that most intermarriages do not work out (*if
you get more than fifteen percent that come out, you're doin' good*), I said
that I was personally interested in the issue for I had a boyfriend of a different religion. Jan then tells a story about a young couple on their street
(one Jewish, one Catholic) whose marriage ended for a reason having nothing to do with religion. She closes her story:

(17)   And, they found they have nothing in common. **Now**, in *their* case, I
        don't think it was religion that broke them up.

Jan's story ends with a coda that establishes it as a specific case to compare
with the general pessimistic view offered by Ira. (Note that Jan's story also
compares my situation to *their case*.) Thus, her coda is prefaced by *now*. In
sum, when *now* occurs with an opinion about a disputable topic, it is displaying the speaker's recognition of interpersonal differences about that
topic.

Consider the third way in which a discourse is implicitly comparative:
the statement of opinions. Note, first, that opinions need not be about disputable topics to be considered as implicitly comparative. Let us define
opinions as verbal representations of internal cognitive states (feelings or
beliefs) concerning a particular state of affairs. What is crucial is that such
states are available for neither observation nor verification. This characteristic makes opinions immutable to either confirmation or disconfirmation
from others: 'it is not clear what kind of substantiation would be sufficient

to ground an opinion in an external reality' (Goffman 1974: 503). Thus, because opinions can be as little confirmed as disconfirmed, the mere presentation of an opinion implicates uncertainty over the facts about which the opinion is held. This means that opinions are inherently disputable: they implicate a comparison between 'my view' and 'another's view'.[4]

Sometimes, of course, the presentation of an opinion does initiate an actual disagreement and thus make the comparison between 'my view' and 'another's view' more overt. In (18), for example, Jack, Freda and I have been discussing old movies. One of Jack's favorites is *Overcoat*, and I state that I have seen the movie.

(18)   Jack: a.   **Now** y'see your age wouldn't appreciate Overcoat.
        Debby: b.   Well I ⌈ saw it. . .about six or seven years– ⌉
        Freda: c.   ⌊ She enjoy– enjoyed it! She thought ⌋ it was
                       ⌈ fine! ⌉
        Jack: d.   ⌊ But ⌋ you'd have t' understand the background,
                 e.   what a coat meant in those days, t'certain people.

In (a), Jack gives his opinion about my ability to like the movie. Note that this is also a comparison between Jack and me (he is in his sixties and had referred to himself as 'old' earlier in our conversation). As I prepare to disagree – to claim that I did like the movie even though I had seen it many years before when I was still younger – Freda more openly claims that I *enjoyed it* (c). Jack then implies that I could not have fully understood the movie.

However, as I noted above, opinions need not be openly disputed to be interpreted as implicit comparisons between 'my view' and 'another's view'. In (19), for example, Irene is describing a recent visitation day at her son's school.

(19)   a.   He was giving a spelling test.
        b.   **Now** to me, if you're inviting parents t'come observe, y'don't give a spelling test!

Irene's opinion (*to me* in b) is that a spelling test is an inappropriate activity for parental observation. Although this opinion neither focuses on an inherently disputable issue, nor initiates a disagreement, it is still a personal evaluation of a particular state of affairs – rather than a neutral description of those affairs – and thus, it is an implicit comparison between what Irene feels and what others feel. It is for this reason that it is prefaced by *now*.

I have suggested that *now* shows a speaker's progression through the discourse time of a comparison, a discourse which is comprised of a cumulative series of subtopics. What has differed in my examples is: (1) the explicitness with which the comparison was identified (openings such as *it depends* were most explicit, and statements of opinion were least explicit), (2) the location of *now* in the comparisons (*now* prefaced the first and/or the second subtopic), and (3) the completion of the comparison (some stopped after the first subtopic). In all these comparisons, however, *now* has the same function: it displays that what is coming next in the discourse is but a subpart of a larger cumulative structure, and thus has to be interpreted as a subordinate unit in relation to a progression of such units. In short, *now* marks the speaker's orderly progression in discourse time through a sequence of subparts.

Now occurs in other discourse in which a subordinate unit is to be interpreted in relation to a larger structure. Sometimes we find *now* with metalinguistic markers of new idea units within such structures:

(20)   **Now**, lemme give you an idea when I talk about fantasy.

or reasons within explanations:

(21)   So Russia was split down the middle. **Now**, the reason why Catholicism was able to creep into Poland [continue]

The meta-linguistic marking of a new idea, or a reason, makes explicit the same **ideational** progression through a discourse of the sort already described for comparisons: a main unit branches into two subordinate units.

Descriptive lists have the same structures: lists add topics which accumulate as specific cases of a more general topic. In (22), for example, Zelda is listing the names of restaurants she and Henry have liked. She follows one restaurant with:

(22)   **Now** where else did we go. Um. . .

In (23), Jack has been describing American movies which have been commercial successes:

(23)   Jack: **Now** another one, eh: what's the other one that eh: they made a lot of money with. And everybody jumped out of their seats.
                 ⌈ Uh: ⌉   Exorcist.
         Debby: ⌊ Oh. .⌋ The Exorcist.

In both of these cases, speakers use *now* to mark the information which will add to a prior collection of items (restaurants, movies). However, because the specific information is not immediately recallable, *now* actually has a dual function here: not only is the next potential item in a list marked, but so too, is the need to maintain focus on **the speaker** for provision of that next item. Thus, in (23), even after I have remembered the name of the movie for which Jack is searching, the turn to talk is still rightfully his, and he is the one who continues with a description of 'The Exorcist'. (See 8.1.3 for discussion.)

My discussion so far has shown that in discourse in which there is an orderly progression through a sequence of subordinate parts, *now* marks one or more parts of that sequence. But *now* does not seem to mark every step in such a sequence (cf. the alternation between *and* and asyndetic connection in Chapter 6, suggesting a tendency toward syntagmatic variation). This suggests that repeated use of *now* is a resource with which a speaker can emphasize the sequential nature of a discourse whose cumulative nature is important for the establishment of a particular point. In other words, repeated use of *now* emphasizes the progression of particular units in discourse time.

(24) and (25) further suggest that repeated *now* occurs when a discourse is based on a comparison of some kind – even if it does not have the explicit comparison structure discussed above. In (24), for example, Henry is arguing that Black students often create classroom trouble for White teachers. He makes his point by asking Sally (who is White) to compare her teaching experience at two high schools, one in which she taught Black students, the other in which she taught White students.

(24)   Henry: a.   Was there colored at your school?
       Sally: b.   Yeh. Jackson High School.
       Henry: c.   Did they give you a hard time there?
       Sally: d.   Yeh.
       Henry: e.   **Now** why? Why? Why should they give you a hard time?
                f.   They– **now** you didn't have a hard time here!
       Sally: g.   No.
       Henry: h.   **Now** why?
                i.   You're the same teacher!

Henry establishes the first part of his comparison: Sally taught at a school with Blacks (a, b) and had *a hard time* (c, d). His question in (e) (*now why*) is then built on these prior facts. The second part of Henry's comparison focuses on Sally's situation at a school with Whites: *now you didn't have a hard time here* (f). After Sally agrees with this (g), Henry again questions *now why* (h). Thus Henry's point is built through his elicitation of responses to a cumulative set of questions and statements which compare Sally's experience with two different groups of students.

The integration of the comparison into the discourse in (25) is slightly more subtle. Here Jack is boasting that he can go to any serious movie and identify the composer of the musical score. This musical talent differentiates Jack from other moviegoers, who cannot even remember the music in movies. In (25), Jack provides the groundwork for his boast through a series of cumulative questions which establish how his talents compare with those of others.

(25)   Jack: a.   **Now** I can go to a movie,
            b.   **now**– it– well it's– **now** look.
            c.   What was the last picture you saw?
      Debby: d.   Um. . .believe it or not, 'One flew over the cuckoo's nest.'
      Freda: e.   We didn't see that one.
      Rob: f.   **Now** that's ⎡ one. ⎤
      Jack: ⎣ Was ⎦ that a serious picture?
      Freda: g.   Oh: ⎡ gosh ⎤ yes!⤚
      Debby: h.   ⎣ Yeh. ⎦   ⟋It was ⎡ serious. yeh.   ⎤
      Jack: i.   ⎣ **Now** can you recall any⎦
            of the music in it. [2.5 second pause]
      Debby: j.   Uh. . .not– no. Not in that ⎡ movie ⎤ I can't.
      Jack: k.   ⎣ See? ⎦
            l.   **Now**, I can go to a movie,
            m.   and I'll tell you any– an' it's um: and I'm talkin' about– y'know a movie that's a big hit, or. . .or. . .like one of the best ten.
            n.   Generally.
            o.   And I'll tell you whose music was played.

Jack begins his boast in (a): *now I can go to a movie*. With *now look* (in b), he then initiates a strategy by which to strengthen his boast by comparing his own ability with others' lack of ability. The strategy depends on the successful elicitation of answers for a series of questions, such that each question fits into the total argument only after the answer to the prior question has been provided. After I answer Jack's first question (c) with 'One flew over the cuckoo's nest' (d), Rob notes (with *now that's one*) that my response fulfills Jack's search for a serious movie – an appropriateness which is in contrast to a comedy which he had himself mentioned earlier. Following his own confirmation of the seriousness of the movie, Jack asks a next question which builds on my answer: *now can you recall any of the music in it* (i). Since I cannot (j), Jack has found evidence for his point that others are unable to remember the music in movies; he invites others to acknowledge this evidence with *see* in (k). He can then return in (l–o) to his initial point from (a): after repeating *now I can go to a movie*, he claims that he can identify the composer of the score. His original boast is thus strengthened: his sequentially elicited comparison has allowed him to elevate his own ability in contrast to the lack of ability which his questions have prompted me to admit.

In sum, this section has shown that *now* marks a speaker's progression through a discourse which contains an ordered sequence of subordinate parts. One crucial aspect of this function that I have not yet focused on is that *now* focuses on the **speaker's** progression. I consider this aspect of *now* as part of a more general discussion of participation framework.

8.1.3 Now *and shifts in participation framework*

Now differentiates parts of discourse which are defined not only by their sequential role in the discourse time of an ordered structure, but by the mode through which the speaker is related to the information being presented. I have spoken before of this plane of discourse organization as the **orientation**: the stance which the speaker is taking toward what is being said.

The most grammaticalized switches in stance are changes in mood, e.g. from declarative to interrogative. In (26), for example, Jack ends his explanation of governmental policies which bail out corporations in financial trouble with a declarative sentence, and then with a question which checks on his hearers' understanding:

(26)   They're using socialism t'fight capitalism. **Now** can you understand that?

Other declarative/interrogative switches marked by *now* occur as the speaker ends a sequence of facts with a rhetorical question – a question whose answer has just been implicitly provided from the prior sequence. In (27), Jack is arguing that the United States is too young a country (200 years) to have a culture, by comparing it with older civilizations:

(27)   That's one breath in history compared. . .England's over a
         thousand. . .uh uh. . .countries like uh Egypt, is almost six thousand
         years. **Now** what's two hundred against six thousand years?

Now also marks changes in speaker orientation which are not grammaticalized. In (28), for example, Jack switches from a narrative to an evaluative mode:

(28)   a.   Finally, he put him in the third time,
         b.   and he pulled out an Oriental,

    c.   he was just brown, toasted, nice.
    d.   **Now** I mean this is just a legend, an n– Oriental legend.

Because Jack's switch in (d) frames his story (as an *Oriental legend*), it can
be seen as a reflexive frame break (Goffman 1974): it provides the hearer
with an interpretive bracket for what has just been said. Another example is
(29). Ira is explaining why he is against intermarriage. He shifts from
recounting hypothetical events (a–d) in a narrative mode to interpreting
them (e).

(29)   a.   For example, eh. . .eh. . .let's assume the husband's a– w– a–
                    a– a– the husband's Jewish,
          b.   and the girl's, say, Catholic,
          c.   and they have an argument
          d.   and she says 'You goddamm Jew!'
          e.   **Now** she wouldn't say something like that, if she was rational.

Because Ira's interpretation brings out the point of his argument, it provides a frame in which to understand what he has just said.

   We have seen thus far that *now* focuses attention on what the speaker is
about to do: in (28) and (29), for example, *now* prefaced the speaker's
upcoming shift into an evaluative mode (even though what was evaluated
was **prior** talk). This cataphoric focus suggests that *now* would also be
used when the speaker needs to negotiate the right to control what will
happen next in talk. Turn-taking struggles are the most obvious example of
such a negotiation. (30) shows *now* with the attention-getter *hold it* as Jack
recycles a turn-initiation:

(30)   Freda: I don't know whether it's the Jew: or the Catholic. Cause
                    they're pretty ⌈ well prejudiced.   ⌉
          Jack: ⌊ No. The Catholic is– ⌋ **now** hold it. It varies.

Control of the topic is another arena for participation negotiation. In (31),
Henry is on the phone with his son. He is giving him instructions on fixing
a drain (their family business). It is clear from what Henry has previously
said that his son is worried about a procedure which Henry finds irrelevant.

(31)   That don't make any difference.
          Now listen to me.
          Take a lead eh eh a chisel, and hit it.

Now occurs with *listen to me* as a way of returning the speaker to a position
in which he can control the topical development of talk.

   Examining the next example in some detail shows how *now* focuses
attention on pivotal moves during still another domain in which partici-

pation statuses are negotiated – interpersonal argument. Although Henry
and Irene agree that it is not wise to spoil children, Irene claims that Jewish
children are often spoiled by their parents. In (32), Henry prompts me to
repeat an earlier statement of his (it is not Jewish girls who are spoiled, but
Jewish boys) which is a partial rebuttal to Irene's claim.

(32) Irene: a. How 'bout the nice Jewish kids ⎡ the parents– ⎤
      Henry: b.   ⎣ All right   ⎦ what
                   would I say?
               c. What was I–
               d. **Now** uh Deborah!
               e. What did I say about the Jew–
               f. did I say anything about the Jewish girls?
      Debby: g. Nothing about the Jewish girls!
      Henry: h. What did I say?
      Debby: i. They're not Jewish princesses, they're Jewish princes!
      Henry: j. The *prince*!
               k. The golden prince!

Henry asks several questions which elicit from me a response to support his
position against Irene. His questions are sequentially ordered, in that the
answers to earlier questions provide the input to later questions (cf. 24 and
25); each question also increases Henry's likelihood of gaining from me the
information needed to defend his position.

Henry begins in (b) with a WH-question with an irrealis modal (*would*).
This question has the same interactional function as those which follow: it
is a prompt for support through a request for information. But because of
its referential meaning, it does not insure that support: the WH format assumes merely that there is a set of options, and the modal defines that set as
possible, not actual. In (c), Henry begins to restrict the possibilities for my
answer, and thus to further prompt the supporting information: he
replaces *would* with *was*, thereby directing me to recall an actual event.

Then in (d), Henry specifically targets his questions to me: *Now uh
Deborah!* This is a pivotal move in the argument because it directly elicits
my participation in the argument, and carries a risk if I do not participate in
a way which supports Henry. Thus, following this move, Henry's
questions to me continue to narrow the field from which my answer can be
drawn. In (e), Henry is still using a WH-question, but he further specifies
the domain of experience (Jews) in which I am to search for the requested
information. Then in (f), Henry shifts to a yes–no question: *did I say anything about the Jewish girls?* Since yes–no questions limit the content of the
question to a two-member pair of options, rather than an open set, this

question is Henry's most direct attempt to elicit supporting information from me. After my answer (*nothing about the Jewish girls* in g), Henry is able to return to a WH-question (*What did I say* in h) because my previous answer has just eliminated from consideration the very group Henry wants to exclude, i.e. Jewish girls. Finally in (i), I repeat what Henry had said – which allows him to state his position against Irene.

Now in interpersonal arguments also focuses attention on the speaker's next move as a contrast with what preceded (cf. discussion of *now* with disputable topics). (33) is an example in which Zelda reports an argument between Henry and herself. Zelda has been complaining that her daughter-in-law does not call her 'Mom'. She states that it is imperative to start using this address term in the beginning of a relationship, and offers three examples which support her point. The third reports a disagreement with Henry about this very issue. (*Now* in (a) introduces her support; see p. 244).

(33)　　a.　　　Now I remember when I first got married,
　　　　　b.　　　and I was in that situation.
　　　　　c.　　　And eh the first– like the first. . .few times, I wouldn't say anything.
　　　　　d.　　　And my husband said to me, '**Now** look, it isn't hard. Just say "Mom".'
　　　　　e.　　　He says, 'And I want y't'*do* it.'

Henry's reported directive in (d) follows Zelda's reported resistance in (c). What is indicated by *now* is Zelda's prior resistance, i.e. Henry would not have issued the directive had Zelda not resisted *the first few times*. Interestingly, Henry uses the same format when he himself reports his own mother issuing a directive to her son (Henry's brother) who was going out with a girl who was not all Jewish.

(34)　　a.　　　And my mother says, '**Now** Jerry,'
　　　　　b.　　　And this is the God's honest truth.
　　　　　c.　　　I'm not gonna hold no punches, y'don't want me to, do y'babe?
　　　　　d.　　　She said, 'I don't want y't'marry that– and I want y' t'break it off right now.'

Again, what is indicated by *now* is prior resistance to the directive.

Consider, now, that because orientation shifts are embedded in conversation, changes in speaker orientation have an effect beyond the speaker's own relationship to information: they also propose changes in the **hearer's** relation to that same information. For example, when a speaker shifts from a neutral description of a state of affairs to an interpretation of those affairs, an assessment of the world is being offered to a hearer. This is an assessment with which the hearer can either agree or disagree, but in either case, one in which he or she can participate. In other words, a speaker's shift from description to evaluation offers a hearer a chance to be evaluative, and to thereby align (or disalign) themselves with a stance toward the world (cf. above discussion on opinions). Similarly, a change from a declarative to an interrogative sentence moves the hearer from a relatively passive position of listening to the speaker's assertion of information, to a more active participation in which he or she is requested to confirm, or at least acknowledge, the prior assertion. Thus, again, a change in speaker orientation simultaneously proposes a change in speaker/hearer footing.[5]

Recall, now, that *now* also marks an ideational shift: we saw in (8.1.2) that *now* marks the speaker's orderly progression through a cumulative sequence of subordinate units. This means that in some discourse, *now* may actually mark a three-part shift – in idea structure, orientation, and participant footing. Arguments through which speakers support disputable positions are an example of such discourse. In (35), for example, *now* occurs as Henry shifts from a general position to a concrete, specific example to support that position:

(35)   Henry: a.   Value. Your sense of value is lost.
         b.   **Now** you take your father's dentist.

What is accomplished here is not only an ideational shift from a general assertion to a specific example (note the indefinite *you* in (a) and the definite *you* in (b)), but an orientation shift and a proposed change in speaker/hearer footing: in (a), Henry asserts a general truth to his hearer, in (b), Henry involves his hearer in the assessment of that truth.[6] These multiple shifts occur whenever speakers use *now* to preface support in an argument. (See (33), line a.)

In sum, *now* not only marks discourse which is a subordinate unit in a cumulative structure, but it marks talk toward which the speaker is shifting orientation and through which a speaker is inviting a hearer to adjust the participation framework.

8.1.4. Proximal time deixis and now

The discourse uses of *now* which I have described are related to its deictic meaning. Recall, first, that temporal *now* establishes a reference time for a proposition in relation to the time of the speaker's utterance, i.e. the speaking time. Another way of saying this is that *now* provides a temporal index from a proposition to an utterance. In its use as a discourse marker, *now* is also indexing a proposition to a temporal world. But the temporal world is not one in which a proposition is related to the speaking time; rather, the temporal world is internal to the utterances in the discourse itself. Thus, the marker *now* provides a temporal index for utterances within the emerging world of talk, i.e. their ideas, the speaker orientation, and the speaker/hearer footing. (I discuss this in more depth in 8.3 and more generally in Chapter 10.)

Second, temporal *now* is a proximal deictic which locates an utterance in a ego-centered space, i.e. a space dominated by the producer, rather than the receiver, of an utterance. The marker *now* is also ego-centered: it focuses on what the speaker him/herself is about to say, rather than on what the hearer says.[7]

Third, as I noted earlier, many proximal deictics have evaluative overlays; for example, the historical present tense, a proximal temporal deictic, is evaluatively used in narrative (Schiffrin 1981). Several examples suggest that *now* is used to highlight interpretive glosses for one's own talk which a speaker him/herself favors. In (36), Jack is about to describe his fondness for a sentimental love story.

(36)   a.   The best picture I think I remember in my mind is—
        b.   maybe it's cause I was a youngster.
        c.   **Now** this'll make y'all laugh. . .
        d.   but I was ver:y, ver:y affected. . .by Wuthering Heights.

Jack gives an explanation for his feelings (b), and clues his audience to his own awareness of how amusing this might be (c). And in (37), Henry follows his argument against intermarriage with a disclaimer about his feelings:

(37)   **Now** I don't hate a Gentile girl, or a guy, I don't *hate*. But I know
        what's. . .what's good, what's good for them, and I know what's good for
        me.

In both examples, the evaluative use of *now* is suggested by the speaker's orientation shift into an interpretation of own talk, and by the fact that the interpretive gloss is one which the speaker him/herself seems to prefer the hearer to adopt.[8]

In sum, *now* is used as a discourse marker in ways that reflect its properties as a time deictic: it provides a temporal index in discourse time, it is ego-centered, and it may be evaluative. My description of *then* in the next section will suggest that its role as a discourse marker can also be explained by its deictic properties.

8.2 *Then*: Speaker/hearer succession

Then indicates temporal succession between prior and upcoming talk. Its main difference from *now* is the direction of the discourse which it marks: *now* points forward in discourse time and *then* points backward. Another difference is that *now* focuses on how the speaker's own discourse follows the speaker's own prior talk; *then*, on the other hand, focuses on how the speaker's discourse follows either party's prior talk. These discourse differences between *now* and *then* reflect their proximal/distal temporal differences.

Another difference between *now* and *then* is that *then* is a member not only of the proximal/distal deictic pair, but of the conditional pair *if/then*. I assume that a relationship of temporal succession is also marked by *then* when it is paired with *if*. The only differences are: (1) the entire sequence is potential (rather than actual) and (2) the temporal succession of the consequent (marked by *then*) is assured given the occurrence of the antecedent (marked by *if*).[9]

Still another difference between *now* and *then* is that *then* can be either deictic or anaphoric. As a deictic, *then* marks reference time: a linguistic event (the proposition) is prior to speaking time. But as an anaphor, *then* marks the temporal relation between two linguistic events, thus displaying temporal connections between events internal to the discourse. After considering the fuzzy boundary between *then* as adverb and *then* as marker (8.2.1), I examine further the difference between deixis and anaphora (8.2.2).

8.2.1 Then: *Adverb or marker?*

We saw earlier (8.1.1) that even though the categories of adverb and discourse marker are mutually exclusive, it is sometimes difficult to decide how a particular token of *now* is functioning. An additional problem develops for *then* – for not only is it difficult to differentiate adverb from marker in actual use, but it is not at all clear whether these two functions **are** totally distinct. It is thus worth considering how our earlier definitional criteria for markers would separate *then* as an adverb from *then* as a marker.

First, since both adverbial and marker *then* are sequentially dependent, they are indistinguishable in this regard. But as I noted earlier (Chapter 2), sequential dependence is a property of other items as well as markers. All anaphors, for example, are cohesive ties which connect prior and upcoming talk, e.g. the interpretation of pronouns presupposes a prior full form in the text (Halliday and Hasan 1976). Thus, consideration of this criterion alone would define many additional items as markers.

Second, both adverbial and marker *then* bracket prior and upcoming talk. We will see that adverbial *then* displays a temporal relationship between two linguistic events internal to the discourse (it is anaphoric), whereas marker *then* displays this relationship not only between linguistic events, but between warrants and inferences, and actions. (Compare my discussion of *so* and *because*, Chapter 7.)

Third, both adverbial and marker *then* may be utterance initial or utterance final. (We will also discuss this issue with *y'know*, Chapter 9.) This distributional difference for adverbial *then* is associated with a meaning difference (p. 250). Similarly, utterance-initial and final positions of marker *then* have specialized discourse uses: initial *then* has wider scope as a discourse marker than final *then*, i.e. it marks global discourse relations between episodes (8.2.3.1), and final *then* is frequently used to mark relationships between actions (8.2.3.2). Still another positional problem is that most cases of *then* in my corpus (at least when it marks actions, 8.2.3.2) are preceded by other markers.

The fourth definitional dilemma is whether the units marked by *then* are always discourse units. This issue is crucial for as long as we found connections between units clearly identifiable as discourse units, there was no question about the functional identity of a word as a marker. Recall that we faced this same issue with conjunctions. For example, we considered *and* to be a marker when it connected narrative sections, actions, or turns. But *and* was not considered a marker when it connected nouns, e.g. *John and Sue went to the beach*, or verb phrases, e.g. *John went to the beach and swam in the ocean*, since the conjoined units in such cases were not discourse units, but clause internal constituents. (Note that I made this assumption even if the conjuncts were reductions of two full clauses.) Yet if the conjuncts were two full clauses, we did consider *and* to be a discourse marker:

(38a)   John went to the beach. And Sue went to the beach.
(38b)   John went to the beach. And John swam in the ocean.

Furthermore, we considered *and* to be a marker in full clauses regardless of whether there was an intonational boundary between the two clauses.

(39a)   John went to the beach. And Sue went to the beach.
(39b)   John went to the beach, and Sue went to the beach.
(39c)   John went to the beach and Sue went to the beach.

In short, regardless of how conjuncts were intonationally packaged, I interpreted every case of *and* between clauses to be a marker of event structure within the discourse. I will do the same for *then*.[10]

In sum, I will treat the following cases of *then* as markers: (1) all clause initial cases (whether in a separate intonational unit or not), (2) all cases following a clause initial marker, (3) all clause final cases which have a pragmatic function (see 8.2.3.2). However, because of the fuzzy boundary between adverbial and marker *then*, my discussion of deixis and anaphora in the next section will also consider clause final adverbial *then*.

8.2.2 Deixis and anaphora

Then is both deictic and anaphoric. (40) to (42) illustrate that deictic uses of *then* indicate reference time, a temporal relationship between a linguistic event and speaking time, and anaphoric uses indicate event time, a temporal relationship between two linguistic events (Reichenbach 1947).

(40)   Q.   When did you visit John?
a.   A: *I visited him now.
b.   I visited him then.
(41)   Q: When are you visiting John?
a.   A: I'm visiting him now.
b.   I'm visiting him then.
(42)   Q: When will you visit John?
a.   A: I'll visit him now.
b.   I'll visit him then.

The answers in (a) show that *now* is deictic: *now* indexes an utterance to a reference time which is coterminous with speaking time (present), or posterior to that time (future), but not prior to speaking time (past). The answers in (b) show that use of *then* evokes a very different understanding. Although *then* seems deictic in (40b) – since it conveys a prior reference time – there is also an anaphoric reading available not only when *then* occurs with the preterit (40b), but when *then* occurs with the present (41b) and with the future (42b). These readings are highlighted when discourse prior to *then* provides another event, e.g. *go to New York*:

(40')   Q: Did you visit John when you went to New York?

b'.	A:	I visited him then.
(41')	Q:	Are you visiting John when you go to New York?
b'.	A:	I'm visiting him then.
(42')	Q:	Will you visit John when you go to New York?
b'.	A:	I'll visit him then.

In each case, the events *go to New York* and *visit John* are understood as coterminous. It is this temporal relationship between two events presented in the discourse which is event time. So although *go to New York* and *visit John* have different reference times in (40b'–42b'), they have constant event times – they are always coterminous.

However, because event time is a relationship between two linguistic events, and has nothing to do with speaking time *per se*, the marking of event time is not deictic. Another way of saying this is that because *then* is relating units **internal** to the discourse it marks an anaphoric, rather than a deictic, relationship.[11] An example from my data illustrating anaphoric *then* is (43).

(43)	Debby:	a.	So, when did they come here?
	Ira:	b.	1906. Um: around 1906.
	Debby:	c.	How old were they **then**?
	Ira:	d.	Um: my dad was about twenty two, my mom was uh: a– about twenty.

Then in (c) is anaphoric: it refers to a time already mentioned in the discourse (1906). My question is thus understood as a request for Ira's parents' ages at that time.

Although my examples thus far have illustrated coterminous event times, this is not the only event time marked by anaphoric *then*: *then* also marks successive event time. In (44), for example, Irene is answering Sally's questions about where she has lived:

(44)	a.	And uh: I lived there 'til I got married,
	b.	and **then**, for about two years after **then**.
	c.	So: uh, and **then** we moved here.
	d.	We've been living here for about twelve years.

In (b), *then* marks both coterminous and successive event times: initial *then* marks the *two years* time period **following** Irene's marriage (a), and final *then* marks the time period co-occurring with the time of the marriage. In (c), *then* marks successive event time. Regardless of which event time is being marked, however, *then* is still anaphoric: it still points to a prior event in the discourse to establish its temporal relationship with a next event in the discourse.

My examples have already suggested a relationship between the position of *then* within the clause and the selection of an event time: clause-final *then* establishes a coterminous event time, and clause-initial *then* establishes a successive event time. An exception to this is when initial *then* figures in a temporal comparison (cf. *now* in temporal comparisons, 8.1.1). In (45), for example, I am contrasting my nephew's behavior this summer with his behavior the previous summer.

(45)   a.   Well my nephew was– was down the shore the last time we were there,
        b.   and he's about fourteen or fifteen months.
        c.   And he had been on the beach *last* summer,
        d.   y'know when he was about *two* months, like your– your other grandson.
        e.   And **then** he just slept in his carriage.
        f.   He didn't know where he was.
        g.   But *this* year, we were really anxious t'see if he would like the water.

(45) compares *last summer* (c) and *this year* (g). *Then* (e) establishes an event time for my nephew's behavior as coterminous with the first time period (*last summer*). Thus, even though *then* is clause-initial, the discourse forces *then* to mark a coterminous event time.

In sum, *then* can be either deictic or anaphoric. In the former case, it marks reference time, which is a relationship between a linguistic event and the time of speaking. In the latter case, it marks event time, which is a relationship between linguistic events within the text itself. Two different event times are marked by *then*: initial *then* marks successive event time, and final *then* marks coterminous event time.[12]

8.2.3 Succession in discourse time

We saw earlier that the properties of *now* as a marker were related to its properties as a time deictic. I suggested that this is because discourse (like events in the world) proceeds forward in time. Discourse time is also relevant to the function of *then*: *then* refers to prior discourse time to establish succession between events (the anaphoric property described in 8.2.2), as well as succession between other units of talks such as ideas, topics, and actions. In short, *then* refers to prior discourse time as a source of information for upcoming talk.

8.2.3.1 Successive ideas in discourse time. Let us begin with discourse in

which temporarily successive events (in real time) are also temporally successive ideas (in discourse time). In (46), Zelda reports a series of events –
episodes – which support her claim that she was tired on the Monday morn-
ing following her family weekend at the beach.

(46) a. So uh: I wanted t'show equal ti– give equal time.
      b. So first, I played with the b– the twins, who're two and a half.
      c. And uh·I went on the beach with them.
      d. **Then** when they went ho–off eh for their nap, I :–
      e. **then** I gave the younger son uh. . .attention.
      f. So it was quite hectic on Saturday.
      g. And we were really ti :–
      h. and **then** we babysat Saturday night, let my younger son go
          out.
      i. And the baby slept in our house.
      j. So that by 10:30 I was really tired.
      k. And I went t'bedhhh.

Zelda describes three episodes in (b–c), (d–e), and (h–i) which are also
reasons for her fatigue. *Then* opens the episodes in (d) and (h).[13] Each episode ends with Zelda's repetition of its outcome (f–g, j–k): she was tired.
This outcome is also the claim that Zelda has been supporting. Thus, in
(46), temporally successive events are also successively presented reasons
in the discourse time of an explanation.

Temporally successive events also coincide with successive topics. In
(47), Zelda describes two episodes with contrasting outcomes. Each episode details how Zelda's twin grandsons reacted to different pairs of toys;
thus, each concerns a different topic. Zelda opens the first episode by introducing the first pair of toys (the different colored buckets).

(47) So w– there's two big red buckets. One has a handle and one doesn't. And
      there was a green bucket, with a handle. [continues]

After reporting the first episode (the twins fought over who would have
what bucket), Zelda contrasts the twins' reactions to the second pair of toys
(a rake and an ordinary shovel). She opens the second episode by introducing the second pair of toys:

> And **then** there was like a blue shovel with r– eh it was a rake. One had–
> there was only one:: like that. The other was an ordinary shovel.

Thus, what is differentiated in (47) are not only two episodes with contrasting outcomes, but two topics: the buckets (red and green) and the shovels
(rake and ordinary). *Then* is used at the simultaneous juncture between

these two coinciding units of talk – the episodes (successive in real time) and the topics (successive in discourse time).

One reason why successive events often coincide with successive units in discourse time is that events often serve as parts of other discourse units. In (47), for example, the episodes involving Zelda's twin grandsons served as two specific examples to support her general point about the unpredictability of twins. Consider, however, that even units of talk which are not themselves temporally successive events **still** succeed one another in discourse time. This succession can also be marked with *then*. (48) illustrates *then* between reasons in an explanation which are not episodic. Ira is explaining Black migration to the North.

(48)   a.   The first Blacks that came on the scene, were uh– as I say they were uneducated,

           b.   no one would give 'em a job

           c.   and they– they started. . .crime.

           d.   Now, when other Blacks heard y'know that the– uh what kind of money they were makin' up here, they left,

           e.   because down South they weren't makin' any kind of money.

           f.   And **then**, the Southerners used t'give 'em carfare t'get 'em the hell outa there.

           g.   So, uh. . .I'm– I– y– you can't say all Blacks are bad.

           h.   Just like all Whites are not good either.

Ira states that the Blacks who first migrated North turned to crime when they faced job discrimination (a–c). Southern Blacks left when they heard about the wealth available in the North (d–e), and Southern Whites encouraged their migration (f). Ira ends his explanation with a disclaimer about its generalizability (g–h): not all Blacks are criminal. *Then* occurs prior to a reason in Ira's explanation. Although it is possible that this reason is a temporally successive event (after some Blacks left, Whites encouraged more Blacks to leave) there are two reasons to suspect that *then* is not functioning temporally here. First, the prior reason (d–e) is marked with *now*: this suggests the opening of a discourse in which the speaker is focusing on the progression of ideas (rather than events). *Then* would thus continue that progression. Second, my understanding of the temporal relationship between the events in (d) and (f) make it unlikely that *then* is indicating successive event time (recall that this is what clause initial temporal *then* marks 8.2.1). Since the events in (d) and (f) are not successive but coterminous (Southern Whites encouraged further Black migration while it was already ongoing), it is doubtful that initial *then* is here functioning as an adverb of successive event time.

(49) illustrates *then* between successive subtopics which are not episodic. The general topic that Zelda and I are discussing is problems facing academic careers. Zelda's first subtopic is *the money part*:

(49)   Zelda: The money part of it isn't eh: anything, is it.

After I agree and elaborate, Zelda continues with her second subtopic, combining family with career:

        Zelda: Oh I see. And **then** say you wanna get married. Cause it makes it hard.

'Getting married' is not a temporally successive event to 'not earning much money'. Furthermore, because I had not recently mentioned my status (single or married), Zelda cannot be suggesting marriage as a successive event to a just mentioned state of being single. Rather, it is a second subtopic which succeeds the first in discourse time.

Then also marks successive subtopics in lists. In (50), for example, Irene is answering my question about her bowling team.

(50)   Debby: How many people are in the team?
         Irene: Four.
         Debby: So it's just t– the two of ⎡ you: and. . .the t–yeh. ⎤
         Irene: ⎣ The two couples, yeh. ⎦
                    And **then** the kids have their own team.

The overall topic of Irene's answer is the membership of the bowling teams. Her two subtopics are the members of each team: first, *the two couples*, and second, *the kids*. Her answer lists the two teams.

We saw in (8.1) that *now* also occurs in lists. This is not the only discourse in which both *now* and *then* occur: the two markers also occur in comparisons. But *now* and *then* have different functions and locations in such discourse. *Then* marks the succession in the discourse from one topic to another, whereas *now* marks the speaker's focus on the next unit *per se*. Another way of saying this is that *then* points backward in talk and *now* points forward.

This backward/forward difference between *then* and *now* leads to a crucial difference in distribution: although *now* can occur with either an initial or next (or last) subtopic, *then* can occur only with a later subtopic. In other words, we find *now* in (b) and/or (d), but *then* only in (d).

(51)   a.   It depends on where you live.
         b.   Now/*then our street is not that nice.
         c.   Because there's so much traffic.
         d.   Now/then their street is nice.

Thus, it is because *now* points forward that it can mark progression to either an initial or later part of a text, and because *then* points backward in talk that it can only mark succession to later parts of a text.

The distributional restriction of *then* helps explain why it can be used by speakers to **repeat** conclusive portions of arguments following another's disagreement. In (52), for example, Irene has stated that common sense is a relative notion: what is right for some people is not right for others. Zelda disagrees, and Irene repeats her point:

(52)   And **then** again, I still feel it's what *they* feel is common. . .I mean what–
        what *you* think is: is not right t'do, and they–y'can't actually say its wrong
        for them.

Then functions here (along with *again* and *still*) to show that Irene's point is not only a repetition of her prior point, but one which follows Zelda's disagreement (statement of a contrasting point). .

In sum, discourse unfolds in a temporal order which is akin to the temporal order presented between real world events. And just as *then* can mark temporal succession between events, so too can it mark temporal succession between the ideas and topics of talk. Another way of saying this is that *then* points to prior discourse time as a source of information not only about events, but about the ideas and topics in discourse structures.

8.2.3.2 Successive actions in discourse time. Another unit whose temporal succession is marked in discourse by *then* is an action, in particular a request from Speaker B which has just been motivated by prior talk from Speaker A. I will speak of such actions as **warranted requests**. Because most warranted requests with *then* are for confirmation, I will first justify my identification of these actions, and then discuss other warranted requests (for action and information) which are also marked by *then*.

The first reason to identify an action as a request for confirmation is its information content: the focus of the request is background information assumed to be either mutual knowledge, or knowledge of the hearer. (Compare Labov and Fanshel 1977: 100 whose rule of confirmation states that 'If A makes a statement about B-events, then it is heard as a request for confirmation.') We can see this best by first observing *then* with repetition and paraphrase, as in (53).

(53)   Sally: a.   Um, how many years of school did you get a chance to
                        finish?
        Zelda: b.   Twelve.

Sally: c.   Twelve. So you went through high school, **then**.
Zelda: d.   Umhmm.

Sally reiterates Zelda's answer that she finished twelve years of school with
the repetition *twelve* and the paraphrase *went through high school*. The
paraphrase is introduced with *so* and closed with *then*. It is because Sally
and Zelda share knowledge about Zelda's education – albeit knowledge recently become mutual – that I interpret Sally's request as one for confirmation, rather than information. (Note that it does not matter that Zelda
had access to the information before Sally – although this issue of other's
prior knowledge would matter for Labov and Fanshel's rule of confirmation.)

Speakers and hearers share access to a great deal of background knowledge which is provided not only by what they tell each other during a conversation (as in (53)), but by their shared membership in a cultural and
social world. In (54), for example, Sally requests confirmation about
Irene's age at the time she met her husband:

(54)   Sally: a.   D'you remember how you met your husband?
        Irene: b.   One of my girlfriends was having a confirmation dinner
                            dance.
                    c.   And I had met him at this party and I asked him to go.
        Sally: d.   So you were younger, **then**.
        Irene: e.   Yeh. I was going with my husband when I was fifteen
                            and a half.

Sally's cultural knowledge of 'confirmation dinner dances' allows her to
infer that Irene met her husband at a relatively young age. Sally requests
confirmation for this inference (d), and Irene provides that confirmation
(e).

(55) illustrates another piece of information whose mutual knowledge is
due to membership in a shared social world. In (55), I request confirmation from Ira about the proximity of one location to another.

(55)   Ira: I was born in South Philadelphia, but I moved to North
                    Philadelphia when I was a year old.
        Debby: Oh, Where in South Philadelphia were you born?
        Ira: 16th and South.
        Debby: Oh! Okay. That's sort of close to center city, **then**.
        Ira: Umhmm.

Since the location about which I request confirmation is a neighborhood
well known to Philadelphians, this is information which I assume is shared
by Ira. Thus, again, this example shows that one reason to interpret

requests as requests for confirmation is the status of the information upon which they focus.

The second reason I identify requests with *then* as requests for confirmation is sequential: A has just presented information which is inferentially related to the content of the request. In (54), for example, it was Irene's recent mention of a 'confirmation dinner dance' which allowed Sally to draw upon her cultural knowledge to infer Irene's age; in (55), it was Ira's mention of a location which allowed me to draw upon my social knowledge to infer the proximity of that location to another. In short, B's assumption of the other's knowledge is recently warranted by A's prior statement. It is the way in which this warrant/inference relation is situated in just-prior talk which also defines these actions as requests for confirmation rather than information.

An examination of how actions are linguistically performed provides the third reason for identifying them as requests for confirmation. In (56), for example, I have been talking with Jack's nephew Rob about jogging, and Jack infers that I am not attending school in the summer:

(56)   Rob: Which is it, near Penn?
        Debby: Yeh. Yeh. Forty third Street.
        Jack: How's your eh:...Oh **then** you don't go t'school in: the
                  summer.
        Debby: Well there aren't any classes. So I can't really get course
                  credits or anything.

Note that Jack's request is presented as a declarative statement with falling intonation. A request for information might have been presented as an interrogative with rising intonation, e.g. *then don't you go to school in the summer?*

(57) provides another example. Ira has just told me that his son started law school that year.

(57)   Debby: a.   How old is he?
        Ira: b.   Twenty one.
        Debby: c.   So he just started **then**.
        Ira: d.   Hm?
        Debby: e.   He just started?
        Ira: f.   Yeh.
        Debby: g.   Yeh. How does he like it?

Like Jack's request for confirmation in (56), my request in (c) in (57) is presented as a declarative statement with falling intonation. And after Ira's *hm?*, I reissue my request again as a declarative (this time with rising intonation) rather than asking a yes–no question (*did he just start?*).

The final reason for identifying requests with *then* as requests for confirmation is that this is what almost always follows them – confirmation in the form of *yeh, uhhuh* and other agreement tokens. Furthermore, the confirmation is then itself followed by agreement tokens from the one issuing the request – thus suggesting that such confirmation is exactly what has been anticipated. In (57), for example, I followed Ira's *yeh* in (f) with my own *yeh*, thus acknowledging the receipt of anticipated information (compare the acknowledgement of unanticipated information with *oh*, Chapter 4). That such information is expected is hardly surprising – given that prior discourse has just provided a warrant licensing its inference.

Requests for confirmation with *then* are often used in interpersonal arguments when one speaker finds a warrant for his own belief in the talk of his opponent. In (58), for example, Freda and Jack have been arguing about the value of coeducation. Freda's position is that the all girls' high school that she attended provides a good academic education, but is not good for more general development. She doesn't clearly formulate this distinction at the outset of her argument, however, and Jack disagrees that the school does provide a good education. (58) shows Jack's efforts to warrant his own position – and the challenge which it poses to Freda's position – in what Freda had said.

(58)	Jack:	a.	But that doesn't make you a better student.
	Freda:	b.	I didn't say it *did*!
	Jack:	c.	Oh! I'm sorry. I thought y'said it did.
	Freda:	d.	No I didn't.
		e.	No I think you're a better student, if you have all of your: uh– uh– y'know if you're one– one sex and you're not looking for ⌈ the: the boy– ⌉
	Jack:	f.	⌊ **Then** y'*did* say that. ⌋
	Freda:	g.	Huh? Oh no I did *not*.
		h.	I said you are a better *student*, if it's all one sex.
	Jack:	i.	**Then** y'*did* say that.
	Freda:	j.	Umhmm.
	Jack:	k.	Well I disagree.
		l.	**Then** I really *do* disagree.
	Freda:	m.	Well– well what d'you mean?

Jack's initial disagreement is in (a). After Freda denies that this is her position (b), and Jack apologizes for the wrong accusation (c), Freda repeats her denial (d) and explains her position (e). Her explanation, however, provides Jack with new grounds for accusation: in (f), Jack accuses Freda of the position with which he had initially disagreed. This accusation is simultaneously a request for Freda's confirmation of the position – which she again denies (g) prior to paraphrasing (h). Again Freda's position provides Jack with grounds for accusation (i) and allows him to request her confirmation – which she this time provides (j). Now that Freda has confirmed what Jack thought to be the position with which he had initially disagreed, Jack restates his disagreement: after prefacing it with *well* (k), he shows that it has been warranted by Freda's recent admission with *then* (1).

Then occurs not only with requests for confirmation, but with any requests which have just been warranted by prior talk. (59) illustrates one way in which a request is warranted: the sudden failure of a prior assumption. Prior to (59), which occurred at the outset of our first interview, I had assumed that both Henry and Zelda would talk to me – because this is what they had agreed to do. But after Irene entered their kitchen, and I said that I wanted to talk to her too, Henry suggested that I no longer needed to talk to him.

(59)   Henry: a.   You go with her. You take *her*.
        Debby: b.   Well when can I talk to you **then**?
        Zelda: c.   She wants t'talk to you too so d–
                  d.   all three of us do it together!
                  e.   C'mere Henry!
                  f.   She needs you too.

My request (b) is warranted by the sudden change in Henry's availability (a): I had assumed Henry would still be available even after I asked Irene to join us. Zelda (c–f) makes explicit my underlying assumption by issuing and justifying a direct request to Henry to stay in the conversation.

Other requests for action hinge upon the receipt of information elicited by prior questions, i.e. they are warranted by a response to a pre-request (a move which checks the validity of a precondition (e.g. Levinson 1983: 345–64)). In (60), for example, Henry is about to tell an off-color ethnic joke, but Zelda stops him to ask him if any members of that ethnic group will hear our conversation. This is a pre-request, for when I respond that I alone hear the conversation, Zelda then goes on to direct Henry to tell me his joke:

(60)   Zelda: Oh! Well **then** tell her about your cruise!

Then in Zelda's request for action marks the fact that this request has been warranted by the information that she has just received from me.

A similar example is (61). I have recently arrived at Freda's house on a summer evening. She and Jack are sitting outside, but they have no outdoor light on – since outdoor lights attract bugs. Freda asks if I will need the light on:

(61)   Freda: a.   Do y'still need the light?
         Debby: b.   Um.
         Freda: c.   We'll have t'go in **then**.
                    d.   Because the bugs are out.
                    e.   We're gonna go crazy with the bugs.

Freda's request for action in (c) is contingent upon the information which I provided (b) to her first request for information in (a): if I do *need the light*, then *we'll have t'go in*. In other words, her request in (c) is warranted by my answer in (b) to her pre-request in (a).

Consider, finally, that *then* is rarely used alone in requests: out of 22 warranted requests with *then*, only 3 used *then* as the sole marker. Figure 8.1 shows the order and the functions of the co-occurring markers. Thus, *then* is preceded by markers which display: (1) either **acknowledgement** of prior information (the information which warrants the request) or **receipt** of that information, and (2) general **participation transition** (*so*) or more specific transition to **respondent** status (*well*). *Then*, the marker of succession, may either precede or follow the request. This order suggests that speakers first admit prior information into their knowledge base, make a transition to a more active participant role, and then perform an action based on that information.[14]

I have shown in this section that *then* has a pragmatic function: it marks Speaker B's request (for confirmation, action, or information) as a request which has just been warranted by A's prior talk. It is important to note that although I have spoken here of requests – which are actions – I have also spoken of them as **warranted** requests. Recall that I spoke of warrants and inferences in my discussion of *so* and *because* (Chapter 7): these markers also display a relationship between a speaker's inference and its warrant which I spoke of as an adjustment in information state. I also suggested that the motive and action chain marked by *because* and *so* (e.g. claim and grounds) rests upon this adjustment in information state. The same suggestion holds for *then* in requests: a request which has just been warranted by prior talk is one which has just been interactionally motivated, but it is also one which is inferentially licensed by what has just been said or done. For both of these reasons, requests with *then* are those whose burden of responsibility – both in terms of satisfying preconditions and assuring the proposed outcome – is shared by both speaker and hearer. Thus, such requests also display a particular division of labor in responsibility for talk,

Figure 8.1. *Markers in warranted requests*

$$\left\{ \begin{array}{l} \text{ACKNOWLEDGEMENT} \\ \text{RECEIPT} \\ \{\text{repetition} \\ \textit{yeh, okay} \\ \textit{oh}\} \end{array} \right\} - \left\{ \begin{array}{l} \text{TRANSITION} \\ \text{RESPONSE} \\ \{\textit{so} \\ \textit{well}\} \end{array} \right\} - \text{(SUCCESSION)} - \text{REQUEST} - \text{(SUCCESSION)} -$$
$$\textit{then} \qquad\qquad\qquad\qquad\qquad \textit{then}$$

Note: {} indicate a choice between items in the brackets; () indicate optional items.

in other words, a particular participation framework. And it is precisely this three part relationship – in information state, participation framework, and action structure – that is marked by the typical sequence of markers in warranted requests: (1) markers which acknowledge or receive prior information, (2) markers which make a transition to a more active participant role, (3) a marker which displays an action based on that information.

8.2.4 Distal time deixis and then

I have suggested that *then* indicates temporal succession between prior and upcoming talk: *then* creates a bridge within the flow of discourse time by pointing away from a current utterance to a prior utterance produced by either the current or prior speaker. It is this reach back to prior discourse time, and to an utterance from either current or prior speaker, which reflects the fact that *then* is a distal deictic.

My interpretation of the function of both *now* and *then* has depended upon an implicit concept of discourse time, i.e. a concept of sequence in which one unit is understood to be 'next' and to follow another. Because this concept is so important to my analysis, I conclude this chapter by way of its more explicit examination. This closer examination of temporal sequences in talk will also allow me to sharpen some of my previous observations about *now* and *then*.

8.3 *Now* and *then*: Deictics in discourse time

Before we consider temporal sequences in talk, it will be helpful to review my observations about *now* and *then*. *Now* marks a speaker's progression through discourse by displaying upcoming attention to a new idea unit, speaker orientation and/or participation framework. *Then* indicates temporal succession between prior and upcoming talk. Whereas *now* points forward in discourse time, *then* points backward. And whereas *now* focuses on how the speaker's own talk is progressing, *then* focuses on how the speaker's talk succeeds either his/her own talk, or the other's talk. These properties of *now* and *then* reflect their status as proximal and distal deictics respectively.

Let us now consider some time sequences (Figure 8.2). Note, first, an important difference between discourse time and other temporal sequences. Events, ideas, topics, and actions are units which are temporally related because they themselves have a linear order according to some independent property which they exhibit. Events, for example, are tem-

Figure 8.2. *Some temporal sequences in talk*

DISCOURSE TIME	OTHER TIME SEQUENCES IN TALK			
Utterance 1	[Event 1]	[Idea 1]	[Topic 1]	[Action 1]
Utterance 2	[Event 2]	[Idea 2]	[Topic 2]	[Action 2]
Utterance 3	[Event 3]	[Idea 3]	[Topic 3]	[Action 3]

porally ordered according to when they occurred in the real world; topics or ideas may logically precede and follow one another; actions may produce a certain outcome only if performed in a particular order. But discourse time emerges only because a speaker is presenting utterances in a certain order: utterances have no independent property which leads to a particular linear order.

Although these time sequences are usually isomorphic – discourse time mirrors event time, and so on – they need not be. For example, discourse and event time may differ:

(62)　**[Utterance 1/Event 3]**　Sue left the hospital today.
　　　[Utterance 2/Event 1]　She was operated on last week.
　　　[Utterance 3/Event 2]　Yesterday she had a relapse.

Although many narratives (at least in Western cultures) assume that discourse time mirrors event time (cf. Labov's (1972a) rule of temporal juncture), a mismatch between discourse time and event time is also common in narratives, e.g. when speakers preface a complicating action with an abstract or when they embed orientation clauses within the complicating action.

Another mismatch occurs when topic time does not mirror discourse time:

(63)　**[Utterance 1/Topic 1]**　My first topic will be phonology.
　　　[Utterance 2/Topic 3]　I'll also discuss syntax.
　　　[Utterance 3/Topic 2]　Before that, I'll go over morphology.

An ensuing discourse may then go on to expand each of those topics in the same order as they were introduced – thus providing a global disjunction between discourse and topic time which reflects the local disjunction.

Similarly, action time may not mirror discourse time. In (64), for example, the sequence of directives produces the desired outcome – reaching a particular destination – only if the action time is the reverse of the discourse time.

(64)   [**Utterance 1/Action 3**]   Turn right onto Broad Street.
        [**Utterance 2/Action 2**]   Before that, pass a bank on the left.
        [**Utterance 3/Action 1**]   And before the bank, you see a park.

Let us use these preliminary observations about temporal relationships in talk to reconsider the role of *now* and *then*. I begin now, with how these issues bear on *now*. Note that I have just (intentionally) provided a use of *now* which illustrates the fuzziness between adverb and marker in actual use. Although this use did not occur at all in my corpus (thus I did not discuss it in 8.1.1), it is common in written discourse (it occurs throughout this book), as well as in somewhat formal, planned (even if loosely planned) discourse modes such as lectures.

(65) provides another example of this discourse use. (Note that I continue to speak of utterances, even though the units in written texts are not verbally produced.)

(65)   [**Utterance 1/Event 1/Topic 1**]   I have so far considered phonology.
        [**Utterance 2/Event 2/Topic 2**]   Now let us consider morphology.

In (65), discourse time mirrors topic time (*phonology, morphology*) and event time, i.e. 'considering phonology' is an event which precedes 'considering morphology'. So *now* marks the speaker's focus not only on a new discourse time, but on a new event and a new topic. And it is this triple focus which makes *now* seem to be both time adverb and discourse marker in this particular type of usage.

This multiplicity of time relations provides another way of describing my observation in (8.1.1) that the distinction between *now* as adverb and marker is neutralized in temporal comparisons. Comparisons consist of a progression of subunits which differ along some topical dimension. Thus, they always display a topic time. But when the topical dimension along which the subunits differ is time – when a speaker is comparing what happened at one time to what happened at another – then the topic time of the discourse is also an event time. It is because of this isomorphism between topic time and event time that I considered the distinction between adverb and marker to be neutralized by the structure of the discourse.

The situation with *then* is slightly more complicated than that with *now*. First, *then* is used when discourse time mirrors event time.

(62a)   [**Utterance 1/Event 1**]   Sue was operated on last week.
        [**Utterance 2/Event 2**]   Then yesterday she had a relapse.
        [**Utterance 3/Event 3**]   Then she left the hospital today.

But *then* is also used when discourse time does not mirror event time.

(62b)   [**Utterance 1/Event 3**]   Sue left the hospital today.
         [**Utterance 2/Event 1**]   Then she was operated on last week.
         [**Utterance 3/Event 2**]   Then yesterday she had a relapse.

But note, crucially, that the use of *then* is appropriate here only if the events are also discourse units of another kind, e.g. idea units which are serving as reasons for a particular outcome, or specific examples supporting a generalization. (62b') suggests the former possibility. (Note also that there may be specific intonational requirements, e.g. *then* with tonic stress in Reason 2.)

(62b')   [**Utterance 1/Event 4/Outcome**]   Sue is in a really bad mood.
         [**Utterance 2/Event 3/Reason 1**]   She left the hospital today.
         [**Utterance 3/Event 1/Reason 2**]   Then she was operated on last week.
         [**Utterance 4/Event 2/Reason 3**]   Then yesterday she had a relapse.

In such cases, what *then* is marking is still discourse time. But instead of also marking event time, it is marking idea time: the ideas are reasons in an explanation.

We can now express the boundary between adverb and marker *then* in a different way. *Then* seems to be an adverb when discourse time mirrors event time (62a), for it is then that it is marking a successive relationship between events. In contrast, *then* seems to be a marker when discourse time mirrors not event time (62b, 62b'), but some **other** successive relationship. What this means is that it is only when the temporal relationships underlying talk *include* event time that *then* can be an adverb. Suppose a speaker orders ideas or topics which are not sequentially ordered events. Such was the case in (49): when Zelda suggested two reasons why an academic career would be problematic, her two reasons were not two temporally ordered events.

(49)   The money part of it isn't eh: anything, is it. And **then** say you wanna get married.

It is because the two reasons are not events which are temporally ordered with each other that I considered *then* a marker rather than an adverb.

However, as I noted earlier (in discussion of (46) and (47)), events can also be functional units in other discourse structures. (62c) illustrates an isomorphism between discourse time, event time, and idea time in our constructed example:

(62c)   Sue is in a really bad mood.
         [**Utterance 1/Event 1/Reason 1**]   She was operated on last week.

[Utterance 2/Event 2/Reason 2]   Then yesterday she had a relapse.
[Utterance 3/Event 3/Reason 3]   Then she left the hospital today.

An example from my data is (66). (See also (46) and (47).)

(66)   Debby: Well who would you invite to a party. Which people.
            Zelda: Em. . .my next door neighbor. And her next door neighbor.
                     And **then** we have eh. . .an old neighbor who we've
                     known. . .y'know, from them. And I guess Jan.

Zelda answers my question with a sequential list of people; the third person in that list is marked with *then*. But note that Zelda's answer is in response to a question about an anticipated action – who she would invite. This means that Zelda may be listing people in the order in which she would invite them. If this is the case, then *then* is marking event time as well as idea time.

In such cases, I would consider *then* a marker even though the isomorphism between discourse time, event time, and idea time could suggest that the distinction between adverb and marker is neutralized (as it was with *now* in temporal comparisons). Regardless of one's position on this, however, it is clear that the problem itself is due to the fact that there are three (or more) different temporal relationships which simultaneously underlie discourse.

Consider, finally, that marker *then* occurs only when discourse time matches **some other** time sequence in talk. Recall that *then* is used with warranted requests, particularly requests for confirmation (8.2.3.2). Although such requests are created by a combination of discourse conditions, it turns out that it is a sequential condition which is most critical in explaining the use of *then*: *then* occurs with requests for confirmation only when they have just been warranted by prior talk. Another way to say this is that *then* occurs only when discourse time matches the action time between warrant and request. Compare (64a) to (64b).

(64a)   **[Utterance 1/Action 1]**   B: I'm looking for boxes to pack my books.
          [Utterance 2/Action 2]   A: You got the new job **then**.

In (64a), the discourse time mirrors the action time of warrant and request: Speaker B says something which warrants A's request for confirmation about *the new job*. But suppose A and B have been discussing a topic unrelated to B's impending move. This means that A's request for confirmation is not immediately warranted and that A cannot use *then*:

(64b)   **[Utterance 1/---------]**   B: I saw Sue yesterday. She looked great.
          [Utterance 2/---------]   A: *You got the new job then.

The reason why *then* cannot be used here is because discourse time does not mirror action time: in fact, the utterances from A and B do not form sequentially implicative actions at all.[15] That *then* is not used under such circumstances shows, again, that it is a marker of temporal succession. But it shows more precisely that *then* is such a marker only when that succession is between utterances in discourse time whose sequential order mirrors some other time sequence of talk.

In conclusion, we have seen in this chapter that *now* and *then* are markers of discourse time. Their functions differ in ways predictable by the proximal/distal difference between time deictics. *Now* marks a speaker's progression through discourse time by displaying attention to what is coming next. Both its focus on the speaker, and on upcoming talk, reflect the proximal quality of the deictic *now*. Similarly, the evaluative use of *now* as a marker reflects the evaluative use of proximal deictics in general. *Then* differs from *now* just as distal deictics differ from proximal deictics: *then* creates a bridge to a prior discourse time created by an utterance from either the speaker him/herself or from the other.

9 Information and participation: *y'know* and *I mean*

This chapter focuses on two markers whose literal meanings directly influence their discourse use. *Y'know* marks transitions in information state which are relevant for participation frameworks, and *I mean* marks speaker orientation toward own talk, i.e. modification of ideas and intentions. Both markers also have uses which are less directly related to their literal meanings: *y'know* gains attention from the hearer to open an interactive focus on speaker-provided information and *I mean* maintains attention on the speaker. I consider these markers together not only because use of both is based on semantic meaning, but because their functions are complementary and because both are socially sanctioned (9.3).

9.1 *Y'know*

Y'know functions within the information state of talk. As I stated in Chapter 1, information states are formed as participants' knowledge and meta-knowledge about the world is redistributed through talk, as different bits of information become more or less salient, and as knowledge about information becomes more or less certain. Although they are initially cognitive in focus, information states have pragmatic relevance since it is through verbal interaction that information state transitions are negotiated and displayed.

9.1.1 Y'know *in information states*

The literal meaning of the expression 'you know' suggests the function of *y'know* in information states.[1] *You* is a second person pronoun (singular or plural) and it is also used as an indefinite general pronoun similar to *one* (or in some of its uses, *they*); *know* refers to the cognitive state in which one 'has information about something'. These component meanings suggest that *y'know* has two possible composite meanings: (1) information X is available to the recipient(s) of talk, (2) information X is generally available.

And these meanings suggest two discourse functions of *y'know*: first, *y'know* is a marker of meta-knowledge about what speaker and hearer share (9.1.1.1), and second, *y'know* is a marker of meta-knowledge about what is generally known (9.1.1.2). Because these functions are realized at slightly different junctures in talk, *y'know* would accomplish two slightly different information state transitions.

9.1.1.1 Meta-knowledge of speaker/hearer shared knowledge. A preliminary problem of talk revolves around the fact that a speaker does not always know whether a hearer shares knowledge about the speaker's topic of talk. Imagine a dialogue in which a speaker is trying to explain a certain procedure, e.g. how to play a game, how to reach a destination. Since the hearer's understanding of such an explanation is likely to depend upon his/her familiarity with particular background information (items, processes, locations, etc.), a speaker must know whether or not the hearer does in fact possess that necessary background.

Four knowledge situations are illustrated in the matrix in Figure 9.1. Each is a different combination of what the speaker knows about hearer knowledge and what the hearer actually knows: thus, each possibility is a different type of meta-knowledge.

Figure 9.1. *Meta-knowledge about speaker/hearer shared knowledge*

| | | Does speaker know of hearer's knowledge? | |
		Yes	No
Does hearer know of X?	Yes	(a)	(b)
	No	(c)	(d)

In (a), the hearer knows the background information and the speaker knows that; in (b), the hearer knows the background information and the speaker does not know that; in (c), the hearer does not know the background information and the speaker knows that; in (d), the hearer does not know the background information and the speaker does not know that. Note that both (a) and (b) are shared knowledge, even though in (b), the speaker does not know that the hearer shares that knowledge. In addition, both (a) and (c) are the speaker's accurate assessments of the hearer's knowledge, even though in (c), the speaker has made an accurate assessment of the hearer's lack of knowledge. Conversely, both (b) and (d) are inaccurate assessments which may require remedial work (although remedial work for b is likely to come from the hearer, e.g. *I knew that already*, and remedial work for d is likely to come from the speaker, e.g. *I thought you knew that already*).

Y'know is used to reach situation (a) in the meta-knowledge matrix, in other words, to create a situation in which the speaker knows about (has meta-knowledge of) knowledge which is shared with the hearer. Furthermore, *y'know* brings about this transition in meta-knowledge regardless of the information state at which speaker and hearer start. Examples (1–4) illustrate the use of *y'know* in transitions from situations (b) (c) and (d) to situation (a).

In (1), Jack is emphasizing his dislike for organized religion. He is saying that prejudice toward religious groups so increases their solidarity that they are unable to abandon their religion.

(1)	Jack:	a.	And when you're a cripple, you're a prej–
		b.	in other words. . .they're cripples because they're so religious is what– is the point I'm trying to make.
		c.	In other words they're *sick*. Religiously.
		d.	Like the: . . .**y'know** what Hasidic is?
	Debby:	e.	Umhmm.
	Jack:	f.	The Hasidic Jew is a cripple in my eyes, a mental cripple.

In (d), Jack begins to illustrate his point about religion by mentioning Hasidic Jews (*like* indicates that Jack is drawing an example from a larger set, Schiffrin 1982b: Chapter 6), but because he cannot be sure that I know of this group, he checks my knowledge with *y'know what Hasidic is?*. Since I do know about Hasidic Jews, I confirm Jack's question in (e), and then Jack continues with his description (f). Thus, (1) illustrates the transition from situation (b), in which the speaker does not know that the hearer has knowledge, to situation (a), in which speaker/hearer shared knowledge is openly attested.

(2) illustrates the transition to (a) from (c), i.e. speaker knows that hearer does not share knowledge. Zelda has been telling me about her daughter JoAnn's first summer away from home.

(2)	Zelda:	a.	Well right now she says, 'I'm so: lonely.'
		b.	She said, 'Everyone went on the boardwalk.'
		c.	And she's ti:red.
		d.	She– just got a job: oh I didn't tell you!
	Debby:	e.	Oh no!
	Zelda:	f.	She got– she– she had applied eh: for a job at the drugstore, as a counter girl?
		g.	**Y'know** ⌈ lunch ⌉ eonette? As a waitress. =
	Debby:	h.	⌊ Yeh. ⌋

Zelda: i.   And they called Sunday.
          j.   So she's workin', ⎡ she's been ⎤ working, =
Debby: k.   Oh ⎣ great!   ⎦
Zelda: l.   = and she says, 'I'm so tired!'

It is in (d) that Zelda opens an information state transition by displaying her realization that I do not know about JoAnn's job: she opens this transition with *oh I didn't tell you* (even though her own realization probably precedes this interactional display: note that both the glottalized stop after *she–*, and an initial background description with *just got a job*, precede *oh*).

Key in the transition in (2) is Zelda's use of rising intonation with two items which are central to her description: the job, *counter girl* (f), and its location, *luncheonette* (g). Bolinger (1982) has suggested that rising intonation is a universal signal that a speaker has not yet completed an information unit (note its use with interrogatives, i.e. incomplete propositions). Sacks (1973) suggests that rising intonation on a particular lexical item solicits hearers' recognition of that item; Sacks refers to this display as a 'try marker'. This suggests that the completion of an information unit presented in a rising intonation would depend less on the speaker him/herself retrieving the needed information, than on the hearer displaying knowledge of that information. In (2), then, rising intonation with *counter girl* and with *y'know luncheonette* display the incompleteness of Zelda's description, and further, the dependency of its completion on my acknowledgement of the two items referred to. Note, also, that this is the same intonation used in (1) with *y'know what Hasidic is?*, a question which my affirmation suggests was a request for recipient knowledge. It now seems that *y'know X?* and *X?* without the additional structural frame of *what X is?*, are also requests for recipient knowledge. (See 9.1.3 on the alternation between reduced and full *y'know* formats.)

(3) is another example in which *y'know X?* marks a transition from situation (c), speaker knows that hearer does not have particular information, to (a), speaker knows that hearer shares knowledge. I include it here because it shows that the information whose reception is sought may need to be reformulated before a hearer achieves recognition.

(3)   Debby: a.   Did you know the doctor that eh they were talking about
                       before, who tried to kill his wife? ⎡ Did=   ⎤
       Zelda: b.   ⎣ Oh no!= ⎦
       Debby: c.   ⎡ = y'know him? ⎤
       Zelda: d.   ⎣ = He's not–   ⎦ he's not a neighborhood doctor. =
       Debby: e.   Oh, oh. ⎡ You had known ⎤ him from. . . ⎡
       Zelda: f.   ⎣ = He's: em. . . ⎦   ⎣ He's from
                 Woman's Medical.

| Debby: | g. | Oh. Yeh, up in: Hen–⎡ on ⎤Henry Avenue. |
| Zelda: | h. | ⎣ Yeh. ⎦   **Y'know**, |

that eh orthopedic doctor?

	i.	**Y'know** that took care of Henry when he had his back?
		⎡ Problems? ⎤
Irene:	j.	⎣ Who, that ⎦ Chinese doctor?
Zelda:	k.	No:: the Italian. Bonzi!
Irene:	l.	⎡ Oh yeh. ⎤
Henry:	m.	⎣ He was ⎦ not Italian, Zelda, he was Spanish.

(3) begins as I ask Irene whether she knows a particular doctor (a); Zelda's answer in (b) shows that she knows that Irene does not have this knowledge. It is after Zelda explains to me why Irene does not know the doctor (d–g) that she provides information about the doctor to Irene by incrementing her knowledge and soliciting her confirmation of that knowledge with *y'know X?* (h, i).

The final example of *y'know* in information state transitions to metaknowledge about shared knowledge is (4), which illustrates a transition from situation (d), speaker does not know that hearer does not share information. (4) begins with my remark that Henry and Zelda's grown children live far from their own home.

(4)	Debby:	a.	Yeh, Zelda was telling me they're about an hour away.
			⎡ That's ⎤ a long drive! ⎡
	Zelda:	b.	⎣ Yeh. ⎦ ⎣ Yeh.
	Henry:	c.	⎡ More ⎤ than ⎡ an hour. ⎤
	Debby:	d.	⎣ Yeh. ⎦ ⎣ Especially ⎦ if you're just going out for a
			⎡ few hours or some ⎤ thing.
	Henry:	e.	⎣ **You know** where– ⎦ **You know** where
			Neshaminy is?
	Debby:	f.	I have an idea. A very vague idea.
		g.	Is it out–
	Henry:	h.	**Y'know** where eh:Street Road is?On the boulevard?
	Debby:	i.	Yeh.
	Henry:	j.	Past Street Roa:d, and then you k– go over the: it says
			Nesh⎡ amin– ⎤ Mo– Washington Motel?=
	Zelda:	k.	⎣ eh: ⎦ Motel?
	Henry:	l.	=Y'cut deep, bear to your right [continues]

Henry begins in (e) with a description of where his children live by locating a central landmark and asking if I know its location: *you know where Neshaminy is?*. Since I have only *a very vague idea*, I cannot respond affirmatively (f), and I begin to ask for further specification (g). Henry locates another landmark (h) and uses the same *y'know where X is?* format, as well as a specification of that landmark (*on the boulevard?*), to elicit my recognition. Once I provide that recognition (i), Henry continues with directions to his children's house.

We have seen in these examples that *y'know* brings about information states in which the speaker knows of speaker/hearer shared knowledge, but that *y'know* does not always work alone in such transitions. In addition to the important role played by intonation and reference to the entity about which hearer recognition is sought, a crucial part of these transitions is for the **hearer** to acknowledge his/her receipt of information either by affirming that information (as in 1 through 4) or by marking its reception with *oh* (as in 2 and 3). In fact, when such markers are not provided, the speaker is likely to try again with a different bit of information (as in the initial parts of (3) and (4)).

Note, now, that a hearer may indicate his/her reception of information following a speaker's use of *y'know* even when *y'know* is presented with neither a rising terminal nor reference to a particular entity. This suggests that *y'know* may create a transition to meta-knowledge about speaker/hearer shared knowledge even when it is not explicitly formulated to do so. In (5), for example, Irene has been answering my question about bowling, when Zelda prompts her to tell me with whom they bowl.

(5)   Irene: a.   We have a team in the summer we bowl.
                 b.   Every summer ⎡ they– husband and wife–
        Zelda: c.   ⎣ Tell her who you bowl with.⎦
        Irene: d.   Who we *bowl* with.
        Zelda: e.   D– **y'know**, the teams.
        Irene: f.   Oh. Wha'd'y'mean ⎡ the kids?
        Zelda: g.   ⎣ The kids.⎦
        Irene: h.   Oh yeh. This year the kids have their own team, and
                      they're...they're eh...they're givin' us a run for our
                      money.

Zelda begins a direct prompt in (c) with her imperative: *tell her who you bowl with*. Irene requests clarification with her repetition (d), and Zelda provides that clarification by specifiying the referent of *who* with *the teams*. Note that *the teams* is preceded by *y'know* – an effort by Zelda to gain Irene's knowledge of what she means – and that it is presented with falling intonation. In (f), Irene displays her recognition of Zelda's referent with *oh* and then requests more specific clarification with *wha'd'y'mean the kids?*. After Zelda confirms this specification, Irene again acknowledges it (*oh yeh* in h), and expands upon the composition of the bowling teams.

(6) illustrates that *y'know?* without reference to a particular entity also

elicits markers of information reception. Irene is explaining to Sally why her son's school class had a special feeling about themselves.

(6)   Irene: Because like uh: . . .eighth grade, they were the only class
                    that he had taken over t'the synagogue, which remained
                    there: **y'know?** ⌈
        Sally: ⌊ Yeh, I remember.
        Irene: It labelled them.

Irene follows the reason for the class's attitude with *y'know?*, to which Sally responds *yeh, I remember*. (Sally had taught at the school so she was familiar with the situation.) Irene then continues with her explanation.

And (7) illustrates that *y'know* with neither rising intonation nor reference to a particular entity can also elicit a hearer's display of information reception.

(7)   Debby: a.   And what d'you do?
        Irene: b.   I'm an N.T.A. In ⌈ school. ⌉
        Debby: c.   ⌊ What's ⌋ that?
        Irene: d.   Uh::really a cop. ⌈ See that the– Yeh. See that= ⌉
        Debby: e.   ⌊ Oh real: ly?!   No kidding? ⌋
        Irene: f.   =the kids behave a little bit. **Y'know.** ⌈ And– ⌉
        Debby: g.   ⌊ I   ⌋
                          didn't know they had those: uh   ⌈ discipline ⌉
        Irene: h.   Yeh ⌊ in the   ⌋
                          Philadelphia schools they do.

Irene describes the job *N.T.A.* after I ask *what's that* (c). (Since I cannot identify her job, her explanation creates a shift in meta-knowledge from a situation in which speaker did not know that hearer lacked knowledge (situation c) to one in which speaker and hearer openly attest to shared knowledge (a).) During my initial evaluative reaction (e) to her preliminary definition of her job (d), Irene continues to describe her duties (d, f); she also affirms my *oh real:ly?!* with *yeh*. I then treat Irene's *y'know* in (f) as another invitation to attest to my increasing knowledge (even though Irene is about to continue; note her interrupted *and*).

Our discussion of the complementary use of speaker's *y'know* and hearer's *yeh/oh* has begun to take us away from the strictly informational role of *y'know*. This is because once we start to acknowledge that the reception of information is verbally displayed, then we may also assume that the marker by which such verbal displays are **solicited** functions not merely as a cognitive marker, but as an interactional marker. The examples in this section suggest that *y'know* is complementary in function to *oh*. We saw in Chapter 4 that *oh* displays a hearer as an information recipient, i.e. one who is actively involved in the production format of talk through the process of receiving information as it is being presented. Because *y'know* induces a hearer to act as an information recipient, it has the complementary function of ratifying the speaker as an information provider but one in a somewhat specialized production format – one whose provision of information is contingent upon hearer reception.

This specialized production format allows us to understand why *y'know* prefaces background explanatory clauses in narratives (cf. *because*, Chapter 7). Speakers may need to introduce background material before an upcoming narrative event will make sense to their hearers. Bracketing such material with *y'know* marks its special status as to-be-shared information, as well as the speaker's dependency on hearer reception of that information prior to his or her continued role as information provider. (8) illustrates. Zelda is answering my question about whether the future is predictable with a story about her youth.

(8)   Zelda: a.   I remember when I was. . .young.
                   b.   And em. . .I'd say like in my earl– it was in my early
                         twenties.
                   c.   I was about twenty,
                   d.   and I was working then.
                   e.   And, **y'know**, how some of the girls we'd go out for
                         lunch,
                   f.   and they'd have these eh. . .they– they read your tea
                         leaves!
                   g.   **Y'know** these tea rooms?

Zelda's story will not be interpretable unless I know about tea rooms and predicting the future by reading tea leaves. Thus her status as an information provider depends on her ability to establish that information as shared. She does this by prefacing it with *y'know*, first in (e), and then in (g) as a try-marker. Zelda then continues to tell her story in her role as information provider.

In sum, *y'know* is used to create a situation in which a speaker knows that a hearer shares knowledge about a particular piece of information. Because it may thereby induce a hearer to attest to that knowledge, *y'know* also displays the speaker as an information provider who depends upon hearer reception of information.

9.1.1.2 Meta-knowledge of generally shared knowledge. Y'know also marks the general consensual truths which speakers assume their hearers share through their co-membership in the same culture, society, or group (cf. T.

Labov 1980).[2] These uses of *y'know* may have the same interactive effect as those discussed above, simply because speaker and hearer are assumed to be included in the set of those who share a general truth; furthermore, speakers can use consensual truths to enlist hearer recognition or agreement.

The easiest way to see that *y'know* is used as a marker of general truths is to find it with formulaic expressions of such truths. In (9), for example, Henry and Zelda have been discussing Henry's upcoming visit to the dentist, to which he is not looking forward. Henry playfully suggests (a, b) that since he is participating in our interview, he should not have to go to the dentist: he does this by defining our interview as a 'mitzvah' (a good deed) and building upon an implicit analogy between the healing powers of a mitzvah and an apple.

(9)   Henry: a.   A mitzvah a day will keep the doctor away.
              b.   So if I can do this mitzvah today, maybe I don't have
                   t'go t'the dentist tomorrow?
      Zelda: c.   No⎡ y'still ⎤ have t'go Henry, tomor ⎡row! ⎤
                    ⎣hhhhhhh⎦   ⎣hhhh⎦ That's a
                   thought though, isn't ithhhhh
              e.   **Y'know** they say an *apple* a day keeps the doctor away?

Henry makes the analogy underlying his joke explicit by stating the formulaic expression of the conventional wisdom: *an apple a day keeps the doctor away* (e). He prefaces this expression not only with *y'know*, but with *they say*, a quotative expression which itself conveys general consensus (*they* here is an indefinite pronoun). That Henry also presents the formulaic expression with a rising intonation, the same terminal rise seen in (1)–(4), shows that he is also proposing his hearers' recognition of the conventional wisdom.

In (10), a consensual truth is presented as a tautology. Although tautologies are often formulaic ways of conveying general truths (e.g. *war is war, boys will be boys*), the tautology in (10) is not in itself formulaic. Henry is saying that one reason why Jewish women should not marry out of their religion is that Christian men are not always faithful husbands. Irene argues that many Jewish men also *treat Jewish women pretty lousy*. (10) is the end of Henry's response to Irene.

(10)   Henry: a.   If a man is lousy to a woman, he's lousy to *any* woman
                    he can get t–
               b.   t'*him*, a woman is only a– a receptacle that he can use,
                    an' the hell with everything!
               c.   'At's all it means to him,

> d.   'At's all it means!
> e.   It doesn't mean anything to him.
> f.   So whether he's a Jew or somethin' else it's– 'at's– 'at's
>   eh– 'at's getting away from the subject.
> g.   A bastard's a bastard regardless, **y'know**

Elsewhere in our conversations, Henry expresses strong opinions on the
rights of women to be treated well by their husbands. The same level of
intensity and involvement with this issue expressed throughout Henry's
discourse is conveyed here: note Henry's use of taboo words (*hell, bastard*)
and his repetitions (c, d, e). Henry then claims that Irene's critique is off
the point (f) and that the point can be summarized with the tautology in
(g): *a bastard's a bastard regardless*. In other words, because this is an inevitable truth with which all would agree, it is futile for Irene (or anyone)
to argue otherwise.

Y'know as a marker of consensual truths occurs not only with formulaic
expressions and tautologies, but with general descriptions (e.g. of situations, states, events). Speakers often use general descriptions to support
their more specific claims and to gain their hearers' endorsement of such
claims. In (11), for example, Zelda, Henry and I have been talking about
husbands' dependencies on their wives' daily presence in the home. Zelda
states that Henry did not want her to continue to vacation at their summer
home when he had to return to the city, and I add that my father sometimes
behaves in a similar way. Henry interrupts my description with the following defense:

(11)   Henry: I'm not a–...we're all not perfect, **y'know**.
                  I'm not perfect Zelda, after all.

By presenting his own individual defense **after** a consensual truth (a play
on *nobody's perfect*), Henry not only increases the likelihood that Zelda
and I will accept his defense, but he cushions himself against having to bear
responsibility for his own specific character: if no one is perfect, certainly
Henry cannot be expected to be so either.

Of course speakers cannot always assume their hearers' endorsement of a
generalization. In (11), in fact, Zelda and I join Henry's later laughter, but
neither of us verbally respond to what he has said. Other consensual truths
with *y'know* do become a basis for further interaction, however, and an
examination of some ways that such truths are situated shows some additional interactional effects of *y'know*.

In (12), Freda provides a tacit endorsement of Jack's generalization by

continuing to describe the specific situation included in it. Freda and Jack
are answering my question about who they go out with.

(12)   Jack: a.   Yeh but uh : . . .that's about it, I guess.
               b.   Come t'think of it we hardly bother with anybody
                    anymore.
               c.   Since I stopped bein' the committeeman, I g– that sort
                    of gave me a break t'get away from everybody.
       Freda: d.   No f– let's face it.
               e.   You do come home tired,
               f.   and I don't feel– I'm not in the mood anyway.
       Jack: g.   See we're old people already. =
       Debby: h.   I know how y'feel.
       Jack: i.   = I guess that–s– that–s what it is.
               j.   **Y'know** when you get older, you just don't keep
                    socializing anymore.
               k.   There's nobody t'social ⌈ize with! ⌉
       Freda: l.   ⌊Well we–⌋ we went through
                    it anyway.

Jack switches from a description with Freda of their own situation (a–g) to
a general statement about older people (j). Thus, he uses a general statement to show that his own situation is not just a single, isolated case, but a
typical instance of a more pervasive and broader generalization. Although
Freda does not openly agree with Jack's generalization, her continued description of their own specific situation shows her tacit endorsement of its
ability to be legitimately described by Jack's general statement.

   In (13), a speaker seeks hearer endorsement of a generalization. Zelda
and I are talking about JoAnn's plans for college. Zelda has said that she
can't afford to send JoAnn to college without some kind of financial assistance, but that matters are complicated because JoAnn doesn't want to go to
the less expensive local college. Nevertheless, Zelda will not argue with
JoAnn about it now.

(13)   Zelda: a.   Well, I'm not even eh: arguing wi– that's why I figure,
                    why should I argue now.
       Debby: b.   Yeh, yeh.
       Zelda: c.   And she hasn't any idea of what she wants to take.
               d.   She's leaning toward optometry.
               e.   But she coul– she: **y'know**: what you lean towards and
                    what you do, are two different things.
               f.   She could go through a year, and then maybe, figure
                    'I'm tired of studying.'
               g.   ⌈Did ⌉ you?
       Debby: h.   ⌊Yeh.⌋   I wanted to stop the first week I started.
       Zelda: i.   Y'see! That's what I said.

After describing JoAnn's lack of direction (c, d), Zelda begins in (e) to continue her specific description, but then switches to a general description prefaced by *y'know*. (Note that although Zelda's general statement is not formulaic, it does reflect a general belief in the tendency of real life concerns to intrude upon people's hopes and dreams, e.g. 'if wishes were horses, beggars would ride'.) Zelda then returns to her specific description (f) and asks me to confirm the general observation through my own experience (g). After I do so (h), she attests to the increased validity of the general truth in (i). Thus, (13) illustrates that general truths can be validated by elicitation and receipt of evidence of speaker/hearer shared knowledge and hearer alignment.

In (14), a speaker seeks to invalidate the other's specific description – an invalidation which the other then denies. Jack and Freda have been discussing their new neighbors' efforts at housekeeping. Jack compares their diligence with the laziness of their previous neighbor, Rose (who was Freda's close friend).

(14)　　Freda:　　a.　These two kids are really scrubbin' and rubbin' even
　　　　　　　　　　　what $\begin{bmatrix} \textit{they} \\ \text{They–} \end{bmatrix}$ scrubbed and rubbed! $\begin{bmatrix} \text{Yeh,} \\ \text{Well} \end{bmatrix}$ *she*
　　　　Jack:　　　b.　never
　　　　　　　　　　　did $\begin{bmatrix} \text{any} \\ \text{Huh?} \end{bmatrix}$ thing. $\begin{bmatrix} ^\prime \textit{Rose} \text{ never did} \\ \text{No she didn't,} \end{bmatrix}$ anything
　　　　Freda:　　c.　　　　　　　　　　　　　　　　　　　　　　　but she
　　　　　　　　　　　had that girl.
　　　　Jack:　　　d.　Oh! Help don't do these things! C'mon.
　　　　　　　　　　e.　**Y'know** they just wipe this off, and wipe that off, and
　　　　　　　　　　　underneath it's dirty.
　　　　　　　　　　f.　**Y'know** it's help!
　　　　　　　　　　g.　And why should they?
　　　　　　　　　　h.　It's *your* house, not theirs.
　　　　Freda:　　i.　No. I think Rose. . .would demand.
　　　　Jack:　　　j.　Ah: Rose was a slob. I was in that house.

Jack switches from a specific discussion of Rose to a general truth about hired housekeepers in (d–h). Note his efforts to enlist Freda's agreement with *c'mon* (d), *y'know* (e, f), and a rhetorical question/answer pair (g, h). But Freda does not agree that Rose's case fits the general description, and the discussion returns to a specific level of description (i, j).

In sum, *y'know* is a marker of meta-knowledge about generally shared knowledge: *y'know* marks consensual truths which speakers assume their hearers are likely to share (because of co-membership in the same culture, society, or group) as well as general descriptions within which specific descriptions are assumed to be included. Because these generalizations are not always openly endorsed by hearers, speaker and hearer may have to negotiate both the informational status (is it shared knowledge?) and the interactional status (is there agreement as to its ability to capture a range of specific situations?). Again we have seen, then, that when *y'know* has an informational function, it also has an interactional function: *y'know* marks not only meta-knowledge, but transitions in participation framework. In the next section, I consider further the link between information state and participation framework.

9.1.2 The interactional relevance of meta-knowledge

Markers of information state transitions have pragmatic relevance in participation frameworks. We saw in (9.1.1.1) that *y'know* has a complementary function to *oh* because it marks a speaker in a complementary participation status – as a producer rather than a recipient of talk. We saw in (9.1.1.2) that *y'know* as a marker of consensual truths can be used to seek particular interactional alignments. To show further how information shifts are interactionally relevant, I focus on *y'know* in arguments (9.1.2.1), and narratives (9.1.2.2).

9.1.2.1 Y'know in arguments. In an argument, a speaker presents support for a disputable position (Chapter 1). Underlying this discourse structure is an asymmetric distribution of knowledge and/or opinion: Speaker A provides information to B about some area of expertise in which B is not equally informed, and/or A provides evidence which leads B to take a position with which he/she was not initially aligned. *Y'know* allows a speaker to check on how the discourse is creating an interactional progression away from an initially asymmetric distribution: is knowledge now more equitably divided? Is opinion now shared? In so doing, *y'know* functions both informationally and interactionally: it allows a hearer to affirm the receipt of information, and it displays the ways in which particular participant roles are undergoing gradual transitions throughout the discourse.

The most obvious use of *y'know* in this dual capacity in arguments is illustrated in (15): *y'know* appeals to shared knowledge as a way of converting an opponent to one's own side in a dispute. Henry and Irene have been arguing about the current disintegration of family structure. Henry blames fathers' decreased authority (*fathers are not the kingpins anymore*), but Irene argues that this does not always have a devastating effect by presenting her own family as an example: her husband's overbearing job responsibilities leave her with the responsibility of housekeeping and child-rearing. What Irene does **not** say is that her own family is stable and well integrated; rather this is an assumption of the argument. (15) is Henry's rebuttal to Irene's challenge. It works by denying another unspoken assumption of Irene's argument: her personal experience can be used as evidence because it is a specific instance of the more general situation under dispute.

(15)   Henry: a.   Irene you gotta remember one thing.
                  b.   You cannot put yourself in that category, because you are in a different circumstance.
                  c.   **You know** you went through, and you went through eh: something else. T'catch up.
                  d.   **Y'know** you got a lot t'catch up.
                  e.   And you're both working hard,
                  f.   but it ain't always gonna be like *that*,
                  g.   it's gonna pay,
                  h.   it's gonna be different.

Y'know in both (c) and (d) has a dual role: since both Henry and Irene are familiar with Irene's economic circumstances, *y'know* appeals to shared knowledge, and since Henry is disqualifying Irene's personal evidence, *y'know* works in Henry's attempt to convert his opponent to his own side. (Schiffrin 1984a, 1985a provides further discussion of this argument.)

(16) illustrates *y'know* at a slightly different juncture in argument, but one which is also definable in both informational and interactional terms. Jack has been explaining to his nephew Rob how Americans are socialized into believing in their country's superiority during war.

(16)   Jack: a.   And I betcha you couldn't picture. . .America losing in Vietnam.
                 b.   In fact you said that.
                 c.   That we were somehow gonna win.
                 d.   **You know** why?
                 e.   Because you're American.
                 f.   and you were already built up in your mind,
                 g.   they built it up for you, whether you know it or not, that we never lost a war!

In (a) to (c), Jack offers Rob's own experience as evidence for the pervasiveness of the American belief. In (d), Jack asks Rob if he knows why he himself held this belief. This *y'know why* question opens a slot in which Jack can insert a reason – the reason which is the point of his whole argument (e–g). The question is a pivotal ideational transition in Jack's argument precisely because of the dual role of *y'know*: by focusing attention on Rob's knowledge about his own belief, *y'know* draws Rob into the interactional process of validating the general point of the argument.

(17) illustrates *y'know* at an ideational transition similar to that in (16). However, rather than go on to state a position, the speaker states the relevance of that support for her general position. Irene is explaining to me why she prefers urban to suburban living; (17) begins with her second reason.

(17)   Irene: a.   I know I have a girlfriend that lives in Hatfield,
                    b.   and she doesn't know her neighbor on either side.
                    c.   **Y'know?**
                    d.   And I'm not that kind of person.

Irene initiates support for her position with *I know* (thus indicating that it is personal evidence for a belief), and then exits from that support with *y'know?* She then states the relevance of that support for her position (d). (See Chapter 6, pages 129–37 for comments on *and* at different structural levels in argument.) Thus, *y'know* not only closes Irene's first piece of support, but it also allows her to go on from that support to state its importance for the argument as a whole. In short, Irene has offered her hearer a chance to receive the information in her argument at a key structural juncture.

In sum, arguments involve an asymmetric distribution of knowledge and/or opinion. *Y'know* allows a speaker to check on how the discourse is progressing away from that initial distribution: a speaker can solicit affirmation of information reception as well as evidence of shifts in the interactional alignment.

9.1.2.2 Y'know in narratives. *Y'know* also occurs when a hearer is invited to share in the information transfer being accomplished through narrative discourse. The interactional effect of *y'know* in narratives differs, however, because *y'know* enlists the hearer not just as an information recipient, but as a particular kind of participant to the storytelling (an audience). This function is suggested by the fact that *y'know* has two primary locations in narratives: with events which are internally evaluative of the story's point, and with external evaluation of the narrative point.[3] (Internal evaluation is within the story frame, e.g. a complicating action clause such as *were laughing so hard it hurt!*; external evaluation is outside of the story frame, e.g. meta-linguistic clauses such as *that was the funniest time I remember*. See Labov 1972a.) The function of *y'know* in these locations is to draw the hearer's attention to material which is important for reaching an understanding of why the story is being told.

Two stories from Henry illustrate *y'know* with an internal evaluation. (18) is the end of a story retelling Henry's conversation with a wealthy man. Henry has previously made the point that giving children too much money is akin to giving them poison, and his story reiterates that point.

(18)   Henry: a.   And I was working very hard,
                  b.   and I told him, I said 'I must save money t'send my children t'college.'
                  c.   **Y'know** what he told me for an answer?
                  d.   He says, 'Henry, children find their *own* way t'go t'college if they want to.'
                  e.   He says, '*They* make better children.'
        Irene: f.   I agree with ⌈ that. ⌉
        Henry: g.   ⌊ And I ⌋ never forgot what he said.
                  h.   Ab ⌈ solutely. ⌉
        Irene: i.   ⌊ I agree with ⌋ that.

The *y'know what* question in (c) prefaces the reported speech in (d) and (e) which conveys the story's point: children should not be spoiled. (See 9.1.3 for discussion of the similarities between different *y'know* formats, and the way in which *y'know what* opens an upcoming slot to hearer attention.) Note that this is the part of the story with which Irene agrees (f, i), and that Henry further intensifies this point (g, h).

(19) shows that *y'know* can work at a deeper level of internal evaluation because *y'know* occurs within the reported speech comprising the central events of the story. Henry has been complaining about the stinginess of his previous next-door neighbor, and his story provides an instance of that stinginess by recounting what happened after Zelda had given the neighbor a tomato in return for one previously loaned to her.

(19)   Henry: a.   And she sat down there,
                  b.   and she says, '**Y'know** I got a problem Zelda.'
                  c.   She says, 'I really got a problem.'
                  d.   So Zelda says, 'What's your problem?'
                  e.   I was sittin' right there.
                  f.   She says, '**Y'know** I gave you a tomato. Your tomato's not as big as the one I gave you. What shall I do with it?
                  g.   What d'y'think I wanted t'tell her t'do with it?!

Y'know prefaces two instances of reported speech in which the neighbor introduces and describes her dissatisfaction with the tomato. Thus, rather than telling his audience about the neighbor's stinginess, Henry transforms his hearers into an audience to the telling – allowing them to hear for themselves the way in which she conveyed her character. Note how he further authenticates his report in (e) with *I was sittin' right there*, and how he draws attention to the neighbor's complaint not only with *y'know* within the quote, but by having Zelda ask *what's your problem* (d). Finally, *y'know* within the quotes also shows the neighbor's own presumption that Zelda should have been aware of the injustice of the unequal trade of tomatoes – or at least Henry's portrayal of the neighbor as one who is that sure of her complaint.

(20) illustrates *y'know* with several different forms of evaluation. Irene has been saying that the Blacks she knew as a high school student were easier to get along with than the Blacks that she now meets. After opening her story with *I'll give you a for instance*, she begins to report a parent visitation day at her son's school. The teacher was giving a spelling test, and Irene started to talk to some of the other mothers. (20) tells what happened after the spelling test.

(20)	Irene:	a.	And on the way out of the door, this v– very fine looking colored woman,
		b.	and she came up t'me and another one of the women,
		c.	and she said eh:, 'You have a child in this room.'
		d.	And I said, 'Yes.'
		e.	She said, '**Y'know** it was really very annoying t'sit here, during visitation, while you people are rattling on.'
		f.	I mean really indignant.
		g.	I don't know the woman from Adam.
		h.	I think she must– her daughter is not– wasn't in the room before this year.
		i.	I really got annoyedhhh
		j.	I was ready t'punch her! This other– **y'know**?
		k.	Like out of the clear blue sky!
		l.	**Y'know** they just have such an arrogant air about them!
		m.	As if they wanna take over
		n.	and they're–it's the first time that they're there!

Y'know in (e) is with an evaluation which is deeply embedded in the narrative structure. Like Henry's *y'know* in (19), it occurs with a direct quote which provides the pivotal event of the story, and through which Irene's story becomes understood as an instance of a more general situation. And also like (19), *y'know* is with quoted material whose initial author would prefer to define as shared knowledge: the indignant woman's complaint is validated if Irene agrees that *rattling on* during visitation was *really very annoying*. *Y'know* in (j) is also evaluative, but it moves slightly out of the story frame: Irene's annoyance is portrayed by her being *ready t'punch her*, and *y'know* opens this internally evaluative event to audience response. Finally, *y'know* in (1) marks Irene's shift from the specific story to the general point of which it was an instance (her *they* refers to Blacks in general). In short, *y'know* here occurs with an explicit statement of the narrative point from a perspective outside of the story frame.

In sum, *y'know* in narrative occurs with internally evaluative events and with external evaluation. *Y'know* enlists the hearer's participation as an audience to the storytelling by drawing the hearer's attention to material which is important for his/her understanding of why the story is being told. The function of *y'know* as a marker of information state transition contributes to this use in narratives. A narrator has an interactional stake in making a story interesting (to avoid, in Labov's 1972a terms, 'the withering response of "so what?"'). By enlisting the hearer as an audience, *y'know* provides the minimum needed for story appreciation – hearer attention. *Y'know* goes even further, however. Since many stories report typical instances of more general propositions (Irene's story in (20) made this explicit through its preface), a dual task facing a storyteller is to get an audience to recognize the typicality of the reported events and the general proposition which is illustrated by those events. *Y'know* helps a speaker in these tasks precisely because it marks meta-knowledge about shared (either speaker/hearer or general) knowledge. That is, once speakers produce in their hearers recognition that a story is about something with which they themselves are already familiar – something which is shared knowledge – then much of the informational and interactional dilemma facing storytellers is resolved.

Note, finally, that the fact that *y'know* occurs with both internal and external evaluation is important for two additional reasons. First, it allows us to see that *y'know* has a more global scope in discourse than we have yet considered. We started with examples in which *y'know* focused on very local entities: nouns, specific propositions. *Y'know* with evaluations also focuses on propositions, but on propositions which are themselves established through an entire discourse unit (the story). This means that the hearer has to filter the main message of the discourse from the entire discourse unit. And although external evaluations explicitly state a point (the message) which has been expanded through the story, internal evaluations force the hearer to piece together the point from assorted clauses throughout the story. Thus, *y'know* with internal evaluations helps the hearer filter through the story and select what is important for understanding of the point.

Second, my analysis is beginning to move from more literal uses of

y'know which solicit hearer knowledge about an entity or proposition
(9.1.1) to less literal uses of *y'know* which solicit hearer attention to propositions derivable from an entire discourse. (This is because *y'know* with
narrative evaluations marks information whose importance is its relation to
other information in the discourse and to the overall point of the entire
story.) We will see in the next section how *y'know* can solicit hearer attention in ways which are even less directly related to its meaning.

9.1.3 Exchange structures and hearer attention

I have suggested thus far that it is because of its literal meaning that *y'know*
marks information state transitions, and because of its role in information
states that *y'know* has interactional relevance in participation frameworks.
Another reason why *y'know* has these functions is that it helps create an
exchange structure which focuses the hearer's attention on a particular bit
of information provided by the speaker. Figure 9.2 shows this structure;
y'know would occur in A1. Observe, first, that A1 and B1 are likely to form
an adjacency pair. For example, A1 may be a *y'know where X is* question
which solicits an affirmation in B1 (as in (4)). A2 can then proceed upon
the assumption that knowledge of X is shared, e.g. *well you go to X and
you...* Note next that A1 is oriented not only toward soliciting hearer
reception in B1, but toward accomplishment of A2. This means that A1 is
not only the first part of an adjacency pair: it is also the first part in another
sequence comprised of A1 and A2.[4] The completion of this sequence is
actually contingent upon the response (the second part of the adjacency
pair) in B1. (We saw examples of these structures, which I referred to as
contingent sequences, in Chapter 5, 44, 45.) It is this dependency between
A1/B1 and A2 that I indicate through the brackets in Figure 9.2.

Figure 9.2. *Exchange structure created by* y'know

A1:	says something which leads B to focus on X	
B1:	focuses on X	
A2:	uses X in a way dependent upon A1 and B1	

A good example of how this exchange structure works is the use of
y'know what? to open narratives. Recall that narratives require a relatively
long conversational space if they are to be completed, i.e. a suspension of
turn-exchange at a number of turn-transition locations (Chapter 1). One
particularly effective method for securing such a space is for Speaker A to

ask a question of the format *y'know what (happened)?* Since answers are
conditionally relevant on questions, A expects a respondent B to answer
along the lines of *(no), what?* But note what this response does: it asks
another question, which then requires an answer. Thus, A's question has
solicited a question from B, and it is then up to A to provide an answer – an
answer which will be given through the story. Figure 9.2' shows how this
negotiated story opening fulfills the exchange structure. In short, *y'know
what (happened)?* fills the slot of A1; it solicits from B1 an answer which
then allows A2 to use a story to expand upon *what happened*. Thus, the
telling of the story is contingent upon the completion of the adjacency pair
in A1 and B1.

Figure 9.2'. *Exchange structure of story opening with* y'know

A1:	says something which leads B to focus on X
	'Y'know what happened the other day?'
B1:	focuses on X
	'No. What happened?'
A2:	uses X in a way dependent upon A1 and B1
	'I was walking home from school and [story]'
	'So that was it. That's what happened.'

One problem with suggesting that *y'know* creates this particular
exchange structure is that A1 in the structure is not always an embedded
WH-question (*do you know WH*) intended to be answered with another
question. Rather, A1 may assert a proposition and ask for B's knowledge
(*do you know that?*) which B1 may then confirm or deny without asking
another question in return. I suggest, however, that eliciting B's confirmation (or denial) of a particular proposition focuses B's attention on that
proposition, and that B would thus assume that his/her attention had been
directed to that information for some reason, e.g. so that A could then use
that information in some way in upcoming talk. It is this assumption which
could lead B1 to expect A2 to use the focused information in a way dependent upon A1 and B1.

Another problem is that A1 is not always a question, and thus, not
always as sequentially implicative as the first part of an adjacency pair.
This is a problem because it is the adjacency pair structure, and the force of
the question in the first-pair-part, which is crucial to the outcome of the
exchange.

I suggest, however, that many cases of *y'know* can be considered as
reduced questions, and thus, that even those cases of *y'know* which do not

initiate questions lead a hearer to focus on particular information. (I have already implied this in 9.1.1.1.) More specifically, I propose that *y'know* focuses on either upcoming or prior information because it is a reduced form of a *do you know* question with either forward or backward discourse scope. Such a question focuses on information in one of three ways. First, a proposition can be prefigured in a WH-complement (21a) or a reduced complement (b). (P= proposition.)

(21)   a.   do you know who/what/where/why/when/how X is? P.
       b.   do you know what (happened to X)? P.

Second, a proposition can be in *that*-complement of *know*:

       c.   Do you know that P?

Third, a proposition can be referred to with anaphoric *that*:

       d.   P. Do you know that?

(21a–c) are *y'know* formats which point forward in talk; (21d) is a *y'know* format which points backward in talk. My suggestion is that both these question formats, and *y'know* without a question frame, lead a hearer to attend to speaker's information, and thus, open an interactive focus on a proposition P.

Support for this proposal would find, in each discourse environment in which a full *do you know* question occurs, also a reduced *y'know* question, and a solitary *y'know*. And in each environment, we would expect to find some *y'know* formats followed first by B's response (e.g. 'No, what?') and then by initial Speaker A's continuation, and other *y'know* formats followed just by A's continuation. Because my corpus does not have examples of all forms in all environments, however, I list the total range of cases which would be needed in Figure 9.3, and then go on to discuss the examples which I do have (listed on the right of the figure).

I start with full *do you know WHAT-COMP* questions when they are used as requests for information about hearer knowledge. (22a) and (b) illustrate the optionality of *do* in this environment.

(22a)   Sally: Have you ever heard of something like mother wit? **D'you know** what that is? Ever heard that expression?
        Zelda: No.
(22b)   Jack: In other words they're *sick*. Religiously. Like the:. . .**y'know** what Hasidic is?
        Debby: Umhmm. [=(1)]

(22c) illustrates a reduction to *y'know NP?*

Figure 9.3. *Expanded and reduced frames of* y'know

A1:	Do y'know WH–COMP	/(B1: No. WH?)	/A2: P		(22a) (23a)
A1:	(Do) y'know WH–COMP	/(B1: No. WH?)	/A2: P	(22b) (23b) (23c) (25a)
A1:	(Do) y'know NP	/(B1: No.)	/A2: P		(22c) (23c) (24)
A1:	(Do) y'know WH	/(B1: No. WH?)	/A2: P		(25b)
A1:	Do y'know that P	/ B1: No.	/A2: P		(26a) (27a)
A1:	(Do) y'know (that) P	/(B1: No.)	/A2: P	(26b) (26c) (27b)
A1: P.	Do y'know that	/ B1: No.	/A2: P		(28a)
A1: P.	(Do) y'know (that)	/(B1: No.)	/A2: P		(28b)

(22c)   Jan: **Y'know** Har Zion Temple in Wynnefield? [what that is]
             Debby: Yeh.
             Jan: Well my grandmother and grandfather one of the– were one of
                      the big contributors when that synagogue went up

Where-complements often occur in direction-giving, where they solicit hearer information about locational knowledge. (23a–c) illustrate formats with *d'y'know where X is* and *y'know where X is*.

(23a)   Zelda: **D'y'know** where the Montclair is? And the Sea View?
                   D'you ever ride down the: ⌈ uh   ⌉
             Debby: ⌊ The ⌋ motels? There?
             Zelda: The motels. On the boardwalk.
                   ⌈ D'you go bike riding? ⌉
             Henry: ⌊ **Do you know** where ⌋ Abe's is?
             Debby: Yeh I know where Abe's is.
             Henry: Right across the street.
             Debby: Oh it's that way.

(23b)   Irene: The New Yorkers tend t'go upstate New York, like to–
                   y'know where Monticello is?
             Sally: Yeh. The Catskills ⌈ and all?   ⌉
             Irene: ⌊ The Catsk ⌋ ills. Right.

(23c) also illustrates that because such complements are existential, there can be further reduction to a single noun phrase (*y'know X*), i.e. *the boatyard*.

(23c)   Henry: **Y'know** where the Mainline: eh Mainline–
             Debby: It's when y'come over the Margate ⌈ Bridge? ⌉
             Henry: ⌊ Yeh:! ⌋
                     Y'know the boatyard? [where the boatyard is]

Debby: You have a boat there?
Henry: Sure!

(24) shows that existentials in who-complements can also be reduced:

(24)   Henry: **Y'know** Laurel and Hardy? [who they are] That's us!

(25a) and (b) show the use of *y'know what* to highlight a new point in an argument. Since neither seems intended to elicit a response as to hearer knowledge (neither speaker pauses after *y'know what*), they illustrate the optionality of a hearer response.

(25a)   Henry: **Y'know** what I like the best? I like the seashore area.
(25b)   Zelda: But see now I'm getting so used to it that I don't even mind it.
                     Well– **y'know** what? And especially when the– when a child
                     comes along. Because what happens, is 'hi Grandmom!'

Examples (26a) to (c) illustrate the optionality of *do* in *y'know that S* formats in evaluative sections of narratives, particularly in external evaluations which close their stories.

(26a)   Henry: He got up and he walked out! Ay:eh: so: eh. . .**don't y'know**
                     boys are like gir: eh worse: than little girls.
(26b)   Irene: Like out of the clear blue sky! **Y'know** they just have such an
                     arrogant air about them![=(20)]
(26c)   Henry: So then the man and wife worked, and the kids were running
                     around. Well **you know** if you get a sixteen– seventeen year
                     old kid and the mother's working, and she's got a boyfriend,
                     they gonna play!

(27a) and (b) illustrate the same two formats in internally evaluative quotes within a story. In (27a), Irene has introduced her story as an illustration of what kids are taught today: *they are taught today that a person is a person, regardless of what they are*. The quote in (27a) instantiates this generalization through the words of Irene's nine-year-old neighbor.

(27a)   Irene: a.   She came home,
                     b.   and they were sitting at the dinner table,
                     c.   and she said t' her parents, '**D'you know**, I'm a *per*son.'
                     d.   And they said, 'Yeh, we know.'
                     e.   '*No. Really. I* am a person in my *own* right.'

Note that *d'you know* is not intended literally here, and that the parents' response is in a playful key which builds upon the obvious truth of their daughter's statement. Compare (27b) in which *do* is absent. Again, the

quotes instantiate the earlier stated point of the story, i.e. that Henry's
neighbor is *a shrew* who *is jealous*.

(27b)   Henry: a.   And she sat down there,
                   b.   and she says, '**Y'know** I got a problem Zelda.'
                   c.   She says, 'I really got a problem.'
                   d.   So Zelda says, 'What's your problem?'
                   e.   I was sittin' right there.
                   f.   She says, '**Y'know** I gave you a tomato. Your tomato's
                         not as big as the one I gave you. What shall I do with it?
                   g.   What d'y'think I wanted t'tell her t'do with it?!

Another example is Irene's quote in (20).

Next consider *P. Do you know that?*. (28a) and (b) show this format with
highly evaluated and intensified points in arguments.

(28a)   Henry: We give *more* money, we give *more* money for donations, than
                   any other nationality in the world! **D'you know** that?
         Debby: No I ⌈ didn't know ⌉ that.
         Henry: ⌊ We're very ⌋   compatible– we're compassionate
                   people.
(28b)   Henry: Well eh eh it– Jewish is a bastard language. **You know** that?
                   Yiddish is a bastard lang– but it's the best– but it's the best
                   language in the *world*.

The previous examples have shown different degrees of reduction of
y'know questions. Although I have not shown final reduction to *y'know* in
all environments, I have suggested that many cases of *y'know* be considered as reduced questions, and thus, that even those cases of *y'know*
which do not actually initiate questions focus hearer attention on the same
information on which speaker is currently focused.

In sum, I have proposed that *y'know* leads a hearer to focus attention on
a piece of information (either prior or upcoming) being presented by a
speaker. Another way of saying this is that *y'know* creates an interactive
focus on speaker-provided information. The general interactional function
of *y'know* is thus similar to that suggested in 9.1.1.1: *y'know* marks the
speaker as an information provider, but one whose successful fulfillment of
that role is contingent upon hearer attention. The discussion in this section
has suggested that *y'know* does so because it is an expression which is
reduced from a *do you know* question.

9.1.4 Different pragmatic effects of y'know

Even though all *y'know* formats open a joint focus on speaker-provided information, such formats do not share all their pragmatic effects. I focus on two pragmatic differences, one in speaker/hearer accountability to information, and one in turn-taking. What is responsible for these pragmatic effects is the intonation of *y'know* (rising or falling) and its location relative to focused information (preceding or following).

Y'know formats can be presented with either rising or falling final intonation. Rising intonation conventionally signals that a speaker has not yet completed an information unit, e.g. it is used with interrogatives (incomplete propositions). As we saw earlier, rising *y'know* solicits hearers' recognition of a particular piece of information; thus, the completion of an information unit framed by *y'know?* depends on the hearer displaying knowledge of that information rather than the speaker him/herself retrieving the needed information. Falling intonation, on the other hand, conventionally indicates that a speaker has completed an information unit.

My data suggest that this intonational difference reflects a pragmatic difference in speaker certainty about hearer knowledge, i.e the degree to which a speaker assumes his/her hearer is mutually accountable to information. More specifically, rising *y'know* reflects less certainty about shared knowledge than falling *y'know*. There are four indicators of this pragmatic difference.

First, consider the distribution of the two intonations when *y'know* marks meta-knowledge about speaker/hearer shared knowledge by prefacing reference to a specific entity (9.1.1.1). There was only one occurrence of *y'know* with falling intonation in such environments:

(5)   Irene: a.   We have a team in the summer we bowl.
                    b.   Every summer ⎡ they– husband and wife–
        Zelda: c.   ⎣ Tell her who you bowl with. ⎤
        Irene: d.   Who we *bowl* with.
        Zelda: e.   D–**y'know**, the teams.
        Irene: f.   Oh. What'd'y'mean ⎡ the kids? ⎤
        Zelda: g.   ⎣ The kids. ⎦
        Irene: h.   Oh yeh. [continues]

The information being marked by *y'know* in (5) (*the teams*) is information which the speaker assumes the hearer should know: not only has Irene already mentioned the *team* (a), but since the teams are something in which Irene (not Zelda) participates, knowledge about their composition is something Irene is expected to have. Irene's response (f, h) shows that Zelda's assumption is warranted. In contrast to the one case of falling *y'know* in this environment, all cases of rising *y'know* were used in such exchanges – and none of the information marked by rising *y'know* was information about which the speaker clearly expected the hearer to be accountable.

The second indication of a pragmatic difference between rising and falling *y'know* is that all of the consensual truths in my data were marked with falling *y'know* except one:

(9)   Henry: a.   A mitzvah a day will keep the doctor away.
                    b.   So if I can do this mitzvah today, maybe I don't have
                          t'go t'the dentist tomorrow?
         Zelda: c.   No ⎡ y'still ⎤ have t'go Henry, ⎡tomorrow!⎤
         Henry: d.   ⎣ hhhhhhh⎦   ⎣hhhhh   ⎦ That's a
                          thought though, isn't ithhhh
                    e.   **Y'know** they say an *apple* a day keeps the doctor away?

Henry states the formulaic expression of the conventional wisdom (e) to explicate the analogy underlying his joke (a, b). But because this explication is after Henry has already used the analogy in his joke, it actually has a clarifying effect – just what we would expect if Henry cannot be sure all his hearers got his joke, i.e. if the speaker cannot be sure of his hearer's shared knowledge of the general truth.

The third indication that rising *y'know* reflects less certainty about shared knowledge than falling *y'know* comes from comparing (6) and (7). In (6), rising *y'know* is a turn-transition device:

(6)   Irene: Because like uh: . . .eighth grade, they were the only class
                    that he had taken over t'the synagogue, which remained
                    there: **y'know**? ⎡
         Sally: ⎣Yeh, I remember.
         Irene: It labelled them.

Irene does not continue until after Sally responds with *yeh, I remember*. In (7), however, Irene continues to talk (note *and* in (f)) while I am responding to falling *y'know*.

(7)   Debby: a.   And what d'you do?
         Irene: b.   I'm an N.T.A. In ⎡ school. ⎤
         Debby: c.   ⎣ What's   ⎦ that?
         Irene: d.   Uh::really a cop. ⎡ See that the–   Yeh. See that=⎤
         Debby: e.   ⎣ Oh real: ly?!   No kidding? ⎦
         Irene: f.   =the kids behave a little bit. **Y'know**. ⎡ And–
         Debby: g.   ⎣ I didn't know
                    they had those: uh   ⎡discipline⎤
         Irene: h.   Yeh ⎣in the   ⎦
                    Philadelphia schools they do.

That Irene pauses in (6), but continues without pause in (7), suggests that rising *y'know* is used to elicit hearer confirmation prior to speaker continuation. And this suggests that rising *y'know* reflects less certainty about shared knowledge than falling *y'know*.

The final indication of a pragmatic difference between rising and falling *y'know* is the relationship between intonation and position of *y'know* relative to the information being focused upon. In all but one case of *y'know* in my data, when *y'know* **preceded** information being focused upon, that information was presented in a rising contour. However, when *y'know* **followed** information being focused upon, that information was presented in either a rising or falling contour.

(29a)   'Y'know X?'
(29b)   'X, y'know?' or 'X, y'know.'

This distribution is important because information is often positioned in an utterance according to the speaker's assumption as to what the hearer knows: old, familiar information precedes new, unfamiliar information.[5] In the rising contour of (29a), X is at the end of the utterance, whereas in the falling contour of (29b), X is at the beginning of the utterance. The information/position correlation suggests that when X ends an utterance, speakers cannot assume hearer's knowledge of X; when X initiates an utterance, speakers can assume hearer's knowledge of X. My data suggest that when speaker cannot assume their hearers' knowledge, they use *y'know X?* (*y'know* in initial and X in final position with rising contour); when speakers can assume their hearers' knowledge, they use either *X, y'know?* or *X, y'know* (*y'know* in final and X in initial position with rising or falling contour).

The location of *y'know* relative to focused information is also responsible for the second pragmatic effect I noted above – in turn-taking – for only utterance-initial *y'know* is a turn-initiator. In (30a), for example, Henry adds utterance-initial *y'know* to his recycled turn entry:

(30a)   Irene: We have a friend of our's who became an architect.
          Henry: [His father died when] he was young. =
                          [I think they have–   ]   **Y'know**
          Irene: Irene. . .   = [I think   ] they have students that are =
                          [= And he–]
          Henry: = on relief.

This addition is especially striking because speakers typically delete utterance-initial markers in recycled turn entries (see Chapter 6).

Note, now, that speakers use not only utterance-initial *y'know*, but also full cataphoric *y'know* questions, to direct the hearer's attention to their turn-initiating efforts. In (30b), Henry uses 'do y'know that S' twice before he gains his turn.

(30b) Debby: Yeh, I'd like to ⌈ see it. I'd like to know. ⌉
        Henry: ⌊ **Do you know** that all of ⌋ those=
        Zelda: Yeh.
        Henry: ⌈ =space⌉ men– **D'you know** that the spacemen up=
        Debby: ⌊ Yeh. ⌋
        Henry: =there were mostly– that the ones that worked on the
                  projects, the biggest ones were Jewish people?
        Debby: No I didn't know that.

And in (30c), Henry uses 'y'know WH–COMP' three times before he gains his turn:

(30c) Zelda: Ice cream sundaes! And not even an ordinary ice cream!
                                  ⌈ We ⌉ had the good life!
        Henry: But **y'know** what ⌊ I–= ⌋
        Debby: ⌈ Yeh it sounds it! ⌉
        Henry: ⌊ =**Y'know** what I ⌋ like the best, though?
                 Y'know what I like the best?
                 I like the seashore area.

That utterance-initial *y'know* is used in the same turn-initiating capacity as full cataphoric *y'know* formats also suggests that utterance-initial *y'know* is the final reduction of those formats (those depicted in 21a, b and c). Perhaps, too, utterance-final *y'know* is the final reduction of those *y'know* formats which point backward in talk (as in 21d). If so, it is not surprising that utterance-final *y'know* seems to end turns – for such occurrences look backward to what preceded rather than forward to what is coming.

In sum, I have suggested that *y'know* formats do not share all their pragmatic effects because of the intonation of *y'know* (rising or falling) and its location relative to focused information (preceding or following). I have described pragmatic differences in speaker/hearer accountability to information and in turn-taking.

9.1.5 Why y'know

We have seen that *y'know* is basically an information state marker: it marks transitions to meta-knowledge about shared knowledge. However, the fact that *y'know* verbalizes speakers' handling of cognitive tasks has interactional consequences. For example, *y'know* may open an interactional negotiation over the informational status of a generalization (is it really shared knowledge?), or, speakers may use *y'know* to enlist hearer agreement when such agreement is not otherwise forthcoming. Informational and interactional roles are also found in arguments: *y'know* allows a speaker not only to solicit hearer affirmation of the receipt of information, but to create a gradual transition in participant roles throughout the discourse. And in narratives, *y'know* helps the hearer filter through the story and select what is important for understanding the narrative point – and thus respond to the story as an audience. These informational and interactional functions of *y'know* are due to the literal meaning of 'you know' (hearer and/or general knowledge) and to the way in which *y'know* helps create a particular kind of exchange structure (*y'know* creates a joint focus on speaker-provided information).

In sum, *y'know* displays the speaker as one whose role as information-provider is contingent upon hearer reception. Since speakers may require different types of hearer reception – ranging from attention to what is said to confirmation of a proposition to relinquishment of the floor – it is not surprising that *y'know* occurs in so broad a range of environments.[6]

9.2 *I mean*

I mean functions within the participation framework of talk. As I stated in Chapter 1, participation frameworks involve not only the different footings through which speaker and hearer relate to each other, but the ways in which producers of talk are related to the units of talk they are producing – their propositions, acts, and turns. It is primarily within this latter aspect of participation framework that *I mean* functions. However, because shifts in speaker orientation have an effect on speaker/hearer relationships, *I mean* also has interactional relevance. And because speaker orientation to ideas is related to knowledge about their content, *I mean* also has relevance for information states.

9.2.1 I mean *in participation frameworks*

I begin by focusing on how *I mean* marks speaker orientation to two aspects of the meaning of talk: ideas and intentions (9.2.1.1). We will see that this dual focus is due to the polysemous meaning of the predicate 'mean', and that it is related to the meta-linguistic properties of 'mean'. I then go on to consider interactional relevancies of the speaker orientations marked by *I mean* (9.2.1.2).

9.2.1.1 Speaker orientation: ideas and intentions. The literal meaning of
the expression 'I mean' influences its function in participation frameworks:
I mean marks a speaker's upcoming modification of the meaning of his/her
own prior talk. The predicate 'mean', however, has several different
senses, and thus the modifications marked by *I mean* include both expansions of ideas and explanations of intention.

When the predicate 'mean' has an ideational meaning (words 'have meaning' because they refer to entities or convey concepts; sentences 'have
meaning' because they express propositions), it influences not only the
marker *I mean*, but also the expression *meaning*. In (31), Jack is explaining
the difference between socialism and capitalism.

(31)   a.   Uh: they do:: hold down: that they control the capitalism.
        b.   You can't have more than two hundred and sixty dollars in the
                  bank.
        c.   Y'see *that's* the difference.
        d.   **Meaning**, that you cannot earn money interest wise.

Jack expands two ideas from (a) and (b) in (d), prefacing that expansion
with *meaning*: the inability to earn interest expands the idea that Socialists
control capital investment. In (32), we find a similar use of *I mean*. Ira is
explaining why he believes racial integration is increasing.

(32)   a.   But I think um ten years from now,
        b.   it's going to be much more liberal.
        c.   I could see it in my own job.
        d.   **I mean**, when I started working for the government, there
                  were no colored people.
        e.   And today eh. . .uh. . .twenty five, thirty percent, forty
                  percent of the people I work with are– are colored.

Ira prefaces an expansion of (c) in (d–e) with *I mean*: Ira finds an increasingly liberal attitude toward the hiring of Blacks in his own job (c) and
expands that idea by comparing his early days at work with the present (d–
e). Thus, (31) and (32) illustrate that 'mean' can have an ideational meaning in both *meaning* and *I mean*, such that both can preface expansions of
speakers' own prior ideas.

Another sense of 'mean' is speaker intention (as in *He didn't mean to
insult you*; cf. Grice's (1957) concept of meaning–nn). *Meaning* and *I
mean* both preface explanations of intention, particularly when the intended force of an action is deemed to have been missed by a recipient, e.g.
because it was too indirect for appropriate uptake. In (33), Zelda is describ-

ing how Henry's card partners were teasing a friend whose younger wife no
longer served coffee and cake at their weekly card games.

(33)   a.   But, the last time they were around she wasn't there.
            b.   And they were kidding him,
            c.   they said, 'Where's your wife?'
            d.   **Meaning,** is she hhrunning round now,
            e.   y'know sorta teasing him.

Zelda uses *meaning* in (d) to preface an explanation of the quoted speakers'
indirectly conveyed intentions in (a). Compare (34). Zelda is describing
how Henry proposed marriage to her.

(34)   a.   He says, 'Oh, I wish you could come with me!'
            b.   And I said– I was very pro– proper, and prim!
            c.   And I said, 'Oh, I couldn't go away with you.'
            d.   And he says, '**I mean** let's get married!'
            e.   And I said, 'Oh okay!'

Here, it is Zelda's *I mean* in (d) which prefaces an explanation of Henry's
indirect proposal in (a). Thus, again we see that the predicate 'mean' has
parallel uses in two different expressions: both *meaning* and *I mean* preface
explanations of speaker intention.

Examples (33) and (34) focused on only one aspect of speaker intention:
intended action. Another aspect of speaker intention is the tone in which a
speaker intends an utterance to be interpreted – what Hymes (1974) calls
the key (e.g. *He didn't mean it seriously*). The next examples show that
both *I mean it* and *I mean* can preface specification of speaker key. In (35),
Jack is explaining why the Irish have to prove their Catholicism more than
the Italians.

(35)   Jack: a.   Cause the Italian don't have t'prove he's a– a Catholic,
                                he has the Pope.
                   b.   The Irishmen never made it– they– Pope yet.
                   c.   and they used t'try so hard.
    Debby: d.   Umh ⌈ hhh. ⌉
    Jack: e.   ⌊ No ⌋ **I mean it**
                     I– I'm serious about this.

Jack uses *I mean it* (e) to preface the key (serious) in which his previous
point (a–c) is to be interpreted. Note that this specification of key overlaps
with my laughter (in d). Thus, *I mean it* does more than just specify Jack's
intended key: *I mean it* has a remedial function – serving to clarify Jack's
misinterpreted intention – and thus helps to reestablish the mood of the interaction as a whole.

Like *I mean it, I mean* is also used to reestablish the tone of a conversation by establishing a serious speaker key. In (36), Irene and Henry are arguing about interracial marriage. At a particularly polarized and competitive stage of their argument, Henry breaks the prevailing mood (see Schiffrin 1984a, forthcoming, for discussion of competition and cooperation in argument):

(36)   Irene: a.   Henry, if they wanna do it, they'll go away and do it!
                  b.   *What'm I gonna do, take a gun and KILL 'em?*
        Henry: c.   I *hate* you!hhhhhhhhhhhhhhhhhhhhhh
        Debby: d.   I didn't mean t'start thishhhhhh
        Irene: e.   ⌈ *No*, we argue about this   ⌉ *all* the time.=
        Henry: f.   ⌊ hhhhhhhhhhhhhhhhhhhhhhhhhh ⌋
        Irene   g.   ⌈ =*All* the time. *Al*ways. Because I really don't–⌉
        Henry: h.   ⌊ If I wanna get my adrenalin   worked up we–⌋ *she*
                        comes in! ⌈ hhhhhhhhhhhh ⌉
        Debby: i.   ⌊ Keeps y'young! ⌋
        Irene: j.   **I mean** *I've* seen girlfriends of mines parents, sit shiva
                        for them, [a mourning ritual]
                  k.   because they were marrying out of their religion.

Henry's frame break begins in (c) where his declaration of hatred is coupled with laughter. Although Irene never really joins in the joking that Henry's frame break proposes, she attempts in (g) to reestablish the serious frame of the argument: after she agrees with Henry that they argue *all the time*, she begins to state a reason for their disagreement and thereby justify her position. Henry, however, continues to joke (h) – thus continuing to display the cooperative undertones of their relationship – until Irene recreates a serious, openly competitive mood (j) by describing the futility of parental protest (this was the thrust of her earlier challenge to Henry). This switch back to a serious frame is prefaced by *I mean*.

(37) shows that *I mean* also prefaces a speaker's intended key even when that key is consonant with prior talk, i.e. when no clarification or reestablishment of frame is required. (37) is from a story in which Irene is comparing the current behavior of Blacks to the behavior of the Blacks she knew as a teenager.

(37)   a.   She said, 'Y'know it was really very annoying t'sit here, during
              visitation while you people are rattling on.'
        b.   **I mean** really indignant. [= 20]

Irene's *I mean* in (b) prefaces her specification of the key of her quoted speaker from (a). Thus, *I mean* is used not only to preface intended key when a prior interactional mood has been disrupted, but to preface speaker key in general.

Note that we have already seen (in (34)) that *I mean* can preface clarifications of misinterpreted meaning (e.g. intended action) other than disruptions in intended key. (38) is another example.

(38)   Debby: a.   Well, if I say 'mixed marriage', what does that mean, t'you?

       Henry: b.   Wha' does that mean t' ⌈ me= ⌉

       Debby: c.   ⌊ Yeh. ⌋

       Henry: d.   =It means a– it means a pain in the heart.

                 e.   ⌈ That's what ⌉ it means t'me.

       Zelda: f.   ⌊ Oh c'mon::! ⌋   Two words! You'll have her here all night!

       Debby: g.   Who marries who.

       Irene: h.   *Who* marries *who*?

       Debby: i.   **I mean** marrying out of your what?

                 j.   That's what ⌈ I'm talkin'– ⌉

       Irene: k.   ⌊ out of ⌋   your religion.

My question in (a) is intended to elicit a definition of 'mixed marriage', not an evaluative reaction to mixed marriages. I paraphrase my question from (a) in (i) – prefacing it with *I mean* – after the initial response from Henry (d–e) fails to provide the information I had intended to elicit. Thus *I mean* clarifies the request for information that I had originally intended to enact through my question. (See also discussion of replacement repairs, pp. 300–2.)

We have seen so far that the meanings of the predicate 'mean' influence its use in several expressions other than *I mean*. Although I have not stated so explicitly, the fact that 'I' in *I mean* is a first person pronoun is also an obvious influence on the uses thus far described: *I mean* focuses on the **speaker's** modification of his/her **own** talk (contrast *you mean*, which allows a speaker to propose a modification of another's talk). One indicator of the focus of *I mean* on the speaker is its tendency to preface propositions through which a speaker predicates something of him/herself (by using a first person subject). Table 9.1 compares *I mean* to *y'know* (a hearer focused marker; see 9.1) with different pronominal subjects. (Note that I have split *you* into definite, second person subjects, and indefinite subjects akin to *one*; see discussion in 9.1). It suggests that in propositions in which speakers predicate something about themselves, they use *I mean* more than they use *y'know* (44% vs. 27%). This reinforces my suggestion that *I mean* is used when the speaker focuses attention on him/herself, and that *I mean* is also adding to that focus on self.

Table 9.1. I mean, y'know *and pronominal subjects*

	First vs. second person marker		
	I mean	*y'know*	Total
PRONOMINAL SUBJECTS			
I/we	34 (44%)	14 (27%)	48
definite *you*	2	2	4
indefinite *you*	18	16	34
he/she/it/they	24	20	44
Total	78	52	130

The composite meaning of 'I mean' is responsible not only for the use of *I mean* as a speaker's modifier of ideas and intentions, but for its use with a particular type of self repair: **replacement repairs**. First, let us differentiate two types of repairs: background and replacement repairs. Background repairs are subordinate asides which provide information to modify and/or supplement hearers' understanding of surrounding material. After the speaker inserts the aside into discourse, s/he repeats or paraphrases the material which had been interrupted. (38a) and (38b) illustrate. In each segment, line (b) contains the background repair; lines (a) and (c) contain the paraphrases surrounding the repair.

(38a) a. Well like I say the only thing different I think may be with–
     b. well in our area, it isn't because of the school.
     c. But the only difference I would think would be maybe the better schools out there.

(38b) a. Well I told–
     b. see my son went to Temple.
     c. And I told Sam, I said, 'Why don't you take her up there and show her around?'

What is crucial about the paraphrases (lines (a) and (c)) is that the speaker is taking as a starting point the ideas of the **prior** discourse, rather than the ideas presented in the inserted asides (line (b)).

Although this is the characteristic that most clearly differentiates background from replacement repairs, there are also prosodic, informational, and structural features which typically occur with background, but not replacement, repairs. Prosodically, background repairs are preceded by a glottal closure which interrupts an utterance prior to its completion. Informationally, the added material provides background information for the surrounding discourse. And finally, the corrective material is structurally subordinate to the surrounding discourse: this status is shown by the frequent use of *and, but* and *so* (see (38a) and (38b), also Chapters 6, 7) to mark the discourse **following** background repairs, but not to mark the background repair itself.

As I noted above, the clearest difference between background and replacement repairs is the way they are followed in discourse: background repairs lead back to the discourse which had been interrupted. In sharp contrast, replacement repairs lead forward to the ideas of the upcoming discourse on the basis of the material in the repair itself. (39a) and (39b) illustrate.

(39a)   a.   I think the best picture–
         b.   I think you were affected by Shoeshine more than
                 anything else.

In (39a), the speaker continues an idea (in (b), *you were affected by*) which substitutes for an idea (in (a) *the best picture*) without returning to the material from (a). And in (39b), the speaker continues the idea prefaced by *he* without returning to the idea prefaced by *we*.

(39b)   I was so affected that when we– he insisted I go back t'see it the second
         time, I knew I couldn't take it!

Replacement repairs may also differ from background repairs in their other characteristics. First, not all replacement repairs are prosodically initiated by a glottal closure. Second, replacement repairs provide different information than background repairs: rather than provide background for surrounding material, they are substitutions of prior material (note that this also excludes repetitive restarts such as *I– I did it*). And third, replacement repairs do not provide subordinate material; rather, they switch the direction of the developing discourse to that initiated by the substitution.

I mean prefaces only the replacement repairs in my corpus. In (40), for example, Irene initiates her substitution of the word *advantage* for *disadvantage* with *I mean*:

(40)   Sally: Were your parents pretty strict or. . .
        Irene: Not at all. And not t'my disadvantage. **I mean** not t' my
                  advantage as I– I see it now because I got everything I
                  wanted then.

In (41), Freda initiates her substitution of *know* for *don't know* with *I mean*:

(41)   But oh I don't know the rabb– **I mean** I know him, but I'm– I– not
        actively, as far as I'm concerned.

In both examples, the speakers continue their discourse on the basis of the substitution – rather than return to what had been interrupted by the repair.

Why does *I mean* preface only the substitutions in replacement repairs? We have just seen that replacement repairs switch the direction of upcoming talk through a substitution of part of prior talk. Another way of saying this is that the speaker is displaying a shift in intention as to what is to be said – a shift which does not occur in background repairs. We saw earlier that one sense of 'mean' is speaker intention, and one use of *I mean* is to preface paraphrases of speaker intention. Thus, the restriction of *I mean* to replacement repairs is due to the compatibility between the function of replacement repairs and the meaning of 'mean' as speaker intention.

This explanation suggests that *I mean* in replacement repairs is functionally parallel to expressions which explicitly introduce an upcoming substitution. In (42a), for example, Jack uses *in other words* to preface two substitutions.

(42a)　　a.　　When *you* keep getting hurt, you become a cripple.
　　　　　b.　　And when you're a cripple you're prej–
　　　　　c.　　**In other words**. . .they're cripples because they're so so
　　　　　　　　religious is what– is the point I'm trying t'make.
　　　　　d.　　**In other words** they're *sick*. Religiously.

In (a), Jack presents the idea that prejudice toward oneself (*you keep getting hurt*) produces religious orthodoxy (which is crippling). In (b), he begins to state that religious orthodoxy produces prejudice toward others. But then in (c), Jack substitutes that idea with the idea that religious orthodoxy is what cripples people: *in other words* prefaces this substitution. And then in (d), *in other words* marks a substitution of *cripples* (c) by *sick*. Now examine (42b):

(42b)　　But he still carries it on and becomes sickening– sickening when y'see it,
　　　　　see. **I mean** he's sick, from that.

Here Jack prefaces a substitution of *sickening* with *he's sick* by *I mean*. Thus, the explicit phrase *in other words* and the marker *I mean* both preface substitutions in replacement repairs.

In sum, the literal meaning of the expression 'I mean' suggests that *I mean* marks a speaker's upcoming modification of the ideas or intentions of a prior utterance. This meaning allows us to understand why *I mean* prefaces repairs which display shifts in speakers' intentions, but not repairs which provide background information designed to supplement hearers' understanding of prior discourse.

I suggested in (42a) and (42b) that the use of *I mean* in repairs is parallel to the explicit meta-linguistic expression *in other words*. Before going on to consider the interactional relevance of speaker orientations, I want to focus briefly on the fact that *I mean* is also a meta-linguistic phrase, for this gives us another way of understanding its use as a marker of speaker orientation toward both ideas and intentions.

I mean is a member of a larger set of meta-linguistic expressions such as *lemme tell you, let's put it this way, like I say, what we call, so called,* and *in other words* (42a) which themselves are discourse markers (Schiffrin 1980; Chapter 10 of this book). These expressions form a functional set because they all focus on properties of the code *per se* (on 'langue') as well as on the language used in a speech situation (on 'parole'). Despite this shared focus, however, meta-language is not easy to define.

Consider, first, efforts to differentiate meta-language from meta-communication. Jakobson (1960) suggests that language has a meta-linguistic function when it focuses on the code as opposed to other components of the speech situation, e.g. the speaker, the hearer, the relationship. But Jakobson also observes that verbal messages do not fulfill only one function: thus, expressions whose primary function is meta-linguistic may also be used to focus on other aspects of a message (albeit to a lesser extent than the code). As Lyons (1977: 55) points out, even utterances that seem to be purely meta-linguistic involve other concerns: for example, asking an interlocutor to define a particular word (a meta-linguistic concern) also involves phatic concerns trying to prevent a communication breakdown) and conative concerns (one speaker is making an appeal to another).

Bateson (1972b) and Ruesch and Bateson (1951) group together as meta-communicative some of the additional functions noted by Jakobson. Bateson defines **meta-language** as discourse whose subject is language *per se*, and **meta-communication** as communication which focuses on language whose (explicit or implicit) subject is codification of the message and the relationship between interlocutors. In Bateson's framework, then, all of the functions served by asking for a definition would be meta-communicative, rather than meta-linguistic, phatic, and conative. Note how the two frameworks differently define *I mean*: in Jakobson's framework, *I mean* is meta-linguistic as well as **emotive** (since it focuses on the speaker); in Bateson's framework, *I mean* is just meta-communicative.

Consider, also, the difficulties of identifying those elements used by a particular language as its own meta-language. Aside from the fact that different speech communities create different meta-linguistic inventories (compare Stross' 1974 study of Tzeltal to Abrahams' 1974 study of Black English), the criteria for including an expression in such an inventory are not uniformly agreed upon. Reichenbach (1947: 58) suggests, for example, that such an inventory would include terms whose designata are aspects of language, e.g. *word, say, mean, conjugate, true*, but Weinreich (1966: 163) expands this to include meta-linguistic operators, i.e. terms such as *real, so-called*, and *strictly speaking* that function as 'instructions for the loose or strict interpretation of designata'. The fact that *I mean* has to do not just with semantic meaning, but with speaker's modification (and hence own interpretation) of that meaning, suggests that it would be included in Reichenbach's narrow inventory and in Weinreich's broad inventory. Another way of saying this is that the polysemous nature of 'mean' leads to the inclusion of expressions with 'mean' in more than one meta-linguistic category.

Let me summarize where *I mean* falls within the different definitions of meta-language and delimitations of meta-linguistic inventories. First, *I mean* can be defined as either meta-linguistic (in Jakobson's sense) or meta-communicative (in Bateson's sense) – the former since it focuses on ideas, the latter since it focuses on the speakers' communicative act. Second, *I mean* can be included in two differently based inventories of meta-linguistic expressions – Reichenbach's narrow linguistic inventory, and Weinreich's broader interpretive inventory – simply because 'mean' refers either to semantic meaning, or to speaker intention. These facets of *I mean* influence the way the expression functions in discourse: it is the narrow meta-linguistic focus of *I mean* which allows it to be a modifier of speakers' **ideas**, and the broader meta-communicative, interpretive focus of *I mean* which allows it to be a modifier of speakers' **intentions**.

In sum, *I mean* marks modifications of both propositional information and speaker intention. This is due not only to the polysemous meaning of the predicate 'mean', but to the meta-linguistic and meta-communicative qualities of the expression which go beyond a focus on the semantic properties of the linguistic code to include a focus on the speaker's use of and reaction to the code. This dual focus is true of meta-talk in general: meta-talk allows not only the identification of chunks of propositional information, but the evaluation of that material (from either one's own or another's talk) (Schiffrin 1980). Since meta-talk in general provides a resource through which speakers display orientations and negotiate alignments, it should not be surprising to find that a specific meta-linguistic expression such as *I mean* does too.

9.2.1.2 The relevance of speaker orientations to interaction. The orientations which speakers display are inherently embedded in interaction: speakers direct their utterances to others, and display their selves to others. Because of this, a speaker's display of an orientation always has interactional relevance. For example, if a speaker displays him/herself as an animator by focusing on the production format of talk, then not only is a different aspect of self made available to the hearer for response, but the response may very well be performed in a parallel productive capacity (see discussion on *oh* and *y'know*, pp. 272–4). Or if a speaker displays a strong commitment to a proposition, then possibilities for speaker/hearer alignment are created which differ from those created by a speaker who displays little commitment to what is said.

Because *I mean* displays speaker orientations, it always has interactional relevance. We have already seen, for example, that a change in speaker key (e.g. a joking vs. serious orientation toward one's one talk) can be associated with a shift in conversational frame: in (36), *I mean* helped return talk to a competitive frame by specifying the speaker's serious key. Examples (43) to (45) illustrate some other ways that *I mean* has interactional relevance.

Prior to (43), I had been requesting information from Jack (about race relations) and Jack had been providing that information in an interview frame.

(43) Debby: a.   Um that's interesting.
            b.   It's probably true.
      Jack: c.   **I mean** what's your opinion? ⎡ Or shouldn't ⎤ we ask.
      Debby: d.   ⎣ Um: ⎦

                   No ⎡ ::   ⎤   ⎡ uh: ⎤
      Freda: e.   ⎣ She's interviewing ⎦ *you*, Jack⎡h⎣ hhhhhh   ⎦
      Jack: f.   ⎣She's of   ⎦ a
                   younger element.
            g.   I wanted to see what the younger element really *think*.
            h.   **I mean** if you *dare* to eh: offer an opinion.

In (a–b), I evaluate Jack's prior statements. This evaluation continues the prior delegation of participant roles in the interview frame. But in (c), Jack switches the participant roles by asking for my opinion; note that he specifically addresses the propriety of doing so with *or shouldn't we ask*. My *no* in (d) is a response not to the literal meaning of his just prior question (i.e. not *no, you shouldn't ask*), but to the indirect request for permission conveyed by that question (i.e. *no, it's okay to ask*). As Freda jokingly reminds Jack of our prior roles in the interview frame (e), Jack justifies the proposed switch (f–g). In (h), Jack requests my opinion for a second time, overlaying this second request as a challenge through *if you dare* (cf. Labov and Fanshel 1977: 95 on repeated requests as challenges). Thus, Jack has switched his own role by shifting his orientation from provider to solicitor of information. This shift is simultaneously a proposal for an adjustment to the **overall** allocation of roles in the interview frame. *I mean* has relevance to this interactional shift because it prefaces both of Jack's requests for my opinion (c, h) – both of the moves proposing the overall shift in participant roles.

(44) also illustrates how *I mean*, as a marker of speaker orientation, is interactionally relevant to the adjustment of frame. The relevance differs from that of (43) in two ways. First, the speaker orientation is centered on commitment to an idea (rather than participant role, i.e. provider vs. solicitor of information); second, the frame adjustment is remedial in nature. (44) begins as Freda is explaining why she prefers black and white pictures (movies and television) to color pictures.

(44) Freda: a. I'll tell you something that's gonna surprise you.
              b. I prefer . . . almost al:ways, that is, a picture that's not in color!
      Debby: c. I ⌈ know. I– that doesn't surprise me. ⌉
      Jack: d. ⌊ Well, I think that could be a– a ⌋ what d'y' call
                  ⌈ it a: ⌉ nostalgic feeling.   ⌈ No. ⌉
      Freda: e. ⌊ I feel, ⌋   No, I feel– ⌊ no. ⌋ I feel,
                  that color: . . . detracts from the picture:,
              f. I also feel that color is not *true* color, it's too much color.
              g. And I fe– find I enjoy . . . what y'don't see often, but a picture that's not in color.
              h. I: ⌈ I: think it's more real. Than color. ⌉
      Debby: i. ⌊ I agree with you. And for this– ⌋ the very same reasons.
              j. I've said the same thing.
              k. I think that the color doesn't look real.
              l. It's too bright.   ⌈ Y'   ⌉ know it's– it's=
      Freda: m.   That's ⌊ right! ⌋
      Debby: n. ⌈ =it's too . . . vibrant! ⌉
      Freda: o. ⌊ We don't have color ⌋ T.V. and I don't *want* it!
              p. I :– **I mean** uh I jus– **I mean** if somebody offered me one,
              q. could use another T.V.
              r. I would take the black and white!
              s. Which is crazy, I know.

Freda prefigures her preference for black and white pictures as *something that's gonna surprise you* (a), and she presents three reasons for her preference (e–g). Neither Jack nor I, however, display whatever feelings of surprise we may have felt from hearing Freda's preference. Jack offers his own reasons for Freda's preference (d) with which she disagrees (e). I say that it doesn't surprise me (c), that I agree with Freda (i), that I have said the same thing (j) for *the very same reasons* (i, k–n). What has happened, then, is a deviation from intended effect; compare a story whose speaker prefaces it with *something funny happened the other day* to which no one responds with laughter or acknowledgement of humor. In short, the supportive responses from me and Jack have actually sabotaged the surprising effect which Freda had intended her preference to have. Thus, in (o–p), Freda strengthens her preference by offering a piece of evidence attesting to her commitment to it: not only does she not want color T.V., but if someone offered her another T.V., she would take *the black and white*. This commitment is prefaced by *I mean* (p). Thus, here *I mean* marks Freda's attachment to an idea when the interactional reception of that idea has threatened her ability to use it as an individual claim for attention. Another way of saying this is that *I mean* is marking an orientation through which a speaker recommits herself to a prior claim when its interactional reception has disrupted its intended effect. *I mean* is thus used remedially (cf. Irene's *I mean* in 36 to reestablish the competitive frame of the argument) to reinvoke an interactional frame in which one speaker is presenting a point of her own, rather than jointly establishing a shared perspective with her interlocutors.

Before we consider (45), let me summarize the importance of the previous examples. (43) and (44) illustrate orientation shifts in which a speaker switched his/her relation to information being presented: in (43), Jack shifted from provider to solicitor of information; in (44) Freda strengthened her commitment to an individual claim. Although such shifts are primarily adjustments in the way individuals relate to their own talk, they simultaneously open opportunities for speaker/hearer realignment *vis-à-vis* talk – in (43) for the delegation of interactional tasks, in (44) for the ownership of ideas. It is because orientation shifts are interactionally embedded in this way that *I mean* has interactional relevance.

(45) suggests an interactional shift to which *I mean* has **less** relevance than the other discourse devices with which it is situated. In (45), Freda and Jack are explaining to me why they don't believe in fate. But rather than cooperatively presenting their beliefs, they are competing for the right to present what are virtually parallel positions.

(45)   Freda: a.   Now if you're drowning, you're gonna fight t'
                         ⌈ t'save s–   ⌉
        Jack: b.   ⌊ You're not ⌋   gonna say 'Well this is it! I'm gonna
                         let go!'
                  c.   It doesn't work that way.
        Debby: d.   Yeh that makes sense.
        Jack: e.   ⌈Your cockroach . . . you wanna⌉ step on a cockroach,=
        Freda: f.   ⌊I mean e– even if– even if–   ⌋
        Jack: g.   =what does it do?   ⌈When you're⌉ ready–=
        Freda: h.   I think even ⌊ a person– ⌋
        Jack: i.   =it'll run! Wouldn't it?
        Debby: j.   ⌈Yeh.
        Freda: k.   ⌊Don't   you think that even a person who wants
                         t'commit suicide . . . will at the last minute, grapple to
                         save himself?

Freda tries to state her position in (f), (h) and (k). She first initiates that
position with *I mean* (f), then switches to a more assertive verb (*think* in
h), and then to a yes–no question which specifically targets her position as
one designed to elicit attention (through *don't you think*). Thus, Freda's
recycled turn entries are progressively geared toward gaining the floor and
gaining attention for her position. The fact that *I mean* is replaced by other
turn-entry devices suggests that it is not particularly effective in Freda's
efforts to shift her role from hearer to speaker. Thus, even though *I mean* is
associated with some shifts in participant role, it is not as relevant to shifts
from hearer to speaker role. In part, this is due to the function of the other
discourse devices in (45) with which *I mean* is situated: *I think* and *don't
you think* are both fairly assertive ways of gaining attention. But the lack of
interactional relevance to turn exchange may also be due to a mismatch between the function of *I mean* and the requirements of turn-taking. If successful turn entry in the face of competition requires a speaker to turn
outward from him/herself to focus on the hearer (cf. *y'know*, examples
(30a–c)), then *I mean* would be less relevant to this interactional task
because of its focus on the speaker's orientation toward his/her own talk.

9.2.2 From participation framework to information state

I have proposed that *I mean* functions within the participation framework
of talk as a marker of speaker orientation, i.e. as a marker of a speaker's
modification of his/her own prior ideas and intentions, and that *I mean* also
has broader interactional effects, e.g. on the creation and evolution of

interactional frames. In conclusion, I would like to merely consider another possibility. We have seen previously that markers of information state transition have pragmatic relevance in participation frameworks: *y'know*, for example, is a marker of meta-knowledge which can be used to seek particular interactional alignments in arguments and narratives (see 9.1.1, 9.1.2). I suggest the opposite possibility: markers of participation framework can be relevant to information states. More specifically, perhaps it is the case that *I mean* also marks two facets of an information state – certainty and salience.

I mean could have relevance for information states for the following reasons. We have already seen that one orientation marked by *I mean* is commitment to a position (43). Since one **source** of speaker commitment is certainty of knowledge, it is reasonable to suppose that a display of speaker commitment can also be interpreted as a claim to certain (rather than uncertain) knowledge. We have also seen that *I mean* marks speaker modifications of ideas and intentions. As such, *I mean* maintains speaker focus on prior material. But note that *I mean* also maintains **hearer** focus on prior material: *I mean* instructs the hearer to continue attending to the material of prior text in order to hear how it will be modified. Perhaps such material is interpreted as more salient simply because of the creation of a stationary focus. If so, then *I mean* can also function as a marker of salient information, i.e. as an indicator of information which is highly relevant for interpretation of the speaker's overall message.

9.3 *Y'know* and *I mean*

I conclude this chapter by discussing some reasons for having considered *y'know* and *I mean* together. First, the semantic meanings of 'you know' and 'I mean' influence the discourse functions of both markers: *y'know* marks interactive transitions in shared knowledge, and *I mean* marks speaker orientation toward the meanings of own talk.

Second, the functions of *I mean* and *y'know* are complementary: whereas *I mean* focuses on the speaker's **own** adjustments in the **production** of his/her own talk, *y'know* proposes that a hearer adjust his/her orientation (specifically knowledge and attention) toward the **reception** of **another's** talk. This suggests that combinations such as *y'know what I mean?* and *I mean, y'know*, may actually accomplish virtually the same interactive task, albeit in the opposite order.

Third, whereas *y'know* works basically within the information state of talk, with secondary effects on the participation framework, the functioning of *I mean* may be the reverse. This would allow us to understand a subtle difference between *y'know* and *I mean* in arguments. We saw that *y'know* marks information in discourse to which a hearer is invited to attend. In an argument, such information is likely to be the general position being established. Focusing hearer attention on a particular position can also reveal the speaker's orientation toward that material, e.g. the speaker believes in the truth or validity of the position being argued, or the speaker has a stake in establishing the position as a shared opinion. Compare *I mean* in arguments. I suggested that material marked by *I mean* is likely to be interpreted as salient, i.e. as information which is highly relevant to interpretation of a speaker's message, simply because it is the object of extended speaker focus. Thus, *I mean* marks information to which a hearer will pay extra attention – even though he/she has not been explicitly invited to do so. Figure 9.4 summarizes how *I mean* and *y'know* affect an argument's outcome. As Figure 9.4 suggests, both *y'know* and *I mean* can lead to hearer assessment of position, i.e. either a shared or disputed opinion. But the means by which they do so differs: *I mean* displays speaker orientation, and as a byproduct it invites hearer's attention; *y'know* invites hearer attention and thus directly invites hearer assessment; as a byproduct, *y'know* displays speaker orientation.

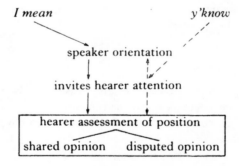

Figure 9.4.   I mean *and* y'know *in arguments*

The fourth reason to have considered *y'know* and *I mean* together is that both are markers which are socially evaluated and negatively sanctioned. For example, newspaper columnists frequently lament about the tendencies of teenagers and football players (two groups thought to be inarticulate) toward excessive use of both *y'know* and *I mean*. Newman (1975), a well-known pop grammarian (Quinn 1980), blames the diffusion of *y'know* throughout American English on outsider groups (poor Black slaves). My analysis suggests a reason for such stigmatization. First, we have seen that *y'know* is used whenever the continuation of conversation hinges upon a hearer giving to the speaker something (e.g. evidence of knowledge, attention) in exchange for speaker's talk. *Y'know* can be interpreted as revealing a speaker's dependence on others for his/her own talk, simultaneously forcing the hearer into a (perhaps unwanted) relationship of exchange and reciprocity. Second, we have seen that *I mean* focuses attention on the speaker's own orientation to his/her own talk. *I mean* can be interpreted as displaying the speaker's own involvement with his/her own talk at the expense of involvement with the hearer and attention to the hearer's right to talk. In short, use of both *y'know* and *I mean* could run counter to standard beliefs about the appropriate division of labor in conversation: use of *y'know* can be interpreted as overdependence on the hearer, and use of *I mean* can be interpreted as overinvolvement with the self. And it could be for these reasons that these markers are stigmatized.

10 Discourse markers: Contextual coordinates of talk

The philosopher Abraham Kaplan suggests that scholary inquiry is guided by two divergent logics: a **logic in use** and a **reconstructed logic**. According to Kaplan (1964): 'A great deal hinges on whether science is viewed as a body of propositions or as the enterprise in which they are generated, as product or as process. An account of the norms bearing on the finished report of an investigation might well be expected to differ from one concerned with the conduct of the investigation itself' (p. 7). Kaplan suggests that 'science as process' is guided by a **logic in use**, and 'science as product' is guided by a **reconstructed logic**. And there is a crucial difference between them: 'we can no more take them to be identical or even assume an exact correspondence between them, than we can in the case of the decline of Rome and Gibbon's account of it, a patient's fever and his physician's explanation of it' (p. 8).

Most academic reports are written according to a reconstructed logic, but much of the work which underlies such reports is the product of a logic in use. Although I have followed a reconstructed logic in most of this book, I think it would be helpful to recount briefly my logic in use – for it not only explains why I included what I did, but it motivates the questions that my inquiry into discourse markers sought to answer, as well as the answers which I present in this concluding chapter.

I have focused on how a particular group of people use certain expressions when talking to each other: *oh, well, and, but, or, so, because, now, then, I mean, y'know*. I began my inquiry by noticing where these expressions were used, and where they were not used, in other words, by paying attention to their distribution in discourse. Trying to describe in a systematic way the discourse in which markers occurred led me toward more detailed analyses of discourse than I had anticipated. For example, I found that I had to examine repair formats for my analysis of *oh* and *I mean*, requests (e.g. for clarification, confirmation) for my analysis of *oh* and *then*, question/answer structures for my analysis of *well, but,* and *y'know*, turn-taking formats for my analysis of *and, but,* and *so*, the relationship between warrants and inferences for my analysis of *so, because,* and *then*, the structure of comparisons for my analysis of *now*, the notion of discourse time for my analysis of *now* and *then*, and the organization of narratives and arguments for my analysis of virtually all the markers. My efforts to understand the distribution of markers also led me toward more detailed descriptions of the speakers and their interactions with one another than I had anticipated. For example, I didn't expect to have to describe my informants' positions on controversial issues, their views of themselves in relation to each other, to their social groups, and to the larger society and culture, or their means of socializing with each other through arguments and stories. Perhaps an alternative approach would have been to start by describing all the different aspects of discourse, and all the characteristics of the speakers and their interactions, which I expected to find relevant. But in the absence of a fully developed and empirically grounded theory of discourse, my 'logic in use' led me to examine just those aspects of discourse and interaction that I needed in my analysis, and furthermore to discover what those aspects were during the course of my analysis. An alternative way of saying this is that my problem ('where do markers occur and why?') guided my analysis, and that it was the process of discovering, and then more clearly defining, specific facets of my problem that forced me to examine different aspects of talk and to incorporate them into my analysis.

In another sense, my problem also guided the development of a broader, more abstract understanding of discourse. It was in my search for underlying characteristics of discourse – characteristics which might explain why the same word was being used in two seemingly different contexts, or why two different words were being used in what had seemed like the same context – that I was forced to attend to the different layers of meaning and structure within discourse. A heightened awareness of those layers of meaning and structure then led me to search for still deeper systems that were responsible for producing coherent discourse. Thus, I began to view discourse as the product of several interlocking components: exchange, action, and idea structures, an information state, and a participation framework. (Hence, my discourse model, and its related views on coherence, which I presented in Chapter 1, were largely an **outcome** of my analysis!) And I began to view markers as having roles within those different components, and as having a function within the overall integration of discourse as a system.

But what of the expressions whose use first led me to examine discourse? Let me retrace the path: the words and phrases are used in certain locations in discourse; discourse has underlying meanings and structures; coherent discourse is produced by the integration of underlying components of talk. Perhaps, then, we can understand why markers are used by locating the utterance containing them within the components underlying talk.

At the same time that this account was beginning to make sense to me, however, I realized that I also had to account for the fact that many of the expressions being examined were not themselves void of their own linguistic properties. Except for *oh* and *well*, for example, all the markers I have described have meanings. The meanings conveyed by markers not only **restrict** the discourse in which they can occur, but also influence the overall meaning of that discourse. Thus, I was also forced to consider how the linguistic properties of markers influence their function.

I transformed this path of inquiry (a logic in use) into several questions (a reconstructed logic):

> What do discourse markers add to coherence?
>> Do markers create, or display, relationships between units of talk (ideas, actions, turns, etc.)?
>
> Do markers have meanings?
>> If so, are those meanings referential and/or social and/or expressive meanings?
>> If so, how do those meanings interact with the discourse slot to influence the total communicative force of an expression?
>
> Do markers have functions?
>> If so, in what discourse component of a discourse system (exchange, action, ideational, information, participation)?
>> Are markers multi-functional?
>> Are markers ever functional equivalents for each other?

Throughout my study, I have tried to show the relevance of my analyses of particular markers to these questions. I now address these questions more directly, first, by discussing how properties of discourse and of particular expressions combine to give markers their functions (10.1), and, second, by suggesting that markers have indexical functions (10.2). It is the combination of discourse plane and indexical function which provides a route toward a synthesis for my analyses of different markers, for it not only highlights similarities and differences among the markers, but it suggests a more theoretical definition of markers as well as the broader role which they play in discourse. And this, in turn, suggests what expressions can serve as markers and a route through which different expressions become markers.

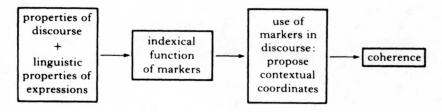

Figure 10.1. *Why use discourse markers?*

Before I begin, it might be helpful to see how these different issues are related to one another. As Figure 10.1 suggests, it is the properties of discourse (the specific discourse location as defined through my discourse model in Chapter 1) together with the linguistic properties of the expression (meaning and/or grammatical properties) which provide markers with their indexical functions: markers index the location of an utterance within its emerging local contexts. It is the indexical function of markers which is the key to understanding why they are used: markers propose the contextual coordinates within which an utterance is produced and designed to be interpreted. And, finally, it is not only because markers propose such coordinates, but because they propose more than one contextual coordinate at once, that they contribute to the integration of discourse – to discourse coherence.

10.1 Discourse contexts and the linguistic properties of markers

How do the linguistic properties of markers interact with properties of discourse to provide markers with their discourse functions? I first discuss the properties of discourse (10.1.1) and then turn to the properties of markers (10.1.2).

10.1.1 Properties of discourse

I have suggested that discourse markers are used on different planes of talk: exchange structures, action structures, idea structures, participation frameworks, and information states. Figure 10.2 summarizes which markers are used on which planes. Note that I differentiate **primary** planes of use from **secondary** planes – all the markers have uses in more than one component of discourse (either separately or simultaneously) – by marking the former with an asterisk.[1]

Figure 10.2. *Planes of talk on which markers function*

Information state	Participation framework	Ideational structure	Action structure	Exchange structure
*oh	oh		oh	
well	*well	well	well	well
		*and	and	and
		*but	but	but
		*or		or
so	so	*so	so	so
because		*because	because	
	now	*now		
then		*then	then	
I mean	*I mean	I mean		
*y'know	y'know	y'know		y'know

The primary function of *oh* is to mark information state transitions. But *oh* also works in the participation framework (since it displays speakers and hearers in particular productive and receptive capacities) and in action structures (since it marks certain actions, e.g. clarifications, which are designed to manage information state transitions). *Well* has its primary function in the participation framework because it anchors a speaker into an interaction as a respondent. But since individuals can respond to anything in talk which temporarily disrupts their expectations for upcoming coherence – ranging from unexpected knowledge, to the ideational content of a question for which they have no unequivocal answer, to a request with which they cannot comply – *well* also functions in information states, idea structures, and action structures. And since *well* is used to implant the speaker in a turn-initiation, more specifically, in one which is the second part of a question/answer adjacency pair, it also has a function in exchange structures.

The primary functions of all the conjunctions are in idea structures. But each conjunction also has additional functions in other components of talk: *and* and *but*, as markers of speaker-continuation and contrast respectively, work in action structures; so do *because* and *so* as complementary markers of motive and motivated action (e.g. grounds and claim). *Or* and *so* also work in exchange structures: both are turn-transition devices, *or* because it is a marker of hearer-option, and *so* because of its broader function in participation frameworks to mark potential participation transitions.

Although *and* and *but* also work in exchange structures, their function, because of their pragmatic effects (continuing and contrasting) are to continue rather than relinquish turns. And in addition to their other roles, *because* and *so* work in information states because they are complementary markers of warrants and inferences – both of which concern the organization and use of speaker/hearer knowledge and meta-knowledge.

Although the primary functions of *now* and *then* are in idea structures, *now* also has a role in the participation framework, because it marks speakers' attention to upcoming talk, and *then* also has roles in both information states and action structures, because it marks warranted requests. And finally, *I mean* and *y'know* both function in the information state (although this is the primary role of *y'know* because of its focus on hearer knowledge) and in the participation framework (although this is the primary role of *I mean* because of its focus on speaker orientation). *I mean* and *y'know* also have roles in idea structures, but *I mean* focuses on speakers' paraphrases of the meanings (referential meaning, speaker meaning) of propositions, whereas *y'know* focuses on the centrality of a single proposition for the overall idea structure of a text. Finally, *y'know* (like *so*) has a role in exchange structures due to its use at potential participation transitions.

As Figure 10.2 shows, then, markers which seem very different if considered just as miscellaneous expressions may actually share functions in the same discourse component (e.g. *now* and *I mean* in participation frameworks), just as markers which seem to be related expressions in other linguistic paradigms may have functions in very different discourse components (e.g. *now* and *then* are both time deictics but only the latter works in action structures).

10.1.2 Properties of markers

Although part of the communicative force of a marker is due to the definition of the discourse slot in which it is used (which is defined by its place in one (or more) discourse components), the linguistic properties of the expressions used as markers are also responsible for its communicative effect. Both referential (semantic) meaning and grammatical (syntactic) properties may contribute.

Many discourse markers are used in ways which reflect their meanings. Conjunctions, for example, have pragmatic effects which are closely tied to their meanings: *but* marks speaker-contrast because of its contrastive meaning, *or* marks hearer-option because of its disjunctive meaning. Similarly, the 'result' meaning of *so* is reflected in its use as marker of potential participation transition, the opposing uses of *now* and *then* are due to their opposing values on a proximal/distal axis, and the use of *I mean* as a marker of speaker orientation, and *y'know* as a marker of information state, is clearly related to the meanings of the predicates 'mean' and 'know' as well as the fact that these expressions contain first and second person pronouns. These core meanings do not fluctuate from use to use; rather, what changes is the discourse slot in which they appear – the position of that slot in an exchange, action, and idea structure, in a participation framework, and/or an information state. This suggests, then, that markers themselves do not convey social and/or expressive meanings. Rather, markers are situated in very different discourse slots, and it is the utterance within that discourse slot which is interpreted for social and/or expressive meaning: *but*, for example, does not itself mean 'challenge' – although the utterance which it precedes may certainly be interpreted as a challenge.

Can we be more precise about how the meaning of a marker contributes to the interpretation of sequential relations in discourse, i.e. the relation between an upcoming utterance and prior talk? I suggest that markers **select** a meaning relation from whatever potential meanings are provided through the content of talk, and then **display** that relation. This means that whatever meaning inheres in the marker itself has to be compatible with the meanings of the surrounding discourse. This does not mean, however, that all discourse meanings are equally likely. Quite the contrary: such meanings may be very strongly constrained. Consider (1).

(1)   a.   Sue dislikes all linguists.
         b.   I like her.

Without any marker preceding (b), which meaning relation is asigned depends on a number of background conditions. One is the identity of the speaker and the speaker's background beliefs. A linguist (or one who liked linguists) would no doubt interpret a contrastive relation between (a) and (b) which would be displayed by *but*. But someone who also dislikes linguists, might interpret a resultative relation, such that *so* would best display their relationship. The meanings of the propositions conveyed in the pair of utterances are vague enough to allow either of these (and other) interpretations. But because the pair would always occur in some context, some interpretation would inevitably be preferred. Another way of saying this is that once utterances are seen within their contexts, the potential meaning relationships between them is already constrained. This means that although a marker may be able theoretically to select any number of implicit and potential relationships, in actuality, that relationship is already fairly constrained, such that the marker acts more to display the relationship.

Before going on to consider the contribution of grammatical properties to discourse function, I want to address a slightly broader question concerning meaning: how does the fact that a marker does (or does not) have linguistic meaning influence the discourse plane on which it used? Figure 10.2 has already given us a hint, for it implied a rough correlation between the semantics of markers and their primary functions. Figure 10.3 makes this correlation more explicit.

Does the expression used as a marker have meaning?	
meaning	no meaning

conjunctions..time deictics....................lexicalized clauses..particles

ideational plane	non-ideational plane
What is the primary function of the marker?	

Figure 10.3. *Meaning of markers and their use in discourse*

It suggests that those markers with meaning have their primary functions on ideational planes of talk, and those without meaning show the reverse tendency. Of course this correlation is not only rough, but it is complicated by (1) the fact that there may be degrees of referential meaning in an expression (thus some cases of *y'know* are less referentially meaningful than others), (2) not all elements at one end of the scale have the same degree of meaning (e.g. although conjunctions are all at the 'meaning' end of the scale, *and* is similar to asyndetic connection whereas *but* has contrastive meaning), (3) a very different scale might result were **all** the functions of markers (not just the primary ones) to be considered. But, in general, what such a scale suggests is that if an expression used as a marker **does** have meaning, its primary use in discourse will be in the organization of referential meanings at a textual level – and that if a marker does not have meaning, its primary use will be elsewhere. What this also suggests is that as an expression **loses** its semantic meaning, it is freer to function in non-ideational realms of discourse.

Consider, now, the relationship between grammatical properties of markers and discourse function. Since it is only conjunctions which have a grammatical (connective) function in sentence grammars, it is really only

and, *but*, *or*, *so* and *because* for which this issue is relevant. We have seen
that the discourse use of conjunctions seems to parallel their grammatical
function: *and*, *but*, and *or* are coordinators in discourse, and *because* and
so are markers of subordinate and main units in discourse. But we have also
seen several features of discourse that point to differences between
discourse grammars and sentence grammars, and thus suggest that the
principles governing use of conjunctions in discourse do not totally parallel
those for conjunctions in sentences.

We saw that the structural units of talk which are marked can be either
referentially defined discourse topics, or idea units which are functionally
related in a larger text. Thus, within an explanation, for example, *and* can
mark the referential topics and/or the functional units. Furthermore,
discourse units vary in size, such that a marker (e.g. *because*) could subordinate very small units, e.g. sentence subjects, as well as larger units, e.g.
an entire narrative in an argument, or sequences of reasons in an explanation. Similarly, structural units can be embedded within each other: a
narrative may be a main unit to which an embedded orientation clause is
subordinated, at the same time that it is itself a subordinate unit, e.g. support for a position in an argument. Thus, markers may work at more than
one structural level at once. Finally, we have seen that because discourse is
multi-structured, what is a main (or subordinate, or coordinate) unit in one
structure, is not necessarily so in another. Thus, as we saw in discussion of
so, for example, what seems to be a marker of a main unit in an adjacency
pair need not be the marker of a main unit in an explanation.

Although conjunctions mark different levels and types of discourse
structure, I do not think that they actually **create** those structures. Rather,
I believe that just as markers select and then display a meaning relation, so
too, do they select and display a structural relation. I illustrate with *so* and
because, which are both semantic and structural converses. Consider the
following.

(2)   a.   I believe in fate.
         b.   I won the grand prize in a sweepstakes.

Without any markers before (b), we can infer several different meaning relations between (a) and (b). For example, (a) may be supported by (b), or
(a) may cause (b). Different structural relations between (a) and (b)
accompany the different meaning relations. If the speaker is using (b) to
argue for the validity of her belief in (a), then (a) is a main unit of position
and (b) a subordinate unit of support. But if the speaker's belief caused her
luck, then (a) is a subordinate unit of cause and (b) a main unit of result.

Either one of these meaning/structure relations is possible without a marker before (b). But once a marker is used, one relation is selected to the exclusion of the other:

(2')   a.   I believe in fate.
          b.   Because I won the grand prize in a sweepstakes.
(2")   a.   I believe in fate.
          b.   So I won the grand prize in a sweepstakes.

Thus, either relation is possible **without** markers, but only one relation is possible with a marker. It is for this reason that I suggest that markers select, and then display, structural relations between utterances, rather than create such relations.

10.1.3 Meaning, grammar, and discourse

Consider, now, that since the content of talk constrains the interpretation of meaning and structural relations, we might expect to find that the larger the discourse unit over which the marker has scope, the less meaning is conveyed by the marker. Recall Irene's story (7 from Chapter 6) in which she reports her personal experience with a local politician as a way of accounting for her general distrust for that politician. She states her general opinion and then prefaces her entire story with *because*. The story coda returns to Irene's general position with *so*. If *because* and *so* were absent from Irene's story, however, we would have no trouble defining the story as specific support for her general position. Thus, my suggestion is that when markers have wide discourse scope, they contribute less communicative force to the overall definition of the discourse than when their scope is limited to a single clause.

The same reduction in individual contribution from the marker would result from the presence in the discourse of multiply reinforcing and redundant cues of meaning and structure – even if the discourse over which the marker has scope is much smaller. Thus, when Jack prefaces his dislike for religion with *but that isn't the point* and *the point is* ((52) in Chapter 6), the contribution of *but* is less than it would be were the meta-linguistic expressions absent.

These two sources of meaning and structure – size of the discourse unit and redundant cues – might help to account not only for a general reduction in the meaning of individual markers, but for the **absence** of markers in particular cases where they might otherwise be expected. Reconsider (3) from Chapter 3. Zelda is explaining that she is strict with her children when it is needed.

(3)   a.   See, she is at the point now where she really doesn't run out
                that much so that there–
        b.   she's not driving a car or anything.
        c.   We *did* have it with the boys, uh: they weren't–they–y–
        d.   when they first started t'drive, they *did* have t'be in by twelve,
        e.   because they had a learner's permit.
        f.   We always did tell the boys. . .
        g.   I always stressed that
        h.   because I went through more with the boys than I did
                with JoAnn.

As I noted in Chapter 3, what gives textual structure to this discourse is lexical repetition (stressed *did*) in (c) and (d), and reiteration of part of the
support (in c and f). Zelda also maintains thematic continuity on a local
basis: topic is continued from clause (a) to (b), a new topic is introduced in
(f) and then maintained through (h). The fact that other devices thus do
much of the same work as markers not only reduces the contribution of the
markers which do occur, but makes it unnecessary for additional markers
to be used. Thus, in general, the more the discourse works toward conveying its own meaning and structure, the smaller the contribution of the
discourse marker, and the more the marker is likely to be absent.

10.2 Indexical functions of markers

Although I have suggested that markers have linguistic properties, and that
markers have functions in particular components of talk, we need another
dimension of analysis if we are to go further in understanding the contribution of discourse markers to coherence. I suggest that this dimension is
deixis, and that all markers have **indexical** functions.[2] Although I already
discussed deixis in Chapter 8, I will do so again to introduce its relevance
here.

Consider, first, that one of the qualities that differentiates utterances
from sentences is that utterances are inherently context-bound: they are
presented by a speaker to a hearer at a certain time and in a certain place.
Speaker, hearer, time, and place are four dimensions of context which are
often encoded through deictic elements: personal pronouns, temporal expressions (including tense) and locative expressions (including verbs of
motion).

Deictic elements define the **deictic center** of an utterance, i.e. the locus
from which speaker, hearer, time, and place coordinates are fixed, and are
thus assigned a context-specific interpretation. In unmarked cases, the
deictic center is the speaker, such that person, time, and place are defined

in relation to the speaker's identity, the time during which the utterance is presented, and the location of the speaker. The grouping of deictics according to whether they point toward or away from the deictic center defines a proximal/distal axis. Those deictics that point toward the deictic center are proximal (e.g. *I*, present tense, *here*), and those that point away are distal (e.g. *you*, past tense, *there*).

Discourse markers also fall into proximal and distal groups – although the deictic center in relation to which this axis is defined is determined not by situational parameters, but by discourse parameters. More specifically, the context to which markers index utterances includes both **participants** and **text**.

The participant coordinates to which markers index utterances are the speaker and hearer: a marker shows that an utterance is focused on either the speaker (proximal), or the hearer (distal), or possibly both. *Oh*, for example, focuses on the speaker – for it marks the speaker's recognition, receipt, and so on, of information. *Well* focuses on both speaker and hearer – for the one who uses *well* is being defined as a respondent (a type of hearer) in relation to a prior speaker's expectations who must also alter his or her expectations about the course of upcoming talk.

The textual coordinates of talk focus on prior text vs. upcoming text: markers index their containing utterance to whatever text precedes them (proximal), or to whatever text is to follow (distal), or to both. In other words, they either point backward in the text, forward, or in both directions. *Oh* focuses on prior text: we saw that *oh* managed information which had previously been presented. *Well* focuses on both for it is the juncture between prior and upcoming text which is being marked – the fact that the expectations proposed through prior text are not being actualized in upcoming text.

Figure 10.4 shows how the proximal/distal opposition classifies markers on participation and textual coordinates of discourse. As I just stated, *oh* indexes an utterance to a speaker, since it is the speaker who is managing information. But *well* indexes an utterance to both speaker and hearer, since its user is defining him/herself as a respondent to a prior interlocutor. *Oh* indexes to prior text, since this is what triggers the information state transition. But *well* indexes to both prior and upcoming text, since it is a mismatch between prior expectations and upcoming material which occasions its use.

And indexes an utterance to a speaker coordinate, because it continues a speaker's action. *And* also indexes an utterance to both a prior and an upcoming coordinate – since it looks forward in a text to a next idea or action, but to one which continues the prior idea or action structure. *But* establishes the same speaker focus, but indexes an utterance only to a prior

Figure 10.4. *Markers as contextual coordinates*

	PARTICIPATION COORDINATES speaker/hearer	TEXTUAL COORDINATES prior/upcoming
oh	speaker	prior
well	speaker/hearer	prior/upcoming
and	speaker	prior/upcoming
but	speaker	prior
or	hearer	prior/upcoming
so	speaker/hearer	prior/upcoming
because	speaker	prior/upcoming
now	speaker	upcoming
then	speaker/hearer	prior/upcoming
I mean	speaker	prior
y'know	speaker/hearer	prior/upcoming

coordinate, e.g. because understanding the contrast marked by *but* requires attention to prior or mutually known information, or because *but* returns a speaker to an earlier point of the text. *Or*, on the other hand, indexes an utterance to a hearer and it looks both backward and forward in a text, since it is the hearer to whom a choice between prior and/or upcoming alternatives is offered.

So targets speaker and hearer (recall its function in potential participation transitions) and prior and upcoming text (since it relates prior causes to upcoming results). *Because*, on the other hand, focuses only on the speaker (since it lacks a function complementary to that of *so* in participation transitions), although it shares with *so* a focus on prior and upcoming text because it is a semantic converse.

Now indexes an utterance to a speaker and to upcoming text, since it marks the speaker's attention to a new subpart of a discourse, or shift to a new orientation. *Then*, on the other hand, targets both speaker and hearer (because it can mark a speaker's request to another) and both prior and upcoming text (because it creates a bridge from current to prior discourse time).

And, finally, *I mean* targets a speaker, since it marks the speaker's orientation to an utterance, and prior text, since it in some way continues the meaning already presented in the text. *Y'know*, on the other hand, targets both a speaker and a hearer since it opens an interactive focus on speaker-provided information. But like *I mean*, it can also mark a speaker orientation – although it opens that orientation for hearer reaction and more general participation transition. Finally, *y'know* indexes an utterance to both prior and upcoming text, because it can look backward to mark previous information as well as forward to upcoming information.

Comparing across groups reveals some interesting similarities and differences among markers. For example, *and* and *I mean* both index an utterance to the speaker, but *and* is upcoming (an addition is coming) and *I mean* is prior (a paraphrase or modification of past text is presented). And *oh* and *I mean* share both coordinates: speaker and prior text. But they differ because of the discourse planes on which such coordinates are fixed: *oh* in the information state, *I mean* in the participation framework. *So* and *then* share the same coordinates. What differentiates them is their meanings: *so* is resultative and *then* is successive.

Viewing markers as having indexical functions allows us to answer our questions about whether markers have more than one function apiece, and whether markers are functional equivalents for each other. First, the question about multiple functions. Throughout my analysis, I have spoken as if each marker has a great number of specific functions – and at the level of detail at which I described particular situated uses of markers, this was indeed the case. That is, each marker had specific **syntagmatic** functions within the particular sequence in which it occurred because of its role within the structure of that particular sequence. But I also suggest, at the more abstract level of analysis which I have been considering here, that each marker has only **one indexical function**. It is because discourse is multiply structured, and its various components integrated with each other, that multiple relations hold between utterances – not because markers **themselves** realize a different function (one devoted to ideas, one to action, and so on) with each occasion of use. Similarly, it is only because utterances are always contextualized in more than one component of talk that markers have the more specific, situated syntagmatic roles which I have described throughout.

Consider, now, the question of functional equivalents. Many markers are functional equivalents if all that is being considered is either their indexical function, or their discourse plane. For example, *so* and *y'know* share their indexical functions; *well* and *I mean* share the participation framework as the primary plane of talk on which they function. But once both indexical function and discourse plane are considered, very few markers remain as functional equivalents. And once the linguistic properties of the marker itself are added in, there are no functional equivalents at all. Thus, what counts as equivalence depends on how finely one tunes one's notion of function.

This observation about the relativity of functional equivalence allows us to realize that although some markers are used in the same broadly defined discourse slots, they are doing very different sorts of work in those slots. *Now* and *but*, for example, are both used in comparisons. But *now* marks the speaker's orientation to an upcoming subtopic, whereas *but* marks the contrastive relationship between the subtopics. Or consider *oh* and *well*. Although both occur with answers whose content is not totally consonant with the ideational predictions of a prior question, they do so for different reasons and with different effect: *oh* marks the speaker's cognitive reorientation to information which is either unfamiliar or not expected to be relevant; *well* marks the speaker's interactional presence despite the lack of an immediately ready response. *So* and *but* provide still another example: both occur when speakers return to the ideational core of an answer to a question. But *so* does so because this is the dominant part of the answer, and *but* does so because this is merely one functionally differentiated part of the answer. The point of these comparisons is that these markers **cannot** be considered functional equivalents – because the close observation of the discourse slot, the indexical function of the marker, and the linguistic properties of the marker, show very distinct functions being realized.

10.3 Contextual coordinates and discourse coherence

Let us turn now to the most general question underlying the study of discourse markers: what do markers add to discourse coherence? Addressing this question will also allow us to consider several remaining issues which are still unresolved.

Consider, first, that the fact that markers function on different discourse planes provides us with clues to discourse contexts, i.e. markers locate utterances on particular planes of talk. I have also suggested, because there is an underlying deictic dimension to their functions, that markers provide participation and textual coordinates within these contexts: the deictic functions locate utterances on two proximal/distal axes within their particular discourse contexts. It is in this dual sense that markers provide **contextual coordinates** for utterances: they index an utterance to the local contexts in which utterances are produced and in which they are to be interpreted. I suggest that this is why markers are used in discourse. And this is what markers are at a more theoretical level of analysis – contextual co-ordinates.

The items which other analysts have defined as markers can also be seen as contextual coordinates: postural changes during interaction (Erickson 1979, Scheflen 1973), particles in American Indian languages which mark verse structure (Hymes 1981, Sherzer 1982), and *okay* in service encounters (Merritt 1984) all provide coordinates to the contexts in which particular verbal and nonverbal moves are produced and designed to be interpreted. What differs is not the function of the marker; what differs is the contexts in which a particular verbal or nonverbal move is to be anchored by the marker. My contexts have emerged from the study of conversational interaction on a local, utterance by utterance basis. Certainly other contexts are more germane to other types and forms of social interaction.

What expressions can be used as markers? One way to answer this question is to begin by focusing on **units** of discourse. Such an approach would first segment the ongoing flow of interaction into a series of identifiable chunks of activity. Attention would then focus on how participants themselves differentiate such chunks – how they display the boundaries between their jointly constituted activities. The result would be a catalogue of discourse markers which is firmly grounded in observations of how participants themselves differentiate interactional units. A key feature of this approach is that entries within such a catalogue would include both verbal and nonverbal markers for both local and global sized units. Another key feature is the likelihood that some segments of interaction would be found to be not marked at all. Assuming one still had confidence in the reality of those units, this feature could be turned to great advantage: one might then begin to look to those locations as favored locations, or key sites, for the emergence of markers.

It is at this point in this first approach that a second approach would be particularly helpful: a delimitation of what elements of language can be used as markers. I have focused here on particles (*oh, well*), conjunctions (*and, but, or, so, because*), time deictics (*now, then*) and lexicalized clauses (*y'know, I mean*). Not only have other analysts found other devices, but there are many which I have not considered:

> the perception verbs *see* (used in explanations), *look* and *listen* (used in repeated directives and challenges, as well as in pre-closings), but not *hear*

the location deictics *here, there* (often used in narratives to mark surprising outcomes in the complicating action)

the adverbial *why* (used instead of *then*, as in *if he wants to come, why let him come!*, or to preface typical instances, as in *why just the other day*...) but not *when, where* or *how*

the interjections *gosh, boy*

the verb *say* (as in *say, can you lend me a dime?*) but not other verbs of saying (except in meta-linguistic expressions such as *lemme tell you*)

meta-talk (such as *this is the point, what I mean is*...; see Schiffrin 1980)

the quantifier phrases *anyway, anyhow, whatever*

This second approach would try to find common characteristics of these items to delimit what linguistic condition' allow an expression to be used as a marker. But such an approach would require not only discovery of the shared characteristics of an extremely diversified set of expressions in English: it would require analysis across a wide body of typologically diverse languages to discover what other linguistic resources are drawn upon for use as markers.[3] And such an approach would require not only a synchronic perspective on the functions of these expressions in discourse: it would require a diachronic perspective which could build from analyses of semantic and pragmatic change (e.g. Traugott, forthcoming) and change from discourse to syntax (e.g. Sankoff and Brown 1976) to trace the processes by which individual expressions with semantic meanings actually gain pragmatic (and other) effects in discourse.

Without the benefit of such scholarship, I offer the following tentative suggestions as to what specific conditions allow an expression to be used as a marker:

it has to be syntactically detachable from a sentence
it has to be commonly used in initial position of an utterance
it has to have a range of prosodic contours
   e.g. tonic stress and followed by a pause, phonological reduction
it has to be able to operate at both local and global levels of discourse, and on different planes of discourse
   this means that it either has to have no meaning, a vague meaning, or to be reflexive (of the language, of the speaker)

More generally, an expression which functions within at least one discourse component can become a marker which functions within other discourse components – simply because of the integration among components. This means that expressions through which speakers display their orientation toward a proposition, e.g. an adverb such as *frankly*, an interjection such as *gosh*, a polarity term such as *yeh*, can become markers of other discourse components, as can expressions through which speakers organize action and exchange structures, idea structures, and information states.

A striking demonstration of the operation of such a process is provided by the adjacent use of two opposing polarity terms. In (4), Freda and Jack are talking about fate:

(4)   Jack: Nobody's really a fatalist when they face it. It's only when it's
                     calm, you're sitting in a . . . the living room dis ⌈ cuss ⌉ ing it=
        Freda: ⌊ Yeh! ⌋
        Jack: =intellectual, you could say that.
        Freda: **No yeh** ⌈ you're gonna fight! You're gonna ⌉ *fight*=
        Jack: ⌊ But not when you're facing it.   ⌋
        Freda: =t'save yourself.

Freda marks her agreement with the negative content of Jack's proposition (*nobody's really a fatalist*) with *no*; in other words, *no* establishes her alignment with Jack by displaying her ideational orientation. Freda marks the same alignment with *yeh*, although *yeh* shows her agreement with what Jack is supporting (*it's only when it's calm*). Thus, (4) shows *no* and *yeh* marking: (1) an ideational orientation toward two different propositions and (2) a single participation framework. Or consider a brief interaction which I observed:

(5)   A is a man sitting on a bus. There is a newspaper on an empty seat next to
        him. B is a man approaching the seat.
        B: Is this your newspaper?
        A: **No yeh** you can have it.

Whereas A's *no* attends to the propositional content of B's question, his *yeh* attends to the request for the newspaper which underlies B's question about ownership. A's utterance can thus be expanded as *No, this is not my newspaper. Yes, you can have it.* The point of these examples is that although *no* and *yeh* are basically polarity terms, once we view them as markers of different discourse components – markers which may begin in one component but gain functions in others – we can understand what would otherwise seem to be a contradiction.

Let us consider, finally, how discourse markers as contextual coordinates add to coherence. Recall that markers often establish more than one contextual coordinate at once. Since coherence is the result of **integration** among different components of talk, any device which simultaneously locates an utterance within several different emerging contexts of discourse automatically has an integrative function. That is, if a marker acts like an instruction to consider an upcoming utterance as speaker-focused on prior text within an information state, with a simultaneous instruction to view that utterance within a particular action structure, then the result is a type of integration between those two components of talk. Note the efficiency of this arrangement. Only one linguistic item – a discourse marker – with one indexical function, anchors an utterance into more than one discourse component at once. By so doing, it provides a path toward the integration of those different components into one coherent discourse. Another way of saying this is that markers allow speakers to construct and integrate multiple planes and dimensions of an emergent reality: it is out of such processes that coherent discourse results.

Notes

1 Background: what is discourse?

1. Leech (1983: Chapter 3) compares formalist and functionalist approaches in linguistics. (See Sadock (1984) for a critique of extreme versions of both approaches.) All of my assumptions are grounded in a functionalist approach.
2. Brown and Yule (1983: Chapter 2) and Levinson (1983: 22–3) discuss the difficulties associated with defining context, and summarize others' attempts to list the contextual parameters necessary for pragmatic interpretation of an utterance. (See also Downes 1983: Chapter 8 and Ochs 1979b: 1–60.) Clark and Carlson (1981) show that the same definitional difficulties have plagued psycholinguists, and they propose a definition of context based on common ground. I explore how some of these issues have both methodological and analytical relevance to discourse analysis in Schiffrin (1986).
3. One reason why context may be so important is that the linguistic sign is arbitrary. De Saussure (1959: 66) defined the sign as 'a two-sided psychological entity': the combination of a concept and a sound image. The concept is the 'signified' (the idea that is represented); the sound image is the 'signifier' (the sequence of sound and syllables which forms a word). Critical in de Saussure's definition is the idea that 'the bond between the signifier and the signified is arbitrary', that is 'the linguistic sign is arbitrary' (p. 67). For de Saussure, however, interpreters are hardly free to supply their own individual meanings: 'every means of expression used in society is based, in principle, on **collective** behavior or – what amounts to the same thing – on **convention**' (p. 67). (Here, de Saussure is drawing upon the concept of social fact, developed by Durkheim (1895).) Although de Saussure does not explicitly discuss context, context enters into the interpretation process in as many different ways as does convention, and in some cases, it cannot be easily separated from convention: for example, some expressions become conventional means of acting only in certain situations (e.g. asking your dinner partner 'can you pass the salt?') or only in certain relationships. The point is that without an inherent (e.g. iconic) connection between signified and signifier, other information (such as that provided by convention and context) has to aid in the interpretation of sound–meaning correspondences.

2 Prelude to analysis: definitions and data

1. Although I will be discussing some other analyses of discourse markers (also

more specifically referred to as particles, conjunctions, connectives and inter-jections) throughout the book, it may be helpful to have a complete list of the analyses which I found particularly helpful even though I will not discuss them all in detail: Auchlin 1981, Barrett and Stenner 1971, Borowski 1976, Brock-way 1981, Dik 1968, Ducrot 1980, Gazdar and Pullum 1976, Goldberg 1982, Hamilton 1983, Heritage 1984, Hurford 1974, James 1972, 1974, Johnson-Laird 1969, Lakoff 1971, Merritt 1984, Oöstman 1981, Owen 1983, Pelletier 1977, Posner 1980, Quasthoff 1979, Schmerling 1975, Schourup 1985, Svart-vik 1980, van Dijk 1977b, Vincent 1983, von Glaserfeld 1974, Warner 1985.

2. See Gazdar (1979) and Levinson (1981) for excellent discussions of many of these difficulties with speech act theory.

3. Tone unit boundaries are indicated in the following ways: a comma, a period, a question mark, an exclamation point, a series of periods, a dash. See Preface for more on transcription conventions.

4. I certainly do not mean to argue here that markers are the only devices that are sequentially dependent: so are anaphors and all cohesive devices which 'pre-suppose' a tie earlier in the discourse. We will see in Chapter 3 that these devices can be considered as coherence options for markers.

3 Questions: why analyze discourse markers?

1. The evaluation of a narrative has a similar function: it shows how the specific experience just reported is an instance of a more general proposition (see Labov and Fanshel 1977: 105 for this view of narrative).

2. Compare Grice's (1957) distinction between meaning and non-natural mean-ing, or his (1968) distinction between sentence-meaning and utterer's mean-ing.

4 *Oh*: marker of information management

1. James (1972) states that *oh* occurs within sentences, but at boundaries which seem to be (according to her transcription of invented sentences) at utterance boundaries. She suggests that in a sentence such as 'The FBI arrested . . . oh . . . Bill Jones', the speaker is 'making a deliberate decision or choice as to what to say next – and that there is not one right way he knows of to complete the sen-tence' (pp. 162–3). I deal with such cases as information searches in (4.1.1).

2. Another self-repair from *coagulating* to *thinning* is marked with *uh*. Two other self-repairs, the addition of background information following *he said*, and re-placement of *that c–* by *this case*, are not marked.

3. Differentiating other-initiated repairs from disagreements often requires in-terpretation of speaker intent, especially when the same phrases are used, e.g. *what do you mean X?*. Because it is not always possible (from either an analyst's or participant's viewpoint) to know whether it is one's information output that is being corrected (repair), or one's knowledge of information that is being assessed (disagreement), I am including any replacement by one speaker of what another has said as other-repair. Note that this ambiguity may be one reason why other-repairs are marked forms of repair.

4. Another possibility is for A to continue talking. Because this follow-up has nothing to do with the clarification *per se* – and nothing to do with information management – we will not consider it any further. This exclusion of four cases accounts for the difference in the totals of the columns in Table 4.2.

5. Although we will focus here on question/answer pairs because they complete a proposition, we should also note a pragmatic reason for the question/answer constraint (on which we focus more in Chapter 5). Questions are among the linguistic means of enacting requests for information and actions, and thus impose – through their underlying appropriateness conditions (Gordon and Lakoff 1971, Labov and Fanshel 1977: Chapter 3) – an expectation of fulfillment. Thus, both completion of a proposition, and compliance with a request, can be enacted through the second-pair-part of an answer.

6. That certain registers, such as teacher talk, use a three-part question/answer/ evaluation format is well-known. See e.g. Mehan 1979.

7. Deciding what to count as 'zero' use of *oh* in acknowledgement was difficult. An overview of question/answer/acknowledgement sequences showed that answers longer that two or three utterances tended not to be followed by acknowledgements. This makes sense for the following reason. Because long answers take more time to process, they would require several acknowledgement markers. But repeated uses of *oh* become heard as back-channel responses because they do not lead to a turn-transition. Another overview showed that acknowledgement markers were more frequent when the speaker continued in a question/answer dialogue format, i.e. asked another question. Thus, I counted the following as 'zero' acknowledgement: (1) other acknowledgement markers (*yeh, okay, right*) without *oh*, (2) the follow-up of a short answer (2–3 utterances) with a questioner's next move unprefaced by any marker.

8. On one level of analysis the uses of *oh* as marker of old information recognition and new information receipt seem contradictory. But note that I have spoken of old information which becomes **newly relevant** in a conversation: so even though the information itself might be familiar, its current salience was not predictable. And on a deeper level, both information tasks concern the management of information transitions in talk. Nevertheless, further study might search for some way in which speakers differentiate these two uses, e.g. through intonation or prosody.

9. Schiffrin (1984b) discusses how Jack uses his relationship with Joey Brenner – a famous comedian who was a childhood friend – for interactional status.

10. Identification of this information as background depends on viewing it in a discourse perspective. That is, even though 'the business that his father was in' is in a syntactically focused position, it is backgrounded information within its story context.

5 *Well*: marker of response

1. I do not want to exclude the possibility that there may be a historical connection between the adverb *well* and the discourse marker *well*. This has been suggested by a variety of people (in personal communication): Joseph Greenberg,

Flora Klein, Elizabeth Traugott. David Harris has also been kind enough to locate many of the same uses of *well* which I identify here in several Elizabethan and Restoration plays, but interestingly, not the most common use following questions. He suggests that this use was too colloquial for the drama of that time.

2. I thank Gail Jefferson for bringing this to my attention.

3. It is important to note that I excluded from my analysis yes–no questions which function as indirect requests for information beyond confirmation or denial. For example, questions like *Could I have your name?* or *Can you think of any games you used to play?* are by form yes–no questions, but by function something quite different. (See the collection of papers in Cole and Morgan 1975.) The use of *well* in answers to such questions seems to follow the pattern for yes–no questions: out of 31 such questions, answers to only 2 were prefaced with *well*.

4. From the standpoint of children in our society, *gym* may very well count as a school topic: it is included in the curriculum, a time is set aside for it, a grade is given, and so on. Yet, I would argue that children become aware that many adults assign a different status to gym, and to physical activities in general: math homework, for example, is often assigned precedence over little league. I thank Don Zimmerman for bringing such issues to my attention.

5. The questions which we examined in (5.1.1) can all be seen as requests for information. I did not highlight this functional role, however, because I wanted to focus on constraints imposed through their form and through their membership in an adjacency pair.

6. *Yeh but* is quite different from *but*. Although I have not analyzed it in detail, *yeh* seems to function here more as a turn-taking device (compare to *uh uh* and *um*) which coordinates multi-turn units of talk. See Schegloff (1981).

7. Further comparisons between these two markers will be made in Chapter 10, where I discuss markers as discourse options for each other.

6 Discourse connectives: *and, but, or*

1. Such syntagmatic contrasts require that neither member of the pair has semantic meaning. For different opinions on this issue as it bears on tense in narrative, see Wolfson (1979, 1982), Schiffrin (1981) and Silva-Corvalan (1983).

2. We would expect other cues (syntactic, prosodic) of idea segmentation in such examples, comparable to those in (14) and (15).

3. Although it is easier to show this meaning by looking at how *and* is used in discourse which is more dialogic, I want to stress that *and* has this meaning even in the monologues examined in (6.1.1): in other words, it is not the speaker's use of *and* which has changed, but the analyst's perspective. I return to this point in (6.1.3).

4. I consider the interplay between closeness and the display of conflict in Schiffrin (1984a), following Simmel (1961, original 1911).

5. For fuller analysis of (25), and of the story which preceded it, see Schiffrin (1984b).

6. Note, here, a parallel to sentence analyses of *and*. We can hardly say that *and* is

'marking' all of the specific idea and interactional units which it precedes than we could say that *and* means temporal succession, simultaneity, causality, and so on. I suggest that it is because *and* can be so freely used that it starts to seem as if it has so many meanings – and the tendency to assign meaning to form may be an unavoidable human proclivity to create signs and symbols. This freedom would then be responsible for the unwieldy meaning-maximalist view that *and* is ambiguous or polysemous (as I discuss in 6.4). But this freedom can also indicate that *and* is an unmarked mode of connection; the unmarkedness of *and* can then explain why it is a discourse option for other, more meaningful, markers.

7. The joint construction of discourse has received little attention. Falk (1979) describes such processes as conversational duets; Tannen (1984) as cooperative overlaps.

8. This suggests, further, that if an individual can briefly counteract the projection of an unfavorable self potentially associated with an objectionable position, he is freed from formulating a less objectionable position in the first place (see Goffman 1981b).

9. By this I do not mean that very few yes–no questions received affirmative or negative responses. Compare my discussion in Chapter 5.

10. Of course, the satisfaction of these different demands may also occur in a single utterance; I don't want to imply that there's a one-form, one-function correlation.

11. *But* also fills the roles of other contrastive expressions, which, again, are not themselves functional equivalents. For example, *but* and *though* are both referentially contrastive, and *but* and *like I said* are both functionally contrastive. But *though* and *like I said* are hardly interchangeable for each other.

12. Jefferson (1974) points out that repairs may have a strategic design other than the replacement of information.

13. On the relationship between arguments and sociability, see Schiffrin (1984a).

14. I do not treat *yeh but* here, but my suspicion is that *yeh* has a turn-taking function and *but* a speaker-return function.

15. This expressive function creates several possible interactional consequences which I can only suggest here: for example, if one is heard as heavily committed to a particular proposition, others may be led to evaluate their own orientation to that proposition, to ask for justifications of such commitment, or to redefine their conversation as a dispute of some kind.

16. Chapter 5, p. 118 presents the same data in discussion of *well*.

17. I do not mean to imply that informationally cooperative entails socially cooperative and vice versa. See Bennett (1978), Tannen (1983).

18. I hesitated to consider *or* in tags as discourse markers because their syntactic distribution is so broad (see Ball and Ariel 1978, Dines 1980). Thus, my remarks apply only to *or* tags which are clause final, and which are prosodically set off as a separate tone unit. (Cf. clause-final *oder* in German.)

19. *Or* was not frequent in my data: I found only 53 tokens of it as a discourse marker. I suggest that this is because *but* and *and* could be used in some of the same environments as *or*. I suggested that *or* presents inclusive options. Since many such options contrast with one another, *but* could thus be used; and

since such options are inclusive, *and* could be used. The fact that there are some differences between *or, but* and *and* even in these potentially similar environments, however, is probably why *or* is used instead: *but* does not open a contrast for hearer choice, and *and* does not offer the possibility of exclusive disjunction.

20. Dik's own position is that coordinators do have semantic values which impose restrictions on what can be connected.

21. Approaching the meaning minimalist/maximalist controversy on a discourse level may also clarify the semantic/pragmatic division of labor by systematizing the contribution of context to communicative meaning.

22. It is important to note that viewing *and* as meaningful beyond logical connection does not necessarily mean that its meanings multiply as rapidly as I have suggested. This conclusion follows only so long as one assumes that *and* **conveys** the meanings of what it connects. One may also argue that *and* has one central sense, e.g. addition, which is compatible with a wide range of textual meanings. Such a view then faces a problem similar to that faced by meaning-minimalist views: accounting for how textual meanings provide both semantic and pragmatic inferences.

23. See Cohen 1971, Johnson-Laird 1969 for arguments about the multiple meaning view, and Kempson 1977, Zwicky and Sadock 1975 for useful tests of polysemy and ambiguity which may be applied to *and*.

24. If the boundary between semantics and pragmatics is differently drawn, then other ways of accounting for the meaning of *but* become possible. Dik (1968: 277), for example, concludes that *but* has a constant semantic value (adversative), and that contrastive readings between propositions are due not only to the semantics of the propositions, but to 'differences in context and situation and other interpretational factors'. Thus, Dik's view is that *but* has a semantic meaning of contrast, and that its use is sensitive to both semantic and pragmatic sources of knowledge (Lakoff 1971).

25. A very different discourse analysis of *and* is suggested by the work of Vincent (1983) on French *et*. She treats *et* just as a coordinator – with no meaning at all. There are three difficulties with this view. First, Vincent does not identify the units which *and* is coordinating (an important prerequisite to any argument that *and* is a coordinator since coordinate structures are not easily found in discourse; cf. Beaman 1984). Second, *and* has interactional uses as a marker of continuation which can be interpreted as a pragmatic effect (6.1.2). Third, the meanings of discourse connectives vary when they are prosodically set off (through stress, pause) from the following utterance. (Try replacing the stressed *or* in 67 with *and* or *but*.) Such meaning differences would not be possible were *and* merely a structural device.

26. Stubbs (1983a: 78) suggests that these two levels may not even be separable for analyses of *and*: 'almost by definition, conjunctions cannot be fully dealt with within syntax, since they are not really part of the structure of syntactic units'.

7 *So* and *because*: markers of cause and result

1. I also include *cause* as a variant of *because*, and *so that* as a variant of *so*.

Although I found no differences between these variants, further study might identify subtle distinctions.

2. In Schiffrin (1985b), I examine further (thematic) constraints on speakers' use of these two causal ordering options.

3. The three-part distinction proposed here differs from the knowledge-based and language-based sources of meaning discussed in relation to *but* (6.2). Whereas the contrast marked by *but* can be either part of lexical meaning (language-based) or part of speaker knowledge (knowledge-based), the causal relations marked by *because* and *so* are never part of lexical meaning (except for analytic truths such as *John$_i$ is a bachelor because he$_i$ is unmarried*). This holds whether the domain of the causal relation is facts or speakers' knowledge.

   Note, also that my distinction is similar to a three-part division often noted for the functions of language: referential (facts), expressive (knowledge) and social (actions), e.g. Bühler (1934). For discussion of the nonseparability of the social and expressive see Lyons (1977a: 50–6). My distinction also expands Halliday and Hasan's (1976) distinction between external and internal meaning (for discussion, see 6.4.1): I consider knowledge-based and action-based to be two variants of internal meaning.

4. This is an intentionally broad definition of the notion of inference and warrant. It is my belief that all semantic and pragmatic inferences are implicitly warranted, in the former case, by linguistic knowledge, and in the second case, by social knowledge. Both linguistic and social knowledge can be considered as background sources of information (warrants) which are used by speaker/ hearers to license a further interpretation (an inference).

5. The notion of claim goes beyond linguistics and beyond the consideration of individuals as speakers: claims involve individuals in their capacities as social beings, and the goods to which access is contested has a property-like value. This explains why the challenge to a verbal claim may be interpreted as a threat to a speaker's status (cf. Labov and Fanshel 1977: 94–6). See also discussion of argument in Chapter 1.

6. Van Dijk (1977a: 73) suggests that *because* 'focuses attention on the interdependencies of facts, whereas the use of sentence-initial *so* and *therefore* is typically used to denote the inferential relations'. However, van Dijk gives little evidence to support this distributional difference. Because many of the examples in my corpus allow both readings, I could not examine his hypothesis. But see Schiffrin (1985b).

7. Henry argues that although there is a great deal of anti-Semitism in the world, Jews themselves are tolerant of religious and cultural differences. He makes this claim several different times during our conversations, and each time, he does so to defend himself against the unfavorable character implications of his own position against intermarriage (see discussion in Chapter 6, pp. 153–5). Henry's point about the tolerance of Jews is contested, then, by his very own position against intermarriage: by not wanting his children to marry out of their religion, Henry can be seen as intolerant of other religions. Note, also that verbal grounds are only one means through which Henry defends his claim to tolerance. At the beginning of one of my visits, for example, Henry requested that I return a brief questionnaire that he had completed in which he

    had ranked his feelings of closeness with different ethnic groups so that he could tear it up and throw it away.

8. Compare Labov and Fanshel's (1977: 100): 'If A makes a statement about B-events, then it is heard as a request for confirmation.' (A B-event is one about which one's hearer is expected to have knowledge.) See also Chapter 8 (8.2.3.3).

9. I have found no uses of *because* other than those which are direct realizations of its semantic meaning of 'cause'.

10. Both *so* and *but* are used with the last idea presented in answers to questions. But whereas *but* functionally differentiates the **segments** of an answer (6.2:1), *so* shows the speaker's forward orientation to the next step after the question.

11. Note that *but* is similar in this regard: when *but* is used alone, its meaning indicates that a contrast is recoverable for some reason. *But* also differs, however: because speakers also use *but* to return to their own points, its elliptical use does not always mark the potential participation transitions marked by *so*: for example, Ira and Jan use *but* to create shared turns in much the same way that they use *and* (see 28 and 29 in Chapter 6), although they do not use *so* in this way.

8 Temporal adverbs: *now* and *then*

1. The relationship between time deictics (including, but not limited to adverbs and tense) and conceptions of time is far too complex for full discussion here; see e.g. Comrie 1985.

2. This simplifies the complexities of *this* and *that*: they too can be used evaluatively.

3. The notion of subtopics captures the idea that comparisons are cumulative – such that a later subtopic is understood in relation to an early subtopic.

4. A recent ruling in Texas forbade public school teachers to ask for students' opinions on moral issues – since the existence of opinions implied uncertainty over ultimate truths. See also Atelsek 1981, Schiffrin 1985d.

5. Such changes are well illustrated in narratives. For example, when speakers shift from the complicating action to the evaluation, they are not only shifting their own orientation, but they are opening a potential shift in participation framework – such that the audience can then respond as evaluators (rather than hearers) of an experience. See discussion in Chapter 1.

6. At another level of analysis, picking a specific example is similar to a comparison: whereas comparisons select two members of a set which differ in some way, examples select a representative member of a set. This explains why *like* can be used to preface both comparisons and examples (discussed in Schiffrin 1982b: Chapter 6).

7. Although I do not consider it here, different aspects of the self may be focused, e.g. animator, principal, etc. (Goffman 1981b).

8. Note the critical role of the *but* phrase following disclaimers with *now*. See discussion in Chapter 6.

9. It is this latter quality which is reflected by the view that the semantic meaning of *if/then* is that of the logical connective →.

10. My interpretation is based on three assumptions: (1) events (or actions, states, processes, etc.) are presented in verb phrases, (2) the agents involved in those events are presented in noun phrases, (3) agents and events are presented in clauses, (4) a string of clauses (containing both noun and verb phrases) represent events which accumulate into the event structure of a discourse.

11. Lyons (1977a, 1977b) discusses the relationship between anaphora and deixis, suggesting (1977a: 676) that it is possible for a deictic term to be used both anaphorically and deictically.

12. Two points. First, there is somewhat of a match between discourse time (see 8.3) and event time. When *then* is clause initial, it reaches forward in discourse time (into the coming utterance), and forward in event time (into the next linguistic event).

    Second, I am treating anaphora here very broadly. Although a narrower treatment might avoid some of the definitional difficulties being faced for anaphora and deixis, I believe that both utterance-final coterminous *then* and utterance-initial successive *then* are anaphoric. (See discussion in 8.3 of utterance-initial successive *then* as a marker of event time, a non-deictic, anaphoric relationship.) Coterminous *then* is clearly anaphoric not only because its temporal understanding presupposes a temporal understanding of a prior event, but because the time of the second mentioned event is supplied only by reference to the first. I would argue that the same holds for successive *then*: one cannot understand when the second mentioned event occurred without knowing that it follows the prior mentioned event.

13. *Then* in (d) and (e) begin the same episode; the *when* clause provides a more local event time overlapping with the initiation of that episode. This is similar to the function of *when* clauses in narrative: they provide a descriptive background overlapping in time with foregrounded, sequentially ordered story events.

14. Halliday (1967, 1976) groups many of the items I discuss as markers as discourse adjuncts. But even though these adjuncts routinely occur in initial position within the information unit, they are not thematic; in fact, they are outside of both the theme/rheme ordering and the given/new ordering distinguished by Halliday. Vasconcellos (1985) has recently argued that both these orderings reveal a progression from a speaker-centered focus to a hearer-centered focus. Some of the same speaker-to-hearer dynamic seems to underlie the order in which markers themselves occur within the 'discourse adjunct' slot: first marked is the information state, which is basically cognitive and thus internal to the speaker; next is the participation framework, which either opens responsibility for information to the hearer, or displays the speaker in a more social capacity; next is the action structure, which is still more directed toward interaction. All of these precede the utterance. The use of clause final markers (see discussion in Chapter 9) is then the most explicit transfer of responsibility for the next move in an interaction away from the speaker to the other (as predicted by Vasconcellos' model).

15. It is possible to see (64b) as coherent if one assumes that there is some connection between 'seeing Sue' or 'Sue's appearance' and 'getting a new job'. However, such a connection requires a more detailed specification of contextual

understandings than the connection in (64a) between 'packing books' and 'getting a new job' – since it is common knowledge that one normally packs books to move, and often moves to take a new job. The difference in required contextual specification may be associated with a different functional load for *then*. In (64a), the commonly known association between packing, moving, and getting a new job may reduce the functional load of *then* as a marker of a warranted request, whereas that load may be maximized when contextual understandings do not readily provide the inferential connection linking two moves (see 10.1.2 for discussion of the contribution of, and relationship between, marker and utterance meaning).

9 Information and participation: *y' know* and *I mean*

1. It is important to note that I am not examining utterance-internal uses of *y'know*, although these occurrences may have the same functions which I will describe for utterance-initial and utterance-final *y'know*. What my limitation means, however, is that I ignore the use of *y'know* in utterance internal repairs.
2. Hamilton (1983) has found that *y'know* is likely to occur with another device through which speakers appeal to general understanding, i.e. set-expanders such as *and stuff like that, and whatever* (Dines 1980).
3. Hamilton (1983) presents quantitative data showing that *y'know* is more likely to occur with evaluative clauses, and in complicating action clauses with evaluative devices, than in orientation clauses and complicating action clauses without evaluative devices. See also Goldberg (1982) who treats *y'know* in narratives as a topic tracker.
4. Another way of saying this is that A1 and B1 form a presequence. See Levinson 1983: 345–64.
5. Vasconcellos (1985) presents a critical summary of the vast and often contradictory literature on information distribution in sentences. See also Prince (1981).
6. This is essentially the conclusion reached by Oöstmann (1981) although her analysis differs in detail.

10 Discourse markers: contextual coordinates of talk

1. Future research should try to be more precise about the relationship between the primary and secondary planes of discourse on which markers function. For example, sometimes I have spoken of the 'influence' that one function may have on another, and other times of the 'relevance' that one function may have for another. Thus, I have assumed that there are different ways in which the primary function of a marker can be related to its secondary functions, and hence different ways that components of talk can be related. Such assumptions should be justified.
2. Levinson (1983: 87) also suggests that many of the expressions I have considered here are discourse deictics: 'there are many words and phrases in English, and no doubt most languages, that indicate the relationship between an utterance and the prior discourse...It is generally conceded that such

words have at least a component of meaning that resists truth-conditional treatment. . .What they seem to do is indicate, often in very complex ways, just how the utterance that contains them is a response to, or a continuation of, some portion of the prior discourse.'

3. See, for example, Auchlin (1981), Hymes (1981), Quasthoff (1979), Sherzer (1982), Vincent (1983) and Zenone (1981).

List of References

Abrahams, R. D. 1974. Black talking on the streets. In R. Bauman and J. Sherzer (eds.), *Explorations in the ethnography of speaking*, 240–62. Cambridge: Cambridge University Press.

Adger, C. T. 1984. Communicative competence in the culturally diverse classroom. Ph.D. dissertation, Georgetown University.

Agar, M. 1982. Toward an ethnographic language. *American anthropologist*, 84:779–95.

Allwood, J., L. Anderson, and O. Dahl. 1977. *Logic in linguistics*. Cambridge: Cambridge University Press.

Aristotle. 1954. *The rhetoric*. Translated by W. Roberts. New York: Random House, Modern Library edition.

Atelsek, J. 1981. An anatomy of opinions. *Language in society*, 10:217–25.

Atkinson, M. 1979. Prerequisites for reference. In E. Ochs and B. B. Schieffelin (eds.), *Developmental pragmatics*, 229–49. New York: Academic Press.

Auchlin, A. 1981. *Mais heu, pis bon, ben alors voilà, quoi!* Marqueurs de structuration de la conversation et completude. Cahiers de linguistique française, Actes du 1er Colloque de Pragmatique de Genève, 141–60.

Austin, J. L. 1962. *How to do things with words*. Cambridge, Mass.: Harvard University Press.

Bach, K. and R. M. Harnish. 1982. *Linguistic communication and speech acts*. Cambridge, Mass.: MIT Press.

Baker, C. 1975. This is just a first approximation, but . . . *Papers from the eleventh regional meeting, Chicago Linguistic Society*. Chicago: Linguistics Department, University of Chicago.

Ball, C. N. and M. Ariel. 1978. Or something, etc. Paper presented at 1978 Penn Linguistics Colloquium.

Barrett, R. B. and A. J. Stenner. 1971. The myth of exclusive *or*. *Mind*, 80:116–21.

Bates, E. and B. MacWhinney. 1979. A functionalist approach to the acquisition of grammar. In E. Ochs and B. B. Schieffelin (eds.), *Developmental pragmatics*, 167–214. New York: Academic Press.

Bates, E. and B. MacWhinney. 1982. Functionalist approaches to grammar. In E. Wanner and L. R. Gleitman (eds.), *Language acquisition: The state of the art*, 173–218. Cambridge: Cambridge University Press.

Bateson, G. 1972a. Why do things have outlines? In *Steps to an ecology of mind*,

27–32. New York: Ballantine Books. (Originally published 1953 in *ETC: A review of general semantics XI.*)

Bateson, G. 1972b. A theory of play and fantasy. In *Steps to an ecology of mind*, 177–93. New York: Ballantine Books. (Originally published 1955 in *A.P.A. Psychiatric Research Reports II.*)

Baugh, J. and J. Sherzer (eds.). 1984. *Language in use*. Englewood Cliffs, N.J.: Prentice-Hall.

Bauman, R. and J. Sherzer. 1974. *Explorations in the Ethnography of Communication*. Cambridge: Cambridge University Press.

Bauman, R. and J. Sherzer. 1982. Case studies in the ethnography of speaking. Working papers in sociolinguistics. Austin, Texas: Southwest Educational Development Laboratory.

Beaman, K. 1984. Coordination and subordination revisited: Syntactic complexity in spoken and written narrative discourse. In D. Tannen (ed.), *Coherence in spoken and written discourse*, 45–80. Norwood, N. J.: Ablex.

Becker, A. L. 1979. Text-building, epistemology, and aesthetics in Javanese shadow theatre. In A. L. Becker and A. Yengoyan (eds.), *The imagination of reality*, 211–43. Norwood, N. J.: Ablex.

Becker, A. L. 1984. The linguistics of particularity: Interpreting superordination in a Javanese text. Proceedings of the tenth annual meeting of the Berkeley Linguistics Society. Berkeley: Linguistics Department, University of California at Berkeley.

Bennett, A. 1978. Interruptions and the interpretation of conversation. Proceedings of the fourth annual meeting of the Berkeley Linguistics Society, 557–75.

Bolinger, D. 1982. Nondeclaratives from an intonational standpoint. *Papers from the parasession on non-declarative sentences of the 18th regional meeting, Chicago Linguistic Society*, 1–22. Chicago: Linguistics Department, University of Chicago.

Boomer, D. 1965. Hesitation and grammatical encoding. *Language and speech*, 8:148–58.

Borowski, E. J. 1976. English and truth-functions. *Analysis*, 36:96–100.

Brenneis, D. and L. Lein. 1977. 'You fruithead': A sociolinguistic approach to children's dispute settlement. In S. Ervin-Tripp and C. Mitchell-Kernan (eds.), *Child discourse*, 49–65. New York: Academic Press.

Brewer, W. and E. Lichtenstein. 1982. Stories are to entertain: A structural affect theory, *Journal of Pragmatics*, 6:473–86.

Bright, W. 1981. Poetic structure in oral narrative. In D. Tannen (ed.), *Spoken and written language*, 171–84. Norwood, N.J.: Ablex.

Brockway, D. 1981. Semantic constraints on relevance. In H. Parret, M. Sbisa, and J. Verschueren (eds.), *Possibilities and limitations of pragmatics*, 57–78. Amsterdam: John Benjamins.

Brown, P. and S. Levinson. 1978. Universals in language usage: Politeness phenomena. In E. Goody (ed.), *Questions and politeness: Strategies in social interaction*, 56–289. Cambridge: Cambridge University Press.

Brown, G. and G. Yule. 1983. *Discourse analysis*. Cambridge: Cambridge University Press.

Bühler, K. 1934. *Sprachtheorie*. Jena: Fischer.

Calfee, R. 1982. Some theoretical and practical ramifications of story grammars. *Journal of pragmatics*, 6: 441–50.

Carlson, L. 1983. *Dialogue games*. Dordrecht: Reidel.

Cattell, R. 1978. On the source of interrogative adverbs. *Language*, 54:61–77.

Chafe, W. 1977. Creativity in verbalization and its implications for the nature of stored knowledge. In R. Freedle (ed.), *Discourse production and comprehension*. 41–55. Norwood, N. J.: Ablex.

Chafe, W. 1980. The deployment of consciousness in the production of a narrative. In W. Chafe (ed.), *The pear stories: Cognitive, cultural and linguistic aspects of narrative production*, 9–50. Norwood, N. J.: Ablex.

Chafe, W. 1984. Speaking, writing, and prescriptivism. In D. Schiffrin (ed.), *Meaning, form, and use in context: Linguistic applications* (Georgetown University Round Table on Languages and Linguistics 1984), 95–103. Washington, D.C.: Georgetown University Press.

Cicourel, A. 1972. Basic and normative rules in the negotiation of status and role. In D. Sudnow (ed.), *Studies in social interaction*, 229–58. New York: Free Press.

Clark, E. 1974. Normal states and evaluative viewpoints. *Language*, 50:316–32.

Clark, H. 1979. Responding to indirect speech acts. *Cognitive psychology*, 11:430–77.

Clark, H. 1980. Polite responses to polite requests. *Cognition*, 8:111–43.

Clark, H. and T. Carlson. 1981. Context for comprehension. In J. Long and A. Baddeley (eds.), *Attention and performance IX*, 313–30. Hillsdale, N. J.: Lawrence Erlbaum.

Clark, H. and T. Carlson. 1982. Hearers and speech acts. *Language*, 58:332–73.

Cohen, L. J. 1971. Some remarks on Grice's views about the logical particles of natural language. In Y. Bar-Hillel, *Pragmatics of natural language*, 50–68. Dordrecht: Reidel.

Colby, B. 1982. Notes on the transmission and evolution of stories. *Journal of pragmatics*, 6:463–72.

Cole, P. 1975. The synchronic and diachronic status of conversational implicature. In P. Cole and J. L. Morgan (eds.) *Speech acts* (Syntax and semantics, vol. 3), 257–88. New York: Academic Press.

Cole, P. and J. L. Morgan. 1975. *Speech acts* (Syntax and semantics, vol. 3). New York: Academic Press.

Comrie, B. 1985. *Tense*. Cambridge: Cambridge University Press.

Crystal, D. 1980. Neglected grammatical factors in conversational English. In *Studies in English linguistics for Randolph Quirk*. London: Longman.

Dik, S. 1968. *Coordination*. Amsterdam: North-Holland.

Dines, E. 1980. Variation in discourse: 'and stuff like that'. *Language in society*, 9:13–31.

Downes, W. 1983. *Language and society*. London: Fontana.

DuBois, J. 1980. Beyond definiteness: The trace of identity in discourse. In W. Chafe (ed.), *The pear stories*, 203–74. Norwood, N. J.: Ablex.

Ducrot, O. 1980. Analyse de textes et linguistique de l'énonciation. In O. Ducrot (ed.), *Les mots du discours*, 7–56. Paris: Minuit.

Duncan, S. 1972. Some signals and rules for taking speaking turns in conversations. *Journal of personality and social psychology*, 6:341–9.

Durkheim, E. 1895. *The rules of sociological method*. New York: Free Press.

Eisenberg, K. A. and C. Garvey. 1981. Children's use of verbal strategies in resolving conflict. *Discourse processes*, 4:149–70.

Ekman, P. 1979. About brows: Emotional and conversational signals. In M. von Cranach, K. Foppa, W. Lepenies and D. Ploog (eds.), *Human ecology*, 169–249. Cambridge: Cambridge University Press.

Ekman, P. and W. V. Freisen. 1969. The repertoire of nonverbal behavior: Categories, origins, usage and coding. *Semiotica*, 1:49–98.

Erickson, F. 1979. Talking down: Some cultural sources of miscommunication in interracial interviews. In A. Wolfgang (ed.), *Nonverbal behavior*, 99–126. New York: Academic Press.

Ervin-Tripp, S. 1976. Is Sybil there?: The structure of American English directives. *Language in society*, 5:25–66.

Falk, J. 1979. The conversational duet. Ph.D. dissertation, Princeton University.

Fasold, R. 1983. *Variation in the form and use of language: A sociolinguistics reader*. Washington, D.C.: Georgetown University Press.

Fasold, R. W. and R. W. Shuy. 1975. *Analyzing variation in language*. Washington, D.C.: Georgetown University Press.

Fillmore, C. J. 1981. Pragmatics and the description of discourse. In P. Cole (ed.), *Radical pragmatics*, 143–66. New York: Academic Press.

Fillmore, C. J. 1982. Story grammars and sentence grammars. *Journal of pragmatics*, 6:451–4.

Firbas, J. 1964. On defining the theme in functional sentence analysis. In *Travaux linguistiques de Prague*, 1:267–80.

French, P. and J. Local. 1983. Turn-competitive incomings. *Journal of pragmatics*, 7:17–38.

Fries, C. 1952. *The structure of English*. London: Longman.

Garvey, C. 1977. The contingent query: A dependent act in conversation. In M. Lewis and L. Rosenblum (eds.), *Interaction, conversation, and the development of language*, 63–93. New York: John Wiley.

Garvey, C. 1979. Contingent queries and their relations in discourse. In E. Ochs and B. Schieffelin (eds.), *Developmental pragmatics*, 363–72. New York: Academic Press.

Gazdar, G. 1979. *Pragmatics: Implicature, presupposition, and logical form*. New York: Academic Press.

Gazdar, G. and G. K. Pullum. 1976. Truth-functional connectives in natural language. *Papers from the 12th regional meeting, Chicago Linguistic Society*, 220–34, Chicago: Linguistics Department, University of Chicago.

Genishi, C. and M. DiPaolo. 1982. Learning through argument in a preschool. In L. Wilkinson (ed.), *Communicating in the classroom*, 49–68. New York: Academic Press.

Giglioli, P. (ed.), 1972. *Language and social context*. New York: Penguin.

Givón, T. 1978. Negation in language: Pragmatics, function and ontology. In P. Cole (ed.), *Pragmatics* (Syntax and semantics, vol. 9), 69–112. New York: Academic Press.

Givón, T. 1979. *On understanding grammar*. New York: Academic Press.

Gleitman, L. 1965. Coordinating conjunctions in English. *Language*, 41:260–93.

Goffman, E. 1959. *The presentation of self in everyday life*. New York: Anchor Books.

Goffman, E. 1961. *Encounters*. New York: Bobbs-Merrill.

Goffman, E. 1963. *Behavior in public places*. New York: Free Press.

Goffman, E. 1967. The nature of deference and demeanor. In *Interaction ritual*, 49–95. New York: Anchor Books.

Goffman, E. 1971. *Relations in public*. New York: Harper and Row.

Goffman, E. 1974. *Frame analysis*. New York: Harper and Row.

Goffman, E. 1981a. Replies and responses. *Forms of talk*, 5–77. Philadelphia: University of Pennsylvania Press. (Originally published 1976 in *Language in society*, 5:257–313.)

Goffman, E. 1981b. Footing. *Forms of talk*, 124–57. Philadelphia: University of Pennsylvania Press. (Originally published 1979 in *Semiotica*, 25:1–29.)

Goffman, E. 1983. Felicity's condition. *American journal of sociology*, 89:1–53.

Goldberg, J. 1982. Discourse particles: An analysis of the role of 'y'know', 'I mean', 'well', and 'actually' in conversation. Ph.D. dissertation, University of Cambridge.

Goodwin, C. 1981. *Conversation organization: Interaction between speakers and hearers*. New York: Academic Press.

Gordon, D. and G. Lakoff. 1971. Conversational postulates. *Papers from the seventh regional meeting of the Chicago Linguistic Society*, 63–84. (Reprinted in P. Cole and J. L. Morgan 1975 (eds.) *Speech acts* (Syntax and semantics, vol. 3), 83–106.)

Grice, H. P. 1957. Meaning. *Philosophical review*, 67:377–88.

Grice, H. P. 1968. Utterer's meaning, sentence-meaning, and word-meaning. *Foundations of language*, 4:1–18.

Grice, H. P. 1975. Logic and conversation. In P. Cole and J. L. Morgan (eds.), *Speech acts* (Syntax and semantics, vol. 3), 41–58. New York: Academic Press.

Grice, H. P. 1978. Further notes on logic and conversation. In P. Cole (ed.), *Pragmatics* (Syntax and semantics, vol. 9), 113–28. New York: Academic Press.

Grosz, B. 1981. Focusing and description in natural language dialogues. In A. Joshi, B. Webber and I. Sag (eds.), *Elements of discourse understanding*, 84–105. Cambridge: Cambridge University Press.

Gumperz, J. J. 1964. Linguistic and social interaction in two communities. *American anthropologist*, 6:137–53.

Gumperz, J. J. 1981. The linguistic bases of communicative competence. In D. Tannen (ed.), *Analyzing discourse: Text and talk* (Georgetown University Round Table on Languages and Linguistics 1981), 323–34. Washington, D.C.: Georgetown University Press.

Gumperz, J. J. 1982. *Discourse strategies*. Cambridge: Cambridge University Press.

Gumperz, J. J. 1984. Communicative competence revisited. In D. Schiffrin (ed.), *Meaning, form, and use in context: Linguistic applications* (Georgetown

University Round Table on Languages and Linguistics 1984), 278–89. Washington, D.C.: Georgetown University Press.

Halliday, M. A. K. 1967. Notes on transitivity and theme in English. *Journal of linguistics*, 3:37–81, 199–244.

Halliday, M. A. K. 1973. *Explorations in the functions of language*. London: Edward Arnold.

Halliday, M. A. K. 1976. Theme and information in the English clause. In G. Kress (ed.), *System and function in language*, 174–88. Oxford: Oxford University Press.

Halliday, M. A. K. 1978. *Language as a social semiotic*. London: Edward Arnold.

Halliday, M. A. K. and R. Hasan. 1976. *Cohesion in English*. London: Longman.

Hamilton, H. 1983. Unlocking the interlocked in discourse: A structural functional analysis of *y'know*. M.S., Department of Linguistics, Georgetown University.

Harris, Z. 1951. *Methods in structural linguistics*. Chicago: University of Chicago Press.

Harris, Z. 1952. Discourse analysis. *Language*, 28:1–30.

Heritage, J. 1984. A change-of-state token and aspects of its sequential placement. In J. M. Atkinson and J. Heritage (eds.), *Structures of social action: Studies in conversation analysis*, 299–345. Cambridge: Cambridge University Press.

Hewitt, J. and R. Stokes. 1975. Disclaimers. *American sociological review*, 40:1–11.

Hockett, C. 1958. *A course in modern linguistics*. New York: Macmillan.

Horn, L. 1984. Toward a new taxonomy for pragmatic inference: Q-based and R-based implicature. In D. Schiffrin (ed.), *Meaning, form, and use in context: Linguistic applications* (Georgetown University Round Table on Languages and Linguistics 1984), 11–42. Washington, D.C.: Georgetown University Press.

Hurford, J. R. 1974. Exclusive or inclusive disjunction. *Foundations of language*, 11:409–11.

Hymes, D. 1972. Toward ethnographies of communication: The analysis of communicative events. In P. Giglioli (ed.), *Language and social context*, 21–44. New York: Penguin. (Originally published 1964 in *American anthropologist*, 66.)

Hymes, D. 1974. *Foundations in sociolinguistics: An ethnographic approach*. Philadelphia: University of Pennsylvania Press.

Hymes, D. 1981. *'In vain I tried to tell you': Essays in native American ethnopoetics*. Philadelphia: University of Pennsylvania Press.

Irvine, J. 1974. Strategies of status manipulation in the Wolof greeting. In R. Bauman and J. Sherzer (eds.), *Explorations in the ethnography of speaking*, 167–191. Cambridge: Cambridge University Press.

Jakobson, R. 1957. Shifters, verbal categories and the Russian verb. Cambridge, Mass.: Harvard University, Russian Language Project. (Reprinted in his *Selected writings*, 2:130–47. The Hague: Mouton.)

Jakobson, R. 1960. Closing statement: Linguistics and poetics. In T. Sebeok (ed.), *Style in language*, 350–77. Cambridge, Mass.: M.I.T. Press.

James, D. 1972. Some aspects of the syntax and semantics of interjections. *Papers from the 8th Regional Meeting, Chicago Linguistic Society,* 162–71. Chicago: Linguistics Department, University of Chicago.

James, D. 1974. Another look at, say, some grammatical constraints on, oh, interjections and hesitations. *Papers from the tenth regional meeting of the Chicago Linguistics Society,* 242–51. Chicago: Linguistics Department, University of Chicago.

Jefferson, G. 1972. Side sequences. In D. Sudnow (ed.), *Studies in social interaction,* 294–338. New York: Free Press.

Jefferson, G. 1974. Error correction as an interactional resource. *Language in society,* 3:181–99.

Jefferson, G. 1978. Sequential aspects of storytelling in conversation. In J. Schenkein (ed.), *Studies in the organization of conversational interaction,* 219–48. New York: Academic Press.

Jefferson, G. 1979. A technique for inviting laughter and its subsequent acceptance/declination. In G. Psathas (ed.), *Everyday language: Studies in ethnomethodology,* 79–96. New York: Irvington.

Johnson-Laird, P. 1969. '&'. *Journal of linguistics,* 6:111–14.

Kaplan, A. 1964. *The conduct of inquiry.* New York: Free Press.

Karttunen, L. and S. Peters. 1979. Conventional implicature. In C.-K. Oh and D. A. Dinneen (eds.), *Presupposition* (Syntax and semantics, vol. 11), 1–56. New York: Academic Press.

Katz, J. 1977. *Prepositional structure and illocutionary force.* New York: Crowell.

Katz, J. and J. Fodor. 1963. The structure of a semantic theory. *Language,* 39:170–210.

Keenan, E. O. and B. B. Schieffelin. 1976. Topic as a discourse notion: A study of topic in the conversation of children and adults. In C. N. Li (ed.), *Subject and topic,* 335–84. New York: Academic Press.

Kempson, R. 1975. *Presupposition and the delimitation of semantics.* Cambridge: Cambridge University Press.

Kempson, R. 1977. *Semantic theory.* Cambridge: Cambridge University Press.

Kempson, R. 1984. Pragmatics, anaphora, and logical form. In D. Schiffrin (ed.), *Meaning, form, and use in context: Linguistic applications* (Georgetown University Round Table on Languages and Linguistics 1984), 1–10. Washington, D.C.: Georgetown University Press.

Kendon, A. 1967. Some functions of gaze-direction in social interaction. *Acta Psychologia,* 26:22–47.

Kirshenblatt-Gimblett, B. 1974. The concept and varieties of narrative performance in East European Jewish culture. In R. Bauman and J. Sherzer (eds.), *Explorations in the ethnography of speaking,* 283–308. Cambridge: Cambridge University Press.

Kirshenblatt-Gimblett, B. 1975. A parable in context: A social interactional analysis of storytelling performance. In D. Ben-Amos and K. Goldstein (eds.), *Folklore: Performance and communication.* The Hague: Mouton.

Kreckel, M. 1981. *Communicative acts and shared knowledge in natural discourse.* New York: Academic Press.

Kroll, B. 1977. Combining ideas in written and spoken English: A look at subordination and coordination. In E. Keenan and T. Bennett (eds.), *Discourse across time and space,* 69–108. Southern California Occasional

Papers in Linguistics, No. 5.

Kummer, I. and W. Kummer. 1976. Logic of action and practical arguments. In
T. van Dijk (ed.), *Pragmatics of language and literature*, 83–106.
Amsterdam: North Holland Publishing Company.

Labov, T. 1980. The communication of morality: Cooperation and commitment in
a food cooperative. Ph.D. dissertation, Columbia University.

Labov, W. 1972a. The transformation of experience in narrative syntax. *Language
in the inner city*, 354–96. Philadelphia: University of Pennsylvania Press.

Labov, W. 1972b. The social stratification of (r) in New York City department
stores. *Sociolinguistic patterns*, 43–69. Philadelphia: University of
Pennsylvania Press.

Labov, W. 1972c. The isolation of contextual styles. *Sociolinguistic patterns*, 70–
109. Philadelphia: University of Pennsylvania Press.

Labov, W. 1972d. The social motivation of a sound change. *Sociolinguistic
patterns*, 1–42. Philadelphia: University of Pennsylvania Press.

Labov, W. 1975. Grammaticality of everyday speech. Paper presented at L.S.A.
annual meeting, New York.

Labov, W. 1978. Where does the linguistic variable stop? A reply to Beatriz
Lavandera. (Working papers in sociolinguistics, 44.) Austin: Southwest
Educational Development Laboratory.

Labov, W. 1984a. Field methods of the project on linguistic change and variation.
In J. Baugh and J. Sherzer (eds.), *Language in use*, 28–53. Englewood Cliffs,
N.J.: Prentice-Hall.

Labov, W. 1984b. Intensity. In D. Schiffrin (ed.), *Meaning, form, and use in
context: Linguistic applications* (Georgetown University Round Table on
Languages and Linguistics 1984), 43–70. Washington, D.C.: Georgetown
University Press.

Labov, W. and D. Fanshel. 1977. *Therapeutic discourse: Psychotherapy as
conversation*. New York: Academic Press.

Labov, W. and D. Sankoff. 1980. *Locating language in time and space*. New York:
Academic Press.

Labov, W. and J. Waletsky. 1967. Narrative analysis: Oral versions of personal
experience. In J. Helm (ed.), *Essays on the verbal and visual arts*, 12–44.
Seattle: University of Washington Press.

Laffal, J. 1965. *Pathological and normal language*. New York: Atherton.

Lakoff, G. 1975. Hedges: A study in meaning criteria and the logic of fuzzy
concepts. *Papers from the 11th Regional Meeting, Chicago Linguistic Society*,
183–227. Chicago: Linguistics Department, University of Chicago.

Lakoff, G. and S. Peters. 1969. Phrasal conjunction and symmetric predicates. In
D. Reibel and S. Schane (eds.), *Modern studies in English*, 113–42.
Englewood Cliffs, N.J.: Prentice Hall.

Lakoff, R. 1971. If's, and's, and but's about conjunction. In C.J. Fillmore and
D.T. Langendoen (eds.), *Studies in linguistic semantics*, 115–50. New York:
Holt, Rinehart and Winston.

Lakoff, R. 1973a. The logic of politeness, or minding your p's and q's. *Papers from
the 9th Regional Meeting, Chicago Linguistic Society*, 292–305. Chicago:
Linguistics Department, University of Chicago.

Lakoff, R. 1973b. Questionable answers and answerable questions. In B. Kachru *et al.* (eds.), *Papers in honor of Henry and Renee Kahane,* 453–67. Urbana: University of Illinois Press.

Lavandera, B. 1978. Where does the sociolinguistic variable stop? *Language in society,* 7:171–83.

Laver, J. 1970. The production of speech. In J. Lyons (ed.), *New horizons in linguistics,* 53–75. New York: Penguin.

Leech, G. 1983. *Principles of pragmatics.* New York: Longman.

Lein, L and D. Brenneis. 1978. Children's disputes in three speech communities. *Language in society,* 7:299–323.

Levinson, S. C. 1981. The essential inadequacies of speech act models of dialogue. In H. Parret, M. Sbisa, and J. Verschueren (eds.), *Possibilities and limitations of pragmatics: Proceedings of the conference on pragmatics at Urbino,* 473–92. Amsterdam: John Benjamins.

Levinson, S. C. 1983. *Pragmatics.* Cambridge: Cambridge University Press.

Lieberman, P. 1967. *Intonation, perception and language.* Research monograph vol. 38. Cambridge, Mass.: M.I.T. Press.

Linde, C. and J. Goguen. 1978. The structure of planning discourse. *Journal of social and biological structure,* 1:219–51.

Linde, C. and W. Labov. 1975. Spatial networks as a site for the study of language and thought. *Language,* 51:924–39.

Lyons, J. 1972. Human language. In R. A. Hinde (ed.), *Nonverbal communication,* 49–85. Cambridge: Cambridge University Press.

Lyons, J. 1977a. *Semantics.* 2 vols. Cambridge: Cambridge University Press.

Lyons, J. 1977b. Deixis and anaphora. In T. Myers (ed.), *The development of conversation and discourse.* Edinburgh: Edinburgh University Press.

MacKay, D. 1972. Formal analysis of communicative processes. In R. Hinde (ed.), *Nonverbal communication,* 3–25. Cambridge: Cambridge University Press.

Malinowski, B. 1930. The problem of meaning in primitive languages. In C. Ogden and I. A. Richards (eds.), *The meaning of meaning.* (2nd ed.) London: Routledge and Kegan and Paul.

Mathesius, V. 1924. Some notes on the function of the subject in modern English. *C.M.S.* 10:244–8.

Maynard, C. 1985. How children start arguments. *Language in society,* 14:1–30.

Meehan, J. 1982. Stories and cognition. *Journal of pragmatics,* 6:487–500.

Mehan, H. 1979. *Learning lessons: Social organization in the classroom.* Cambridge, Mass.: Harvard University Press.

Merritt, M. 1976. On questions following questions (in service encounters). *Language in society,* 5:315–57.

Merritt, M. 1984. On the use of 'okay' in service encounters. In J. Baugh and J. Sherzer (eds.), *Language in use,* 139–47. Englewood Cliffs, NJ: Prentice-Hall.

Moerman, M. 1977. The preference for self-correction in a Tai conversational corpus. *Language,* 53:872–82.

Morris, C. W. 1938. Foundations of the theory of signs. In O. Neurath, R. Carnap and C. Morris (eds.), *International encyclopedia of unified science,* 77–138. Chicago: University of Chicago Press.

Newman, E. 1975. *Strictly speaking*. New York: Warner.

Ochs, E. 1979a. Social foundations of language. In R. Freedle (ed.), *New directions in discourse processing*, 207–21. Norwood, N.J.: Ablex.

Ochs, E. 1979b. Introduction: What child language can contribute to pragmatics. In E. Ochs and B. B. Schieffelin (eds.), *Developmental pragmatics*, 1–17.

Ochs, E. and Schieffelin, B. B. (eds.) 1979. *Developmental pragmatics*. New York: Academic Press.

Oöstmann, J. 1981. *You know: A discourse-functional approach*. Amsterdam: John Benjamins.

Owen, M. L. 1983. *Apologies and remedial interchanges*. The Hague: Mouton.

Oxford English Dictionary, 1971. Oxford: Oxford University Press.

Pelletier, F. J. 1977. Or. *Theoretical linguistics*, 4:61–74.

Perelman, C. and L. Olbrechts-Tyteca. 1969. *The new rhetoric: A treatise on argumentation*. London: University of Notre Dame Press.

Pike, K. L. 1945. *The intonation of American English*. Ann Arbor: University of Michigan Press.

Polanyi, L. 1979. So what's the point? *Semiotica*, 25:207–41.

Polanyi, L. 1982. Linguistic and social constraints on storytelling. *Journal of pragmatics*, 6:509–24.

Polanyi, L. and R. J. H. Scha. 1983. The syntax of discourse. *Text*, 3:261–70.

Pomerantz, A. 1984. Agreeing and disagreeing with assessments: some features of preferred/dispreferred turn shapes. In J. Atkinson and J. Heritage (eds.), *Structures of social action: Studies in conversation analysis*, 57–101. Cambridge: Cambridge University Press.

Posner, R. 1980. Semantics and pragmatics of sentence connectives in natural language. In F. Kiefer and J. Searle (eds.), *Pragmatics and speech act theory*, 87–122. Dordrecht, Holland: D. Reidel and Co.

Prince, E. 1981. Towards a taxonomy of given-new information. In P. Cole (ed.), *Radical pragmatics*, 223–56. New York: Academic Press.

Prince, G. 1973. *A grammar for stories*. The Hague: Mouton.

Propp, V. 1968. *Morphology of the folktale*. (Revised edition.) Austin: University of Texas Press. (Originally published 1928.)

Quasthoff, U. 1979. Verzogerungsphanomene: Verknupfungs– und Gliederungssignale in Alltagsargumentation und Alltagserzahlungen. In H. Weydt (ed.), *Die Partikeln der deutschen Sprache*, 36–57. Berlin: De Gruyter.

Quinn, J. 1980. *American tongue in cheek*. New York: Penguin.

Quirk, R., S. Greenbaum, G. Leech, and J. Svartvik. 1972. *A grammar of contemporary English*. London: Longman.

Reichenbach, H. 1947. *Elements of symbolic logic*. London: Macmillan.

Romaine, S. 1981. On the problem of syntactic variation: A reply to B. Lavandera and W. Labov. (Working papers in sociolinguistics, 82). Austin: Southwest Educational Development Laboratory.

Ross, J. R. 1967. Constraints on variables in syntax. Ph.D. dissertation, M.I.T.

Ruesch, J. and G. Bateson (eds.). 1951. *Communication*. New York: Norton.

Rumelhart, D. 1975. Notes on a schema for stories. In D. Bubrow and A. Collins (eds.), *Representation and understanding*, 211–36. New York: Academic Press.

Sacks, H. 1971. Lecture notes. School of Social Science, University of California at Irvine.

Sacks, H. 1973. Lecture notes. School of Social Science, University of California at Irvine.

Sacks, H., E. Schegloff, and G. Jefferson. 1974. A simplest systematics for the organization of turn-taking in conversation. *Language* 50:696–735.

Sadock, J. M. 1974. *Toward a linguistic theory of speech acts*. New York: Academic Press.

Sadock, J. M. 1984. Whither radical pragmatics? In D. Schiffrin (ed.), *Meaning, form, and use in context: Linguistic applications* (Georgetown University Round Table on Languages and Linguistics 1984), 139–49. Washington, D.C.: Georgetown University Press.

Sankoff, G. 1974. A quantitative paradigm for the study of communicative competence. In R. Bauman and J. Sherzer (eds.), *Explorations in the ethnography of speaking*, 18–49. Cambridge: Cambridge University Press.

Sankoff, G. 1984. Substrate and universals in the Tok Pisin verb phrase. In D. Schiffrin (ed.), *Meaning, form, and use in context: Linguistic applications* (Georgetown University Round Table on Languages and Linguistics 1984), 104–19. Washington, D.C.: Georgetown University Press.

Sankoff, G. and P. Brown. 1976. The origins of syntax in discourse. *Language* 52:631–66.

Sankoff, D. and H. Cedergren. 1981. *Variation omnibus*. Alberta, Canada: Linguistic Research, Inc.

Sapir, E. 1916. Time perspective in aboriginal American culture: A study in method. Canada, Department of Mines, Geological Survey, Memoir 90; Anthropological Series, No. 13, Ottawa, Government Printing Bureau. Reprinted in D. Mandelbaum (ed.), 1949, *Selected writings of Edward Sapir*, University of California Press.

de Saussure, F. 1959. *A course in general linguistics*. New York: Philosophical Library. (Originally published 1916.)

Saville-Troike, M. 1982. *The ethnography of communication*. Oxford: Basil Blackwell.

Scheflen, A. E. 1973. *Communicational structure: Analysis of a psychotherapy transaction*. Bloomington: University of Indiana Press.

Schegloff, E. 1972. Sequencing in conversation openings. In J. Gumperz and D. Hymes (ed.), *Directions in sociolinguistics*, 346–80. New York: Holt, Rinehart and Winston.

Schegloff, E. 1981. Discourse as an interactional achievement: Some uses of 'uh huh' and other things that come between sentences. In D. Tannen (ed.), *Analyzing discourse: Text and talk* (Georgetown University Round Table on Languages and Linguistics 1981), 71–93. Washington, D.C.: Georgetown University Press.

Schegloff, E., G. Jefferson, and H. Sacks. 1977. The preference for self-correction in the organization of repair in conversation. *Language*, 53:361–82.

Schegloff, E. and H. Sacks. 1973. Opening up closings. *Semiotica*, 7:289–327.

Schiffrin, D. 1977. Opening encounters. *American sociological review*, 42:671–91.

Schiffrin, D. 1980. Meta-talk: Organizational and evaluative brackets in discourse. In D. Zimmerman and C. West (eds.), *Language and social interaction.* Special edition of *Sociological inquiry*, 50:199–236.

Schiffrin, D. 1981. Tense variation in narrative. *Language,* 57:45–62.

Schiffrin, D. 1982a. Cohesion in everyday discourse: The role of nonadjacent paraphrase. (Texas working papers in sociolinguistics.) Austin: Southwest Educational Development Laboratory.

Schiffrin, D. 1982b. Discourse markers: Semantic resources for the construction of conversation. Ph.D. dissertation, University of Pennsylvania.

Schiffrin, D. 1984a. Jewish argument as sociability. *Language in society*, 13:311–35.

Schiffrin, D. 1984b. How a story says what it means and does. *Text,* 4:313–46.

Schiffrin, D. 1985a. Everyday argument: The organization of diversity in talk. In T. van Dijk (ed.), *Handbook of discourse analysis,* vol. 3, *Discourse and dialogue,* 35–46. London: Academic Press.

Schiffrin, D. 1985b. Multiple constraints on discourse options: A quantitative analysis of causal sequences. *Discourse processes,* 8:281–303.

Schiffrin, D. 1985c. Conversational coherence: The role of *well. Language* 61:640–67.

Schiffrin, D. 1985d. Framing truth and sincerity in argument. Paper presented at an American Anthropological Association meeting, Washington, D.C.

Schiffrin, D. 1986. Discovering the context of an utterance. In N. Dittmar (ed.), Special issue of *Linguistics*.

Schiffrin, D. forthcoming. Cooperative conflict. In A. Grimshaw (ed.), *Conflict talk.* Cambridge: Cambridge University Press.

Schmerling, S. 1975. Asymmetric conjunction and rules of conversation. In P. Cole and J. L. Morgan (eds.), *Speech acts* (Syntax and semantics, vol. 3), 211–32. New York: Academic Press.

Schourup, L. 1985. Common discourse particles in English conversation: *like, well, y'know.* New York: Garland.

Schutz, A. 1970. *Alfred Schutz: On phenomenology and social relations.* Chicago: University of Chicago Press.

Scollon, R. 1979. A real early stage: An unzippered condensation of a dissertation on child language. In E. Ochs and B. B. Schieffelin (eds.), *Developmental pragmatics,* 215–27. New York: Academic Press.

Scribner, S. 1979. Modes of thinking and ways of speaking: Culture and logic revisited. In R. Freedle (ed.), *New directions in discourse processing,* 223–43. Norwood, N.J.: Ablex.

Searle, J. R. 1969. *Speech acts.* Cambridge: Cambridge University Press.

Searle, J. R. 1975. Indirect speech acts. In P. Cole and J. L. Morgan (eds.), *Speech acts* (Syntax and semantics, vol. 3), 59–82. New York: Academic Press.

Sherzer, J. 1982. Poetic structuring of Kuna discourse: The line. *Language in society,* 11:371–90.

Silva-Corvalan, C. 1983. Tense and aspect in oral Spanish narrative. *Language,* 59:760–80.

Simmel, G. 1961. The sociology of sociability. In T. Parsons *et al.* (eds.), *Theories of society*. New York: Free Press. (Originally published 1911, *American journal of sociology*, 55(3):157–62.)

Slobin, D. 1975. The more it changes. . .On understanding language by watching it move through time. *Papers and reports on child language development*, 1–30. Berkeley: University of California at Berkeley.

Sperber, D. and D. Wilson. 1984. Pragmatics: An overview. In S. George (ed.), *From the linguistic to the social context: Suggestions for interpretation*, 21–42. Bologna: Cooperativa Libraria Universitaria Editrice.

Stein, N. 1982. The definition of a story. *Journal of pragmatics*, 6:487–507.

Stross, B. 1974. Speaking of speaking: Tenjapa Tzeltal metalinguistics. In R. Bauman and J. Sherzer (eds.), *Explorations in the ethnography of speaking*, 213–39. Cambridge: Cambridge University Press.

Stubbs, M. 1983a. *Discourse analysis: The sociolinguistic analysis of natural language*. Chicago: University of Chicago Press.

Stubbs, M. 1983b. Can I have that in writing, please? Some neglected topics in speech act theory. *Journal of pragmatics*, 7:479–94.

Svartvik 1980. *Well* in conversation. *Studies in English linguistics for Randolph Quirk*, 167–77. London: Longman.

Tannen, D. 1979. What's in a frame? Surface evidence for underlying expectations. In R. Freedle (ed.), *New directions in discourse processing*, 137–81. Norwood, N.J.: Ablex.

Tannen, D. 1981. New York Jewish conversational style. *International journal of the sociology of language*, 30:133–9.

Tannen, D. 1983. When is an overlap not an interruption? In R. Di Pietro, W. Frawley and A. Wedel (eds.), *The first Delaware symposium on language studies*, 119–29. Newark, Del.: University of Delaware Press.

Tannen, D. 1984. *Conversational style: Analyzing talk among friends*. Norwood, N.J.: Ablex.

Tannen, D. forthcoming. Introducing constructed dialogue in Greek and American conversational and literary narrative. In F. Coulmas (ed.), *Direct and indirect speech*. Berlin: Mouton.

Tannen, D. and M. Saville-Troike. 1985. *Perspectives on silence*. Norwood, N.J.: Ablex.

Thompson, S. 1984. 'Subordination' in formal and informal discourse. In D. Schiffrin (ed.), *Meaning, form, and use in context: Linguistic applications* (Georgetown University Round Table on Languages and Linguistics 1984), 85–94. Washington, D.C.: Georgetown University Press.

Thompson, S. Forthcoming. Grammar and written discourse: Initial vs. final purpose clauses in English. *Text*.

Thorndyke, P. 1977. Cognitive structures in comprehension and memory of narrative discourse. *Cognitive psychology*, 9:77–110.

Toulmin, S. 1958. *The use of argument*. Cambridge: Cambridge University Press.

Traugott, E. 1979. From propositional to textual and expressive meanings: Some semantic-pragmatic aspects of grammaticalization. Paper given at the First International Conference on English Historical Linguistics.

Traugott, E. Forthcoming. On the origins of 'and' and 'but' connectives in English. *Studies in language*.

van Dijk, T. 1972. *Some aspects of text grammars*. The Hague: Mouton.

van Dijk, T. 1977a. *Text and context*. London: Longmans.

van Dijk, T. 1977b. Connectives in text grammar and text logic. In T. van Dijk and J. Petofi (eds.), *Grammars and descriptions*, 11–63. New York: De Gruyter Press.

van Dijk, T. 1985. *Handbook of discourse analysis*, vol. 3, *Discourse and dialogue*. London: Academic Press.

van Eemeren, F. and R. Grootendorst. 1982. The speech acts of arguing and convincing in externalized discussions. *Journal of pragmatics*, 6:1–24.

Vasconcellos, M. 1985. Theme and focus: Cross-language comparison via translations from extended discourse. PhD. dissertation. Georgetown University.

Vincent, D. 1983. Les ponctuants du langage. Dissertation, Université de Montréal.

Von Glaserfeld, E. 1974. *Because* and the concept of causation. *Semiotica*, 12:129–44.

Warner, R. 1985. *Discourse connectives in English*. New York: Garland.

Watzlawick, P., J. H. Beavin and D. D. Jackson. 1967. *The pragmatics of human communication*. New York: Norton.

Weinrich, U. 1966. On the semantic structure of language. In J. Greenberg (ed.), *Universals of language*, 142–216. Cambridge, Mass.: M.I.T. Press.

Wilensky, R. 1982. Story grammars revisited. *Journal of pragmatics*, 6:423–32.

Wolfson, N. 1976. Speech events and natural speech: Some implications for sociolinguistic methodology. *Language in society*, 5:189–209.

Wolfson, N. 1979. The conversational historical present alternation. *Language*, 55:168–82.

Wolfson, N. 1982. *The conversational historical present in American English narratives*. Dordrecht, Netherlands: Foris Publications.

Wootton, A. 1981. The management of grantings and rejections by parents in request sequences. *Semiotica*, 37:59–89.

Zimmerman, D. 1984. Talk and its occasion: The case of calling the police. In D. Schiffrin (ed.), *Meaning, form and use in context: Linguistic applications*. (Georgetown University Round Table on Languages and Linguistics 1984), 210–28. Washington, D.C.: Georgetown University Press.

Zimmerman, D. and C. West. 1975. Sex roles, interruptions and silences in conversation. In B. Thorne and N. Henley (eds.), *Language and sex: Difference and dominance*, 105–29. Rowley, Mass.: Newbury House.

Zenone, A. 1981. Marqueurs de consécution: Le cas de *donc*. Cahiers de linguistique française, Actes du 1er Colloque de Pragmatique de Genève, 113–40.

Zwicky, A. and J. M. Sadock. 1975. Ambiguity tests and how to fail them. In J. Kimball (ed.), *Syntax and semantics*, vol. 4, 1–36. New York: Academic Press.

Author index

Subject index

Printed in the United States
73552LV00006B/208-213

9 780521 357180